D0328731

STUDIES IN INTERNATIONAL POLITICAL ECONOMY
Stephen D. Krasner, Editor
Ernst B. Haas, Consulting Editor

Managing the Frozen South

# MANAGING THE FROZEN SOUTH

The Creation and Evolution of the
Antarctic Treaty System

M. J. PETERSON

UNIVERSITY OF CALIFORNIA PRESS
Berkeley · Los Angeles · London

University of California Press
Berkeley and Los Angeles, California

University of California Press, Ltd.
London, England

©1988 by
The Regents of the University of California

**Library of Congress Cataloging-in-Publication Data**

Peterson, M. J., 1949–
    Managing the frozen south.

    (Studies in international political economy)
    Bibliography: p.
    Includes index.
    1. Antarctic regions—International status.
2. Mining law—Antarctic regions. I. Title. II. Series.
JX4084.A5P48 1988 341.2′9′09989 87-5078
ISBN 0-520-05997-2 (alk. paper)

Printed in the United States of America

1 2 3 4 5 6 7 8 9

*For B. Jean and Carl A. Peterson*

# CONTENTS

# FIGURES, TABLES, AND MAPS

## Figures

## Tables

## Maps

# ACKNOWLEDGMENTS

The idea for this project was formed, and much of the initial research was done, at Harvard University in the spring and summer of 1983. Its completion was made possible by a two-year research fellowship at the Woods Hole Oceanographic Institution's Marine Policy Center. I am extremely grateful to the Center and to the Pew Memorial Trust, which funded my fellowship, for this unusually long period of research and writing during which two successive drafts were completed. Later drafts were completed at Brandeis University, where the Politics Department kindly tolerated heavy use of the photocopier by a visitor, and at the University of Massachusetts, Amherst.

All research projects have authors, who are responsible for the final form of the work, but none would get far without a circle of aiders and abettors providing hard-to-find information, detached readings of drafts, and moral support. The aiders of this project include Peter J. Beck, Ann Hollick, Christopher C. Joyner, Gerard Julienne, Lee Kimball, Andrew Palmer, Wolfgang Rudolf, and William Westermeyer, who shared information from their own researches or access to official materials, and John E. Cook, who prepared the maps and figures. Robert O. Keohane had the kindness and persistence to read and comment extensively on the entire first draft. Later drafts were improved by suggestions from Stephen Krasner, University of California Press readers, Paul S. Herrnson, and audience comments at colloquia in Woods Hole and Amherst. Moral support was provided by James Broadus, Steve Edwards, Nat Frazer, Porter Hoagland, Mark Meo, Kurt Schusterich, Michael J. Smith, and William Westermeyer. The enthusiasm and encouragement of first Allan Graubard and then Naomi Schneider kept the author going when the process of manuscript review and revision seemed endless. To all the aiders and abettors my thanks, and the customary absolution from responsibility for the study's remaining errors and shortcomings.

# 1

# Introduction

$A$ntarctica has seldom been in the news since 1959. Not until 1983 did it figure on the agenda of the United Nations General Assembly even though each fall that body discusses events or situations in every part of the world. This lack of attention stems, not from an inability to visit or carry out activity on the world's southernmost continent, but rather from the success of the cooperative mechanisms established in the Antarctic Treaty. By that treaty a continent and its surrounding ocean, which would otherwise have become a field for superpower and other conflict, was transformed into a nonmilitarized, nuclear-weapons-free, joint scientific laboratory.

Since the mid-1970s, however, questions about the long-term prospects for continued cooperation have arisen. Greater interest in utilizing Southern Ocean marine life and in the possibilities of Antarctic mineral and hydrocarbon resources have led many observers to doubt that the Antarctic Treaty will work as successfully in the future. These doubts have three sources. First, the whole treaty rests on a compromise between the seven states claiming territorial sovereignty over parts of Antarctica and the other signatories to the treaty under which both groups agreed to lay sovereignty questions aside and use the continent jointly. So long as Antarctica is basically a scientific laboratory, this compromise means no serious deprivation for any state. Once resource activity becomes an issue, however, the balance of costs and benefits shifts. National sovereignty over land and adjacent marine areas is the normal method of organizing the current international system. The Antarctic Treaty creates an exception supported by all participants, particularly the claimants, because the cost of conflict then outweighed the benefit of exercising sovereignty. Resource activity would change this by making the possession of territory more valuable. Everywhere else in the world the sovereign state has the right to regulate resource activity and to collect taxes, royalties, and other fees from anyone, foreigner or national, permitted to undertake resource activity. There would be significant benefits to having sovereignty over Antarctic territory if resource exploitation occurred, and these might be deemed greater than the cost of conflict ensuing from efforts to assert that sovereignty.

Second, the Antarctic Treaty is silent on resource questions, and many observers doubt that its provisions can be read as justifying joint regulation of resource activity by either the eighteen Consultative Parties or all thirty-seven signatories. The participating states themselves acknowledge the gap and are trying to cover it in a set of auxiliary agreements. Third, some observers believe that even if these auxiliary agreements prove effective, the whole Antarctic Treaty system is unstable. Some point to the fact that the treaty itself can be revised any time after 1991 at the request of any one Consultative Party. Others note the fact that a number of Third World states are calling for replacement of the existing treaty by a "common heritage" regime in which all states would participate with equal votes.

Both the quarter century of successful cooperation among states of very diverse outlooks and interests and the current uncertainty about the future make the Antarctic case one meriting study. The Antarctic Treaty set up an international regime—an interrelated set of principles, norms, rules, and procedures—around which participating states have structured their conduct in Antarctica and the Southern Ocean.

Students of international regimes accept the fact that the international system today lacks a world government, that is, a set of central institutions with the moral legitimacy and material predominance that would permit effective regulation of state conduct. Though admitting that the international system is an anarchy in which self-help is prominent, they reject the idea that self-help is the only mechanism for maintaining order. They realize, as have earlier generations of scholars, that the daily operation of the international system depends more on institutionalized patterns of cooperation established among states than on the exercise of naked power. Unlike many of those earlier scholars, however, they do not believe that the institutionalized patterns must necessarily evolve into a world government or lead to wider co-operation. They begin instead with the assumption that states are and will remain basically self-centered. States, in their view, are also constantly balancing the costs and benefits of cooperation or conflict in essentially rational fashion. Building on insights from game theory, learning theory, and the rational-expectations school of economics, they view cooperation among states as something that rises and declines as conditions in the international system and states' calculations of their own interests change.

The Antarctic Treaty and related agreements provide illuminating material for understanding international cooperation. No single case study is sufficient to definitively prove or disprove a theory, though "critical cases" can have a major impact on evaluations of a theory's strength. Yet even a noncritical case can help refine theoretical propositions. Two features of the Antarctic case make it particularly useful in efforts to further refine accounts of when, why, and how international cooperation emerges. First, most studies of international regimes have focused on economic issues such as trade, monetary questions, or the transfer of technology.[1] Though Antarctic affairs now have a growing economic component, security concerns have always been prominent in participants' thinking about Antarctic cooperation. Thus the Antarctic case can contribute to efforts to apply the notion of international regimes to security issues as well as economic ones. Such an extension of the theory is difficult, but it is necessary if the concept "international regime" is ever to become a central part of our understanding of how the international system works given the continued significance of security issues in the world.

Second, much of the existing literature focuses on international regimes that were initially established in the period immediately following World War II. Though most of these studies do pay attention to later changes, the explanations advanced for the emergence and later evolution of these regimes, particularly the "hegemonic stability theory" advanced by Charles Kindleberger and others,[2] are influenced by the circumstances of 1944–45. The Antarctic Treaty was concluded in 1959, and efforts to write supplementary agreements were begun in the mid-1970s. Since many analysts of the postwar regimes believe that conditions had already changed in important ways by 1960, the difference of time should be sufficient for testing whether some of the existing theories overgeneralize from a temporary set of circumstances.

## The Phases of International Regimes

An international regime is a set of principles, norms, rules, and procedures resting on mutual expectations and commitments that govern relations among states (and, where relevant, other actors) on some matter of common concern.[3] The phrase "international regime" usually calls to mind the image of an issue or a geographical area where the interactions of states are pursued through an intergovernmental organization that helps apply the rules and provides mechanisms for their adjustment. Thus, one thinks of the international monetary regime centered around the International Monetary Fund (IMF), or of the international aeronavigation regime centered around the International Civil Aviation Organization (ICAO).

In fact, five possible situations should be distinguished, only two of which are international regimes. In the first, governments do not feel a common concern, so they make no effort to explore the shape of mutual expectations or of the rules and organizations that might be created to assure their fulfillment. Environmental questions fell into this category before 1970. While a number of individuals, some private organizations, and a few governments were concerned about the damage being caused by various forms of human activity, most did not see the problem as one meriting international attention. In such a situation there will be no international regime, because no one sees the need for it. Governments have no incentive to begin the difficult task of searching for common ground or negotiating the rules and institutions that would best assure common goals.

Second, there may be agreement that some issue or area is a common concern, but no common expectations and no agreement on rules or goals. This is probably a relatively short-lived situation, ending as governments go through the process of determining their own policy and consulting with others. Yet acknowledging a common concern does not always lead to the creation of an international regime. Governments may agree that the matter is best left alone, discover that disagreements about what to do are too strong to allow joint or common action, or find that the cost of creating and operating an international regime would far outweigh the gain from doing so.

Third, there can be a common concern, a set of mutual expectations, and a set of common rules, but no intergovernmental organization. Today this probably occurs more often when interaction need not be continuous. For instance, the law of the sea has long included a rule that a warship of any nation may capture any pirates it encounters outside the territorial sea of another state. Rather than create a global anti-pirate patrol,[4] governments have been content to define pirates in fairly clear terms and to authorize each other to take unilateral action in the expectation that the interest of each maritime power in safe ocean travel will inspire the proper action whenever pirates are sighted. Given the size of the oceans and the relatively small number of pirates, this was and remains a more efficient solution than the creation of a special patrol. For similar reasons, there is no global organization dealing solely with the suppression of aircraft hijacking. Yet in these situations an international regime does exist. Even without an intergovernmental organization, written or tacit agreement on norms and rules guides individual actors' behavior and structures mutual expectations.[5]

Fourth, there can be a situation in which common concern, mutual expectation, and agreement on common rules and goals lead to the creation of an intergovernmental organization for dealing with an issue or a geographic area. This is fairly common when interaction must be continuous. While governments will still interact directly with one another on specific transactions, the intergovernmental organization serves as a central forum for discussing general problems and as a mechanism for enlisting help in getting a recalcitrant participant to live up to its agreements. This is the situation most frequently studied in the current literature on international regimes. Occasionally, an organization appearing relevant to some international regime proves irrelevant on closer inspection. The IMF was established in 1944, yet it did not become very important to the international monetary regime until 1958 when the Western European states had recovered to the point of being able to dismantle their postwar currency controls. Until that time the international monetary regime was essentially run by the United States, sometimes operating through organizations but usually dealing directly with one or more other countries.[6] Even in these cases there is an international regime, though it more closely approximates the third type of situation.

Finally, there is a confusing form of nonregime situation. Here there is some common concern and an intergovernmental organization giving expression to it, but very little in the way of mutual expectations, common goals, or common rules. In this situation the organization becomes an arena in which governments struggle to gain support for their own ideas, erode the support given to others' contradictory ideas, or both. The UN Security Council provides a good example of such a nonregime situation. The Security Council expresses the commonly held idea that states should settle disputes peacefully and that a war anywhere is a danger to the security of all. There is even ritual acceptance of the UN Charter norms dividing all resorts of force into self-defense (accepted), collective action organized through the UN or a regional organization (preferred), and aggression (prohibited). Yet any specific conflict quickly shows that there is no real agreement on goals or rules. What appears to one government as self-defense is to another a clear act of aggression. Some governments even adhere to theories that justify certain first resorts to force on grounds they are the necessary prelude to destroying some unacceptable situation (usually colonial or white racist rule) rather than aggression. Thus, what might seem a well-functioning international regime proves to be merely a heavily decorated stage for playing out vast disagreements.

Thus of five possible situations in international relations, only the third and fourth are characterized by the existence of international regimes. Before 1959 Antarctica fell into the first or second category. Initially there was no agreement that the continent should be a common concern; after World War II there was some agreement on the need for a common solution but no consensus on what that common solution ought to be. The experience of scientific cooperation in the International Geophysical Year (IGY) of 1957–58 heightened common concern and pointed the way toward a common solution. Since 1959 Antarctica has been governed by a regime with a rudimentary intergovernmental negotiating forum but no permanent intergovernmental organization until the establishment of fisheries-management institutions in 1982.

Whatever its precise form, no international regime is static for very long. Global conditions, the interests of individual states and other actors, and the ideas about proper conduct and organization held by those individuals controlling policy all change. Any of these changes can put pressure on an international regime. If these pressures become great enough, they can lead either to the transformation or to the breakdown of the regime. Thus, a dynamic theory of international regimes must take into account the different phases of a regime's existence.

The first phase, obviously, is creation—elaboration of an international regime for an issue or a geographic area where none presently exists. Since creation requires extensive activity or negotiation,[7] it tends to occur only when the governments of powerful states decide that continuing to do without an international regime is costly or dangerous. The example of international chaos in the 1930s provided the background against which the postwar economic regimes were elaborated in 1944–46. The initial hope that the UN would provide a working security regime was clearly inspired by thoughts that a third world war would prove too dangerous for all states.

Once the outlines of an international regime have been agreed upon, the new regime enters its establishment phase. This is also a time of relatively great effort, for it is only at this point that governments find out whether their notions actually work. Similarly, each national bureaucracy has to learn the new rules for interaction on the affected issue. Those individuals given responsible positions as delegates to or officers of the new intergovernmental organization have to learn their tasks. Thus, a new international regime goes through a period, not unlike the sea trials of a newly built ship, where everyone involved learns how the equipment will work under actual operating conditions.

If an international regime passes successfully through establishment, it then enters the more comfortable maintenance phase. Here actors need simply to apply the existing rules and procedures to situations with which they are familiar. At this point operating the regime and remaining within its bounds are quite easy. The rules have become standard operating procedure for the relevant national and international bureaucracies. Political leaders know which decisions they may or may not make unilaterally, which means they may employ, and how much blame they can shift to other countries, to the rules, or to the intergovernmental organization. As long as conditions in the international system, the international distribution of power, governments' calculation of their own interests, and governments' ideas remain basically stable, the international regime operates with a minimum of fuss, as "part of the furniture."

Yet things do not remain stable. International conditions, the international distribution of power, governments' calculations of interests, and ideas can all change. Change in one can lead to change in another, or each can change independently.[8] If one or more change is sufficiently large, then the international regime is put under stress. Initially, governments will try to ignore the change and act as if regime maintenance is the proper response. This economizes on effort in general and proves particularly effective if the change proves to be temporary. If the change proves lasting, however, at some point the governments and organizations involved will have to face the question of what to do.

When governments get to this point, they face the question of regime modification. They may decide, for one reason or another, to do nothing. More usually, however, they end up choosing among amendment, replacement, and termination of the regime. Amendment consists of modifying norms, rules, and procedures of the regime so that it continues to serve governments' interests.[9] Replacement consists of substituting one set of basic principles for another and then elaborating supplementary norms, rules, and procedures to match. If, for example, governments agreed that they should stop issuing national currencies and entrust the issuance and management of an international currency to the IMF, this would mean replacement of the current regime based on freely convertible national currencies. Termination consists of dropping an existing regime without providing any replacement, putting states back in the normal anarchy of the interational system on the issue concerned.

Amendment or replacement can be as difficult as creation because agreement must be attained not only on the need for change but on the precise level and content of the change. This explains the difficulties of international monetary negotiations in the 1970s. Large-scale amendment or outright replacement is also complicated by the fact that it occurs in a crisis atmosphere where "don't just stand there, do something" becomes a common urge well before there is wide agreement on what to do. If the scale of the required modification is more modest, it can proceed more easily. There the more difficult part may be getting enough participating governments to agree that a change is needed.

Like initial creation, amendment has an establishment phase in which all the actors must learn and test the new rules and procedures. This is probably shorter than the initial establishment phase, however, because amendment seldom affects every part of the regime. Thus, a fair amount of old knowledge can still be applied. It is possible for an international regime to go through successive phases of amendment, establishment, and maintenance. The history of the international monetary regime since 1960 shows just such a pattern. Economic conditions or members' preferences have never remained the same for very long, and the IMF has found itself adding or shedding procedures, committees, and rules quite frequently.[10]

However, change may overwhelm a regime, or a sufficiently large number of participants may withhold support. Both of this century's world wars disrupted quite a few international regimes. Some were simply reconstituted afterwards. Yet others, like the gold standard for international exchange, were not. Even when change is not so great, governments' responses can doom regimes. League of Nations efforts to promote monetary cooperation in the early 1930s ended in March 1933 when Franklin Roosevelt decided that the United States would not participate. The interwar collective security system died in the early 1930s from both outside attack (Axis aggression) and inside neglect (British and French failure to apply it against Japan or Italy). In either case, the choice is usually between replacement and termination.

Replacement occurs when governments decide that a different set of principles, norms, rules, and procedures will meet their common concerns. The process is like amendment, but the activity or negotiation involved deals with the more basic problem of defining the principles of future interaction, not just with adjusting norms, rules, and procedures. The newly substituted regime then begins its course through the various phases of existence. Experience under the previously existing regime is less directly relevant here, though it will generally suggest practices that should be avoided. Thus, the amount of new learning involved is almost as great as with the establishment of a newly created regime.

Termination of an international regime may happen in either of two ways. There may be a dramatic disintegration in which a number of governments publicly denounce the regime and the others find themselves unable to continue it on their own. Or there may be a quiet erosion in which most participating governments stop conforming at about the same time without publicly challenging the regime. Should termination occur, governments and other actors are thrown back on themselves. They may find this situation congenial and go without any international regime. However, they may decide later that they do need some type of regime. If so, they have to begin again at creation. Creation after an interval following the termination of a previous international regime can benefit, however, from the lessons of the past. The history of the earlier international regime may suggest approaches that will not work or outcomes that should be avoided. Yet even this effect fades with time. If a new generation of policy makers creates the new regime, they may be unaware of the previous history.[11]

## Phases of Regime Existence Explained

Understanding the dynamics of international regimes requires identifying the factors that help or hinder their creation, establishment, maintenance, amendment, replacement, and termination. This enterprise is complicated by two things. First, the various phases have different explanations, if only because a successfully established regime itself becomes a factor in its later evolution. To the extent it succeeds in structuring expectations and guiding conduct, the regime becomes one of the things actors consider in making their policies.

Second, analysis requires looking simultaneously at a triangular set of mutually influencing processes. Individual governments and other actors arrive at particular preferences according to their own internal decision-making processes. At the same time, an international regime seldom stems from the preferences of any one government. Rather, it results from interactions among the governments and others in which some preferences are satisifed, some partly satisfied, and some ignored. This process of interaction occurs within an international system that affects the outcome by helping determine which preferences are given more or less weight. Explanation of regime outcomes thus requires simultaneous attention to national politics in the individual participating states, to the interactions between participating states, and to the influence of the international milieu.

This poses some problems for the analyst. The structure and process of different domestic political systems are not understood equally well, because relevant information is not equally available in different countries. Some governments and other actors make great efforts to hide information from outsiders.[12] Others only provide information as requested, a process requiring acquisition of some basic level of knowledge elsewhere. Yet others routinely disclose information on bureaucratic organization, decision-making processes, budgets, working assumptions, and policy goals. In dealing with the international economic regimes of the postwar period, this has not been a severe problem, because the main states involved are all industrial ones with open societies. There governmental officials and citizens are accustomed to having their political system made rather transparent. For an issue like Antarctica, where the relevant actors include a number of dictatorial governments highly interested in hiding much of their domestic process, the problem is more severe. The analyst ends up with highly detailed information about some actors and very vague information about others. The only recourse, therefore, is to keep the analysis of domestic systems fairly broad.

Three factors account for the various phases of international regimes: the relative salience of the issue involved, the interests of individual states, and the distribution of power among them. All three play a role in determining each phase of a regime's existence, though the relative weight of each changes in different phases.

Salience is the sense of urgency attached to doing something about a particular matter or issue. It is based on perceptions both of the immediacy with which interests are affected and of the importance of the interests affected. An invasion has very high salience for the victim state: the problem exists now and threatens the most important state interests. Toward the other extreme, some change that is estimated to reduce national income by one percent twenty years from now has very low salience. Even if the one percent is deemed important, the lapse of time makes it difficult for decision makers to get excited about the matter, because other changes may intervene to prevent or compensate for the loss. Most issues and problems fall in the broad range between these two extremes. This double nature of salience suggests that it fluctuates for two reasons: changes in perception of immediacy and in perception of the importance of the affected interests. Perceptions of the importance of the interests affected, in turn, can hinge on either a reevaluation of the interests affected or a decision that the matter affects more or fewer interests than was originally believed.

In addition, two forms of salience should be distinguished: restricted and widespread. An issue may be salient to those charged with conducting a state's foreign policy in general or on the particular matter at hand without being deemed important by other government agencies, interest groups, or the general public. This restricted form of salience means that the issue will be handled by small groups of decision makers in conditions approaching those of nineteenth-century "cabinet diplomacy." Today, however, many international issues attain widespread salience.[13] The issues, or the policy chosen to handle them, are important to actors in the domestic political system as well. The general public, interest groups, and various government agencies vie for influence in determining the foreign policy to be pursued. The handling of issues that have attained widespread salience is far more complicated. Not only is there competition for control of policy within the domestic political system, but the competition is likely to spill across national borders. Different agencies and even domestic interest groups may use ties with counterparts abroad to increase the likelihood of their state's adopting the policy they prefer by getting other governments to adopt that preferred policy and urge it on their own government in bilateral or multilateral negotiations.

Interests are those things that a government regards as valuable. They may be material things to be possessed (like territory), opportunities for activity (such as access to fish stocks), or environmental conditions to be enjoyed (such as safety from invasion). Even though governments are not fully rational actors, their appreciation of interests is usually sharp enough to channel decision making in a rational direction.

Sometimes a state possesses sufficient power to protect or enhance a particular interest unilaterally. In most cases, though, a state in the international system, like an individual in a domestic political system, cannot protect or enhance interests alone. Rather, the state must make a coalition with likeminded others. Even great powers, which can serve a wider range of interests unilaterally than other states, often find cooperation necessary.

Coalition formation is a two-tier process aimed at finding a coalition that is both congenial and effective. Even among the basically like-minded, interests are compatible more often than identical, forcing prospective coalition partners to compromise. Compromise is even more essential when the likeminded lack sufficient power and must, therefore, recruit additional states if their coalition is to prevail. This can place governments in real dilemmas. There is little value in being part of a coalition that cannot protect its interests, yet there is also little value in compromising interests so far that the gains of winning either do not exceed or barely exceed the costs of the compromises required.

Attempts to create international regimes occur when an issue that looks as though it will persist and require cooperative management attains enough salience—whether restricted or widespread—to be regarded as requiring attention by several governments. Success in regime creation depends on a perception of shared or compatible interests among a coalition of states possessing sufficient power to protect the regime from challenge by nonparticipants. Clearly, the amount of power necessary will vary according to the number, power, and activity of the outsiders. The postwar economic regimes established under United States leadership were never seriously challenged by the Soviet Union, since it was not expected to participate in them. As the postwar history of superpower relations in the politico-military realm shows, the fates of these regimes would have been quite different had the USSR mounted a challenge.

Successful establishment of a regime depends on whether the principles, norms, rules, and procedures of the regime simultaneously reflect the interests and power of the leading coalition and prove workable in the international environment at the time of creation. There is no guarantee that either condition will be met. Sometimes, as at the Third UN Conference on the Law of the Sea, characteristics of the negotiating forum deviate so much from power realities in the international system that the agreements reached do not have the support of a coalition with sufficient resources to implement them. More often, participants in regime creation assume circumstances other than those actually existing in the international system. When the Bretton Woods Agreements were signed in 1944, participating governments assumed that postwar monetary dislocations would be relatively small and temporary. In fact, the needs of Europe were large and relatively long-lasting; the international monetary regime operated outside the IMF until 1958.

Regime maintenance depends on persistence of the shared or parallel interests and power constellation underlying the regime. At this point high salience is not necessary. In fact, successful establishment will decrease salience, since the issue appears to be resolved. A subsequent rise in salience is cause for concern, for it indicates problems with all or part of the regime. Maintenance does not require that interests or the distribution of power be frozen, but it does require that any change in interests be compatible with the elements of the regime and that the changes in power do not result in a preponderance accruing to states actively opposing the regime.

Attempts at regime modification, whether in the form of amendment, replacement, or termination, follow a new rise in salience. This renewed salience may stem from changes in international conditions, making the old principles, norms, rules, and principles difficult to apply; from reevaluation of interests by some or all participating governments; or from redistribution of power giving predominance to states unhappy with or actively opposed to the international regime.

Whether the new rise in issue salience leads to attempts at amendment, replacement, or termination, or to more than one of these simultaneously, depends on the level of dissatisfaction and the potentials of coalition formation among the dissatisfied. Attempts to amend either a universal or a limited participation regime are most likely when dissatisfaction is relatively low or if supporters calculate that they can rescue the regime from attack by changes that will attract enough inactive or hitherto nonparticipating states to maintain the predominance of the supporting coalition. Attempts at replacement or termination are more likely when participant dissatisfaction is higher or, in limited participation regimes, when a coalition of nonparticipants is able to enlist enough support from dissatisfied participants to form a coalition capable of replacing or ending the regime.

Success at amendment or replacement depends on conditions similar to those required for creation: perception of shared or parallel interests by a coalition of states with enough power to protect their agreements from challenge. Amendment and replacement differ from creation, though, in that they are affected by the existing regime. Amendment must be perceived as consistent with or at least accommodatable within the existing regime, whereas replacement is an effort to replace something that no longer works with a new mechanism of international cooperation that will work.

## The Phases Explained

Thus far, only the basic outline has been given. It is not enough to say that changes in salience, definitions of interest, and coalition formation produce results. It is necessary to explain how salience changes, how governments define state interests, and how the process of coalition formation operates.

### Salience

Changes in the relative urgency attached to particular issues have attracted less systematic study than either governmental definitions of interest or processes of coalition formation. Recent efforts to delineate an "international issue cycle" are tentative and require considerable refinement.[14] On reflection, however, the lack of systematic inquiry is easily explained: the mechanisms of rising and falling salience are many and for the most part are not linked to one another in any particular way.

Technological change frequently leads to a rise in the salience of new issues by posing new challenges or opening new possibilities that require international cooperation for most effective management or exploitation. The nineteenth and twentieth centuries are replete with examples: railways, telecommunications, nuclear arsenals, and pollution from new industrial processes. Technological change has played a role in increasing the salience of Antarctica. Better ships, aircraft, shelter, and equipment all help people do more in the harsh Antarctic environment. Today nearly a thousand people work in the Antarctic through the winter, with several thousand more active in the summer months. Technology today is proving important in moving Antarctic issues toward widespread rather than restricted salience. Exploitation of fish and krill is a reality, and many observers believe that exploitation of fuel and mineral resources is likely by the end of the century.

Though some technological advances can transform an existing issue on their own, most issues acquire new salience when technology permits some change in the process of international politics. Improved transport and communications have led to greater interconnectedness among states and peoples, in many cases amounting to a real interdependence among them. This means such things as more international trade and more cultural contact with others. Incrased interconnection also creates new problems of regulating or facilitating those contacts, and the shift of many issues to widespread salience as the public or particular interest groups acquire stakes in the policies pursued.

Changes in ideas about what is just, effective, or factually correct are another form of exogenous change. These can operate at both the domestic and the international level, and are particularly important if taken up by several governments. Starting in the late eighteenth century, groups in a number of countries challenged the age-old notion that slavery was an acceptable form of human relations. This gave rise to intergovernmental agreements to end the slave trade, requiring a new exception to the rule that ships of one state's navy may stop only ships flying that state's flag on the high seas. The spread of ideas that the government is responsible not only for fostering the wealth of the state but the welfare of each individual in it has led to a new set of international concerns. As governments discovered that the rules governing international transactions affected their ability to manage the domestic economy, they have sought international rules that do not unduly inhibit performance of their domestic tasks.

Changes at the domestic level have also contributed to the creation of new issues or transformed old ones by substituting widespread for restricted salience. The rise of mass interest in politics has made appeal to foreign public opinion a more powerful instrument in international politics. This gives old concerns about propaganda, espionage, and subversion whole new dimensions unforeseen in the days when influencing policy choices meant suborning a few courtiers. At the same time, nationalism has given the individual state a source of legitimacy that generally strengthens it in confrontations with foreign states or private groups. Where it is accepted, mass participation in politics has permitted growth of transnational networks by which interest groups can raise issues before several governments simultaneously. This allows the process by which some matter becomes an international issue to be accelerated, as is shown in the environmental movement of the late 1960s.

Changes in the domestic structure of states, particularly on the question of who rules, can lead to new or renewed interest in some issue by changing the definitions of state interest guiding policy. This is most vivid in the wake of great social revolutions but can occur after less dramatic changes as well.

The decentralized and competitive nature of the international system itself sometimes contributes to rising salience. If a shift in the distribution of power brings to the fore governments preferring different outcomes, then issues will be raised or raised again in efforts to change those outcomes. Actual change may not occur, but the issue will have to be faced nonetheless. In fact, a change in the distribution of power is not always necessary to the raising of issues. Matters often lie dormant until one state shows interest, at which point others decide they had better do the same. The political history of Antarctica yields several good examples. The British decision to make a formal territorial claim attracted French, Argentine, and Chilean attention and rival claims. German activity prompted the formal Norwegian claim in 1939; that claim, in turn, prompted the first official Soviet statement on Antarctic affairs.

Changes affecting related issues, or the operation of related international regimes, can cause the salience of an issue to rise. The increasing volume of international trade in the 1950s and 1960s put pressure on the regime government management of currencies, because the larger volumes of payments accompanying trade created need for greater funds of credit to assist states caught in temporary balance-of-payments deficits. This contributed to the 1971 Smithsonian Agreement ending adherence to the fixed peg system of exchange rates, and became particularly acute after the increases in oil prices after 1973.

The rules of general international law sometimes provide a special reason for increased salience. Stipulations that the agreements on which a regime is based will expire or be reviewed after a particular interval require governments to devote at least cursory attention to the agreement. The extent to which this leads to changes in the regime depend, of course, on whether participating governments believe change to be desirable and opportune. The United Nations Charter provided for holding a review conference after ten years (that is, in 1955), but all members agreed that any attempt to rewrite the charter would cause the collapse of the UN. Thus, they avoided even convening the conference. Yet a deadline may be used to open discussions or revise the basis on which a state participates in a particular agreement. France used the twenty-year-renewal clause in the North Atlantic Treaty to continue within the Western alliance but to pull out of the specific arrangements for defense coordination embodied in the North Atlantic Treaty Organization.

Declines in salience come about for at least as many reasons as do increases. Some result from the permanent or temporary disappearance of whatever caused the initial contention. The partition of Poland in 1770–90 and the final breakup of the Ottoman Empire after World War I removed issues from the international agenda. Some declines in salience result from the closing of opportunities. For example, the internal strengthening of China after 1949 ended a Western competition for influence that had been going on for a century. Some, such as the fate of Hitler's plans for conquest, are settled by war; some are superseded by or subsumed under broader issues.

Quite often, however, salience decreases because governments find a way to manage a problem or an issue that meets their immediate needs. International civil aviation is now sufficiently well regulated that the only questions regularly posed today concern fare setting and protection from hijackers. International agreements on allocation of frequencies deal successfully with problems of interference between broadcasts and communications uses within and among countries.

It is easy to recognize increases and decreases of salience, and shifts between restricted and widespread salience, once they occur. It is much harder to predict them in advance, because of the multiplicity of pathways involved. Since, however, changes in salience determine only the timing of attempts to create, establish, maintain, or modify international regimes, the lack of predictive hypotheses need not stymie inquiry into the success or failure of attempts or the content of regimes achieved in particular cases.

### Interests

The way governments define interests determines how they will react to a rise in the salience of a particular issue. Students of foreign policy have long attempted to determine how governments define their interests. Many take a structuralist position, viewing the definition of state interests as simple equivalence with the interests of whatever group or coalition of groups is most powerful within the government. This basic structuralist position is then elaborated in different ways by five major schools of thought.

Today the Marxists, especially if neo-Marxists are included, form the most numerous school of structuralist analysts of domestic politics. Whatever else they may disagree about, Marxists classify national political systems according to their underlying economic structure, the "relationship of the means of production." The basic theory is straightforward: the character of the political system and the policies the government is likely to pursue can be determined by the kind of economic system that a state possesses. Further, different policies are appropriate to the growth and maintenance of different economic systems. Most Marxists distinguish four types of economic (and hence political) systems: slave, feudal, capitalist, and socialist. Some add a fifth type, an "Asiatic mode of production" in which the most important resources for economic activity are controlled and allocated by a central bureaucracy rather than by a particular class or (in socialism) by the whole society.

Another modern structural tradition analyzes governments in terms of their relation to the individual citizen. Adherents to this view distinguish among totalitarian, authoritarian, and democratic regimes, sometimes using only these three categories but sometimes elaborating subcategories as well.[15] While some adherents employ rather unsophisticated versions that label all rightist or all leftist governments totalitarian, there is an analytical version in which the term "totalitarian" is used to denote governments that seek not only secure tenure and predominance in the political realm, but control over virtually all aspects of people's lives. Hitler's and Stalin's are the most frequently cited examples of such governments, but the term can also be applied to those of Perón in Argentina, Franco in Spain, Mao in China, or Pol Pot in Cambodia. Governments that seek only to protect their tenure and their political predominance by limiting citizen freedom are considered authoritarian. Those that allow the citizens great freedom in the political realm and accept the possibility of replacement in periodic elections are considered democratic.

This school has not elaborated a systematic theory of how policy differs under the various types of government, other than an appreciation of the different degrees of central direction likely to be applied and the different amounts of citizen freedom likely to be tolerated. It tends to assume that definitions of interest in totalitarian states will always sacrifice the interests of individuals to those of the government, that definitions of interest in authoritarian states will sacrifice individual interests only where the continued tenure of the government is at stake, and that in democratic states the interests of individual citizens will be constantly taken into account.

A third structural school deduces policy and calculations of interest from the identity of the social group, or coalition of social groups, controlling the government. In simple versions, this school is almost identical to much Marxist analysis. Classical Marxism regards all governments established before attainment of socialism simply as mechanisms by which the owners of the means of production assure their position and preserve the economic system against domestic or foreign challenge. The government is simply the "executive committee" of the predominant economic class.

Yet there is a more subtle version of this theory: While accepting the basic notions that some people rule while others are ruled, and that rulers tend to use their power to benefit the social group from which they were recruited or on which they depend for their political base, it assumes that rule is usually shared by a number of social groups. Rather than the two-class model of slave, feudal, or capitalist society propounded in classical Marxism, it views society as more differentiated and fluid. In its view, the government might well be controlled by a cross-class coalition consisting of, for example, military officers drawn initially from the lower middle class, large landowners, and technocrats in charge of the country's largest nationalized industry. Some Marxists have edged toward this approach in realizing that finance capitalism is different from industry-based capitalism, or that the interests of large and small feudal landlords can differ.[16] Yet on the whole it has been more popular with those students of democracy who recognize that democratic systems offer opportunities to social groups on a differential basis.[17]

Though defining their social groups by finer categories and leaving open the possibility of a wide variety of coalitions, this more subtle school also assumes that government calculations of the national interest and choices of policy will reflect the needs of the ruling group or coalition. This, however, is a far more complicated structural model than the Marxist, requiring a lot more information about the particular domestic system or systems being analyzed and resulting in far less broad predictions. In fact, this school produces domestic analogues to the overall and issue-specific structure models used in international relations. Some interest theorists assume that the balance of influence among groups is stable most of the time, so the group making decisions on one issue makes decisions on all others until it gets pushed out of its place by changes in society that give other groups more power. The theorists who come to this model out of pluralist theory tend to assume that ruling coalitions can change, depending on the issue involved. This is probably more often true in the Western industrial states, but should not be written off in advance elsewhere.

A fourth school, developed mainly by analyzing differences in response among Western industrial states, explains policy in terms of the government's ability to make and implement a consistent policy vis-à-vis its own society.[18] These ideas cut across all the other structural theories presented thus far, because any type of government ruled by any social coalition can display different levels of strength. Stalin in 1924 was freer to impose his preferences on Soviet society than Gorbachev is today. In the 1920s the October Revolution and ensuing civil war had destroyed the old noble and capitalist classes, but the Bolsheviks had not yet put any definite ruling elite in their place. In the intervening sixty years, a new society with well-entrenched party, ministerial, military, security police, and industrial interests has formed in the USSR. Similarly, some authoritarian governments are relatively efficient and able to give their policies effect, as in Indonesia, while others are a disorganized shambles, as in Haiti.

The fifth structuralist school, that of bureaucratic politics, explains policy choices as the result of a competition among the various offices and agencies of government to control decisions.[19] It assumes that governments consist of related but competing parts, each out to maximize its own resources, power, and area of authority. While each part does have an area of activity clearly falling within its purview, there is still room for competition. Some issues do not fall clearly within the purview of any one agency or office. Other issues have multiple aspects, each of which falls within the purview of a different agency or office. Analysts using this bureaucratic politics approach assume that in either case the policy choice can be explained by identifying the agency or office able to garner the most support for its preferences. This is done by appeals to friendly members of the top political leadership, friendly members of the legislature, or affected interest groups.

A few theories of domestic politics stress the independent constraints imposed by certain aspects of the domestic political process. The organizational-process theory views policy as constrained by the routines through which government agencies operate when carrying out decisions.[20] Essentially, it builds on the common observation that people and organizations react even to new situations by doing things they have done before. Internal coordination requires that governments deal with events according to preset routines that specify who does what when. Set routines are particularly useful when dealing with emergencies or with large numbers of ordinary events because they reduce the amount of time needed to get a response. Yet routines can also limit choice. It may be impossible, at least in the short run, to take certain actions because they are not built into routines and bureaucrats refuse to take the responsibility for departing from the routine. For example, the United States Navy had great difficulty carrying out President Kennedy's instructions for the 1962 "quarantine" of Cuba because they did not fit within any of the kinds of blockading action already detailed in Naval Regulations.

Theorists of organizational process also stress the extent to which routines may delay responses to change. In their view, organizations even more than individuals tend to fit new perceptions into old patterns by ignoring or explaining away the inconvenient facts because the creation of routines represents a large "sunk cost" in terms of energy and resources. This gives the organizational process an inherent inertia that prolongs whatever exists. Adherents of this theory tend to assume that only very large changes, which can no longer be explained away or ignored, or extremely grave emergencies will lead to a reworking of routines.

A second theory of process looks at politics a little more broadly and explains what governments do by identifying what choices of goals and means remain open after the restraints of national customs and laws are taken into account. These restraints may involve prohibitions of particular activities (such as censorship) or of particular methods (such as torture to get confessions from suspected criminals). The restraints may also involve complications arising from divisions of power such that the national executive cannot act alone in some matter (as in Western Europe where the parliament must approve all taxes and spending) or that decisions and actions are left to local rather than national authorities (as in the United State where state and local authorities control decisions about where to site most nuclear power plants).

A third theory of process looks at the relative openness of a society. This has developed somewhat differently in the analysis of domestic and of international politics. Students of national politics have tended to use the notion as a shorthand for contrasting the behavior of individuals and groups in democratic and in dictatorial countries, with leaders in democratic systems seen as more susceptible to private pressures and more open to suggestions "from below" (whether "below" be subordinate officials or citizens). Yet this difference seems amply captured in the structural theories differentiating types of national polities. Students of foreign policy or international relations use a different variant, where "open" means susceptible to influence from abroad. For international economic relations the distinction between "open" and "closed" economies is one of different susceptibility to influences stemming from international markets or from other governments' economic decisions. These, in turn, stem from different levels of dependence on or interrelatedness to other countries. Thus, adherents to this theory acknowledge that the Soviet Union is less susceptible to global economic developments than the United States or Japan because of its greater self-sufficiency and fewer outside trade links, and the United States less so than Belgium, since foreign trade and transactions form a smaller part of the U.S. national economy. For foreign policy generally, the distinction is one between those states where the national government is able to control all or most public interaction with foreign governments or private groups, such as China, and those where private individuals, groups, and firms are relatively free to form their own cross-border ties, such as Switzerland.

The fourth theory of process explains policy by looking at the ideas held by those who influence or control it. This school begins with the notion that people do not react to the facts, because the facts must first be filtered through their preexisting perceptions and ideas. For this school, perceptions of power, openness, sensitivity, and vulnerability are more important than their actual extent. Thus, while an outside observer may think a particular Third World economy relatively closed, the decision makers in that country may not. Many Third World decision makers believe one or another theory stressing how the small exporter of raw materials is at the mercy of the large lender or the large exporter of manufactured goods, whether that lender or exporter is a government or a transnational corporation. The same differences can apply in any state. When the first oil crisis began in 1973, most Americans looked at it in terms of the Organization of Petroleum Exporting Countries (OPEC) against the entire West. Only as the crisis continued, and even more as postcrisis analyses began to appear, did Americans perceive that while an oil shortage was a problem for all the Western industrial states, a cutoff of Middle East oil was a bigger problem for Western Europe than for the United States. This led to a shift in perceptions that introduced a new tension into the Western alliance. Americans realized that if military force had to be used or threatened, only their country had the requisite military resources, but the allies had greater need of success in keeping the oil flowing. This built another strain into the alliance by giving domestic critics of the North Atlantic Treaty Organization (NATO) another reason to think that the United States was being forced to bear a disproportionate burden.

Each of these theories can explain, with greater or lesser success, individual governments' definitions of their own interests when each is left to itself. Yet international relations pose two problems not always addressed by these schools. First, the existence and attitudes of other states, equally committed to advancing their own interests, must be taken into account. In addition, governments must cope with the international system's lack of centralized governing institutions. In domestic politics individuals can compete for control of central institutions and then use those institutions to secure interests. At the international level governments are forced to protect their state and its interests by whatever combination of unilateral action, alliance with others, or establishment of common ground-rules for activity that seems workable and attainable.

Most adherents to structural models assume that states having similar structures will find it easier to cooperate with each other than states having different structures, because states with similar structures define interests in similar ways. This is not true of all structuralists, however. Lenin always assumed that despite their similarity capitalist states would not be able to maintain stable cooperation with one another because each had to expand continually in order to maintain a capitalist economy at home.[21] In his view, similarity leads to limitless desire for the same things in a finite world where all parties cannot be satisfied simultaneously.

Most theorists viewing state interests as defined solely by dominant groups at home fail to consider the effect of international competition on those definitions. The need to protect interests from competing nation-states and the socializing impact of constant interaction with them often leads to similar behavior by states with vastly different domestic structures. International politics imposes certain requirements for success to which governments respond. The Antarctic case demonstrates this very clearly: such things as possession of a territorial claim or the presence of a large distant-water fishing fleet in the Southern Ocean determine alignments among states far more than similarity or difference in domestic structures.

The theories attributing definitions of interest to certain features of a state's domestic political process also fail to address international relations directly. Yet a number of propositions can be derived from them. The organizational-process theory suggests that individual governments often accept continuation of an international regime longer than a fully rational evaluation of their interests might mandate, simply because it has become part of the routine. Amendment, replacement, and termination all require the overcoming of inertia, so they are begun only for serious reasons. Theories calling attention to constraints on choice imposed by national laws or customs help indicate areas where intergovernmental bargains will be difficult to make or to keep. For instance, in 1976 the United States government agreed to permit the Concorde, the British-French supersonic passenger jet, landing rights in New York and Washington so long as it obeyed the rule requiring all civil aircraft to fly at subsonic speed over U.S. territory. However, the Port Authority of New York and New Jersey, which operates all the international airports near New York City, would not issue the necessary permits for use of its airports because the Concorde exceeded local limits on aircraft noise during takeoff and landing. The British and French governments initially insisted that the federal government force the Port Authority to change its position. Only after considerable discussion did they accept the fact that the federal government lacked the legal authority to do so, and decide to confine flights to Washington where the federal government itself set the relevant noise standards.[22]

A stress on the relative openness of different societies and governments suggests variations in the way different states approach the general problem of regimes. A weak state hoping to persuade a strong state to change its position will have a better chance if that strong one has an open society rather than a closed one. Open states are likely to notice signals of trouble sooner—because subnational actors are allowed greater autonomy and the government's tenure depends in part on satisfying all or some subnational actors' needs—but may not manage to adopt a new course of action as quickly as a closed state. This suggests that states with open societies are likely to propose amendments to regimes sooner. A stress on initiation or early adoption of new ideas also leads one to expect the initiatives for regime creation or change to come from governments that have adopted new conceptions of the problem rather than from those content to continue thinking about it in the old way.

While features of the domestic political system are important to a government's definition of state interests, these definitions are also influenced by the need to cope with other states in an anarchical international system. The process of forming coalitions thus exercises an important influence on definitions of interest.

## Coalitions

As in domestic politics, an individual actor's possession of interests is not sufficient to secure their protection and promotion. Rather, the individual must band together with a sufficient number of like-minded others in the international system. While domestic politics dilutes the interest-power relation by filtering it through central institutions capable of redressing power differentials among social groups and discouraging the most extreme forms of self-help, international politics leaves the interests-power connection far more obvious. There extreme forms of self-help always remain a possibility, and no institutions capable of redressing power inequalities exist. This obvious importance of power has led many theorists of international politics to adopt a rigorously structural position, attributing all outcomes to unilateral or group possession of sufficient power to overawe opposition.

Though agreed on this basic point, international-level structuralists are divided on the question of what sort of power is most relevant to the formation of coalitions capable of creating and maintaining international regimes. Some stress the relevance of overall power, arguing that general military or economic capability is the key to success. Others stress the relevance of issue-specific power, arguing that the ability to do the specific things most relevant to determination of the issue at hand is more important than all-round capability.

Emphasis on the overall international distribution of power, whether power is defined as military capability[23] or as size and relative advancement of the national economy,[24] is the oldest and simplest way to analyze and predict the course of any international interaction. As applied to international regimes, a stress on the overall distribution of power takes two forms. The first is the more recently developed theory of hegemonic stability. The Great Depression and postwar experience in the economic field has suggested to a number of observers that the existence of a hegemonial power is necessary to the creation of international regimes, and probably to their successful adaptation.[25] The older, and probably more widely accepted, form of structural explanation does not insist upon the existence of a hegemonial power, but does predict that shifts of phase in an international regime's existence will follow from shifts in the distribution of power, and that the principles, norms, rules, and procedures included in the regime at any particular time reflect the desires of the states with the greatest overall power. To these theorists, power is universally fungible and may be shifted from one issue or geographical area to another without much cost or delay.[26]

The other variant of structural explanation asserts that the best explanation of the phases and content of any international regime is the distribution of capabilities directly related to the issue or the geographical area at hand. For adherents of this view, the most significant variable for predicting the future of the international monetary regime is not overall capacity but the size of different states' reserves, the extent to which various currencies are used in international transactions, and the extent to which different states can raise additional resources by borrowing from private capital markets, other governments, or international financial institutions. In a study of Antarctic regimes, such theories would look at a state's past level of activity, its previous assertion or challenge to territorial claims, and its ability to maintain a level of activity in the future commensurate with that of others.

Either of these structural theories assumes that the strong make the rules and that others accept those rules because they are unable to do anything else. These theories further assume that as the number or identity of the strongest states changes the international regime will change. The overall-structure theory is the more parsimonious; it permits a greater number of predictions on a smaller amount of information. One need know only the overall distribution of power to be able to predict the course of any international regime. Yet the overall-structure variant is also less discriminating. It cannot explain, for instance, why the Soviet Union is essential to any security regime but virtually irrelevant to trade regimes. The issue-structure theory requires more information but is able to distinguish more finely among international regimes. It can explain not only the differences in the Soviet position just mentioned, but also why Switzerland is important in any discussions of the international monetary system but far less important in discussions of trade.

The Antarctic case shows the importance of power in international relations, since the outcomes at each stage of the Antarctic regime's existence are compatible with the interests of the strongest participating states. Yet it also illuminates two limits to the usefulness of power-based theories. First, as will be seen, some outcomes cannot be explained solely by reference to power. Supposedly weaker participants have often found ways to influence stronger ones and get outcomes closer to their preferences than would have been the case if the stronger had adhered to their initial preferences. Second, it also shows that the conditions for operation of power-based theories are not always present in international relations, leaving many outcomes to be explained in other ways.

The strongest assertions of power-based theories about international regimes posit not only that outcomes reflect the desires of the strong but also that international regimes are created, established, and modified or terminated as a result of shifts in the distribution of power which bring to the fore new coalitions with different interests. This assertion cannot be tested fully in the Antarctic case, because, as will be shown later, the distribution of power has not changed very much since 1945. Yet that case suggests that changes in regimes can result from other things. A number of theorists have suggested a number of other factors that affect coalition building and hence outcomes. These notions rest on the assumption that the process, how governments interact in the international system, influences how they perceive their own interests and form their coalitions.

The first such theory focuses on the effect of broad changes in the global economic process, particularly technological change and changes in the level of interdependence among states. While some studies using this explanation use the term "interdependence" in the contemporary sense of a relation that would be costly for both sides to break off,[27] many seem to use the word as equivalent to interconnectedness—the mere fact of having a higher level of cross-border transactions. However defined, changed levels of interdependence, like changes in technology, are assumed to have some effect on all economies.

Though that is true in principle, a general effect seldom has the same impact on all national economies. In most cases, the relative size or advancement of the economy makes a significant difference in the way the effects are felt. Satellite technology offers great potential benefits to all, but only those who have and use telecommunications and data systems most intensively will reap the fullest benefit. A general increase in the level of interconnectedness will have a greater effect on a small economy, since the same change in the absolute level of international transactions will mean a greater proportional change in a small than in a large economy. But all such changes, whether reinforcing or eroding existing structures, do point up new possibilities and lead to new calculations of interests which can affect all states' willingness to create, maintain, amend, replace, or terminate a particular international regime.

This theory of changes in the general economic process as the motor of international regime change posits a simple relation between the level of interdependence (or interconnectedness) and the desire for an international regime. The basic argument is that increases in the level will be noticed by governments and significant domestic interest-groups and make them more interested in international regimes. Since interdependence or interconnectedness is usually very difficult to escape, governments will be keen to regulate the new relations so that benefits are maximized and costs minimized. One important cost is the loss of ability to make unilateral decisions. International regimes can minimize this cost by creating a set of common rules and procedures that limit everyone's choice of goals and means, thereby making the most costly forms of outside behavior less likely. Under such circumstances, governments can be persuaded that giving up some of their own discretion in a general surrender is better than trying to assert an unlimited right to "go it alone" likely to be challenged by others.[28]

This theory also posits that later changes in the level of interdependence will put serious strain on international regimes, leading either to adaptation or to termination. As governments perceive the change and see that it is affecting the balance of benefits and costs arising from the international regime, they will desire change. This theory tends to assume that adaptation will be the response, since the fact of interdependence remains and governments will still wish to capture the benefits interdependence brings. At least implicitly, termination is assumed to occur when the level of interdependence falls enough that it is not providing benefits worth the cost of maintaining an international regime. Yet this theory does not exclude the possibility of governments deciding that the value of "going it alone" is higher than the value of cooperation whatever the level of interdependence.

A second theory of process focuses on something that appears relevant to any issue or area, namely the activity of intergovernmental organizations able to assert a mandate for addressing the issue or regulating activity in the area. This theory can be applied without assuming that every regime has an organization or that every organization is part of a regime. It does assume, however, that since international regimes stem from interactions among states, and since intergovernmental organizations structure certain interactions in certain ways, they have an influence on all interactions coming within their purview. International organizations provide places where governments—or even bureaucratic actors within governments—can create coalitions of the like-minded in other governments or the staff of the organization. They also provide a set of norms and procedures that may be used at any phase of a regime's existence.

This organization-process theory assumes that once created, an international organization is unlikely to disappear; hence an investment in learning the organization's procedures and norms will pay off in greater ability to affect outcomes. There have been many examples of just such a phenomenon. No other theory could have predicted that Singapore would have had major influence in the law of the sea negotiations, yet the procedural knowledge and diplomatic ability of its chief delegate, Tommy T. B. Koh, assured that country a critical role.

This focus on organizationally based influence can take two forms. Most work to date has focused on the way in which organizations created as part of a particular regime contribute to the implementation, maintenance, or adaptation of that regime. Yet it is also possible to trace influences from other international organizations, whether general-purpose ones like the UN General Assembly, or special-purpose ones set up as part of international regimes in related issues or areas. Thus, one could study the functioning of the internatinal trade regime by focusing on the General Agreement on Tariffs and Trade (GATT), but a fuller study would also take into account the activities of the UN General Assembly, the UN Conference on Trade and Development, the IMF, and the World Bank, all of which deal with issues that can impinge on the conduct of international trade or negotiations within GATT. This second variation on the organizational-process theory permits its use even for nonregimes or regimes without organizations.

In either variant, the theory assumes that the organization will generally work to slow down regime change and reduce the likelihood of termination. On the whole, organizations change more slowly than do conditions in the international system, governments' calculations of their own interests, or ideas. The governments and bureaucratic actors benefiting from the existing organizational networks will be loath to change them. Even those who are not benefiting as much will be loath to change simply because the familiar is more comfortable in most situations. Thus, organizations provide more inertia to be overcome in efforts to make changes. Additionally, organizations promote inertia by encouraging participants to fit changes into existing patterns as long as possible. This means that an organization will be a useful force for stability during temporary changes, but an additional hurdle to be overcome when the change is permanent and the regime must be adapted.

Obviously, organizational processes are relevant to the creation of a new international regime only if creation is effected through, or meant to prevent involvement by, particular organizations. Such processes are more relevant in other phases of the regime's existence. As long as a regime persists, any organization created within it affects outcomes. However, outside organizations may also affect outcomes even when they have no formal role. The Antarctic now provides a good example of this latter phenomenon. The fact that an outsider campaign for replacement is being waged through the UN General Assembly is helping the Consultative Parties avoid carrying their disagreements so far as to endanger the regime's stability while they work to amend it.

A third theory of process takes a slightly different focus, paying attention not to organizations but to the operation of any or all related international regimes as a whole. This theory has the advantage of capturing the effects of regimes that lack organizations, though it fails, unlike the second theory, to take account of organizations that do not form part of a regime. This theory assumes that the ordinary working of one regime can assist in the various phases of another's existence, either by suggesting that the latter regime needs to be created or by contributing strains that help force its adaptation or termination. This theory also assumes that strains in one regime are likely to spill over into related areas. Under this theory it is not surprising that the relative undervaluation of the yen and overvaluation of the dollar in the international monetary regime pose serious problems for the international trade regime because they work together to badly distort Japanese and American trade.[29] There has been little thought about whether stability in one regime can assist the maintenance of another; the prevailing assumption seems to be that stability "stays home" while strain "travels."

Recent developments in Antarctica provide a very clear example of strain's traveling. Changes in the law of the sea during the mid-1970s provide the second main explanation for the timing of efforts to amend the Antarctic regime. This was done indirectly, by changing the value of access to Antarctic fisheries for distant-water fishing fleets and by changing the possible economic benefits of having sovereignty over a piece of Antarctic territory. While these effects have been unusually dramatic, the Antarctic example suggests that the effects of changes in related international regimes can explain activity that otherwise appears meaningless.

A fourth theory of process explains change mainly as the result of shifts in the ideas widely shared among governments and other actors. Such ideas may be no more specific than "we can't let that happen again," or may posit particular relations of cause and effect and suggest ways to get rid of the effect by removing the cause. A good example of this latter type is the Prebisch thesis of international trade. It says that the position of developing countries in international trade will progressively worsen because the prices for raw materials and agricultural goods will not increase as quickly as the prices for manufactured goods in a competitive market. It then says that the solution to the developing countries' problem is the creation of market-regulating devices that will assure at least a commensurate rise in the prices of raw materials and agricultural commodities whenever the prices of manufactured goods rise. This suggests the formation of intergovernmental producers' associations or the negotiation of producer-consumer price-support agreements.

This theory does not deny all relation between ideas and position in the political structure. Obviously a state with global interests looks at security issues differently than does a state whose main problem is keeping one or more neighbors on their own side of the mutual border. Obviously, too, a state that reaps great benefits from existing rules is going to look at them differently than will a state that does not. The theory does assert, however, that ideas have an existence independent of structure, and spread for reasons unrelated to structure or changes in structure. Individuals, groups, and governments all explore, experiment, and learn. Demonstration effects of others' successes or failures, national histories and traditions, and new ideas arising in the global community of scholars and scientific investigators all contribute to changes in the ideas held by governments, and these changes can lead to changes in policy. Changes in policy are one of the ingredients of change in international regimes.

Theories that pay attention to the influence of ideas posit that regime creation depends not only on perceiving a common concern but on having a notion of how to deal with it. In the nineteenth century people knew that trade between different countries having different currencies could occur only if there was some way to tell what each currency was worth. The prevailing economic ideas of the time gave a simple solution: the value of each currency should be expressed by some weight of gold, and these gold equivalents could then be compared. If a government erred in assigning the value, or if developments in trade indicated that foreigners valued the currency more or less highly than the official figure, adjustments would come through the market. Government management of the money was deemed unwise as well as unnecessary. Today, ideas about how to deal with this same problem are very different, and go far to account for the differences between nineteenth-century and contemporary international monetary regimes.

Though offering various explanations, these theories of process taken as a group illuminate ways in which governments can be brought to reevaluate their interests and re-form their coalitions. Again, the simple structural model seems inadequate, though a stress on issue-specific power explains more than focusing solely on overall power. Power is important, but it operates within an international system having processes that limit choice even for the most powerful states or coalitions.

With these tentative hypotheses in mind, it is time to turn to an examination of the Antarctic Treaty system. The Antarctic case illuminates the processes of creation, establishment, maintenance, and amendment, since all of these have occurred during the Antarctic Treaty system's quarter century of existence. It also sheds some light on replacement, at least when offered as an alternative to amendment, because of the recent Third World effort to bring Antarctica under a "common heritage" regime.

Since the Antarctic case is unfamiliar to most people, chapters 2 and 5 summarize the history of Antarctic activity and negotiation between 1945 and the present. Chapter 2 takes the story through the signing of the Antarctic Treaty in December 1959, since that act marks the transition between regime creation and later phases of regime existence; Chapter 5 brings the story to the present. Chapters 3 and 4 explore the conditions of regime creation by examining both the unsuccessful effort of 1948–49 and the successful effort that produced the Antarctic Treaty. Chapter 6 explores the conditions of regime maintenance by focusing on the period 1961–70 when the Antarctic Treaty came into force and its institutions were given their initial tests. Chapter 7 explores the dynamics of current participants' efforts to amend the Antarctic regime. Chapter 8 focuses on efforts by outsiders to replace it, paying particular attention to the special conditions arising from the fact that replacement is being offered as an alternative to amendment. Chapter 9 applies lessons from the Antarctic case to the refining of theories about international regimes.

# 2

# Regime Creation

The Antarctic Treaty was negotiated in a lengthy process culminating in the Washington Conference held between 15 October
and 1 December 1959. The Conference followed several years of intermittent
discussions among governments of the twelve states most active in Antarctica.
These discussions, in turn, followed several decades of individual activity and
assertion by the governments involved.

## Antarctic Politics before 1959

Though geographically contiguous, the Southern Ocean and the Antarctic
continent have distinct histories because activity in the ocean has always been
easier than activity on the continent. Their geographic proximity has ensured,
however, that the politics of the two has always been intertwined.

In the nineteenth century little thought was given to legal regimes for the
continent. Explorers who saw it, whether on government service, like the
Englishman Ross, the American Wilkes, or the Russian Bellingshausen, or in
search of commercial opportunity in whaling and sealing, like the American
Palmer or the Englishman Biscoe, might lay claim to the areas they saw, but
their governments generally did not follow up these claims in any way. The

31

continent appeared so inhospitable that most early nineteenth-century explorers and statesmen assumed that human activity on it would be impossible. The Southern Ocean and many of its islands seemed a bit more promising. Both sealing and whaling operations required coastal bases—sealing because seals were most easily taken when they were on land to breed, and whaling because all rendering of whale fat into oil took place on land or in harbors until the development of factory ships able to operate at sea in the mid-1920s. Yet even here governmental attention was quite uneven. In part, this may be attributed to the whalers and sealers themselves, who generally kept discoveries secret lest rivals exploit the seals and whales before they could, and who often preferred to maintain order and settle disputes among themselves. Yet it also resulted from the long distance and slow communications that made administration extremely slow and costly.

This pattern of sporadic attention is well exemplified in the histories of both Macquarie Island (now ruled by Australia) and the Kerguelen Islands (now ruled by France). Macquarie Island was first sighted in 1810 by sealers based in Sydney, Australia, and sometime later was attached to Tasmania for administrative purposes. This administration was not very active, however. Concerned about overexploitation of the seals, New Zealand authorities asked London in 1890 if they could take over administration of the island. They were then told that it was already attached to Tasmania. Despite prodding from the New Zealanders, Tasmanian authorities showed little interest in the island until after the turn of the century. They first banned sealing, then granted a ten-year license for exploiting penguins for oil in 1902, and then made the island a wildlife sanctuary in 1933.[1] The Kerguelen Islands were discovered by French navigators in 1772 and 1775, who landed briefly and left plaques claiming the islands for France. But the authorities in Paris took no active interest in the islands until 1904 when permits for sealing were issued. A number of attempts to introduce agricultural settlements followed, the first in 1911.[2]

The area between the southern tip of South America and the Antarctic Peninsula was always an exception to this lack of attention. It had been a focus of imperial rivalry even in the seventeenth and eighteenth centuries because the shortest route from one coast of South America to the other was either through the Strait of Magellan or farther south between Tierra del Fuego and the northern tip of Antarctica. With Portugal, Spain, England, and France all seeking colonies in the Americas, it is not surprising that the islands lying relatively close to these major navigation routes were discovered early and were more quickly perceived as valuable by governments. The early history of South Georgia Island (54°15′S, 36°45′W) was typical. It was sighted successively by

Portuguese (1502), English (1675), Spanish (1756), and English (1775) navigators. Though uninhabited, it was formally annexed by the English in 1775 after Captain Cook's first voyage.[3] Yet active administration did not follow even though it soon became a favorite shore station of British and American whalers. Even here, active exercise of sovereignty had to await the revival of Antarctic whaling in the 1890s when the new technology of steamship and harpoon gun allowed killing of the previously uncatchable rorqual whales.[4]

At about that time the Antarctic continent came into new prominence as explorers successively landed (1895), wintered over (1899–1900), and then began to explore the interior of the continent.[5] The "race" between the English expedition under Scott and the Norwegian expedition under Amundsen to be the first to reach the South Pole in 1911–12 focused wide public attention on the area. This combination of renewed interest in the Southern Ocean and new interest in Antarctica itself led governments to consider the problem of providing a legal regime. Most governments involved reacted in familiar ways, by asserting sovereignty over those lands and islands to which they could make the strongest claim because of discovery, later exploration, or geographical proximity.

A number of governments were considering Antarctic claims at the same time, but the first to take any public action was the British, which defined a number of its preexisting claims and added a few more in 1908. Britain formally laid claim to all islands lying south of 50°S between 20° and 80°W, as well as the part of the Antarctic Peninsula they called Graham Land.[6] This claim was refined and modified in 1917 to include all land and islands lying between 50°S and the South Pole within an area enclosed by the meridians at 20° and 50°W, and between 58°S and the Pole enclosed by the meridians at 50° and 80°W.[7] This change not only excluded the Falklands and parts of the South American mainland from the claim, but was the first to define a claim by the wedge converging at the Pole so familiar today.

This British action caused a brief flurry of diplomatic activity. The French government reminded the British of its interest in various subantarctic islands as well as in Adélie Land, a stretch of the Antarctic coast between 136° and 142°E.[8] The Argentine government proposed an agreement under which the British would cede the South Orkneys in 1913, but brief negotiations on the question led nowhere.[9] The Chilean and Argentine governments held consultations meant to establish a common position on their own and other states' Antarctic claims, but these did not succeed.[10] However, nearly all diplomatic activity was interrupted by World War I and the subsequent peace negotiations.

After World War I, Britain was again the first to act. The British government decided in 1920 that "it is desirable that the whole of the Antarctic should ultimately be included within the British Empire."[11] This decision led to Orders-in-Council defining additional British claims based on the activities of British explorers. In 1923 Britain laid claim to all land and islands lying between 60°S and the Pole enclosed by the meridians at 160°E and 150°W.[12] In 1926 this was followed by a claim to all areas between 60°S and the pole enclosed by the meridians at 20° and 80°W.[13] Antarctica was also the subject of consultations between Britain and the Dominions at the Imperial Conference of 1926, where the Dominions endorsed the 1920 policy.[14]

Again, this activity brought forth rivals. After the 1923 Order-in-Council was issued, France again asserted its rights to Adélie Land. After considerable correspondence, the British agreed to respect the French claim. France then issued decrees defining the claim and including it with the Crozet and Kerguelen islands in the "Terres australes françaises" administered through the governor of Madagascar.[15] Norway began to fear that if Britain extended its claims all the way around the continent, Norwegian whalers might be excluded from the Southern Ocean.[16] The Norwegian government thus laid formal claim to Bouvet Island (54°26'S, 3°24'E) in 1928[17] and Peter I Island (69°00'S, 91°00'W) in 1931.[18]

A number of developments increased interest in Antarctic questions and precipitated another round of diplomatic activity. Public interest sparked by the second Byrd expedition led the United States government to undertake a lengthy review of policy toward both polar regions in the spring of 1938. Almost simultaneously the Norwegian government invited governments of states whose citizens were active in Antarctic exploration to participate in a Polar Exhibition and Congress in Bergen, scheduled for 1940. Though canceled once World War II broke out, the invitation provided an opportunity for official comment on Antarctic affairs. By the end of 1938 press speculation that the United States would make an Antarctic territorial claim also came to the attention of other governments. Both Japan, which had reserved the right to be consulted on Antarctic affairs when responding to the Norwegian invitation,[19] and Germany were expected to make claims.

The German announcement in 1939 that an Antarctic expedition was being sent to explore areas near 35°W precipitated more activity. Norwegians had surveyed the coast in that area and had been the only explorers of it. To head off any possible claim by Nazi Germany, the Norwegian government decided to lay formal claim to the Antarctic coast and hinterland between 20°W and 45°E.[20] This claim brought an additional participant into the discussion when the Soviets sent the Norwegians a note insisting that the future of Antarctica should be settled in negotiations by all interested states, among which the Soviets included themselves.[21]

The Norwegians were not the only ones frightened by the possibility that Hitler would make an Antarctic claim. The United States government was worried enough to approach Latin American governments with a proposal to jointly assert some form of rights in the part of Antarctica lying directly south of the Western Hemisphere. This was reinforced by Secretary of State Hull's statement in May 1940 that the American republics need to ensure that no extrahemispheric power had stronger territorial rights in that area than they. This speech was followed by the dispatch of expeditions to establish summer camps at both edges of the unclaimed area.[22] The Norwegian claim and these United States actions precipitated formal territorial claims by Argentina and Chile in 1940. Argentina had been asserting sovereignty over the South Orkneys since the 1920s, claiming that the British had effectively ceded the islands when they turned over operation of the weather station on Laurie Island to Argentinians in 1904.[23] Argentine spokesmen had referred to wider Antarctic claims but had never defined their precise limits. Discussion in the Argentinian press identified the area south of 60°S enclosed by the meridians at 25° and 68°34'W as the focus of Argentine interest.[24] Though some of the initial government acts defining Argentina's Antarctic interests used these limits, by 1946 government statements placed the western boundary at 74°W.[25] The Chilean decree of 6 November 1940 defined a claim to all "lands, islands, islets, reefs, ice packs and other things known and unknown, as well as their territorial waters" lying between Chile and the South Pole enclosed by the meridians at 53° and 90°W. No particular northern limit was set.[26] This Chilean claim overlapped both the Argentine and the British claims. Although there were no discussions with the British, the two South American governments held talks in 1941 aimed at reconciling their differences. These proved only partly successful; the two did agree that each had rights to territory in Antarctica but could not agree on a common boundary between their respective claims.[27]

Despite the overlapping of Argentinian, British, and Chilean claims, it might have been possible to negotiate a division of Antarctica among the claimants if they had been the only states involved. While claimants were divided on the question of who had sovereignty where, they all did agree in principle that Antarctica, like all other land areas, was open to national appropriation. However, a number of other states with strong interests in the future of Antarctica did not accept the idea of national appropriation. The United States government, whose influence grew through the interwar period because Americans became the most active explorers of the continent, expressed doubts that any state had a right to claim sovereignty over any portion of Antarctica. As first enunciated by Secretary of State Hughes in 1924, this opposition was based on a belief that since legal title to sovereignty depended on effective occupation of the territory claimed, and no part of Antarctica could be effectively occupied owing to the harshness of the climate, no state could rightfully claim territory there.[28]

Though in 1939 there was some American interest in making a claim,[29] the official position remained that of making none for the United States and refusing to recognize those made by others.[30] Three other states, Belgium, Japan, and the Soviet Union, also objected to existing claims and asserted a right to be consulted.[31]

At the outbreak of World War II, then, there was no agreement on the legal regime that should apply to Antarctica. Although claims to subantarctic islands had not inspired much difficulty, except where the governments of Argentina, Chile, and the United Kingdom asserted conflicting claims to the same islands, claims to the continent had been challenged. The seven claimant states clearly felt that Antarctica was *terra nullius* open to appropriation by whatever state might find and administer territory there. At least two states, the Soviet Union and the United States, had challenged that idea. While the Soviets had only insisted that there be general discussions among all interested states, the Americans had challenged the legality of making claims, at least for the present. Though some private individuals had proposed that Antarctica be treated as *res communis,* whether under League of Nations administration or in some other way, no government had yet adopted such ideas. The prevailing view among international lawyers was that although land might occasionally be administered by more than one state under a condominium, the notion of common space applied only to the oceans and the air above them.

Though World War II directed attention and energy elsewhere, a number of incidents during the conflict influenced early postwar thinking about the Antarctic. German surface raiders and submarines successfully preyed on shipping in the Indian Ocean from bases in the Kerguelen Islands. The Argentinian and British navies spent many years patrolling their Antarctic claims, more to outdo the other than against the Axis submarines and raiders in the area.[32]

In 1946 Antarctic problems seemed most acute to the Argentinian, Chilean, and British governments. A second round of Argentine-Chilean discussions in 1947–48 got the two governments no closer to their goal of a common front on Antarctic questions, in large part because both sides felt that the drawing of an Antarctic boundary would affect their sixty-year-old border dispute in the Beagle Channel.[33] At the same time, the British government approached the Latin Americans with the idea of submitting their respective claims to the International Court of Justice for a definitive determination of their respective rights. This both Latin American governments rejected.[34] The Argentine government simply reasserted its view that its rights were unassailable. The Chilean government, however, was prepared to defuse the territorial question at least temporarily. It proposed a "freeze" of limited duration on all claims, during which nationals of all interested states could pursue scientific research. This idea was first raised with the United States government in 1948,[35] and revived in later discussions.

A number of things led the United States government to take Antarctic questions seriously in 1946. First, it planned a major Antarctic expedition in 1947 (to make up for an expedition that had been canceled in 1941), and needed to consider whether to make any formal territorial claims. Second, the Argentinian and Chilean governments were both trying to enlist its support against the United Kingdom. They argued that British activity in the Antarctic Peninsula area amounted to threats by an outside state meriting joint response under the Interamerican Treaty of Reciprocal Assistance (Rio Pact) of 1947.[36] They even entered declarations to that effect when ratifying the Rio Pact.[37] The United States government did not want to get caught between its British and its South American allies in any disputes they might have. In 1947 the best way to avoid problems seemed to be dissolution of all claims, whether by merging them in a condominium or placing Antarctica under a special UN trusteeship. A third concern among many American policy makers was keeping the Soviets, who were beginning to show interest in the form of greater whaling activity,[38] out of any discussions.[39]

Near clashes between Argentinian or Chilean and British naval forces in 1948 sped up American activity.[40] After some preliminary discussions with the claimant governments, the Americans floated proposals for a UN trusteeship in July of 1948, and followed them with proposals for a condominium in August. The trusteeship proposal met with general rejection. Though some individual Labour party leaders were sympathetic,[41] the British government as a whole felt it would be undesirable because it would necessarily mean allowing the Soviets a role and would deny the validity of claims.[42] The Argentine and Chilean governments both rejected it quickly.[43] The condominium proposal also received little support. While the British and New Zealanders thought it a reasonable basis for discussion, the Australian government opposed and made its views known in Commonwealth conferences.[44] The Norwegians and French also seemed uninterested in any solution except an agreed division of the continent.[45]

Though they did not lead to an agreement about Antarctica's future, these discussions had two results. First, the Chileans renewed their notion of a limited-duration "freeze" on claims, coupled with cooperation in scientific research and cessation of British efforts to control whaling by requiring licenses.[46] Second, publicity given the discussions brought other countries into the arena.[47] In October 1948 both the Belgian and the South African governments told the U.S. State Department that they should be included in any discussion about the future of Antarctica. Belgium pointed to its long history of exploration, beginning with the Gerlache Expedition of 1899,[48] while South Africa pointed out its sovereignty over the subantarctic Prince Edward Islands (46°S, 38°E) and its relative proximity to the continent.[49]

The United States and the seven claimants might still have kept discussions to themselves had not a far more powerful state expressed its concern. The Soviet government began expressing strong interest in February 1949 through the "unofficial" medium of the All-Union Geographical Society. That month, the president of the society read a paper asserting that the Russians Bellings-hausen and Lazarev had discovered the continent, and that this gave the USSR a valid claim to all of Antarctica. The Society then adopted a resolution stating that in its view any discussion of Antarctica's future without Soviet participation would lack legal force and that the USSR would be justified in ignoring any agreement that came out of such discussions.[50] This was followed by an active press campaign. When the eight governments involved took no notice, the Soviet government sent them a formal memorandum in June 1950. This repeated the statements made earlier and concluded that "in accordance with international practice, all interested countries should be entitled to participate in the discussion of the regime for any area of international importance."[51]

Yet the other governments still hoped to avoid including the Soviets. Not all authorities agreed that Bellingshausen and Lazarev had discovered the continent. Even if they had, the other governments and most international lawyers outside of the USSR believed that the lack of Russian or Soviet activity for more than a hundred years afterward eroded any Soviet legal claims stemming from discovery. Although it was increasing, Soviet whaling activity was still relatively minor.[52] Therefore, the eight went ahead with their negotiations,[53] with only the Argentine and Chilean governments making any formal response to the Soviet memorandum.[54] The United States government began to see great promise in the Chilean proposals and began drafting what was intended as a joint presentation to the other six governments.[55] However, this work proceeded slowly.[56] First, the Korean War distracted American attention. Then the Chileans wanted to delay until after their 1952 presidential elections. Negotiating efforts did receive a new impetus in February 1953 when British marines tore down Argentine and Chilean huts that had been built very close to the British runway on Deception Island.[57] By then, however, the United States government was distracted by internal arguments over policy. These arguments had not been settled when the U.S.–Chilean initiative was swamped by developments in another quarter.

In 1952 scientists began discussing the possibility of having a third "Polar Year" in which expeditions from as many countries as possible would mount a cooperative effort to study both polar regions. As the idea was discussed among individual scientists, in national scientific academies, and in the International Council of Scientific Unions, the initial proposal was broadened until plans for a cooperative research program covering the whole earth and running for eighteen months appeared under the name International Geophysical Year. This wider proposal included polar components, including the establishment of fourteen to twenty research stations on the Antarctic continent. Though aware of the political complications that might ensue, the scientists felt that such an ambitious program of research had to include Soviet participation, given the location, size, and scientific resources of the USSR. Accordingly, the Soviet National Academy of Sciences was invited to participate.[58]

The Soviets accepted the invitation, in part to demonstrate the new Soviet policy of "peaceful coexistence," but also because it offered a chance to get into the Antarctic with a minimum of fuss. The participating national and international scientific bodies had already decided that their activities should be kept as separate from politics as possible, and a number of potential squabbles were kept from disrupting planning during the first IGY regional planning conference for Antarctica, which met in Paris in July 1955.[59] At the end of that meeting the scientists passed a resolution that sought to avoid any further political complication. It recorded an understanding that IGY activities were temporary measures that "do not modify the existing status of the Antarctic regarding the relations of the participating countries."[60] This resolution was intended to avoid the diplomatic exchanges that had followed previous traverses of claimed areas by expeditions from states that did not recognize the claims involved and so did not ask for permission to enter the territory.[61] The resolution was supplemented by a decision at the second planning conference, held in Brussels that September, which provided for exchange of personnel among the various stations.[62] The second meeting also allocated station sites in a way that satisfied most of the participants.

Once launched, scientific cooperation under the IGY proved very successful. Quite early on, in December 1956, the U.S. National Academy of Sciences proposed that Antarctic work continue even after the scheduled end of the IGY in December 1958.[63] Despite misgivings from the Commonwealth governments, scientific interest in the proposition was so great that they came to support it. The Soviets helped settle matters when they announced that they intended to continue operating their Antarctic research stations no matter what others did.[64] This made it imperative for other states to do likewise, lest their legal claims be weakened by failure to match the newcomer's activity.[65] This permanent, qualitative change in Antarctic activity also made the creation of some common legal regime imperative. The "gentlemen's agreement" made in Paris would expire at the end of the IGY, and in the absence of common rules the political situation would become very difficult indeed. Conditions for creating some regime were also promising. Relations between the superpowers were better than they had been in the early 1950s. All participants also acknowledged that the Soviets would have to participate if any regime were to be effective.[66]

Several attempts to negotiate a new, more permanent Antarctic regime got under way almost simultaneously. Beginning in the summer of 1957, the British, Australian, and New Zealand governments began reconsidering old ideas of creating some sort of Antarctic consortium. The existence of these talks was made public in February 1958 by the British prime minister during a visit to Australia. Though no details were released, the mere statement that talks were under way was enough to elicit unfavorable reactions from the Argentine and Chilean governments and a loud nationalistic clamor in the Argentine and Chilean press. That same month, the United States government again began informal soundings. By reviving the old Chilean idea of a temporary "freezing" of the legal status quo and coupling it with proposals for disarmament and inspection, the Americans were able to secure Argentine and Chilean particpation. The existence of these talks was made public in late April, and the lack of hostile reaction to the news encouraged the Americans to further efforts.

In May 1958 the United States government invited eleven states—the seven claimants (Argentina, Australia, Chile, France, New Zealand, Norway, and the United Kingdom) and four other states sponsoring stations or expeditions in the IGY program (Belgium, Japan, South Africa, and the USSR)—to join it in negotiating an Antarctic regime. While based on actual interest,[67] this choice of participants meant that strongly contrasting views on the sovereignty question would have to be accommodated. The Argentinian and Chilean governments remained adamant in their assertion of sovereign rights to their claims.[68] The Australian government, while less demonstrative publicly, was no less convinced that any regime must include protection of national sovereignty over the claims, though it was ready to assure scientific cooperation.[69] The British, French, and New Zealand governments appeared ready to yield their claims in favor of international administration if all other claimants did likewise.[70] The governments of both superpowers also preferred some form of international administration, though they reserved the right to make claims should it prove unattainable.[71] The Belgian and Japanese governments, whose position was weak given the relatively small amount of activity by their nationals, also preferred an international arrangement.[72] Further soundings, some sixty preliminary meetings held between mid-June and mid-October of 1959, and six weeks of formal negotiations at the Washington

Conference were sufficient for the parties to overcome their differences on sovereignty and other issues. The Conference produced the Antarctic Treaty, which was signed by delegates of all twelve participating governments on 1 December 1959, and which entered into force on 23 June 1961 when the last three of the twelve governments ratified. This treaty created the international regime that continues to govern Antarctica today.

## The Antarctic Treaty Regime

The Antarctic Treaty created a set of principles, norms, rules, and procedures providing a framework for common activity in Antarctica and the Southern Ocean.[73] This was not a comprehensive framework, as will be seen, but it did form the basis on which the governments involved could organize their co-operation. It also provided the starting point for further elaboration, first as implementation of the new international regime, and later as its modification.

### Principles

The Antarctic Treaty embodies three basic principles for the regime. First, more by implication than by any direct statement in the treaty, it establishes the principle that there is an Antarctic community that should share the continent and its governance. Second, the preamble to the treaty establishes the further-ance of scientific cooperation as a major purpose of the regime. Third, the preamble also establishes the principle that Antarctica should be used only for peaceful purposes. At the same time, the treaty avoided any pronouncement on the one issue where the parties accepted no common principle, namely, the issue of territorial sovereignty. This issue was handled at the lower level of norms, where it was possible to formulate a compromise that would guide behavior without affecting anyone's position on the principle.

### Norms

The Antarctic Treaty creates a larger number of general norms for behavior. Most derive from and help implement the principles, while some help the parties avoid disagreements on principle that could destroy the regime. The community principle is implemented in a number of norms, expressed most clearly in Articles II, VIII, and XI of the treaty, which provide for open access to the continent, peaceful settlement of disputes, and joint management by certain of the participating states. The principle of scientific cooperation is reflected in Article II, which stipulates freedom of scientific research and an obligation to cooperate in scientific endeavor.[74] The principle of peaceful use is directly reflected in the Article I bans on establishing military bases or installations, holding military maneuvers, or testing weapons of any kind. An additional norm, an obligation to protect the Antarctic environment, is established by implication from certain of the treaty's specific rules.

The most interesting normative provision of the treaty treats the sovereignty issue. Article IV avoids endorsing either of the determinative principles advanced during negotiations. It adopts neither the claimants' notion that territorial claims and national sovereignty apply in the Antarctic as elsewhere, nor the nonclaimants' notions that claims and sovereignty do not or cannot now apply there. Instead, it creates a "suggestive norm" that the parties should avoid conflict on territorial sovereignty by leaving the issue alone while they cooperate on matters where they can agree.[75]

*Rules*

To stabilize the norms and provide answers to other questions likely to arise in day-to-day activities, the treaty also provides a series of rules for conduct in specific situations. Unlike the norms, which admit of differing interpretations, these rules tend to be fairly clear-cut, allowing each participating government and its nationals to determine on their own whether actual or proposed activity conforms to the treaty.

The first specific rule, expressed in Article VI, states that the treaty's provisions shall apply to all land and ocean areas south of 60°S latitude. This rule thus determines the geographical extent of the regime and represents an important political choice by leaving the large number of "subantarctic" islands lying between 45° and 60°S out of the regime. Thus, states can continue to assert sovereignty over those islands they claim and to pursue any conflicts over them (e.g., the Falklands) without disturbing the Antarctic regime directly.

Other rules help the Antarctic community maintain itself. Article IX establishes a coordinating group, subsequently known as the Consultative Parties, to hold periodic meetings for exchange of information, consultation, and the framing of further rules for Antarctic activity. This group has authority to recommend measures "furthering the principles and objectives of the Treaty" generally. This authority is then defined in Article IX (1) as including measures for (a) ensuring that Antarctica is used only for peaceful purposes, (b) facilitating scientific research, (c) facilitating scientific cooperation, (d) facilitating exercise of the right of inspection, (e) resolving questions of which government has jurisdiction over what activities or persons, and (f) protecting the Antarctic environment. In case the consultative parties take a long time to act on some question, Article IX (5) specifies that the exercise of rights established in the treaty does not depend on adoption of measures through the consultative parties.

The treaty is also unusual, though not unique, among post-1945 international agreements in establishing two tiers of membership, one with and the other without the right ,to participate in decision making. Participation is reserved to states eligible for consultative party status. Article IX (1) provides that the twelve original parties have that status permanently. Article IX (2) permits states that ratify the treaty later (acceding states) to acquire consultative status when, and for as long as, they demonstrate serious interest in Antarctica by conducting "substantial scientific research" there.

Several rules are meant to assist the community in maintaining the compromise over sovereignty questions. Article IV (1) (a) and (c) together provide that the treaty shall not be interpreted as either endorsing or denying validity to territorial claims. Article IV (1) (b) provides that the treaty will have no effect on any rights acquired or claims asserted before it came into force in 1961, while Article IV (2) bans the assertion of any new territorial claims or the enlargement of existing territorial claims while the treaty remains in force. Article IV (2) also provides that activity undertaken while the treaty is in force will have no legal effect on preexisting claims, whether to weaken or to strengthen them. By these rules, then, the participating governments hope to separate political from other, mainly scientific, considerations in the planning of expeditions and other activity, and to decrease claimant-state worries about the activity of others within the areas they claim.[76]

The treaty also provides a number of rules for enforcement of its provisions both among participating states and vis-à-vis others. It expresses or implies several rules apportioning jurisdiction over ships, expeditions, stations, and individuals in Antarctica. Article VIII (1) specifies that observers named by consultative parties to carry out the inspections provided for in Article VII, and scientists exchanged between stations and expeditions, remain under the jurisdiction of their own state. By silence on the matter, the Antarctic Treaty confirms that states retain jurisdiction over ships and aircraft flying their flag, as is already provided in aerial law and the law of the sea. By silence and the implications of Article IV, the treaty continues the IGY rule that states retain jurisdiction over their stations, their nationals working at or out of the stations, and the scientific expeditions organized from their bases or their home territory. Nothing in the treaty prevents a claimant from claiming terrtorial jurisdiction over any person, station, ship, or aircraft within the limits of its claim, but any attempt to exercise such jurisdiction would meet with stiff opposition from the nonclaimant states.

The treaty also establishes a few rules for settlement of any disputes arising among the parties. Article XI provides that all such disputes must be settled peacefully. Participating states are first encouraged to settle by direct negotiations or any other peaceful method (such as requesting mediation or going to arbitration) they may choose. They are also given the option of submitting the dispute to the International Court of Justice for a ruling, but only if all parties to the dispute agree to take that step. Yet refusal to submit a dispute to the ICJ does not absolve a party from the general obligation to settle the dispute peacefully. Articles VIII (2) and IX (1) (e) read together apply the general rules to disputes about jursidiction over observers and give the Consultative Parties authority to formulate further rules on this particular question.

The treaty also establishes three mechanisms for intracommunity enforcement of rules: inspection, prior notice of activity, and exchange scientists. The inspection system created by Article VII is the most formalized of the three. Each consultative party has the right to name an unstated number of its own nationals as observers. These observers are to enjoy "complete freedom of access at any time to any or all areas of Antarctica" for the purpose of inspecting the area, all "stations, installations, and equipment" there, and all ships or aircraft at points of embarking or disembarking passengers or cargo in Antarctica. Additionally, any consultative party may at any time undertake aerial observation of any part of Antarctica. Article VII creates a second system applicable to all parties. It requires that each party notify all others of all expeditions to or within Antarctica by its own ships and nationals, of all expeditions to Antarctica organized in or proceeding from its territory even if they do not include any of its nationals, of the location of all stations occupied by its nationals, and of any military personnel or equipment being taken to Antarctica for purposes allowed by the treaty. Article III (1) (b) provides that parties shall exchange scientists between stations and expeditions. While not directly established as an enforcement mechanism, this is a device for monitoring behavior because the size of most Antarctic stations makes it impossible to hide major violations from someone who spends several months there.

The treaty also creates a few rules for the more problematic matter of enforcing the Antarctic regime against nonparticipating states and their nationals. In general, international law denies that a treaty may be enforced against states that are not parties to it.[77] Yet in Article X each party undertakes to exert "all appropriate efforts, consistent with the Charter of the United Nations" so that "no one" (whether a government, a private group, or an individual) engages in activities in Antarctica that violate treaty provisions.

This rule was established in part to protect the regime from being upset by outside states, and in part to provide justification for consultative party efforts to ensure that all states active in Antarctica accede to the treaty. Enforcement against individuals on the continent poses few problems, for it remains impossible to stay there for long without using facilities belonging to states that are parties to the treaty. Enforcement against states is another matter; this question has seldom arisen because serious Antarctic activity is an expensive proposition beyond the resources of most states and of no interest to many others.[78] The Southern Ocean poses a more difficult problem in this regard, since it is possible for ships and nationals of nonparty states to remain there for considerable periods of time.

Article III contains a number of rules intended to further freedom of scientific research and scientific cooperation. First, it requires that each party notify all others of plans for scientific activity. While related to enforcement and similar to obligations in Article VII (5), this provision also seeks to avoid unnecessary duplication of effort. The same article calls for the exchange of scientists among bases and expeditions, as a further mechanism of internationalizing Antarctic research, and requires parties to exchange and publish or otherwise make freely available scientific data and results. Additionally, the parties agree that they should "give every encouragement" to cooperative working relations with UN specialized agencies and other international organizations having a scientific or technical interest in the Antarctic.

Several rules give more precise content to the norm that Antarctica is to be used only for peaceful purposes. Article V bans all nuclear explosions, including weapons tests. It also provides that the rules included in any other agreement regulating any use of nuclear technology to which all consultative parties are also parties shall apply in Antarctica as well. Article I (2) also restricts the use of military personnel in Antarctica to supporting scientific research and other peaceful purposes. Thus, military units may be used for such tasks as providing air transportation or breaking ice so that ships may reach the coast.

A number of rules permit the inference that the original regime did include some notion of responsibility to protect the Antarctic environment. Article V, which also bans the disposal of any radioactive wastes in Antarctica, was inspired as much by environmental as by military concerns.[79] The rule granting the consultative parties authority to recommend measures for protection and conservation of Antarctic living resources also rested on environmental concerns.

Finally, a number of rules set forth agreements on how some questions of air and ocean use should be regulated. First, Article VI incorporates much of the law of the sea into the Antarctic regime by providing that nothing in the treaty affects the possession or exercise of rights on the high seas by any state south of 60°S. By implication, the same article also solves the perplexing question of whether ice should be treated as water or as land for jurisdictional purposes by listing ice shelves among land formations. This indicates that the original parties intended to determine which areas were high seas by measuring from the coast or the edge of an ice shelf rather than from the outer edge of the highly variable pack ice.[80]

Normally, overflight of land requires permission from the subadjacent state. Civil aviation is regulated by a number of multilateral treaties which provide a framework of rules within which pairs of states agree on overflight and stopping rights for their respective civil carriers. Military flights, too, require special agreement, either within the framework of an alliance or on a case-by-case basis.[81] With the agreement not to exercise territorial sovereignty in the Antarctic, the treaty had to include a number of rules on flying. Article VII (3) provides that aircraft of the consultative parties have the right to fly freely over the continent for purposes of aerial observation supplementing the on-site inspection by observers. Article VII (2) implies freedom of overflight for the purpose of conveying observers from place to place as they carry out inspections. Article II implies freedom of overflight for the purpose of assisting in scientific work, whether for delivering scientists and their equipment to the field, picking them up again, taking support personnel from place to place, or evacuating sick or injured personnel needing medical treatment unavailable at their camp or station. Thus, there is wide freedom of overflight on the continent and in waters that would otherwise form part of some state's territorial sea.

The treaty contains no provisions that directly or indirectly establish rules for ordinary civil aviation within or over Antarctica. Though there had been discussions about the possible uses of Antarctic great-circle routes between Southern Hemisphere cities, the lack of airfields and navigation facilities in Antarctica and the relatively short range of civil airliners at the time made this a future possibility rather than a current reality in 1959.[82] The Article I ban on military activity does mean that there is no such freedom of overflight for military missions.

*Procedures*

Finally, the treaty outlines a number of procedures to be followed in particular situations. Most relate to the status or modification of the treaty itself, but a few guide the deliberations of the consultative parties.

The treaty gives minimal procedural guidance to the consultative parties.

Article IX (1) specifies that their meetings should be held at "appropriate intervals," leaving them to determine just what such an interval might be. While there is no express provision defining the majority necessary for adoption of decisions in consultative meetings, the delegates at the Washington Conference assumed that a unanimity rule would apply.[83] This was the custom in any international meeting limited to small numbers of states, and is the rule specified for proposing amendments to the treaty except at the specially provided Review Conference. Additionally, Article IX (4) provided that measures recommended by the consultative parties would become effective only when ratified by the governments of all states having consultative party status.

Several procedures for interpreting and modifying the treaty are laid out in advance. When the consultative parties all adopt and ratify a measure for implementing the treaty or furthering its principles and objectives under Article IX (1), that measure becomes binding on all parties. Thus, one group of parties has the legal right to make authoritative interpretations of the treaty for all. This was compatible with the customary international law of the time which required the unanimous agreement of all parties for such an interpretation unless they agreed in advance to a different rule.[84]

The treaty can be amended by one of two procedures. Under the ordinary procedure outlined in Article XII (1), an amendment may be proposed by unanimous agreement of the consultative parties and enters into force for them when all ratify the amendment. These amendments enter into force for each of the nonconsultative parties (as the other participating states are now called) when that state ratifies, but failure to ratify within two years of the date the amendment entered into force for consultative parties is deemed equivalent of withdrawing from the treaty. Thus, other parties have the choice of accepting the consultative parties' handiwork or leaving the group.

Article XII (2) provides an alternate procedure, a special review conference. Such a conference may be convened at the request of any consultative party once the treaty has been in force for thirty years (that is, after 23 June 1991). All parties, not just consultative ones, have the right to participate in this conference. Amendments may be proposed at the conference by a simple majority so long as it also includes a simple majority of the consultative parties.[85] These amendments then enter into force in the same way as ordinary amendments, ensuring consultative party control of the process.

Like all treaties, the Antarctic Treaty specifies how states may join or depart from the group of parties. Article XIII (1) provides that the treaty must be ratified by the original parties, a procedure by which governments confirm the work of their representatives at a diplomatic conference. Paragraph 5 further specifies that the treaty enters into force when all twelve of the original parties have ratified. Article XIII (1) specifies that any state which is a member of the United Nations or is specially invited by unanimous vote of the consultative parties may accede to the treaty,[86] becoming a party even though it was not represented at the conference. Paragraph 5 then provides that the treaty enters into force for an acceding state either on the date when all the twelve original parties have ratified or the date when it deposits a notice of accession, whichever is later.[87] In order to symbolize the separation of the Antarctic regime from the United Nations, and in conformity with prevailing international practice regarding limited participation multilateral treaties, one of the parties, in this case the United States, was designated the depositary in charge of receiving notices of ratification, accession, acceptance of amendments, and withdrawal.

The treaty itself specifies only two ways in which parties may withdraw. The first is the Article XII (1) (b) provision that failure to ratify an amendment within two years of its ratification by all consultative parties is deemed a withdrawal. The second is the Article XII (2) provision that if an amendment adopted by the review conference has not been ratified by all consultative parties within two years of the conference's proposing it, any party may give notice of withdrawal. This notice takes effect two years after the date on which it is given to the depositary government. Yet it would be difficult to argue that these provisions so exhaust the question that the customary right of withdrawal at any time after due notice could not apply.[88]

The treaty is also silent on another important matter, the ways in which it could be terminated. There, too, customary international law applies. Customary law allows termination (a) by agreement of all parties, (b) when all parties have withdrawn (essentially a nonsimultaneous agreement of all parties), (c) when conditions have changed so much that continuing to uphold the treaty obligations proves impossible, or (d) when all parties become party to a later treaty on the same subject which supersedes the older treaty.[89]

### Omitted Topics

No description of the Antarctic Treaty can ignore the fact that it is silent on a number of questions. Though the treaty provided a clever compromise of conflicting principles on sovereignty over territory, it provides no guidance for settlement of that question should it again become acute. Nor does it provide any clear legal guidance on how to evaluate the effect of treaty-era activity on claims should the treaty lapse. Thus different commentators give different answers to the question of whether common use under the treaty is itself a precedent eroding all claims.[90]

The treaty also fails to provide clear guidance or a firm legal foundation for specific actions taken by individual parties to ensure that third states and third-state nationals do not violate the treaty. Some commentators have attempted to invoke broad interpretations of "self-defense" or of the doctrine that certain treaties create "objective regimes" that must be respected by third states even though they have no direct obligation to obey their rules.[91] None of these arguments is fully convincing.

Questions of jurisdiction over persons engaged in nonscientific activity, such as tourism, are also unanswered. Though Antarctic tourism seemed a remote possibility in 1959, cruises in the Southern Ocean with short visits to coastal areas or charter flights over the continent are now common. The greater range of civil airliners and the development of better navigational facilities make use of Antarctic great-circle routes between South America and Australasia a real possibility.[92]

Most important, the treaty is silent on the questions of whether to permit and how to regulate the exploitation of Antarctic and Southern Ocean resources. This was a conscious omission,[93] made to ensure that the compromise on sovereignty would be accepted, and based on the assumption that by the distant date when resource activities became feasible the Antarctic community would be ready to make a new agreement on the subject.

The negotiations of 1958–59 thus accomplished what discussions during the 1940s had not, the creation of an international regime for Antarctic and Southern Ocean activity. An examination of the contrasting circumstances of each decade will show why these very different results occurred.

# 3

# The Failure of
# Regime Creation in 1949

Though various ideas were suggested and several governments took part in discussions, no Antarctic regime was created in 1948–49. Failure stemmed from both the relatively low salience of Antarctic issues and the large differences of interest between the governments involved. Salience was high enough to inspire some governmental attention but not high enough to inspire the effort that would have been required to bridge the differences involved. These lay at the level of principle; participating governments could not agree on either dividing the Antarctic landmass between them or treating it as a common area. This being so, questions of regime norms, rules, and procedures were hardly discussed.

## Salience

On the whole, Antarctic issues had low restricted salience in the late 1940s. Though a slightly wider set of policy makers and scientists were paying attention to Antarctic issues after World War II, there was nothing about the continent or its resource prospects to inspire sustained public or interest-group attention. Even among those policy makers paying attention to Antarctic issues, a settlement of the outstanding territorial questions was seen as desirable but not as an immediate necessity. At the same time, many other issues that were seen as requiring immediate action competed for governmental and public attention.

Considered on their own, Antarctic issues had acquired increased importance in the late 1940s. Cold weather operations during World War II had led to improvements in clothing and equipment for very cold climates and had demonstrated how important the ability to mount operations in the extreme cold could be during wartime. These notions retained currency after the war. As in World War I, German surface and submarine raiders had preyed on Allied commerce from bases in Arctic or subantarctic waters. The shortest routes between the homelands of the superpowers lay across the Arctic, and a number of Americans regarded the Antarctic as useful for carrying out cold weather exercises without raising major political complications.[1] At the same time, Argentine-British tensions had inspired a considerable amount of activity aimed at ensuring that the other did not gain a decisive advantage in arguments over conflicting claims. Countering Argentine moves probably absorbed as much British attention between 1940 and 1945 as countering German activity. After the war Argentina, Britain, and Chile all stepped up their scientific and naval activity in order to buttress territorial claims.

The immediate economic importance of Antarctica did not increase in this period. Whaling, which was recovering slowly from wartime destruction of whaling fleets, was the only significant economic activity in the Antarctic. Inclusion of Antarctic whaling in the global International Convention for the Regulation of Whaling[2] meant that there were no immediate economic values at stake in any Antarctic negotiations at this time.

Except in Argentina and Chile, where support for asserting jurisdiction over a fishing zone of two hundred nautical miles was widespread, most governments saw little reason to consider Antarctic claims as a way to acquire control over more ocean resources. The existing law of the sea encouraged policy makers to view Antarctic issues in terms of the possibilities of the continent rather than of the Southern Ocean around it. Coastal states had begun to assert jurisdication over resource activities on the continental shelf, but in 1948 the idea of asserting jurisdiction over fishing in broad stretches of the sea was confined to a few Latin American states. Though other states were departing from the old three-mile rule, this was being done hesitantly, in the form of conservation zones in particular areas of a twelve-mile territorial sea.[3] Antarctic whaling occurred much farther offshore, and there was no other Southern Ocean fishing at the time. Thus, even if Antarctic territorial claims had been accepted by the rest of the international community, most states would still have conceded that whaling needed to be regulated by some form of international agreement, and there was no other reason to exercise jurisdiction over fisheries in the Southern Ocean. Thus, coastal states had little incentive to think of Antarctic fisheries as a potential source of riches for themselves. Similarly, the harsh conditions of the continental shelf and the lack of information about resources there did not encourage thinking about the continental shelf as a source of significant resources.

On their own, then, Antarctic questions were not viewed as sufficiently pressing to inspire either a settlement of the policy debates within the United States government or a clear agreement among the eight governments concerned. Even worry about the possibility of Soviet involvement in Antarctic affairs was insufficient to hasten efforts or to precipitate a resolution either of the internal United States policy debate or of disagreements among the eight governments.[4]

This relatively low intrinsic salience was powerfully reinforced by the far greater salience attached to a plethora of other issues. Even Argentina and Chile, which viewed Antarctic questions as extremely important, had other boundary issues to worry about and a whole host of economic problems arising from the fact that the revival of more normal international trade was eroding their earlier prosperity. Both were also involved in the negotiations revising the Inter-American system by creating the Organization of American States and a series of related agreements. Though greatly worried about Argentine and Chilean activity in the Antarctic, the British government had a large empire to run, an exhausted economy to revive, and the whole question of its future relations with Europe to settle. The Labour government also remained divided about what attitude to take in the cold war, with an important faction still hoping to pursue dialogue with the Soviet Union while avoiding overly close ties to the United States. Even under a Democratic administration the United States was regarded as far too capitalist in outlook by Labour's left wing.

For other countries, Antarctic issues came even farther down the agenda. In France, the problems of punishing collaborators, reconstructing the country, and reviving democratic governance after the Nazi occupation absorbed much attention. All these issues were complicated by the continuation of sharp ideological struggle, with a clearly pro-Soviet Communist party enjoying support from much of the trade union movement and of the population as a whole. For the United States, all sorts of other issues were far more pressing. Having decided that conflict with the Soviets was serious and was going to require considerable effort, the United States government was engaged in pursuing the Marshall Plan in Europe, assisting the Greek government in the Greek civil war, encouraging efforts to achieve Western European unity through various defense arrangements and, if possible, economic union. The year 1948–49 was a time of extreme tension in Europe, symbolized most vividly by the Berlin blockade. Meanwhile, Asian problems, particularly the Chinese civil war and the problem of reconstructing Japan along democratic lines, were also absorbing great amounts of American energy.

## Interests

The eight prospective partners were not able to agree on a definition of shared or parallel interests sufficient to create an international regime. They could agree that they wanted to exclude the Soviet Union, but on nothing else. In particular, the United States on one side and the seven claimants on the other (with some wobbling by New Zealand and the United Kingdom) were not able to agree on how to define the legal status of the Antarctic continent. Without agreement on this point, it was difficult to discuss any of the more specific Antarctic questions, because their resolution would depend heavily on whether the continent was divided into national pieces and, if it were, who owned what piece.

The territorial question was largely, though not completely, an argument between the United States on one side and the other seven participating governments on the other. The United States government not only made no territorial claim in the Antarctic, it also refused to accept as valid the claims of others. This position rested on an argument that since sovereignty to previously unoccupied lands accrues only after effective occupation, and no one had yet effectively occupied any part of Antarctica, no territorial claim there was valid. Behind this determination lay a calculation that United States interests in exploration and scientific research were best served by maintaining free access to the whole continent. Asserting a claim would make free access impossible, since such an act would necessarily imply acceptance of other states' rights to make claims and then control access to the areas they claimed.[5]

Argentina, Australia, Chile, France, New Zealand, Norway, and the United Kingdom had all made claims. Though their size and location did not always conform to the patterns of interest and activity developed by 1948, the claimants did all agree that the Antarctic landmass should be treated like any other and divided among countries according to the traditional rules of international law. They were so sure that this was the right solution that they even left the area between 90° and 150°W empty to accommodate a United States claim.[6]

Neither side in this argument had the power to overcome resistance by the other. The claimants still possessed more issue-specific power in 1948, but it was clear that the United States was increasing its Antarctic activity at a pace that would soon make it the most active nation there. At the same time, the claimants compensated for their relative weakness by pursuing linkage strategies. They attempted to constrain United States power by calling on their alliance ties. Though they were the weaker parties in the alliances, they knew that American policy makers regarded the alliance ties as important in the cold war. The Americans did not want to weaken any of those ties, either by letting conflict among Argentina, Britain, and Chile get out of hand or by attempting to impose a regime the claimants would not accept. So long as the linkage was kept implied and not given any specific form that would have stiffened American opinion against a particular claimant, the emotional appeal of these alliance ties could be used to great effect. Their effect was enhanced by the depth of the cold war; the Berlin blockade was simultaneous to much of this Antarctic effort.

The stalemate was also encouraged by the fact that both sides were internally divided. New Zealand, and to a lesser extent the United Kingdom, had expressed willingness to give up claims if an agreement internationalizing Antarctica could be reached.[7] Beyond that, the overlap in territory sought meant that Argentina, Chile, and the United Kingdom were unable to form a firm coalition. Argentina and Chile had agreed that both had rights to make a claim in the Antarctic Peninsula area and set mutually recognized outer boundaries of their claims. However, their inability to agree on an inside boundary hobbled their efforts to work together. This boundary problem was, in fact, part of a larger set of border disputes in the Andes and the Beagle Channel area. Tensions between Argentina and the United Kingdom also made it very difficult for those two states to collaborate. Argentine leaders spent more time in 1947–48 trying to get support for their claims vis-à-vis the British than on negotiations for an Antarctic regime. In particular, they sought to enlist United States support by arguing that the United Kingdom was an interloper in an area defined as falling within the Western Hemisphere security zone under the Rio Pact. The Argentine-British dispute also caused a rift with Australia and New Zealand, loyal members of the Commonweath supporting the British claim.[8]

Division on the nonclaimant side of the argument was at least as great, even if it was internal to one government. It was obvious then, as later, that the United States government had great difficulties in making coherent policy. From 1946 through 1949 Antarctic issues were the subject of serious debate among U.S. officials. They were arguing about three basic ideas: holding a conference with the seven claimants in order to divide up the continent, placing Antarctica under some form of UN or other international administration, and asserting claims unilaterally. Officials in the Interior Department were interested in whatever solution would best secure access to Antarctic resources.[9] Officials in the Defense Department preferred having the United States make a territorial claim, but would accept other solutions so long as the Soviets were kept out.[10] Others were not keen on asserting a claim for two reasons. First, avoiding quarrels with other friendly states would confine the United States to the unclaimed area between 90° and 150°west, the least accessible and hence least desirable area of the continent. Second, assertion of a claim would mean accepting others' claims, giving up the previously asserted right of free access to any place in the continent.

Given this division of U.S. opinion, it is surprising that resistance to the notion of accepting claims persisted and was sufficient to prevent adoption of a regime based on dividing Antarctica into national territories. Certainly both the institutional and the conceptual climate favored division over other solutions to the problem of defining the legal status of the Antarctic landmass.

Even within the United States government, proposals to place Antarctica under a United Nations trusteeship failed to win much support. At first glance this seems surprising. The United States and its allies then controlled a majority of the votes in both the General Assembly and the Trusteeship Council, the two UN organs that would be most closely involved in any such plan. Additionally, most U.S. policy makers remained confident that this situation would last indefinitely. Two other sets of concerns limited American enthusiasm for trusteeship.

First, any mention of discussing Antarctic affairs at the United Nations—much less giving the UN any role in governing the area—aroused vehement Argentine and Chilean opposition. Both governments regarded their Antarctic claims as integral parts of their national domain. This meant, among other things, that they regarded any UN discussion of Antarctic affairs as violating Article 2, paragraph 7, of the UN Charter, which prohibits UN intervention in the affairs of member states.[11]

Second, proposals to create a special trusteeship for Antarctica were inhibited by many governments' opinion that the trusteeship system was designed to help bring inhabited areas to some form of self-government, not to deal with uninhabited lands.[12] Additionally, many British and American policy makers viewed trusteeship as a bad solution because there would be no way to prevent the Soviets from having a role. The Soviet Union sat on the Trusteeship Council by virtue of being a permanent member of the Security Council, and would have been able to use that position to advance its views, even if it were not given a place in whatever committee of states might be set up as the actual administrator of an Antarctic trust territory.[13] All these negative reactions helped shift United States policy away from internationalization under UN auspices well before the end of 1948.

The ideas commonly held by governments also discouraged any internationalization of Antarctica. There were no precedents for long-term international administration of land areas. The League of Nations administration of the Saar ended, as was planned, after fifteen years when the local population chose to be reunited to Germany. League administration of Danzig, though competent, was not a happy memory, given beliefs that the Polish corridor had only contributed to German grievances against the Versailles settlement. Trieste was then under an international administration, though well on its way to being united with Yugoslavia. There were proposals to put Jerusalem under a UN administration, but none of the governments and other groups involved in Middle Eastern affairs had any great enthusiasm for the idea. The UN trusteeship system was clearly intended as a temporary thing, a form of supervision to hasten the day when colonial populations would secure self-government. The only "international" administrations with long-term stability were condominia in which two states shared the administration of a particular, usually small, territory.

The basic norm in legal arrangements for land areas remained national sovereignty. Colonial peoples hoped to attain this. All governments thought in terms of sovereignty whenever any land area—continental mass or island—was discussed. Few saw any reason to make an exception for Antarctica. Rather, because of its lack of native human population and its completely undeveloped state Antarctica seemed to meet the strictest definition of the *terra nullius* traditionally deemed open to appropriation by whatever state was willing and able to provide effective administration. A few private individuals might argue that the era of land-grabbing was over, or that this pristine continent should be set aside for common scientific use, but most governments were not interested in such ideas. This was especially true among the claimants, which contended that nothing stood in the way of acquiring territory in Antarctica. The farthest any claimant was prepared to go officially in 1948 was the Chilean proposal that territorial questions be set aside temporarily while interested states cooperated in pursuit of scientific knowledge.[14]

The failure of the 1948–49 negotiations clearly shows the limits of any theory attempting to explain governments' definitions of state interest by analyzing features of the state's domestic structure. Whether attempted along Marxist, governmental type, ruling social coalition, relative strength of the governmental apparatus vis-à-vis the society, or bureaucratic-politics lines, the history of Antarctic negotiations in this period demonstrates no clear relation between structure and definition of interest.

In Marxist analysis, the 1948–49 negotiations provide the spectacle of eight capitalist—or in some classifications six capitalist and two dependent capitalist—states unable to agree among themselves on an international regime. In this case, a similar economic and class basis did not make cooperation easy; the states involved arrived at different policy preferences despite their similar economic structures.

Obviously, Marxist theory could be rescued by arguing that disagreement resulted from imperialist rivalry, which in turn stems from the inherent contradictions within and among capitalist states. At first glance this appears a poor explanation, since some of the states involved were advocating internationalization of the Antarctic continent rather than its division into national parts, each ruled by an individual capitalist state, Marxist theory could still be rescued by arguing that the ostensible policies of the United States were really a cover for a long-term American effort to dominate the continent. Rather than accept the relatively unattractive unclaimed sector, one might argue, the United States was really attempting to ensure that it had access to all parts of the continent and would then use its greater resources to dominate—directly, by maintaining a high level of activity in the Antarctic, or indirectly, by making claimant governments depend for support on their readiness to accommodate American desires. Similarly, the British and New Zealand interest in internationalization can be viewed as attempts by claimants with weak claims and little inclination to defend them to get something out of the negotiations rather than lose their claim to a more active and aggressive rival.

If Antarctic politics in this period were simply an example of the Leninist model of imperialism at work, one would expect to see eight imperialists sitting down at a table and negotiating about who would get what territory, rather like the way the Congress of Berlin partitioned Africa in 1885. However, disagreements arose, not over shares but over whether there ought to be shares. The Congress of Berlin met under a common assumption that any place in Africa not already ruled by Europeans or under a European protectorate was open for new colonizing ventures. The problem was simply dividing something everyone had agreed was available for the taking. Yet in the Antarctic negotiations there was no agreement whether international administration or division into national territories should be the basic principle of the international regime. Since this prior question had not been settled, it was impossible to go on to dividing it up.

A very different model of decision making, rational-choice theory, might be invoked in support of notions that the Antarctic negotiations of 1948–49 represent nothing more than imperialism at work. Certainly, it suggests a very plausible explanation of United States, United Kingdom, and New Zealand interest in internationalization. Like the other participants, these three governments faced the question of whether to divide up an area of real but unknown resource potential. Rather than opt for a slice of territory of indeterminate value, any government involved might decide instead to opt for a share of the whole.[15] One-eighth of the total Antarctic resource potential might well seem more attractive than all of the resources of a portion of the continent. Several American policy makers did view the unclaimed area as unpromising. For the British, the fact that virtually all of their claim was contested by Argentina or Chile or both would make division less attractive. For New Zealand, calculation could well rest on an appreciation of the fact that protecting its Antarctic claim against unfriendly incursion might prove impossible. Yet even this model cannot explain all attitudes. Despite the relative smallness of their claim, the French had no interest in internationalization, and low capabilities had not lessened Norwegian interest in dividing Antarctica.

Structural theories focusing on the type of political regime fare no better, though this might stem from the small number of states involved. Three democracies, New Zealand, the United Kingdom, and the United States, preferred internationalization.[16] Advocates of dividing the continent included democracies (France, Australia, Norway, and Chile) and one authoritarian state (Argentina).[17] There is no simple correlation between democracy (or lack of democracy) and attitude toward dividing Antarctica.

The theory that policy and attitudes toward international regimes in general vary by the strength of the governmental machinery vis-à-vis the domestic society does receive some confirmation and yield some insight into the 1949 result. A rough ranking would order the governments of the eight main participants from strongest to weakest as follows: France, United Kingdom, and Norway first, then Australia, New Zealand, and Argentina in the middle,[18] and Chile and the United States weakest.[19]

In 1949 the expectation that states with weak governments would be the most interested in establishing an international regime was borne out. The United States and Chile were the most interested in reaching some agreement on the future of Antarctica. The Chilean case is particularly interesting. Perhaps domestic weakness made that government more sensitive to the weakness of its Antarctic position vis-à-vis other states as well. However, that is not a universal phenomenon; the spectacle of weak governments trying to shore up their domestic positions through foreign adventures is too common to allow confident generalizations in this regard.[20] American interest in an international regime, particularly one providing internationalization, is obvious; agreement on such a regime would get the U.S. government out of the dilemmas caused both by squabbles among its allies and by its own inability to frame a policy.

Differences in bureaucratic structure also fail to account for the way in which governments perceived their interests. By 1948 most of the claimant governments had created central policy bodies for Antarctic affairs. Argentina and Chile had evolved rather similar structures. Argentina created an interdepartmental National Antarctic Commission chaired by an official from the Foreign Ministry for formulating general policy. The Antarctic territory itself was deemed a "national territory" outside the normal provincial administration, ruled directly by the central government through the maritime governor of Tierra del Fuego. All activity in the Antarctic was carried out or supplied by the navy, acting through the Melchior and Decepción Naval Detachments.[21] In Chile, the Chilean Antarctic Commission, also chaired by an official from the foreign ministry, not only provided policy guidance but was responsible for overall administration of the Antarctic claim. As in Argentina, most Antarctic activity was carried out by the navy, but the Chilean navy was less able to hold a commanding position than its Argentine counterpart. Though it kept operational responsibilities, planning functions were taken over by the general staff when the Antarctic section was transferred to it from the naval staff.[22] In both Argentina and Chile, this organization of activity reflects the more general Latin American tendency to concentrate oceanographic and other maritime scientific activity in the navy. Yet in Argentina the navy was able to translate this general tendency into far greater influence over policy. The Perón government depended heavily on military support for its existence, and one method of keeping the various services happy was farming out particular policy realms to them. The navy essentially "owned" Antarctic policy. In Chile naval influence was constrained by the fact that civilian rule and civilian control of the military had been the norm since at least 1890.

The United Kingdom also had a strongly organized machinery for Antarctic policy because of the need to defend Antarctic claims from Argentine and occasional Chilean challenge. The South American Department of the Foreign Office included a Polar Regions Section which oversaw diplomatic and legal aspects of policy. Civil administration of the claim, then part of the Falkland Islands Dependencies, was handled by the governor of the Falklands, who reported to the Colonial Office. The Colonial Office was also home to the Falkland Islands Dependencies Survey, which operated Antarctic stations and carried out scientific work. While the Foreign Office handled most of the diplomatic work, consultations with Australia and New Zealand continued through Commonwealth channels.[23]

Australia and New Zealand had less elaborate bureaucratic structures: in both countries, administration of the claim and formulation of general policy were entrusted to the Department of External Affairs, which maintained an Antarctic Division to handle the work. Australian scientific activity had grown sufficiently to justify the establishment of an interdepartmental coordinating committee in 1947.[24] New Zealand lacked any such committee until the International Geophysical Year, and created a standing committee only in 1958.[25]

France had an even less unified machinery for policy. The Foreign Ministry dealt with the political and legal implications of Antarctic questions. Adélie Land and the subantarctic islands were administered by the governor-general of Madagascar, who reported to the Ministry of Colonies. The Ministry of Marine (navy) was responsible for defense of the territory. An interdepartmental committee chaired by the minister of education had charge of planning and supervising scientific work, but the initiative and all operational responsibilities still lay with Expeditions polaires françaises, a private body headed by Paul-Emile Victor. Though the EPF received most of its funds from the government, through the Conseil national de recherche scientifique, it also accepted private donations and operated autonomously of both the government and the university system.[26]

For a claimant, Norway's policy apparatus was particularly fragmentary. In 1948 Norwegian legislation provided for civil administration of Bouvet and Peter I Islands, but not for Queen Maud Land, an omission not repaired until 1957. Perhaps reflecting the fact that whaling was long the major Norwegian interest in Antarctica, scientific work was coordinated by the Norsk Polarinstitutt, an autonomous body reporting to the Commerce Ministry. Any diplomatic or legal difficulties that arose were handled by the Foreign Ministry.[27]

Since the United States had no Antarctic claim, it did not have to create a real or a fictive administrative structure. As in other countries, political and legal questions were handled in diplomatic channels, through the State Department. The State Department also sought to coordinate policy through ad hoc exchanges with other departments. Government-sponsored Antarctic activity was undertaken by the navy.[28]

In 1948, then, there was still a good deal of diversity in bureaucratic organization. While all governments needed Antarctic experts in their foreign ministry to deal with international aspects of the issue, the organization of domestic Antarctic operations differed greatly. Argentina and Chile regarded their Antarctic claims as integral parts of the national domain. This stemmed in part from the legal justifications put forward for the claims, but also from the fact that neither had any other colonies and so lacked any special bureaucratic structure for administering them. Nor did either government want to create any colonial-style administration, given their opposition to colonialism. Britain and France both treated Antarctic claims as part of a wider colonial empire, even to the point of delegating the task of administering Antarctic and subantarctic areas to a particular colonial governor. Britain reinforced this by charging the Colonial Office with the task of maintaining an active scientific program. In France scientific activity was separate from administration in 1948, a luxury permitted by the fact that no other state was challenging French claims directly. Australia and New Zealand also lacked any colonial administrative structure, so they had to graft Antarctic tasks onto existing structures in their respective foreign ministries. Norway, too, lacked any separate administrative structure.

Then, as later, Antarctic science and Antarctic politics went hand in hand. This was particularly true for Argentina, Britain, and Chile, since each used a scientific program as the excuse for a wider presence meant to bolster its own claims and weaken those of rivals. In those countries the government provided generously for scientific activities. In other countries, where the political pressures were less immediate, the government had to be prodded by private groups. This was particularly true in New Zealand, where the New Zealand Antarctic Society's bylaws listed the encouragement of greater government activity as a goal of the organization;[29] in the United States, where navy work was supplemented by the private expedition led by Finn Ronne; and in France, where much of the actual scientific work was left to a private organization.

Yet it is hard to derive much policy significance from these differences in organization. Bureaucratic politics may explain some of the claimant resistance to an international regime. Most had one or more agencies concerned with administering the territorial claim, and these agencies would lose work and influence if the claim were given up. However, there is no full correlation between the strength of claim administration and national possessiveness. Britain is the most obvious example. Further, the agencies in charge of scientific research could be kept busy, and perhaps even gain influence, under a nonterritorial regime.

Because of the relatively low and definitely restricted salience of Antarctic issues, differences in domestic political processes had little effect on Antarctic policy. The Antarctic continent was far enough away, and Antarctic issues involved so few people, that there was little meaning in differences of domestic legal or customary constraints on government action or in the relative openness of each national society to outside influence. All eight governments were able to formulate their policy in isolation from the pressures of interest groups or extensive public discussions. Though public attention was higher in Argentina than elsewhere, this was the product of a governmental decision to use the issue for seeking the continued support of ultranationalist groups. Though this might have caused difficulties, it is clear that the Perón government could shift their attention elsewhere, such as the various boundary disputes with Chile or general anticommunist agitation, should Antarctic policy require. The incoherence of United States policy was encouraged by the fragmentation of power in the U.S. political system, but the United States government had shown itself capable of making and following coherent policies in other areas when the issue was deemed sufficiently important.


## Coalitions


The failure to create an Antarctic regime in the late 1940s does not disprove structuralist contentions that the distribution of power determines which interests prevail. Clearly, the stalemate between those rejecting and those supporting the notion of dividing Antarctica into national territories was possible only because of the great overall and rising issue-specific power of the United States. Operating alone, the dispute over claim boundaries among Argentina, Chile, and Britain would not have prevented division into claims; in that case, the problem would have been treated as one of boundary delimitation within the framework of prevailing international law on acquisition of territory.

The failure does, however, point out the conditions necessary for proper use of structuralist theories. Power counts only if and insofar as it is activated. The United States government did act sufficiently to prevent a result it did not like. However, its own internal division made it unable to bring enough power to bear to secure its first choice. United States power was not brought to bear because the relatively low salience of the issue allowed policy makers to continue arguments over goals (or, from another point of view, did not force top decision makers to put an end to the squabbling by imposing their views).

Some features of the international process may have affected outcomes by constraining the use of power. This is suggested by the Argentine and Chilean efforts to secure United States endorsement of notions that their Antarctic claims were covered by the mutual-assistance obligations of the Rio Pact. They hoped in this way to win acceptance of their view that the United Kingdom was an interloper with no rights in the area. Had the United States government accepted this interpretation, it would have found it hard to remain neutral or to side with the United Kingdom in any Antarctic and subantarctic territorial disputes (including that over the Falkland Islands). More seriously, it would have amounted to a tacit acceptance of claims. It is also possible that some policy makers in various countries resisted the Chilean notion of converting Antarctica into an area for the pursuit of cooperation in science, because it would have been very hard to use force against any outsider desiring to join in the cooperation. Be that as it may, it is clear that process restraints on use of power work most effectively at low or medium salience. If salience is perceived as very high, the restraints become less effective, a phenomenon long noted in the realization by international lawyers that states will not settle disputes affecting "vital interests" by arbitration or adjudication.

In both overall and issue-specific terms, a coalition of the United States and the seven claimant states possessed sufficient overall and issue-specific power to maintain any agreement they made against outside challenge. In 1948–49 the United States was clearly a hegemonial power in the economic realm. It had the only industrial economy that came out of World War II enlarged rather than exhausted (like the British economy) or heavily damaged (like the Soviet, German, Japanese, or French economies). The dollar was the most desired currency, supplanting the British pound sterling as the main reserve and trading currency in the world. There were vast markets for American industrial and agricultural goods. While the Soviet bloc resisted U.S. economic power by shutting itself off from the global market, all countries felt and most acknowledged U.S. economic preeminence.

The United States military position was also enviable, though not hegemonial. Its nuclear monopoly was lost after Soviet explosion of an atomic bomb in August 1949, and Soviet conventional forces were larger in numbers. Yet the United States still had great advantages in the ability to project power rapidly far from home because of foreign bases on allied soil, the world's largest navy, and the world's greatest long-distance airlift capacity.

Britain, too, remained an important global power, though its position was weaker than anyone (including the British themselves) realized at the time. France was clearly weak, but this condition was seen as temporary, since it retained its overseas empire and remained an industrial state. The other negotiating partners were not significant as global powers, but were important in Antarctic affairs.

Restricting negotiations and participation to the United States and the seven claimants was equally plausible at the time because between them they virtually monopolized issue-specific power. In 1948 issue-specific power on Antarctic questions had four components: geographical proximity to the continent, historical level of activity in Antarctica, current level of activity in Antarctica, and the potential to continue that activity at an equal or greater level in the future. Proximity favored Argentina and Chile the most, with Australia, New Zealand, and South Africa also in the running. Sovereignty over subantarctic islands was not enough to put Britain, France, and Norway on the same footing in this regard. These islands could service as staging points for logistics and communications, but did not significantly reduce the cost of Antarctic activity, because all personnel and equipment still had to be sent from the home country.

In terms of historical activity, Britain had the longest and strongest record in 1948. British subjects were among the most active early explorers, and one has a good claim to being the first to actually sight the continent. Britons were very active in both sealing and whaling in the nineteenth century, and the British government commissioned thirteen expeditions in the course of the century. A British party led by Scott was second at the South Pole. British or Commonwealth expeditions also were very active in the interwar exploration of the continent.[30]

The United States and Norway also had long traditions of south polar explorations in 1948. Americans had been the most active participants in nineteenth-century sealing and whaling, and the United States government sent the Wilkes expedition in 1841–43. American activity picked up again in the interwar period with the various Ellsworth and Byrd expeditions. Norwegian activity began later, but quickly reached a high level. A Norwegian party led by Amundsen was the first to reach the South Pole. Norwegians also came to dominate whaling by the 1920s, since the most advanced technology had been developed in their country.[31] Norwegians also undertook several expeditions that cruised off, flew over, or traversed parts of the continent in the late 1920s and early 1930s. Argentinian and Chilean activity had included encouraging some whaling (usually by foreigners incorporating companies in those countries), some cooperation in efforts to rescue expeditions in trouble, and, in the Argentine case, operation of a weather station on Laurie Island in the South Orkneys just north of the Antarctic Peninsula. Australians and New Zealanders participated in a number of Commonwealth expeditions, most notably the British, Australian, and New Zealand Antarctic Expedition under the Australian Mawson in 1929–31. Germans had led and financed expeditions in 1873, 1882–83, 1901–3, 1928–29, and 1939–40, as well as participating in Antarctic whaling after 1935. Russian navigators had a good claim to being first to sight the continent in 1821, but there was no further Russian or Soviet activity until fleet-scale whaling was taken up in 1946. Belgium could claim an Antarctic tradition of exploration going back to the Gerlache Expedition of 1899. The Japanese government sent an expedition under the naval lieutenant Shirase in 1911–12, and Japanese whaling fleets began Antarctic operations in 1935.

By 1948 the United States had taken the lead in current activity with "Operation Highjump" of 1946–47, which involved 4,000 men, thirteen ships, and aircraft operating from a base on the continent as well as from aircraft carriers; "Operation Windmill" of 1947–48; and the Ronne Expedition of 1949. The United Kingdom was not far behind with the 150 men, two ships, and five stations of the "Falkland Islands Dependencies Survey." Argentina and Chile each maintained two stations in the Antarctic Peninsula.

Australia, France, and New Zealand had no current activity, though plans for various expeditions were under way.[32] Germany, still under four-power occupation, lacked the resources for Antarctic research, and might not have been permitted to undertake any activity even if it had found the resources. Japan had been allowed to resume whaling by the American Occupation authorities. However, that decision was motivated by the need to supply the Japanese with more food and did not appear to presage wider activity, at least until such time as Japan was released from the Occupation and allowed to make decisions on its own.

Members of the proto-coalition were, rightly, apprehensive that the Soviet Union would launch a serious challenge to their monopoly. The Soviet government had indicated interest in Antarctic affairs during the 1930s. By 1949 it was engaged in a propaganda campaign preparatory to a more public pronouncement on the area. The postwar whaling expeditions were a token of the sort of activity the Soviets could organize if they decided to devote the necessary resources to it. Yet in all probability, the eight participating governments could have beaten back any Soviet challenge if they had been able to agree on a regime and decide that Antarctic affairs merited the necessary commitment. These two things, however, were just what the eight were unable to do. Since they were unable to create a regime, there remained greater opportunities for external challenge to their position.

## Summary

The failure to create an Antarctic regime in 1948–49 stemmed from a combination of low salience and great differences of interest among participants in the negotiations. If they had not been divided on the basic question of whether Antarctic lands were open to national appropriation, low salience probably would not have hindered the formation of a regime. The negative interest in keeping outsiders (mainly the Soviets) out of Antarctic affairs was not enough to bridge the difference in conception of positive interests. If salience had been higher, the participants might have been able to bridge those differences along the lines proposed by the Chilean government before the International Geophysical Year.

This inability to arrive at some mutually acceptable resolution of the territorial question prevented any discussion of norms, rules, and procedures for an Antarctic regime. This lack of resolution stemmed mainly, though not entirely, from the United States government's inability to arrive at a set policy. If the pro-claims faction had been able to carry the day, there would have been a regime based on the division of Antarctica into eight national areas, the reciprocal recognition of sovereignty, and a united effort to protect that sovereignty against all outside challenge. If the anti-claims faction had prevailed, the United States would probably have backed the Chilean proposal to hold claims in abeyance while pursuing cooperative scientific research. This, of course, would have depended on being able to frame the proposal in such a way as to prevent Soviet participation. In 1948–49 the cold war was too intense to allow any American policy maker to take a public stand that would open any opportunity for Soviet activity in another area of the world.

The 1948–49 negotiations also demonstrate that most theories of how governments make foreign policy fail to explain the positions of the eight participating governments. It is possible to argue that this failure occurred only because the restricted salience of Antarctic issues meant that discussions were confined to small groups of officials and a few others ready to make Antarctic policy on strictly rational calculations. Yet there is some evidence that even on issues of widespread salience, governments act on ideas and perceptions which develop in ways not fully determined by the structure or process of their domestic systems.[33]

# 4

# Successful Regime Creation in 1959

$A$decade after the first attempt to create an Antarctic regime tapered off in failure, a second attempt with an enlarged set of participants succeeded. There remained important differences of interest among the now twelve participants, but the increased salience of Antarctic affairs inspired the efforts necessary for creating a mutually acceptable international regime. Though increased salience forced governments to continue discussion until they reached acceptable understandings, success was also aided by the fact that there was wide agreement on a number of norms that should apply in the Antarctic. This eased the compromise on territorial sovereignty that permitted creation of a viable Antarctic regime.

## Salience

The United States pursued its initiatives in 1958–59, and other participants responded positively because Antarctic issues had acquired greater relative salience by then. This stemmed in large part from the increased governmental and scientific attention inspired by the International Geophysical Year. Yet that increase in the intrinsic importance of Antarctic affairs might not have been sufficient for success at regime creation but for the fact that it occurred at a time of relative calm in the wider international system.

Antarctica had gained new importance in the 1950s. Further improvements in technology made it easier to explore Antarctica and maintain year-round manned stations there. The International Geophysical Year had led to the establishment of new year-round scientific stations in Antarctica, and many of the sponsoring governments planned to continue using them afterward. Even if the level of activity dropped off somewhat after the IGY, it would remain much greater than in previous years. The Soviet decision to continue using their stations posed an additional problem for the eleven other participants. Few had the power to throw the Soviets out, and there was little inclination to do so, because of both the intrinsic difficulties of doing so and the political unacceptability of using force against peaceful scientific research. Unless Antarctica were to become a new venue for the cold war, some more enduring arrangement than the IGY understandings would have to be negotiated. For their part, the Soviets also needed a more enduring arrangement to impart a measure of security to their newly established activity. For both practical and political reasons, then, continued year-round activity forced governments to negotiate a longer-term understanding about access to and use of Antarctica.

At the same time, salience had not risen so high that governments were unable to reach compromises on questions that divided them. In particular, nothing had happened to make the claimants insist on division of the continent rather than the revised Chilean proposal that became Article IV of the Antarctic Treaty. Neither developments in related international regimes nor improvements in technology had markedly increased the immediate economic value of claims.

Though elements of the law of the sea had been revised in 1958, these changes did not add materially to the value of Antarctic claims. The first UN Conference on the Law of the Sea did register general acceptance of the already developed doctrine of the continental shelf, under which coastal states had exclusive jurisdiction over living and nonliving resources on the ocean floor just off their coasts. Article 1 of the 1958 Convention on the Continental Shelf[1] defined that area as referring

> (a) to the seabed and subsoil of the submarine areas adjacent to the coast but outside the area of the territorial sea, to a depth of 200 meters or, beyond that limit, to where the depth of the superadjacent waters admits of the exploitation of the natural resources of the said areas;
> (b) to the seabed and subsoil of similar submarine areas adjacent to the coasts of islands.

Article 2 (3) accepted the notion, first advanced in the United States's Truman Proclamation of 1945, that "the rights of the coastal state over the continental shelf do not depend on occupation, effective or notional, or on any express declaration." The International Court of Justice endorsed this view, stating that Article 2 (3) expressed a rule of customary international law benefiting all states, not just the then forty parties to the Convention,[2] in 1969 when it said, "the rights of the coastal state in respect of the continental shelf . . . exist *ipso facto* and *ab initio* by virtue of its sovereignty over the land."[3]

All claimants were therefore free to regard their Antarctic territory as including control over any resources on the seabed and subsoil in at least those areas lying under no more than 200 meters of water. A few of them acted on the doctrine by express proclamation before the Antarctic Treaty was concluded.[4] Those which had not acted could argue from the 1958 Convention (especially as interpreted later by the International Court of Justice) that their territorial claim included a claim to the continental shelf as well. Nonclaimants would, of course, have a different view. Starting from the same assumption that continental-shelf jurisdiction is an extension of territorial sovereignty, they concluded that nonacceptance of territorial sovereignty means that offshore areas are part of the high seas.[5]

Yet this difference had little practical import in 1959 because of the particular characteristics of the Antarctic continental shelf. In most areas of the world, the seaward edge of the geological continental shelf, which can be anywhere from forty to hundreds of nautical miles from shore, lies under 100 to 200 meters of water. The Antarctic geological continental shelf lies under 400 to 800 meters of water at its most seaward points.[6] In fact, only small areas of the total Antarctic continental shelf lie at depths shallower than 200 meters. These extend no more than twenty miles from shore and are covered by pack ice almost all of the year.[7]

Nor did changes in the rules governing coastal-state jurisdiction in the water column affect Antarctic claims very much. Majority opinion, embodied in the 1958 Conventions on the Territorial Sea and Contiguous Zone and on Fishing and Conservation of the Living Resources of the High Seas,[8] held that except under very special circumstances fisheries jurisdiction should not extend more than twelve nautical miles from the coast. The territorial sea was limited to a band somewhere between three and twelve nautical miles as well, with the major maritime states favoring the older three-mile rule. For most claimants, then, claims to fisheries jurisdiction were not a source of stubbornness over sovereignty. It is true that a number of Latin American states, Argentina and Chile among them, were already

claiming the right to control all fisheries and other resources within two
hundred nautical miles of their shores. Argentina and Chile had even extended these assertions to their Antarctic claims.[9] However, this posed no
particular problems in 1958–59, both because such doctrines enjoyed very
little international support and because neither Argentina nor Chile attempted to act on them in the Antarctic beyond entering reservations to the
International Whaling Convention.[10]

The physical and technical barriers to resource exploitation remained
formidable. Offshore production of hydrocarbons had begun, but only in
areas lying under less than 70 meters of water and with favorable climate
and water conditions.[11] There was some mining in Arctic areas, but it was
confined to fairly small operations close to the coast, with shipping of
product limited to the summer months.[12] No one had yet figured out how
to cope with either exploring or mining through thick ice, a major hindrance in the Antarctic. Whaling in the summer months was the only current economic activity in the Antarctic, and it was already regulated by the
International Whaling Convention.[13]

In 1959 most experts estimated that resource exploitation was at least a
generation away. They also agreed that much remained to be learned about
Antarctica's resources before the economic feasibility of exploitation could be
assessed. None disagreed with Laurence M. Gould, chairman of the U.S.
National Academy of Sciences' committee on Antarctica, who said: "The
point is that we don't know, and to predicate a program or presume that there
are vast resources there is nonsense. We haven't examined one percent of the
area geologically. We have only scratched the surface of our ignorance. So
that for many years to come, perhaps as many as thirty years, the most
important export of Antarctica is going to be scientific data."[14] Widespread
expert agreement on this point meant that even the most resource-minded of
the participating governments were able to concentrate on fostering scientific
research. They were also able to agree that science is a positive-sum activity in
which anyone's acquisition of new knowledge benefits all, and that it had to
be a cooperative activity, since no one country could bear the entire cost of
unlocking Antarctica's secrets.

The year 1959 was a good time for creating an Antarctic regime because
there were not too many other issues on the participants' foreign policy
agendas. The great postwar economic adjustments and reconstructions had
been completed. The Bretton Woods institutions were operating roughly as
planned. Europe, Japan, and the Soviet Union had all recovered from wartime devastation. At the same time, North-South issues had been raised but
had not yet attained the prominence they would have in the mid-1960s,

because the Afro-Asian and Latin American groups of countries had not yet coalesced into a stable Third World coalition. Decolonization still had a long way to go, so economic concerns were not yet at the top even of the Afro-Asian agenda. The cold war had abated considerably since 1949, though the superpowers remained in competition with one another. Thus, the Antarctic Treaty was negotiated late enough not to become embroiled in the worst of the cold war and early enough not to become a North-South issue.

## Interests

The compromise on sovereignty forming the basis of the Antarctic regime was not the first choice of most participants. The claimants would have preferred acceptance of their claims. For New Zealand and the United Kingdom, which remained ready to yield their claim if a stable form of international control could be established, the compromise was a way to see whether this would in fact happen before they made any definitive legal commitments. For other claimants it was probably less desirable, being a second choice that held real hazards of eventually turning into something worse: full loss of sovereignty. However, the terms of the compromise were such that they believed they could still protect their positions. It was also a second choice for the smaller nonclaimant states—Belgium, Japan, and South Africa. They would have been better off under endorsement of some type of joint control, since none were ever likely to attain a level of activity that would justify their raising a claim in the future. For South Africa, the fact that those parts of Antarctica lying closest to its territory were already claimed by others provided an additional incentive.

For the superpowers, the compromise might have been their first choice. Neither had made a claim or recognized any claim made by another state, and both had supported the idea of "international" solutions. At the same time, however, neither was prepared to exclude the notion of territorial sovereignty entirely. Both "reserved all rights" growing out of their Antarctic activity,[15] indicating that if Antarctica were to be divided up in the future, they expected a share. They were thus positioned to support either some form of international control or a territorial division in the future, depending on which would best serve their interests. Given the paucity of information about the continent, it was too early to make a definitive choice in 1959. The sovereignty compromise meant that choice could be deferred until there was better information about the resources and until the general political situation was allowed to develop further. Both could feel that given their ample resources and the increasing importance of current activity, time was on their side vis-à-vis the other participants.

The willingness of participants to accept the compromise was also increased by the fact it was given a definite term. The possibility of holding a review conference in thirty years meant that any participant could reopen the issue later if it so desired. Since this interval corresponded to the interval most of the experts believed was needed to learn enough to assess the resource potential of the continent, governments could read into the provision an acknowledgment that the compromise could be renegotiated if material interests changed.

The compromise was probably made easier by the fact that other norms enjoyed unanimous support, particularly nonmilitarization of Antarctica and the Southern Ocean, cooperation in scientific research, and protection of the Antarctic environment. Each of these either advanced or was compatible with each participating government's interests.

Nonmilitarization attracted unanimous support because it conferred advantages on every participant. It is not hard to see why the superpowers agreed to this. In 1959 Antarctica was seen (at least by Western commentators) as having five potential military uses: (1) as a base for surface or submarine raiders preying on commerce in the Indian Ocean or the areas around Cape Horn and the Cape of Good Hope (particularly important if the Panama and Suez Canals were blocked);[16] (2) as a base for launching attacks on Southern hemisphere states;[17] (3) as a base for long-range bombers or missiles carrying nuclear weapons;[18] (4) as a site for weather and satellite tracking stations;[19] and (5) as a possible storage depot or refuge in the event of global nuclear war.[20]

Yet for every claim of significance, there were counter-assertions stressing the great disadvantages posed by cold climate, isolation, and distance from other countries.[21] Thus, any military use of Antarctica was extremely problematical. It might be easy to establish a base, but very difficult to defend it from attack. Further, both superpowers lay in the Northern Hemisphere, and the main lines of confrontation between them ran across Europe and the Arctic. This meant that the Antarctic was very far away from what would be the main theaters of war. The possession of Antarctic bases might prove irrelevant. Yet the logic of bipolar competition between the superpowers meant that if one established any Antarctic bases, the other would feel impelled to follow suit. Whatever advantage such a base might confer would thus be cancelled. Each would be better off, if only by being able to concentrate more military resources closer to home, if both agreed to leave Antarctica out of the military competition.[22]

American preferences are well documented, both in the Senate debates over ratification of the Antarctic Treaty and in statements by leading officials. Soviet preferences are less well documented, though some appear in statements during and after the Conference. Probably the best evidence that the Soviets really wanted demilitarization is the fact that they were prepared to accept the very sort of on-site inspections they routinely rejected in other arms-control negotiations. Grigori Tunkin explained away the apparent inconsistency with an argument about the significance of Antarctica's distance from Soviet home territory by noting that "the specific conditions prevailing in the Antarctic, where inspection cannot be used against national security, permitted agreement on unlimited inspection."[23]

The Argentines, British, and Chileans had attempted to control their own conflicts between 1948 and 1956 by agreements that they would avoid sending warships into the Antarctic Peninsula area except as needed to support scientific work. However, these had broken down temporarily in 1952–53 when several incidents occurred. The Falklands dispute between Argentina and Britain and the Beagle Channel dispute between Argentina and Chile, both of which had strong Antarctic implications, meant that conflict might revive at any time. The British, operating at the end of very long supply lines, were keenly interested in controlling this conflict. They had even attempted to get a resolution of the underlying issues by asking the International Court of Justice to rule on the respective territorial claims, an idea rejected by both Latin American states.[24] For the Argentinians and Chileans, demilitarization yielded advantages. In a real confrontation, neither one alone, and probably not even both together, could hope to defeat the British. Further, they could not be sure of winning support from the United States. At the same time, territorial disputes between themselves in the Antarctic, the Beagle Channel area, and along their common Andean frontier had led to incidents and mobilizations in the past and could do so again.[25] Demilitarizing Antarctica would remove one source of potential conflict between them.

For all the Southern Hemisphere states, demilitarization meant not having to worry about an attack launched from Antarctica. Both Australians and New Zealanders had expressed fears of being caught from behind.[26] The specific inclusion of a ban on all types of nuclear explosion also appealed to them as promising protection from danger of radiation. There had been enough talk about the advantages of Antarctica as a test site to make this danger seem real.[27]

Demilitarization also benefited any state that maintained an Antarctic station or sovereignty over a subantarctic island, by removing the most immediate threats to those stations or islands. This gave France, Norway, Belgium, and Japan positive material reasons to desire demilitarization.

All participants also endorsed the broad principles and norms of scientific cooperation. The claimants might have preferred a regime specifying that scientific expeditions could be sent or scientific stations established only with the consent of the state on whose claim they would operate, but the other participants all supported unqualified open access. In this situation, a relatively weak claimant could best protect its legal position against erosion from the activities of more powerful outsiders by agreeing to a deal whereby access would be traded for insurance in the form of the understanding that activities during the time the treaty was in force would have no legal significance if it were terminated and a division of the continent were to ensue.[28] While some of the nonclaimants might prefer internationalization or a declaration that Antarctica was a common area, open access gave them most of what they wanted. They could pursue exploration and scientific study without political hindrance.

Both superpowers were also highly interested in science, not only for itself but as a sign of power and a source of prestige. The Soviets were still enjoying advantages from the launching of Sputnik, and the Americans were still smarting under the embarrassment of having been beaten. For the Soviets in particular, science had been the key that unlocked the door to their participation in the Antarctic community. Howard J. Taubenfeld concluded in 1960 that the IGY "did perhaps make what was the inevitable Soviet entrance into the area more graceful—and also, it might be acknowledged, more internationally limited and more exposed to the scrutiny of others than has usually been the case"[29] This extra scrutiny was important, for the Soviets' highly secretive methods of operation were in themselves the cause of much nervousness among other countries. Once the basic norm of open access was accepted, it was not difficult to agree on the more specific rules governing scientific cooperation. They flowed logically from the needs of science and the need for mutual assistance in a harsh environment.

All twelve participating governments could easily agree that measures should be taken to protect the Antarctic environment. In the first place, the undisturbed environment of the Antarctic was viewed as a major asset to research, particularly on questions of climate change and the dispersion of atmospheric pollution or radioactive fallout from atomic tests. Second, protection of the environment was seen as important in its own right. Governments in the Southern Hemisphere feared that disturbing the Antarctic environment would lead to serious climate changes in their part of the world. Even governments in more distant states realized that any major warming would lead to the melting of the ice cap, at the very least causing sea levels to rise all around the world and likely having great effects on the overall global climate as well. Here were obvious "bads" that all governments could agree were worth avoiding.

Agreement on regime procedures was made easier by the widespread aversion to the creation of an elaborate set of institutions. The other participants rejected British proposals to create an Antarctic organization,[30] and even refused to give the consultative parties any permanent staff. Instead, necessary secretariat functions, such as preparing documents and providing simultaneous translation into the four working languages of the group (English, French, Russian, and Spanish), were to be provided by the government acting as host for each meeting.[31] The claimants' legal position was stronger if there were no organization actually taking an active role or even exercising some forms of jurisdiction in the Antarctic. Creation of an organization would encourage notions that Antarctica's long-term future lay with internationalization. For the Soviets, lack of an organization meant the absence of an international staff, which might acquire independent influence in Antarctic affairs and have few Soviet members. This had been their experience in other international organizations, and they were interested in avoiding that situation whenever they could.[32]

These areas of broad agreement demonstrate again the weaknesses of theories deducing governments' definitions of national interest solely from the structure or process of domestic politics. If anything, this demonstration is stronger in these negotiations than in the earlier ones. Inclusion of the Soviet Union in the later negotiations widens the diversity of systems available for comparison, making possible a more rigorous test of the structural explanations.

Marxist theories deriving policy from the needs of the economic system would not predict that the world's leading capitalist state and the world's leading socialist state would adopt virtually identical policies, but that is what happened in 1959. The similarities of the two superpower's policies are even more stiking in 1959 than they were in 1949, if only because the USSR began describing its preferences in greater detail. Both superpowers wanted an international regime for Antarctica which would avoid endorsing territorial claims (or at least existing ones), remove Antarctica from military competition, ensure continued scientific cooperation, and keep Antarctic decisions out of the UN or any forum with a large number of participants.

Again, Marxist theory might be rescued. First, the parallelism of result might be viewed as the accidental congruence of two very different sets of material and moral calculations. Under this view, cooperation would be expected to break down once the accidental congruence was broken for any reason, such as the imminence of economic activity. The 1959 result could be seen as stemming from the lack of immediate prospects for economic activity. This lack of prospect for early economic gain, then, would weaken the normal capitalist drive for profit and permit other considerations to have more influence over policy.

Obviously, Marxist theory could also be rescued by denying that the Soviet Union is really a socialist state. If the USSR is defined as being a "state capitalist" system,[33] the similarity of policy is not hard to explain. The differences of emphasis in American and Soviet policy then become material for elucidating the differences between the two types of capitalism and the contradictions likely to arise when states of different capitalist types attempt to cooperate.

Again, however, rational-choice theory offers a simpler and more persuasive explanation of superpower preferences. Both face a situation in which the resource potential of a continent, and of the various regions within it, are unknown and in which others have staked out claims to most of the land involved. If those claims are accepted, the superpowers close themselves out of most of the potential resource activity, since at best they can share the unclaimed area. Their failure to endorse division in 1959 allows them the possibility of a share in joint activity covering the whole continent or of delaying division until such time as they can apply their greater power to Antarctic activity in ways that permit them to insist on being given larger or more desirable territories.

Theories tracing policy to the type of political regime fare no better. Dictatorships and democracies appear on both sides of the claimant-nonclaimant divide. Coalitions of democracies and dictatorships also formed on other issues. For instance, the Southern Hemisphere interest in banning all forms of nuclear explosions joined three democracies, one dictatorship and one partial democracy in common cause.[34] All participants accepted not only nonmilitarization but also a system of on-site inspection to go with it.

In 1959 there was also no relation between a government's place on the right-to-left political spectrum, or the composition of social coalition supporting its government, and its Antarctic policy. While Argentina, the most vociferous claimant, also had the most right-wing government, the almost equally right-wing South Africa did not endorse division. The leftist USSR, the right-of-center Liberal Democratic government of Japan, and the right-of-center Republican administration in the United States all sought to avoid the endorsement of claims. A structuralist could insist that if a larger number of solidly leftist governments had been involved, there would have been an explicit internationalization instead of an agreement to put claims on "hold." There is no way to prove or disprove this contention, though twentieth-century history suggests that holding territory has an appeal that even the most leftist of governments feels strongly. On this issue, possessing or lacking a previously asserted claim was far more important to attitudes than ideology.

Structuralist notions relating policy to political ideology cannot be rescued by asserting that the more rightist the claimant government, the more likely it is to insist on maintaining its claims, or the more leftist the nonclaimant government, the more likely it is to insist on some form of internationalization. Argentina, Chile, and Australia were the most insistent claimants, whereas New Zealand and the United Kingdom had expressed a willingness to surrender claims. Right-of-center governments ruled Chile, Argentina, and Australia. However, the United Kingdom was also ruled by a center-right government, New Zealand by a center-left one (see figure 1).

The participants in the Washington Conference can be divided into four groups in terms of governmental machinery. The Soviet Union stood by itself in having a state machinery able to dominate society constantly on all issues. Japan, France, the United Kingdom, South Africa, and Norway had governments responsive to social pressures but generally able to frame and implement coherent policies. Of this group, Japan had the strongest governmental machinery. Australia, New Zealand, and Belgium had yet weaker governments, with Argentina, Chile, and the United States (in that order) having the weakest. Neither the dependency nor the more general version of theories explaining policy by relative strength of the governmental machinery explains much in the creation of the Antarctic region.

A dependency theorist would be tempted to view Argentinian and Chilean (and perhaps even Australian and New Zealand)[35] insistence on claims as a sign of those governments' weakness. In this view, these governments would inspire nationalist clamor on an issue of no importance to the foreign investors and elites so strongly influencing their basic policies. This would allow them to play a double game of appearing nationalist at home while protecting the basic interests of their foreign bosses. The acceptance of the Antarctic Treaty by all four governments is fully compatible with this argument, since the treaty did not require an explicit renunciation of claims. With economic questions thus put aside for later consideration, the more dogmatic dependency theorists would expect them to be settled on the industrial countries' terms after the precedents of cooperation had become strong enough to permit the local elites to survive any lingering nationalist clamor.

Yet it is equally plausible to view Antarctic policy as one of the areas in which even a dependent government is able to pursue an independent policy. The provisions of the Antarctic Treaty are compatible with efforts to exploit the tendency of Western governments and elites to regard "political" and "economic" questions as separate realms while attacking economic domination through political decisions. They are also compatible with exploiting respect for formal notions of sovereignty to gain room for maneuver.[36]

No matter which process is at work, a government's position as dependent or central does not bear much relation to its Antarctic policy. Argentina and Australia were more insistent upon their rights as claimants than Chile and

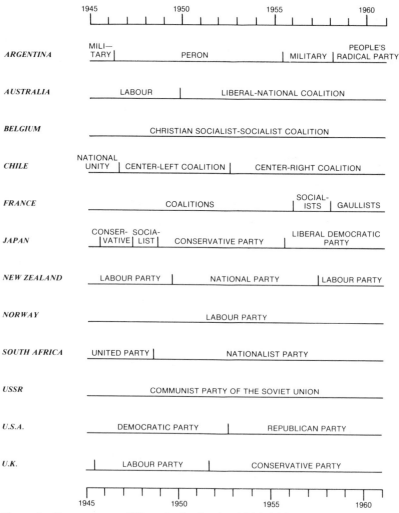

Figure 1. Governments of Consultative Parties, 1945–1960

New Zealand. On other issues, economic dependence was not particularly relevant; avoiding unwanted wars and serious environmental damage has appeal that transcends differences in place within the global economic system.

The more general version of the theory, which looks at a government's strength vis-à-vis its own society, also fails to explain policy. Yet this does not necessarily discredit the theory. Antarctic issues still had only restricted salience. They were not inspiring the mass or interest-group efforts to influence policy which would make differences of domestic political process relevant to outcomes.

The relative strength of the governmental machinery does not even identify the participants most keen on creating a regime in 1959. The high interest of the United States confirms the notion that weak governments want international regimes. Yet the Soviet Union (for all the difficulties its representatives raised before the Washington Conference opened) was just as keenly interested because a regime would give greater legitimacy to its presence in Antarctica. This suggests that states newly arrived to some geographical area or issue want international regimes when they will serve as a vehicle for securing participation in decisions. Similarly, newcomers would oppose any regime threatening to perpetuate their exclusion. This was precisely the Soviet attitude in 1948–49.

The 1959 experience demonstrates that differences in bureaucratic structure do not account for differences in perception of interests. It further shows that the line of causation often runs in the opposite direction, with foreign challenge or international negotiations having a strong impact on domestic bureaucratic structures. The rise of new issues to salience often requires adjustment of the policy machinery, especially if international agreements specify certain procedures. Comparisons with foreign bureaucratic structures deemed particularly successful at dealing with some problem often lead to emulation in the hope that some of that success will be transferred.[37]

The impact of newly salient issues on bureaucratic structures is most apparent in the reorganization of scientific coordination made necessary by the IGY. The overall IGY effort was coordinated by the International Council of Scientific Unions (ICSU), with its member national academies of science. Antarctic activity during the IGY was coordinated through the ICSU's Special Committee on Antarctic Research, which brought together representatives of the science academies of those nations sponsoring the active Antarctic programs. This structure was not affected by the Antarctic Treaty, except in that the ICSU changed the name to Scientific Committee on Antarctic Research in recognition of its continuing existence. The SCAR was then brought informally into the treaty system as an advisory body for the consultative parties.

The 1955 decision to mute political differences by running IGY programs through the ICSU and its national members brought scientists more directly into policy making than had been the case in many countries. This did not erase national differences, since each national scientific academy stood in a different relation to the government, and each national committee for Antarctic research included a different mix of government- and university-employed scientists. The Argentine, Chilean, and South African governments kept this activity pretty much within government circles. The government influence in Austra-

lia, New Zealand, France, and Japan was also strong, given the high proportion of universities run by the state. In the Soviet Union the connections were
particularly thorough, as is true throughout its system. The differences do not
rob SCAR of all significance, however. SCAR created and encouraged a
transnational network of scientists who had a role not only in coordinating
national scientific work but in helping define international cooperation and
advising the consultative parties. Here was a fairly large and usually influential
group of people who would benefit greatly from and want to protect the
Antarctic Treaty regime.

The overall increase in the salience of Antarctic issues led to more far-
reaching bureaucratic reorganizations in several countries. Most of the new
participants (Belgium, Japan, South Africa, and the USSR) had to create
policy machinery. Argentina, France, New Zealand, and the United States all
reorganized their existing machinery to strengthen it.

The more general reorganization of Argentine bureaucracy after the fall of
Perón included making the lines of authority on Antarctic affairs somewhat
clearer. Overall policy guidance was lodged specifically with the presidency
("executive power" is the exact term used), taking advice from the National
Defense Council as desired. The older National Antarctic Commission,
chaired by the Foreign Ministry, remained in existence as an arm of the Foreign
Ministry but reported directly to the president. The navy both gained and lost
in struggles over control of Antarctic activity. The Argentine Antarctic Institute, created in 1951 to oversee scientific work, was moved from the Ministry
of Technical Affairs to the Ministry of Marine in 1957. However, the navy lost
its monopoly on the operation of scientific and other stations that same year.
This had been confirmed in 1956 decrees, but was reversed in a 1957 decree
authorizing each ministry that had established Antarctic stations to continue
operating them. Both the Ministry of Marine and the Ministry of War had
Antarctic Divisions in their secretariats. The Ministry of Foreign Affairs moved
its Antarctic specialists into a new Division of Antarctic and Malvinas Affairs
within the Directorate of Territorial Affairs. In 1959 Argentina had not yet
established a standing national committee for SCAR; this task was given to the
Argentine Antarctic Institute in 1960.[38]

The Chilean government made more modest changes in its Antarctic bureaucracy. The major change before 1959 consisted of shifting civil administration of the Chilean Antarctic Territory from the Chilean Antarctic Commission to the governor of the Magallanes. This brought its civil administration
into line with the rest of the country, a unitary state divided into districts
under governors appointed by the central government. Like Argentina, Chile
was slow in establishing a national committee for SCAR; liaison with that
body was effected through an individual government-employed scientist.[39]

The French government, busy changing administrative organization in a number of areas, acted to remove a number of actual or anticipated problems. Since Madagascar was to become independent in 1960, civil administration of the subantarctic islands and Adélie Land was transferred from the governor-general of Madagascar to a newly established chief administrator of a separate entity, the Terres australes et antarctiques françaises. The Academy of Sciences, France's national member of the ICSU, became responsible for representation in SCAR and established a French Committee for Antarctic Research to carry out these duties. Meanwhile, the Antarctic Expeditions Office of the Ministry of Overseas France was beginning to take on more activity. It concentrated on maintaining programs on the Kerguelens and Crozets, while Expeditions polaires françaises was well on its way to becoming a simple contractor for work in Adélie Land.[40]

The increase of activity inspired by the IGY precipitated a thorough renovation of New Zealand's Antarctic bureaucracy. Administration of the Ross Dependency remained entrusted to the governor-general working through the Foreign Ministry, but the conduct of scientific activities was entrusted to the minister in charge of scientific and industrial research, who set up a separate Antarctic Division of his department for the purpose. The minister also had a Ross Dependency Research Committee, an advisory group of government-employed and university scientists. It also served as the National Committee on Antarctic Research of the Royal Society of New Zealand, which was the local body naming New Zealand's member of SCAR.[41]

The Norwegian government hardly reacted to the changes. The Norsk Videnskapsakademi represented Norway on SCAR, while the existing Norsk Polarinstitutt continued its work. Activity during the IGY had, though, induced the government to revise its legislation defining civil administration of southern dependencies to cover the Antarctic claim (Queen Maud Land) as well as Bouvet and Peter I Islands.[42]

The British government did not yet feel that any major changes were needed. The Royal Society as national adherent to the ICSU took on the task of representing the United Kingdom on SCAR.[43]

In the United States the IGY brought about greater involvement of civilian scientists, which required modification of the operational organization previously dominated by the navy. Civilian scientists were reluctant to submit to naval discipline, and naval officers were equally reluctant to have military personnel commanded by civilians. American stations thus developed a dual command structure where the scientific staff worked under the direction of a chief scientist while the support personnel (exclusively navy at this time) were commanded by an officer-in-charge of the relevant ship or station. In Washington this change was accommodated by setting up a separate U.S. Antarctic

Projects office within the Operations Coordinating Board based at the White House. Representation on SCAR was handled by the National Academy of Sciences, which formed a Committee on Polar Research handling both Arctic and Antarctic aspects of IGY activity.[44]

The nonclaimants previously uninvolved in Antarctic negotiations had to create policy machinery, either by assigning new tasks to existing bodies or by creating new ones. The Belgian Foreign Ministry found its Antarctic experts far more busy than they had been. The requirements for national representation in SCAR were met by having the French-speaking Académie Royale de Belgique and the Flemish-speaking Koniklijke Vlaamse Akademie jointly appoint a National Antarctic Committee to coordinate activity and provide members of SCAR.[45] Since the older Japanese Polar Research Institute (established 1934) no longer existed, the Japanese government had to create new machinery. The Foreign Ministry again became involved in the diplomatic aspects of Antarctic affairs. The Science Council of Japan, under the Ministry of Education, was Japan's national adherent to the ICSU and thus the body responsible for representing Japan in SCAR.[46] South Africa had established a National Antarctic Research Committee within the government's Council for Scientific and Industrial Research, but appointed no member of SCAR until 1960. The Ministry of Transport continued to support actual activity on the subantarctic Prince Edward and Marion Islands.[47] The USSR quickly established a special Antarctic committee, called the Council for Antarctic Investigations in 1959, within the USSR Academy of Sciences for purposes of representation at SCAR. Actual scientific work was undertaken by scientists attached to the whaling fleets and expeditions sent by the Arctic (later Arctic and Antarctic) Institute of Leningrad, an organ of the Ministry of Merchant Marine.[48]

It is difficult to relate differences in Antarctic policy to these differences of bureaucratic organization in any systematic way. For instance, Argentina, Chile, and the United States permitted their militaries the greatest direct role in decision making. The consequences for policy varied according to the different general civilian-military relationships in each government. On most Antarctic questions the three shared similar ideas with each other and with other participants. Like other participants, they divided on the claims questions provoking the most controversy during the 1959 negotiations. Rather, the surest bases for distinguishing the policy preferences of participating governments are location (Southern Hemisphere governments tended to be more concerned about preventing nuclear tests) and possession or lack of a previously asserted territorial claim.

The influence of the international level on domestic organization can also be seen in the relative size and coherence of the bureaucracies of different countries. The claimant governments facing direct challenge to their territorial pretensions still maintained the largest and most coherent bureaucracies. This is particularly clear in the cases of Argentina and Britain. The focus of Argentine and Chilean interest can also be seen in their relative slowness to organize a proper national committee for SCAR. The possibility of new external challenge also seems to have helped inspire Norwegian rationalization of the status of Queen Maud Land. French reorganization was inspired more by the impending independence of Madagascar, to which the Antarctic and subantarctic territories had been attached for administrative purposes, than by Antarctic considerations.

Variations in the domestic political processes of individual states are also not very helpful for understanding how governments framed their Antarctic policies. The relative economic or political openness of different societies still had little impact on Antarctic affairs. Relative economic openness remained irrelevant because no activity of immediate economic significance was being undertaken on the continent. Whaling continued in the Southern Ocean, but this remained a separate issue. Relative political openness still made little difference, since Antarctic issues attracted so little public attention.

Because the Antarctic regime was embodied in a treaty (the strongest form available under international law), the results of negotiations had to be submitted for legislative approval in the democracies, giving interested citizens a chance to comment. This process was most significant in the United States because the executive could not be sure of its ability to muster the necessary two-thirds vote in the Senate. Public discussion was beginning in Australia and New Zealand, where high interest in the media and among some legislators opened up the debate. There was less public debate in France, Britain, and Norway even though the treaty had to be submitted for approval. For whatever reason, it did not become a major issue in those countries. However, the negotiations took place in private, with very little media coverage. Even those governments that had to present the treaty for legislative approval were presenting a finished agreement, not a set of suggestions about what might be done. Legislators were in the position of having to accept or reject the treaty as a whole, not of being able to offer amendments.

Similarly, creation of institutionalized transnational links among scientists in SCAR did not reduce differences in scientists' influence over policy in the various countries. Scientists were free to discuss their concerns and to go home with whatever reinforcement could be gained by being able to say that foreign colleagues agreed with them. Yet governments wishing to ignore their scientists could still do so. Alone, the SCAR would not have had a lot of direct influence. The Antarctic Treaty's formal acknowledgment of SCAR's expertise gave its opinions on scientific and technical matters political weight, though it would be greatest when scientific advice was incorporated in consultative parties recommendations. The extent to which governments listened to scientists would depend on the relevance of the latters' expertise to the question at hand.

## Coalitions

Coalition building during the 1958–59 negotiations was made much easier by two procedural decisions, which had a major influence on the substance of the talks. The first was restricting participation to the twelve states that had actually operated Antarctic stations during the IGY. The second was applying a unanimity rule for decisions in both the Washington conference and the Antarctic Treaty Consultative Meetings. The two decisions were linked in many respects, each decision helping participating governments accept the other one and the overall regime.

The link was obvious in the Soviet case. The Soviets initially advocated open participation at the Washington Conference, but accepted limited participation with a minimum of fuss;[49] nor did they oppose limiting participation in future Antarctic decisions. No doubt this was made easier by general acceptance of the unanimity rule in decision making. With the unanimity rule, the Soviet Union could be sure of protecting its interests even though outnumbered eleven to one in the original group by the United States and its allies. This freed it from the need to ensure that the total membership included enough Soviet bloc or other sympathetic states to block any American-inspired initiatives inimical to Soviet interests. The United States had always supported limited participation, both in the conference and in the subsequent regime, and was prepared to accept the unanimity rule when so many other participants insisted upon it.

The link between limited participation and unanimity was obvious in the case of the claimants as well. In a conference of twelve, they outnumbered nonclaimants seven to five. In an open conference, they would have been greatly outnumbered. In addition, an open conference would probably have adopted rules permitting decisions by either a simple or a qualified majority, since this was the prevailing practice at large international conferences. With such a rule the claimants could be outvoted at every turn. Even in a conference of twelve, an individual claimant could be outvoted if two claimants joined with the nonclaimants on an issue. Any fear of this was also removed by adopting a unanimity rule. Thus, the same fear of being outvoted that led the Soviet Union to insist on a unanimity rule led each of the claimants to the same conclusion.

However, limited participation had wider appeal. Only Japan joined the Soviet Union in proposing an open conference, and retreated when the opinions of others became apparent. The United Kingdom was prepared to accept an open conference, but wanted limited participation in later decision making. The United States made clear its preferences for limited participation in both the creation and the implementation of the regime.[50] There was a general disposition to restrict participation to states demonstrating a serious interest in the Antarctic.

Limited participation facilitated the far more important compromise on sovereignty by making it operate within a small group rather than in the whole international community. Claimant governments would have resisted harder if the whole community of states had been involved, because it would have been harder to specify what they were getting in return for agreeing not to assert sovereign rights. Vis-à-vis five other states, it was possible to specify clear material benefits that seeemed to be worth a temporary agreement to set territorial arguments aside.

The results of the Washington Conference are generally compatible with structural theories of international politics. Most provisions of the Antarctic Treaty fully reflected the shared preferences of the superpowers. This is not to say that they exerted conscious efforts to impose a mutually acceptable international regime on other participants. On further examination, it is seen that most of the interests shared by the superpowers were also shared by the others.

The overall power structure may account for the compromise on sovereignty, depending on how superpower preferences are read. It is clear that both preferred open access to the whole continent and wanted that norm endorsed as strongly as possible.[51] Yet it is not clear whether either desired full internationalization of the Antarctic. The Soviet position might be viewed cynically as a maneuver to delay ratification of claims until the USSR was in a position to advance one of its own. Though the United States had let slip opportunities to assert a claim, there remained a strong pro-claim faction within the government. If the superpowers were biding their time before pressing for a division of the continent, then they were getting their first choice in the wording of Article IV. If, however, either viewed condominium or some other form of explicit joint jurisdiction as necessary to open access, they deferred to the opinions of other participants in accepting Article IV.

The hegemonic-stability theory cannot be applied to creation of the Antarctic regime, because there was no hegemon at work. In 1959 the United States was still the most economically powerful state in the world, though its preeminence was not as commanding as it had been in 1948. Japan and Western

Europe had rebuilt their economies and were at the threshold of a decade of rapid growth. The Soviet economy had also been rebuilt, and the Council for Mutual Economic Assistance (CMEA or COMECON) facilitated Soviet efforts to maintain its independence from world markets. Yet, despite Soviet boasts that the USSR's production of key goods, such as steel, would exceed that of the United States by 1980, the closest rival to the U.S. economy was the newly formed European Economic Community. Though its program of integrating the economies of its six member states had just begun, the six clearly had the potential to rival the United States economy in size before long. In economic terms, therefore, it was still possible to consider the United States a hegemon even though its position was beginning to erode.

By 1959 the Soviet Union had succeeded in narrowing the military gap between itself and the United States. It, too, had a hydrogen bomb. It may have had an advantage in the development of intercontinental ballistic missiles. However, both superpowers had missiles capable of delivering nuclear bombs to targets on the other's territory within half an hour of launch. The Soviets still had larger conventional forces, but the United States had the technological edge in weapons other than missiles and a greater ability to project its power far from home. In military terms, therefore, the situation was one of duopoly rather than hegemony.

The Soviet government was fully aware that its entry into the Antarctic had provoked great concern in other countries. Once it also realized that the United States government was prepared to accept it as a participant in Antarctic discussions, its best policy was to let the United States persuade its friends and allies that the Soviet Union should be included. By the end of 1958, if not in 1955 when the IGY was being planned, most of those friends and allies realized that, for better or worse, the Soviet Union would have to be included. Thus, the fact that the United States assumed the initiative publicly was an effort to act before all room for initiative was lost, not the product of any hegemony giving it unchallengeable leadership.

American actions to bring the Soviets in can be seen as an acknowledgment that the Soviet Union had enough power to barge in or even wreck a regime it did not like. Once admitted to participation, the Soviet government was able to translate its overall power into an effective voice in the negotiations. Had the Soviet Union not been included, it could have shifted to support of the Indian initiatives in the General Assembly. While the United States was still able to win in any General Assembly vote where it let others know it had strong views, any such Soviet action could have made things more difficult. A Soviet-bloc, African, and Asian coalition on the issue could not yet muster even a simple majority of the votes in 1958, though it would be able to do so after the admission of seventeen African states and one Asian state in 1960.[52] Although this remained short of the two-thirds needed to make a decision if the question were defined as "important," there were enough votes to pose real opposition to any Antarctic regime. As the Third World coalition grew in the 1960s, a Third World and Soviet-bloc alliance could have established a rival UN-based regime able to create many political complications for the Antarctic Treaty system. Including the Soviet Union in the latter was one way of helping keep such opposition weak.

The course of the Washington talks demonstrated again the link between overall and issue-specific power. This time the Soviet Union was converting overall into issue-specific power, a process greatly assisted by another increase in the scale of Antarctic activity. The IGY had led to a vast increase in the amount and intensity of activity on the Antarctic continent. For the first time in Antarctic history, expeditions from more than three states were on the continent simultaneously. Some of the scientific parties involved stayed on the continent for the whole eighteen months, a longer period than usual. This change made current activity the most important element of issue-specific power. The Washington Conference confirmed this by including only states that had participated in the IGY. Claimant governments realized this and were careful to participate in the IGY. The relation between current activity and ability to maintain claims was widely perceived. As the *Economist* noted in November 1957, "thirst for science is not the only reason for this flurry of activity. The United States and the Soviet Union are pouring in money and scientists in an Antarctic form of sputnikitis—and, too, with a view to establishing the basis for territorial claims should the Antarctic turn out to have any practical use."[53]

Geographical proximity gained significance because it lowered the cost of increasing activity. At the same time, historical activity became less important in determining current political influence. The claimants realized this, which is one reason they insisted that the compromise on sovereignty specifically include a proviso that activity during the period the treaty was in force would not be counted toward the making or weakening of territorial claims.[54] The shift also permitted other states to change their place within the issue-specific hierarchy. Belgium and Norway found it very difficult to keep up with the new levels of activity common during and after the IGY. Japan and West Germany had the resources and the freedom to renew their older activity. New participants could appear on the scene. Only Poland took advantage of the possibility in 1959, but it remained open to other states.

The fact of having previously asserted a territorial claim also retained political significance. Though it needed to be buttressed by ongoing activity, a claim meant that the holder had an additional "bargaining chip" in negotiations for any regime that attempted to bypass or supersede claims. No govern-

ment gives up territorial claims lightly, and all realize that formal abandonment would require making serious concessions in return.

The increased scale of activity helped bring about a closer relation between
issue-specific and overall power. Before 1945 a state could make up for small
size with intense effort, particularly since Antarctica and the surrounding
oceans were such unappealing places. After the IGY, costs increased to a
point where intensity could not as easily substitute for resources. Antarctica
was now a field for "big science," and that is essentially a rich country's game.

Taken as a whole, the 1959 negotiations may support the idea that issue-
specific power is more important to acquiring influence over the process of
regime creation than is overall power. This is the only way to account for the
compromise on sovereignty in strictly structural terms if explicit joint jurisdiction is assumed to have been the superpowers' first choice. Though American
and Soviet issue-specific power was increasing, it had not yet grown to the
point of overwhelming the issue-specific power of all other participants.
Bringing in Belgium, Japan, and South Africa to further buttress the nonclaimant side did not alter the negotiating situation all that much, since their
issue-specific power was weak in 1959. Yet it is an intriguing indication that
the superpowers did not care to confront the claimants alone. However, such
weighing of issue-specific versus overall power cannot be pushed very far,
given the wide agreement among participants on all other issues.

Characteristics of the international political process help explain a few
points. As in 1948–49, the claimants relied on alliance ties with the United
States to ensure that there would be no superpower coalition forcing renunciation of sovereignty in Antarctica. This task may not have been as difficult in
1959 as in 1949, since the claimants themselves were ready to accept a
compromise, the United States government had lost all interest in placing
Antarctica under UN auspices, and the earlier effort showed just how much
the claimants resisted a complete surrender on the issue. In addition, the
extreme nervousness about Soviet involvement displayed by Australia and the
two Latin American claimants suggests that the United States had to exert
influence to secure their acceptance of it.[55] This would leave the United States
less political capital for other questions.

Related international regimes also had some influence. General norms of
scientific cooperation had guided the organization of the IGY. Once participants had seen that it was possible to cooperate in scientific endeavor despite
deep political differences, IGY practices became precedents that could be
drawn upon. The international law on attribution of sovereignty helped shift
the definition of issue-specific power in favor of current activity. In general,
international law provides that no claim to sovereignty is valid without "effective occupation" of the territory involved. Just what constitutes "effective

occupation" remains open to debate; the standard varies by the size and habitability of the territory involved and to some extent by the absence or presence of rival claims to sovereignty over the same area.[56] Antarctica's remoteness and climate make plausible the arguments that the usual definition of establishing permanent settlements does not apply. Yet, however "effective occupation" is defined, a claim to sovereignty is a claim to exclusive authority over a piece of territory. It is difficult to maintain such a claim if some other state sponsors an equal or a larger amount of activity in the area claimed. With IGY acceptance of open access, claimants had to worry that others might outdo them in activity and then use that fact to overturn previous claims or to advance claims of their own.[57]

While the ideas held by most governments still favored dividing Antarctica in 1959, there was a fair amount of private discussion moving away from the traditional view that all land areas should be placed under the sovereignty of particular states. A few observers asserted that Antarctic territorial claims were holdovers from a now-dead colonialist past.[58] A growing literature was treating the high seas, outer space, and Antarctica as areas that should be held in common and remain open to all.[59] For the high seas, this was simply a continuation of the doctrines that had dominated thinking since the early nineteenth century. For outer space, this was an attempt to look ahead as new technology opened up new possibilities. For Antarctica, the experience of the IGY had inspired thoughts that the continent could remain open. However, there were no preexisting claims to sovereignty over the high seas or outer space. While the analogies appealed to a few governments,[60] the claimants could insist that Antarctica, both as a landmass and as an area where there were preexisting claims, was different from the oceans or outer space. This was a factor that hindered internationalization.

As was noted above, the existence of an alternate forum for Antarctic discussions, the UN General Assembly, helped the Soviets win a place at the Washington Conference. The General Assembly's existence also helped encourage compromise once negotiations got under way. If the negotiations had failed, any of the twelve participants could have joined India in raising the issue at the UN. Though this was not the main spur to negotiations,[61] it did serve to remind the participants that they needed to reach agreement.

## Summary

An Antarctic regime was created in 1958–59 for two principal reasons. First, the prospect of year-round scientific activity after the IGY gave Antarctic issues sufficient salience to inspire real efforts at compromise, while in the absence of immediate economic value no state had strong material incentives to block agreements that did not involve an immediate surrender of territorial claims. True, compromising rather than deciding the basic question of principle is a weak basis for an international regime, but that weakness was not regarded as a serious problem in 1959. Participating governments did acknowledge that it might become a problem later, hence the provisions for reviewing the Antarctic Treaty any time after it has been in force for thirty years. Second, the success of the IGY had demonstrated the viability of the Chilean notion of using the continent jointly while avoiding conflict over claims. Wide parallel interests among the participants on other questions, particularly nonmilitarization of the continent and environmental protection, greatly assisted the compromise on sovereignty by providing positive incentives to agreement. The process of reaching a compromise was greatly facilitated by the decision to limit participation, yet without the IGY, limiting participation would have led to lengthy wrangles about who should be included. The IGY provided, among other things, an "objective" way to identify states with a serious commitment to Antarctic affairs.

The immediate prospects of the newly created Antarctic regime were favorable because the participants formed a coalition with sufficient overall and issue-specific power to sustain their creation. This, too, resulted from selecting those states sponsoring Antarctic research during the IGY. Operating an Antarctic station was (and remains) a form of "big science." Since "big science" requires considerable resources, it attracts only the very powerful or the very interested.

The 1959 outcome also reaffirms the inadequacy of explanations resting solely on the latent capability of states. The Soviet Union was not co-opted simply because it had power; it was co-opted because it had shown a strong disposition to use that power in Antarctic affairs. The importance of demonstrating the will to apply power is obvious from a comparison of the Antarctic regime with those governing international monetary transactions or trade. Although the Soviet government offered a theoretical alternative to the latter two regimes, it was not sufficiently interested in global markets to interfere in their operations or to secure a place in the councils of GATT or the IMF. It was content to let these regimes operate while it offered other countries an alternative set of economic relationships based on its own economic maxims and practices, confident that at least some others would eagerly seek that alternative.

The results of the 1959 negotiations also demonstrate again the limited utility of theories attempting to derive governments' definitions of national interest and choices of policy from the structure or process of their state's domestic systems. Both experiences show that governments define interests very largely in terms of actual or potential material possession. It also shows the way in which international rivalries or the requirements of international agreements can produce organizational and policy similarity even in widely diverse types of domestic system.

# 5

# Antarctic Politics since 1961

The Antarctic Treaty established the barest outline of a regime. Participating governments had to work out a number of procedures and add a number of rules before the regime could function effectively. Until 1970 this activity involved relatively minor additions necessary for maintaining the regime. Since 1970 growing interest in resources has forced participating governments to go beyond the original framework and make adjustments that amount to amending the regime. This same interest in resources has also inspired private and governmental proposals to replace the regime altogether.

All the changes of the 1970s made the initially weak principle of protecting the Antarctic environment more important to the regime. The greater interest in resources also turned the Antarctic Treaty's silence on the matter into a significant gap in the regime. That interest has also put new strain on the norm that participants should cooperate without attempting to resolve the issue of sovereignty. Changes in the number of independent states and the development of new normative ideas about the proper regulation of various activities have put new outside pressures on the regime. Some Third World governments would like to see the Antarctic regime replaced by one open to equal participation by all states and using majority rule for decisions. The governments participating in the existing Antarctic regime remain content

with it, though aware that it needs modification. While outsiders raise occasional calls for replacement of the regime, the Antarctic Treaty states are busy
with projects for regime amendment.

## Establishing and Maintaining the Regime

The task of establishing the regime created by the Antarctic Treaty proceeded
so smoothly, for reasons discussed in chapter 6, that establishment soon
merged into maintenance. Participating governments had two tasks in the
1960s: further elaboration of the procedures under which they would act
together through the consultative meetings, and the addition of more specific
rules for various activities necessary to attaining the principles and goals of
the regime.

Since the First Consultative Meeting, held in Canberra in July 1961, the
consultative parties have used a very stable set of procedures.[1] The main
features include the following:

1. *Unanimity:* All substantive decisions must be approved by all consultative parties. Rules of procedure, except the one specifying the unanimity rule,
may be adopted by a two-thirds majority, and meeting reports may be
adopted by a simple majority, but in practice even these decisions are usually
taken unanimously.[2]

2. *Confidentiality:* All negotiating sessions and most plenary meetings are
held in closed session. Participants undertake not to discuss specific proposals
(or at least the comments of specific delegates on them) outside the meeting.
Initially, participation was limited to the consultative parties, but since 1983
representatives of other parties to the treaty have been permitted to attend.

3. *Flexibility:* Negotiation proceeds in whatever way and with whatever
group that seems most appropriate. Over the years, consultative meetings
have used a bewildering array of negotiating groups, working groups, expert
bodies meeting before or parallel to main sessions, and extra sessions. Regular
consultative meetings have usually been held every two years, though another
aspect of flexibility has been a willingness to defer a consultative meeting if
preliminary talks were not quite ready.[3]

4. *Informality:* No permanent international secretariat is attached to the
consultative parties. Staff services are provided by the host government of any
particular consultative meeting or related session. Additionally, there is no
permanent chairman. Each consultative meeting is held in the capital of a
different member, with the rotation mainly in alphabetical order; each related
session is held in the capital of whatever member volunteers to act as host.
Negotiation proceeds by free-flowing discussion, with drafts of proposals

emerging from group deliberations more often than being tabled in advance by single delegations.

5. *Integrity:* Building on the implied premise of the treaty, participating governments avoid linking Antarctic and non-Antarctic issues in their negotiations or interactions.

All of these are common practices in regimes having a small number of participants, and most are seldom a subject of comment. All participants value flexibility, a practice that even large-membership organizations have attempted to adopt through informal discussions, preparatory meetings, chairman's drafts, and other devices.[4] The unanimity rule has remained undisturbed because it is essential to the continued existence of the regime. Without it, neither claimants nor nonclaimants would be confident that the other side could not win enough support for some measure that would undo the compromise on sovereignty.

Only the rule of confidentiality has been repeatedly criticized, probably because it goes so much against the late-twentieth-century notion that states should have only "open covenants openly arrived at." In fact, confidentiality eroded to some extent in the late 1970s as resource questions brought into Antarctic politics a number of groups, particularly environmental organizations, interested in securing adoption of certain decisions.[5] Third World campaigns to replace the regime have also encouraged greater dissemination of information about ongoing negotiations. They also helped open participation in meetings to nonconsultative parties and, to a much lesser extent, international organizations. Despite these changes, however, deliberations in consultative meetings and related sessions remain far more private than in most other international meetings.

Outside commentators tend to regard confidentiality as a screen behind which the consultative parties can hide various misdeeds. In a relatively mild comment, F. M. Auburn has noted: "General confidence in the work of the meetings is not encouraged by the secrecy of the actual proceedings. As both the United States and the Soviet Union participate, there is no question of national security. Presumably, the purpose is to avoid appraisal and possible criticism by the general public."[6] Those who have participated in the meetings tend to view confidentiality more favorably. Alfred van der Essen regards it as "indispensable to the maintenance of the spirit of understanding" that characterizes the regime because it allows delegates to consider all proposals and hold frank discussions.[7]

The informality and flexibility of the regime is also demonstrated in relations between the consultative parties and the Scientific Committee on Antarctic Research. The SCAR is an organ of the International Council of Scientific Unions (ICSU) founded before and run independently of the Antarctic Treaty.[8] Although it is never mentioned in the Antarctic Treaty, SCAR provides the consultative parties with the scientific information they need for many of their decisions and often serves as a forum for preliminary discussion of science-related rules the consultative parties are considering. Its close relation with the consultative parties is manifested in the fact that until 1978 the national members of SCAR were the scientific academies of states with consultative status. The West German academy was added in 1978, three years before its country attained consultative status, and the East German one was added in 1982, though its country remains a nonconsultative party. Observers from a number of other national science academies attend SCAR meetings, and SCAR is actively considering the possibility of having associate members. The fact that SCAR is technically an organ of the ICSU means that the consultative parties can get advice from an international body of scientists while maintaining a clear separation of science from politics, which helps sustain the principles and norms of the regime.[9]

Even in the early 1960s the participating governments discovered some difficulties with the procedures for rule making. Over the years they took the bare outline of authority granted in the Antarctic Treaty and created a system of rule making that so far has served the needs of all parties. The first procedural problem stemmed from the initial assumption that any rule adopted unanimously by delegates at consultative meetings would be quickly accepted by all of their governments. Within a few years it became clear that this was not the case. The consultative parties found two ways to overcome the lag. First, expanding on the customary rule of international law providing that states which have signed but not yet ratified a treaty should do nothing to frustrate its object and purpose in the interim, they began applying recommendations informally even when they had not been ratified by all consultative parties.[10]

However, the customary rule only creates an obligation to ensure that activity does not make later application of the agreement impossible. This usually falls far short of obeying the full provisions of the rule. Thus, the consultative parties developed a second, more formal mechanism for speeding the application of rules. When the Agreed Measures for the Conservation and Preservation of Antarctic Flora and Fauna were adopted in 1964,[11] a number of the consultative parties indicated that ratification would be delayed because they would have to pass special legislation enabling them to enforce the rules against nationals in Antarctica first.[12] Agreeing that it was important to have the rules in place as quickly as possible, the consultative parties sought to get around that problem by passing an additional recommendation stating that all treaty parties should apply the Agreed Measures on an interim basis pending their ratification. This second recommendation was ratified quickly, permitting application of the Agreed Measures beginning in 1965 even though they have not yet been ratified by all consultative parties.[13]

The consultative parties also found it useful to supplement the formal recommendations with other types of decision making. These have taken two forms: mention in the report of a consultative meeting, and procedural decisions by representatives at a meeting. The first appeared almost at once, as the consultative parties began to see that drafting the report of a meeting could be given diplomatic significance. When discussions were in a very early stage and some participants were hesitating—either because they were not sure the issue should be handled within the regime or because there was little agreement about what ought to be done—an issue might go unmentioned in the report.[14] Once all accepted the idea that an issue fell within the competence of the consultative parties, it would at least be mentioned and formally listed among the items to be discussed at a later meeting. The consultative parties may also indicate that they are using a report from an expert working group or from SCAR as the agreed basis of discussion by mentioning it in the report. Of course, including a matter or mentioning a report in a formal recommendation remains a far stronger endorsement.[15] Final reports of meetings have also been used to make statements elaborating on past recommendations or making points intended to guide future negotiations.[16] For instance, the consultative parties agreed in 1977 that the word "conservation" in any agreement on marine living resources would be read as including "rational use" allowing exploitation under management plans assuring the long-term viability of the fish populations.[17] This was important in reaching agreement, since it assured the major fishing states that the term would not be defined as strict preservation precluding all fishing.

The formal rule that reports of consultative meetings may be adopted by a simple majority creates the possibility of a more flexible decision-making mechanism than recommendations. So far, this potential remains quite limited. Any final decision would have to form the basis of a recommendation requiring unanimous approval. Further, the consultative parties have generally adopted even the reports unanimously, since the benefit of having the majority endorse some idea in a report is likely to be outweighed by the cost in minority resentment at being overridden.[18]

A second new form of decision appeared in 1977, when the First Special Consultative Meeting decided that Poland would be included among the consultative parties. The delegates at the meeting simply announced this decision and gave it immediate effect, without going through the formalities of ratification by their governments. It is clear that the delegates were not deciding something their governments would not accept, because all had been able to think about the issue between the time Poland claimed consultative status in late 1976 and the date of the meeting. Yet some lawyers inferred from this an agreement that the delegates to consultative meetings can make certain procedural decisions[19] or interpret the Antarctic Treaty[20] on their own.

Recommendations themselves can be used to indicate several levels of agreement depending on the detail and specificity of their text. Some register little more than agreement to talk about the matter, like Recommendation VII-6 on mineral exploration.[21] Others initiate more detailed studies, like Recommendation I-VIII on logistics.[22] Others, like the Agreed Measures for the Conservation of Antarctic Flora and Fauna (Recommendation III-8) set forth a comprehensive set of rules that serve as the basis for national policy.[23]

More of the consultative parties' time has been devoted to elaborating or supplementing treaty rules on various activities. This has generally been accomplished through the medium of recommendations. Table 1 classifies the recommendations adopted at the First through the Sixth Consultative Meeting (1961–70) under eleven headings.

In the first decade, most of the consultative parties' attention was devoted to measures for handling matters previously agreed upon. Only the recommendations on pelagic sealing and tourism represented efforts to deal with questions not explicitly mentioned in some provision of the Antarctic Treaty. The concept of specially protected areas, while not foreshadowed in the treaty, represented an interesting way to assure the protection of areas deemed particularly significant for conservation or science because they served as breeding grounds, contained particularly abundant plant life, or were important to some major ongoing scientific program. Another clear trend was the increasing attention being given to environmental matters, a trend that accelerated further in the 1970s.

## Amending the Regime

In its first decade of operation, the Antarctic regime proved quite successful. Antarctica remained nonmilitarized, and continuing disagreements about territorial claims, either in general or in specific cases, did not lead to conflict among participating states. There were no incidents comparable to those which had occurred among Argentina, Britain, and Chile in the 1940s and 1950s. Scientific activity increased and provided a great deal of new knowledge about such questions as climate change, continental drift, the amount and dispersion of pollutants through the atmosphere, and the physiology of life in extremely cold climates. The Antarctic community took on stronger form and developed its traditions of cooperation. More attention

98

Table 1.    Consultative Parties' Recommendations, 1961–1970

|                              | I  | II | III | IV  | V | VI | Total |
|------------------------------|----|----|-----|-----|---|----|-------|
| Scientific cooperation       | 4  | 3  | 0   | 0   | 0 | 1  | 8     |
| Logistics and support        | 4  | 2  | 4   | 2   | 1 | 2  | 15    |
| Conservation/environment     | 1  | 1  | 3   | 18* | 2 | 5  | 30    |
| Pelagic sealing              | 0  | 0  | 1   | 4   | 2 | 0  | 7     |
| Marine living resources      | 0  | 0  | 0   | 0   | 0 | 0  | 0     |
| Mineral and fuel resources   | 0  | 0  | 0   | 0   | 0 | 0  | 0     |
| Historic sites               | 1  | 0  | 0   | 0   | 1 | 1  | 3     |
| Tourism                      | 0  | 0  | 0   | 0   | 1 | 1  | 2     |
| Marine science               | 0  | 0  | 0   | 1   | 1 | 1  | 3     |
| Meetings and procedure       | 4  | 3  | 2   | 2   | 1 | 0  | 12    |
| Other                        | 2  | 1  | 1   | 0   | 1 | 3  | 8     |
| TOTAL                        | 16 | 10 | 11  | 28  | 9 | 15 | 82    |

SOURCE: Author's classification; texts in *Polar Record* as follows: First Meeting, 11:73–78; Second Meeting, 11:465–69; Third Meeting, 12:435–72; Fourth Meeting, 13:629–49; Fifth Meeting, 14:663–86; and Sixth Meeting, 15:729–42.

*Each of sixteen specially protected areas declared separately.

was given to protecting the Antarctic environment as policy makers and scientists alike came to understand its uniqueness and special characteristics better.

By 1970, however, maintenance alone was insufficient for the effective management of Antarctic affairs. The consultative parties recognized this fact, as can be seen from the recommendations adopted after 1970. While many still addressed problems of regime maintenance, there was considerable discussion of new topics, as is shown in table 2. A number of changes began to put real stress on the regime. Increased interest in resources made the consultative parties realize that the regime would have to be expanded in some way to deal with resource use or be replaced by another that would deal with the issue. This pressure had been felt in the mild form in 1964 when some Norwegians undertook an experimental seal harvesting. Though they decided against further activity, their efforts provoked concern that others might attempt to revive the industry, even though seal populations remained fairly low.[24] This

Table 2.　Consultative Parties' Recommendations, 1972–1985

| | VII | VIII | IX | X | XI | XII | XIII | Total |
|---|---|---|---|---|---|---|---|---|
| Scientific cooperation | 2 | 3 | 0 | 4 | 0 | 3 | 1 | 13 |
| Logistics and support | 2 | 1 | 2 | 0 | 0 | 0 | 0 | 5 |
| Conservation/environment | 2 | 6 | 2 | 1 | 0 | 2 | 11 | 24 |
| Pelagic sealing | 0 | 0 | 0 | 0 | 0 | 0 | 0 | 0 |
| Marine living resources | 0 | 1 | 1 | 1 | 1 | 0 | 0 | 4 |
| Mineral and Fuel resources | 0 | 1 | 1 | 1 | 1 | 1 | 0 | 5 |
| Historic sites | 1 | 0 | 0 | 0 | 1 | 1 | 1 | 4 |
| Tourism | 1 | 1 | 0 | 1 | 0 | 0 | 0 | 3 |
| Marine science | 0 | 0 | 0 | 0 | 0 | 0 | 0 | 0 |
| Meetings and procedure | 0 | 0 | 0 | 0 | 0 | 2 | 3 | 5 |
| Other | 0 | 1 | 0 | 1 | 0 | 0 | 0 | 2 |
| TOTAL | 9 | 14 | 6 | 9 | 3 | 8 | 16 | 65 |

SOURCE: Author's classification; texts in *Polar Record* as follows: Seventh Meeting, 16:593–612; Eighth Meeting, 18:201–32; Ninth Meeting, 19:85–94; Tenth Meeting, 20:85–100; Eleventh Meeting, 20:590–93. Twelfth Meeting, 21:113–24; and Thirteenth Meeting, 23:223–52.

led the consultative parties to their first venture in regime amendment, the Convention on Conservation of Antarctic Seals. In the early 1970s there was far greater interest in both fisheries and fuel or mineral resources. The consultative parties decided fairly quickly that if they were to avoid serious quarrels over resources, they would have to negotiate some agreement on resource-related activity before it became a commercially viable proposition. At the same time, visions of Antarctic wealth as the common property of mankind caused some Third World governments to take greater interest in the area and to propose replacement of the Antarctic Treaty.

The consultative parties have sought to deal with the new stresses on the regime in three ways: (1) developing new negotiating methods allowing states engaged in some resource-related or other activity to participate in its regulation without having to include them among the consultative parties, (2) expanding the number of states participating in system deliberations, and (3) adding new rules, usually embodied in separate treaties, to cover activities not regulated by the Antarctic Treaty itself.

*New Negotiating Methods*

The development of new negotiating methods goes back to the late 1960s
when the Seal Convention was being discussed. The issue of concluding such
a convention was raised at the Third Consultative Meeting in 1964 during
discussion of the Agreed Measures. The Agreed Measures included protection for seals located on land, islands, ice sheets, and breeding areas. Some
members felt that the consultative parties could not regulate the taking of
seals in open waters by a recommendation, since that would involve making
rules for the high seas.[25] At the Fifth Consultative Meeting in 1968 they
agreed that the problem would best be handled by a separate treaty. Much
preliminary work was done at a meeting of experts parallel to the Sixth
Consultative Meeting in 1970, but the final convention was the product of a
separate diplomatic conference held in London in 1972. Though this meeting
included only representatives of governments of consultative parties,[26] the
Convention was open for accession by any state sufficiently interested in the
problem.

The same negotiating pattern was used with the Convention on the Conservation of Antarctic Marine Living Resources (CCAMLR), except that
three states not among the consultative parties—Poland, East Germany, and
West Germany—were permitted to join the discussions and were invited to
the final conferences.[27] In that case discussion of the subject began at the
Eighth Consulative Meeting in 1975, continued in a meeting of experts in
1976, the Ninth Consultative Meeting in 1977, three sessions of the Second
Special Consultative Meeting in 1979–80, and a separate conference in
Canberra in 1980. This Convention gives acceding states a real role in part of
the regime, since any state actively engaged in research on marine creatures or
in the taking of any of the species covered may become a member of the
separate commission established to regulate fisheries. A similar pattern may
emerge from negotiations for a minerals regime, though perhaps it may
restrict accession to states whose nationals or state-owned enterprises are
involved in exploration and exploitation.

*Expansion of Participation*

The Antarctic Treaty never set up an exclusive regime; any state belonging
to the United Nations or specifically invited by a unanimous vote of the
consultative parties can accede to the treaty at any time. However, the regime
does have the unusual feature of dividing participants into two classes—those
with consultative status and those without. The latter are bound by the rules

of the regime, but had no direct role in elaborating them until 1984 when they were permitted to observe consultative meetings and the talks on mineral and fuel resources.

Yet even the Consultative Parties is not a closed group, because any state pursuing "substantial scientific activity" in the Antarctic can be added to it. The actual exclusivity of the regime thus depends on the way in which the consultative parties interpret Article IX (2) of the treaty. While at least one lawyer and one government have argued that the applicant state can determine for itself when it qualifies,[28] the consultative parties as a group have successfully maintained that they have the right to determine the conditions of eligibility and the merits of a particular case. The applicant state initiates the process by informing the Unites States government (as depositary of the treaty) that it deems itself qualified, but the current consultative parties decide the matter at a Special Consultative Meeting preceding the next regular meeting.[29]

The consultative parties have defined "substantial scientific activity" in fairly rigorous terms and insist upon the treaty provisions allowing an original party to retain consultative status even if it stops supporting research, but specifying that an acceding party retains its consultative status only as long as it continues research.[30] Though sometimes criticized as inequitable, this rule helps maintain the character of the regime. As a longtime Norwegian participant explained, it

> does prevent a development where new parties accede to the Treaty and mount brief, onetime research programs to achieve consultative status only to abandon their interest in the Antarctic region as soon as they have acquired a right to participate in the formulation of measures for Antarctica. Such practices clearly would tend to emphasize the political element in the Antarctic development at the cost of a more "professional" approach based on knowledge and appreciation of the unique characteristics of the Antarctic region.[31]

However, the "entrance fee" is set informally and has fluctuated over the years. Poland in 1977 and West Germany in 1981 were not accorded consultative status until they had supplemented their existing marine research with the establishment of a year-round station on the continent. Poland thus spent an additional $3 million on construction of Arctowski Station.[32] West Germany undertook a $100 million continental program including the construction of Georg von Neumeyer Station, new icebreakers, the acquisition of related equipment, and the establishment of the Alfred von Wegener Institute for Polar Research in Bremerhaven.[33] In 1983, however, the prior opening of a year-round scientific station was not made a condition of consultative status for Brazil and India. Brazil had sent two small expeditions to the continent, maintained an active Antarctic institute, operated a small marine-research program, and sent scientists to join others' expeditions or to work at others'

stations before 1983.[34] It established its own summer station on King George
Island in the South Shetlands in January 1984.[35] India dispatched its first
expedition to the continent in January 1982 and set up an automated weather
station, at 70°S, 11°07′E. A second expedition recovered data and began
work on construction of the summer-only Dakshin Gangotri Station near the
same site in 1983. Indian scientists also worked at other stations and pursued
some marine research in the Southern Ocean.[36] In 1985 the consultative
parties moved back on a more restrictive direction. Both China and Uruguay
opened summer stations on the relatively accessible King George Island in the
South Shetland Islands before applying for consultative status.[37] Both countries had also sent scientists to participate in other expeditions, the Chinese
including four who wintered over. The Chinese also acquired two ships and
sent their own summer expeditions on which several hundred scientists and
crew undertook continental and marine research.[38]

Even the level of activity demanded of Brazil and India represents significantly greater effort than is now undertaken by states like Taiwan or South
Korea, which confine themselves to active participation in Southern Ocean
fisheries, or Sweden, which plans to support Swedish scientists working with
other countries' expeditions or stations.[39] Yet the contrast with what was
asked of Poland and West Germany is clear, and represents a conscious effort
to broaden the coalition of consultative parties by including more Third
World states.[40]

Besides adding new members, the consultative parties decided in 1983–84
to permit the other states that are parties to the Antarctic Treaty (now generally called the nonconsultative parties) to send observers to consultative meetings and negotiating sessions on the mineral and fuel resources regime. The
nonconsultative parties sent observers to the Twelfth and the Thirteenth
Consultative Meeting in 1983 and 1985, and under Recommendation XIII-
15 will have the same right at all future consultative meetings.[41] They also
began observing the resources talks at the February 1985 session.[42] The
nonconsultative parties have not been passive onlookers. Though they are not
included in meetings of the heads of delegations in either forum, they have
tabled papers and taken an active part in all other debate.[43] Since the consultative parties make no decisions until discussion reveals unanimity on some
proposition, participation in debate can mean real influence.

*New Rules*

To date, the addition of rules covering activities not mentioned in the
treaty has been restricted to the subjects of tourism and the exploitation of

living resources. The first topic has been handled through consultative party recommendations, since it entails stopping on or flying over the continent itself. Thus regulation can be justified to other states as being necessary for preserving scientific cooperation, protecting the environment, and promoting the safety of individuals. The second topic has been handled in separate treaties because of the need for special management institutions, the initial hesitation over extending consultative parties authority to the high seas, and the weight of precedent once the Seal Convention was adopted.

*Tourism*    Tourism first became the subject of discussion among the consultative parties at the Fourth Meeting in 1966. The consultative parties sought to control tourist activity in Recommendation IV-27 by requiring that the government of a consultative party state where a tourist excursion was being organized notify the government of any party whose stations the tourists hoped to visit. Governments of stations were asked to set out the conditions under which they would permit visits, but were not obliged to grant permission unless there were "reasonable assurances" that the tourist group would comply with the Antarctic Treaty, the recommendations, and the conditions for visiting the station. It was clear, then, that science came first and that tourists would be welcome only as space and time permitted. This has remained the basic attitude toward tourism ever since. Recommendations VI-7 of 1970, VII-4 of 1972, VIII-9 of 1975, and X-8 of 1979 continued this trend, differing from the first only in the amount of detail about prior notification and rules for tourist groups provided. They also sought to maintain consultative parties control, even over tourist flights or cruises originating in other countries, by requiring prior requests for visits directly from the tour operator.[44]

Though there have been a number of experimental civil flights over the Antarctic from Argentina and Chile to New Zealand, and several excursion flights looping over the South Pole from Australia and New Zealand, civil aviation has not yet become a routine matter in the Antarctic, owing to the paucity of emergency and navigational facilities. The consultative parties have discussed the issues raised by tourist flights in their meetings, but the only pronouncements related to aviation came in Recommendation X-8, where part IV sought to discourage such flights on grounds that the necessary facilities were lacking.[45] Their warning was confirmed in November 1979 when storms delayed rescuers several days even though McMurdo Station was only thirty miles from the site of the Air New Zealand crash on Mount Erebus.[46]

*Conventions on Marine Living Resources*    The first of the consultative parties' ventures into regulating the exploitation of Antarctic marine resources was the Convention for the Conservation of Antarctic Seals of 1972.[47] This was a change in the regime because it was intended to apply rules in the high seas. It also marked the first use of a procedural innovation that would soon become characteristic: regulation of a specific activity by a distinct treaty to which states not party to the Antarctic Treaty could accede even if they had not or did not accede to the latter. The Seal Convention is linked explicitly and implicitly to the Antarctic Treaty. Article 1 of the Seal Convention reaffirms the sovereignty compromise laid out in Article IV of the treaty. Article 4 of the Seal Convention also carefully leaves undisturbed the permit system regulating noncommercial taking of seals under the Agreed Measures of 1964.

The principles and norms of the Seal Convention are fully compatible with, and derived in the main from, those of the Antarctic Treaty. By implication the former establishes that the Antarctic community and the existing regime should be preserved. In addition, it sets goals of preventing the overexploitation of seals and ensuring acquisition of the scientific information necessary to framing sound management plans. The norms, too, emphasize ecological concern and define the rational use of seals as a management system that assures taking no more than the "optimum sustainable yield" of seals in any year.[48]

The rules of the Seal Convention bear great resemblance to those of the Antarctic Treaty. First, despite the fact that seals range north of the line, the Seal Convention follows the Antarctic Treaty definition in applying only to waters south of 60°S. It also mirrors the main treaty's jurisdictional clauses by providing that it is the responsibility of each party to ensure that its nationals and ships flying its flag obey the rules laid out in the Convention (Article 2). Article 1 (2) specifies that the Convention applies to the taking of Southern Elephant, Leopard, Weddell, Crabeater, Ross, and Southern Fur seals, while Article 3 and the Annex specify the precise regulatory measures (closed seasons, closed areas, size limits, catch quotas, etc.) that will govern commercial sealing. Article 4 provides for a permit system by which each party may authorize nationals to take limited numbers of seals for noncommercial use as emergency rations for humans or dogs in Antarctica, in scientific studies, or as specimens for zoos and scientific laboratories away from Antarctica.

The Convention also includes a number of procedures, some related to the regulation of sealing and others related to the status of the Convention itself. Article 5 (1), (2), and (7) provide for an annual reporting system in which parties must indicate by 31 October of each year the number of ships and nationals engaged in sealing and the number, types, and biological data on seals taken in the twelve-month period running from 1 July to 30 June. These reports must also cover any sealing in areas of floating ice above 60°S as well as in the Convention area, an acknowledgment of the fact that the Southern Ocean's actual northern edge is not the 60° line but the more northerly Antarctic Convergence. The Scientific Committee on Antarctic Research is given the formal role of assessing the data provided by parties, recommending programs of scientific research, and warning when sealing is doing "significant" harm to stocks of any species in any given locality. In a provision borrowed from the International Convention for the Regulation of Whaling, it is also given the task of warning if the limit of a season's catch will be exceeded before the end of the season, so that parties may bring sealing to a halt as soon as the limit is reached even if the normal season has not yet ended (Article 5 [4] and [5]).

The Convention provides for meetings of the parties every five years after commercial sealing begins, or at the request of any one of them if SCAR has indicated that sealing operations are causing substantial harm to any species. It also provides for amendment of its own terms and of the specific rules included in the Annex. These are complex rules, but they may be summarized as providing a quick way to make noncontroversial changes, and as a longer process for changes to which any party objects.[49] The Convention provides that all parties are eligible to attend all meetings, but controls participation by allowing accession only to those states invited to accede by unanimous vote of all the current parties.[50] Any party may withdraw from the Convention effective on 30 June of any year if it gives notice of withdrawal by the preceding 1 January. Upon receipt of such a notice, any other party may also withdraw by the same day if its notice is received within a month of the first party's notice. In this way, no party can get an extra advantage in a season by withdrawing before the others.

Here, then, is a Convention that maintains the Antarctic regime tradition of restricting participation, maintaining the compromise on sovereignty, doing no more than is necessary at the moment, and keeping open options for greater formalization in the future if necessary. The desire to avoid institutionalization is demonstrated by the use of SCAR as a temporary sealing commission. Though this broke with the usual practice of not giving SCAR any formal rule-making tasks, it operates in an area of science, and the Convention does provide that if the level of commercial sealing merits, SCAR's tasks may be taken over later by a specially created sealing commission. Today it would be logical to give that role to the commission created under the Convention for the Conservation of Antarctic Marine Living Resources. So far there has been no commercial sealing in the Antarctic. The Seal Convention remains unused and untested. Its main significance lies in the precedents provided for later negotiation of a broader agreement on Antarctic fishing, negotiations on which began even before the Seal Convention entered into force.

By 1977 the consultative parties found that the problems raised by krill harvesting and other fishing in the Southern Ocean required another set of additions to the regime. As with the Seal Convention, the Convention on the Conservation of Antarctic Marine Living Resources (CCAMLR) formed a separate treaty open to those states actively interested in fishing or fishery-related research.[51] It, too, contained a number of innovations, but in the main it conforms to the basic features of the Antarctic regime and borrows directly from the Antarctic Treaty in a number of places.

The CCAMLR establishes four principles: (1) the Southern Ocean and fishing activities there must not be allowed to become the subject of international discord; (2) the Antarctic Treaty regime must be preserved, and other parties should recognize the prime responsibility of the consultative parties for governing the Antarctic; (3) the ecosystem of the Southern Ocean and the environment of Antarctica must be protected; and (4) rational management of krill and other marine species requires cooperation among all states involved.

Consequently, the Convention establishes a number of norms to guide rule making and behavior. Article II (2) defines conservation as including rational use of marine resources, thus rejecting notions that there should be no fishing in the Southern Ocean. Article II (3) establishes standards of management that adopt an ecosystem approach rather than the more usual species-by-species approach used in other international fisheries agreements.[52] Article XXV requires that all parties settle their disputes peacefully. Article IV binds all parties to the compromise on sovereignty embodied in Article IV of the Antarctic Treaty by repeating its provisions almost word for word. Thus, the norms set by the Convention mirror those of the Antarctic regime as supplemented by the Seal Convention.

The rules established by the CCAMLR include some innovative and some familiar features. One important innovation, foreshadowed in the SCAR definition of "Antarctica" as including all areas south of the Antarctic Convergence and the Seal Convention protection of seals on floating ice north of the 60° line, appears in Article I. This defines the area of application as including all waters south of a line roughly following the Antarctic Convergence. This is a sound ecological decision, though it introduced another complication into existing arguments about sovereignty, as is noted below. A second innovation is the establishment of a separate commission to oversee application of Convention rules and make more specific regulations as fishing activity or new scientific information warrants. This immediate establishment of new institutions reflects the fact that the commercial harvesting of krill and the fishing of finned species had already begun when the Convention was signed, whereas the Seal Convention was concluded at a time when no commercial ventures were under way. The commission is also authorized to establish a system of inspection by on-board observers who report any violations to the commission, which then relays the information to the appropriate party for enforcement. While there is precedent for on-site inspection in the Antarctic Treaty, this feature derives more from the system of inspectors already familiar to distant-water fishing fleets from international fisheries agreements and the fisheries laws of many coastal states.[53]

The other rules incorporate familiar features of the Antarctic regime. Article IV specifically incorporates Articles IV and VI of the Antarctic Treaty, on sovereignty and on dispute settlement, making them binding on all parties. Article V incorporates the Agreed Measures for the Conservation of Antarctic Flora and Fauna and all other environment-related recommendations of the consultative parties with similar effect. This means that any state desiring a say in the regulation of fishing has to accept the main principles and norms as well as many of the rules and procedures of the Antarctic Treaty system even if it does not accede to the Antarctic Treaty at the same time. Article XXI provides the usual Antarctic regime solution to problems of jurisdiction: each state is charged with enforcing the rules against its own nationals and ships flying its flag. Article XXII adopts the familiar approach to dealing with activities of states not parties to the Convention. Each party is to make "all appropriate efforts, consistent with the Charter of the United Nations" to ensure that "no one" violates the Convention, a word-for-word adoption of Article X of the Antarctic Treaty.

Establishment of the commission means that the Convention contains a large number of procedural provisions. Borrowing and making more explicit the scheme used for consultative status under the Antarctic Treaty, the Convention provides that original parties will be permanent members of the commission,[54] and that acceding states will be members so long as their fleets do a significant amount of fishing or engage in significant research on living marine resources. Acceding states gain such status only if all states already members of the commission agree that they deserve it. The Convention departs from the Antarctic Treaty in providing that regional economic-integration organizations may also be members of the commission if all current member states agree. In concession to states, particularly the Soviet Union, opposing their participation, their voting rights are limited. Article XIX (1) does permit them equal say in budget decisions, since they must contribute to commission and Scientific Committee expenses. Article XII (3) and (4) permit the regional organizations to vote only on questions that fall within their competence and provide that if the organization casts a vote, one member state shall not vote on the question.

The commission is charged with ensuring the coordination of fishery-related marine research; formulating conservation measures on the basis of the best scientific information available; implementing the inspection system; monitoring fishing by nonparty states and informing parties when this affects application of the Convention; monitoring the activities of nationals and ships of the parties and reporting to the party concerned when they violate the Convention or regulations established under it; and cooperating with coastal states or international bodies charged with regulating fishing in waters adjacent to the Convention area to ensure consistency of approach.

The Convention also outlines the main aspects of commission procedure. Unlike other institutions in the Antarctic Treaty system, it has a permanent headquarters (in Hobart, Tasmania, Australia) and staff, and is to meet at least once a year. Since commissioners are delegates from governments, the commission also has a Scientific Committee consisting of fisheries experts appointed by the members. Most significantly, Article XII specifies that substantive decisions must be made "by consensus," whereas others may be made by a simple majority of the members present and voting. As in other limited-participation international regimes, "consensus" is defined as meaning unanimity.[55] Using the term "consensus" in this context is simply a way of indicating that members will make every effort to reconcile their differences before making a decision. This does not signficantly weaken an individual state's ability to prevent decision, though it does remind each member of the Antarctic Treaty system's tradition that each must take seriously the others' positions.

Other procedural clauses deal with more general matters. Article XXV sets out procedures for dispute settlement which copy Article XI of the Antarctic Treaty except for creating the possibility of submitting disputes to arbitration rather than to the International Court of Justice. Article XXIX opens the Convention for accession by any state "interested in research or harvesting activities in the Southern Ocean" and to any regional economic-integration organization with competence in fishing issues having one or more members among the states that are parties to the Convention. Article XXXI adopts the same rule for withdrawal that appeared in the Seal Convention. Any party may withdraw effective on 30 June of any year provided it gives notice by the preceeding 1 January. On receipt of such notice, any other party may withdraw effective the same day by giving notification within thirty days of the notice.

Again, the Convention on the Conservation of Antarctic Marine Living Resources expands, but does not replace, the regime established in the Antarctic Treaty. It carefully preserves the primacy of that regime and of the consultative parties. It maintains the sovereignty compromise and jurisdiction rules. As in the Antarctic Treaty, accession is open, but membership in the organ charged with formulating rules and coordinating activity is closely limited to ensure that only states with a real material stake in the regime participate in making decisions. The inspection system is compatible with Antarctic Treaty precedents. The relation between the commission and the scientific committee is much like the relation between the contracting parties and SCAR in the Seal Convention. The Convention did have to give a role to regional economic organizations because members of the European Community insisted, but that role is limited in important ways.

The fishing regime created in the CCAMLR has a number of weaknesses. Some commentators regard them as so serious that Antarctic fisheries will never be regulated effectively.[56] The rules on decision making and jurisdiction have inspired the most criticism, while particular portions of the article reaffirming the Antarctic Treaty compromise on sovereignty are believed by some to cause an additional political problem.

The rules on decision making give every state holding membership on the commission two opportunities to impede management. First, the requirement that all commission decisions be adopted by consensus allows any single member to prevent the adoption of a rule. This allows the delegate of any fishing state to prevent the adoption of a rule it deems too restrictive. Given the interrelatedness of all Southern Ocean marine life, many observers regard this as seriously weakening, if not destroying, the possibilities for effective ecosystem management. Second, any state represented on the commission may decide after a decision has been adopted to withhold cooperation in implementing a particular measure by invoking the "opting out" clause of Article IX (6). This gives each state represented on the commission ninety days to register formal objection to all or part of any measure adopted by the commission. If one objects, then any other may request a meeting of the commission to reconsider the measure and also has thirty days from the end of this second commission meeting to file a formal objection of its own. Opting out does not prevent all application of the contested measure; it simply means that it cannot be applied to vessels flying the flag of an objecting state. However, allowing such uneven enforcement may be sufficient to deprive the measure of all effect if the fleets of objecting states are large or active enough, or the fish population involved is vulnerable to the sort of activity the objectors insist on continuing.

Even when no state files an objection, there is no assurance of effective enforcement. The inspectors and observers are appointed not by the commission as a whole but by the individual members. The inspectors and observers then report to the commissioner who appointed them. The commissioner informs the whole commission, which in the case of violations is confined to notifying the flag state of the violator. While participating states are pledged to establish punishments for proven violations, nothing in the CCAMLR or the commission's structure ensures that flag states will prosecute violators or impose penalities sufficient to deter violation of fishing rules. The strength of enforcement thus depends on the efforts of each state, and that level of effort will be determined by the least active, since one fishing state is unlikely to want its fleet operating under more restraints than anyone else's.[57]

Reliance on flag-state jurisdiction in most of the Convention area (an exception is discussed below) also means that it could be difficult to control the activities of ships flying the flags of states not parties to CCAMLR. While a state can prevent its nationals from using foreign flags of convenience, nothing prevents third states from sending their own fishing fleets or encouraging nationals to establish Antarctic operations. Article XXII permits parties to take peaceful measures to ensure that "no one engages in activity contrary to the objective" of the CCAMLR. Some representatives of claimant states and a few international lawyers of other nationalities have argued that claimants could legally assert jurisdiction over ships of third states operating within a 200-mile zone seaward of their claimed territory, since the compromise on sovereignty only operates among states parties to CCAMLR or the Antarctic Treaty.[58] Yet even if nonclaimants tolerated such activity—and they might not, on grounds it gave away too much to claimants—such activities would cover only part of the Southern Ocean. They might suffice to protect finned fish, since these generally live close to shore, but they would not protect the more wide-ranging krill. In addition, attempts by Argentina, Britain, or Chile to assert jurisdiction in disputed areas would generate severe conflicts with the rival claimants. Thus, it is difficult to envision measures that would succeed against a determined third state. In this light, Soviet objections to South Korean and Taiwanese participation in CCAMLR make little sense, since the best way to get control over a particular state's activities is to secure its participation.[59] Since the technology for distant-water fishing is widely held and the necessary investments are within the capacity of many countries, the problem of controlling third-state activity is very real.

Finally, there are doubts about the long-term viability of the sovereignty compromise. Article IV of the CCAMLR reaffirms it in these terms:

> Nothing in this Convention and no acts or activities taking place while the present Convention is in force shall:
> (a) constitute a basis for asserting, supporting, or denying a claim to territorial sovereignty in the Antarctic Treaty area or create any rights of sovereignty in the Antarctic Treaty area;
> (b) be interpreted as a renunciation or diminution by any Contracting Party of, or as prejudicing, any right or claim or basis of claim to exercise coastal state jurisdiction under international law within the area to which this Convention applies;

(c) be interpreted as prejudicing the position of any Contracting Party as re-gards its recognition or non-recognition of any such right, claim or basis of claim;

(d) affect the provision of Article IV, paragraph 2, of the Antarctic Treaty that no new claim or enlargement of an existing claim, to territorial sovereignty in Antarctica shall be asserted while the Antarctic Treaty is in force.

However, the fact that the Convention dealt with marine areas, and was intended to apply to the waters around several subantarctic islands over which individual states do hold undisputed sovereignty, gave rise to new difficulties.

References to marine jurisdiction opened the question of whether asser-tion of a 12-mile territorial sea, a 200-mile exclusive economic zone, and a 200-mile continental shelf, particularly if initiated after 1961, constitutes an enlargement of claim contrary to Article IV of the Antarctic Treaty. Some commentators have argued that such assertions are enlargements.[60] For their part, claimant governments maintain that they are not, because all of those concepts are now part of customary international law as appurtenances to sovereignty over the land.[61]

Extension of the area of application north of the 60° line brought under CCAMLR islands over which individual states hold undisputed sovereignty—the Crozets and Kerguelens (France), the Prince Edward Islands (South Af-rica), Bouvet (Norway), and Heard and McDonald (Australia).[62] These states, particularly France, wanted freedom to prescribe national regulations tougher than those established by the commission and to retain enforcement powers in the 200-mile zones around these islands. This question was handled not in the Convention itself, but in an agreed statement included in the Final Act of the Canberra Conference affirming these rights.[63] Some commentators regard it as encouraging the views of claimants that they may assert similar control in 200-mile zones off the coasts of their Antarctic claims, but it is hard to sustain this view, for the statement refers specifically to islands.

The Convention came into force in 1982, and the commission held its first meeting in September of that year. Its first two meetings were devoted to organizational matters and discussion of the types of information needed for managing the Southern Ocean ecosystem effectively. The CCAMLR goal of ecosystem management imposes rather onerous requirements for informa-tion. As in traditional species-by-species management, both direct fishing effort and the activities of predators must be taken into account. In addition, and particularly since CCAMLR commits the parties to restoring depleted stocks, managers must also take account of indirect effects from fishing other species or stocks. The mathematical models and knowledge of population parameters (such as size of stock, age distribution, reproductive rate, and age of maturity) necessary for such ecosystem management do not yet exist. In

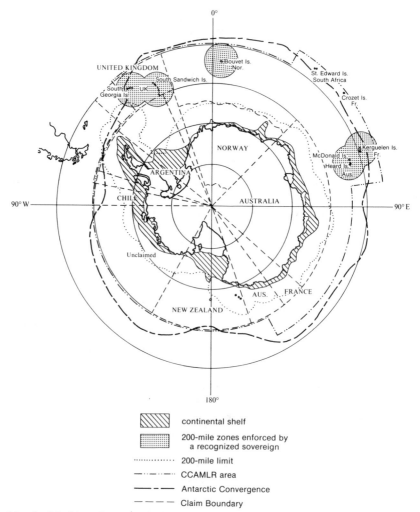

continental shelf

200-mile zones enforced by
a recognized sovereign

200-mile limit

CCAMLR area

Antarctic Convergence

Claim Boundary

Map 1. Maritime Zones in the Southern Ocean

the meantime, the commission must rely on rougher rules of thumb, such as
keeping a target stock within some percentage of its current size.[64]

At its third meeting, in 1984, the commission agreed on several measures.
Because the interval between September and the start of the Antarctic fishing
season in early December is less than the 90-day minimum needed for bringing a rule into effect, the commission requested that all fleets avoid taking fish
of the species *Notothenia rossi,* whether as the target species of fishing effort or

as by-catch of efforts to fish other species, in the waters around South Georgia, and to avoid fishing within twelve miles of that island altogether during the 1984–85 season. The same measures were adopted as a rule to be effective in the 1985–86 season.

The fourth meeting, in 1985, urged members to submit their reports on time and considered reports from the Scientific Committee on fish stocks, methods for estimating the sustainable yield of krill, and designing systems for cooperative ecosystem monitoring. It also discussed the conditions under which additional states could become members of the commission, and nongovernmental groups send observers to meetings. Fears that a combination of the commission restrictions on fishing around South Georgia and French rules limiting catches around the Kerguelens[65] would only divert effort elsewhere led the commission to request for 1985–86 and to rule for 1986–87 that fleets avoid directed fishing of *Notothenia rossi* off the Antarctic Peninsula, the South Orkneys, and the Kerguelens, as well as avoid by-catch in the first two areas.[66]

*Minerals Discussions*     All participants at the Washington Conference in 1959 were aware that Antarctica contained mineral deposits.[67] However, the precise size and concentrations of these deposits were unknown, and the physical and economic obstacles to their exploration appeared formidable.[68] The immediate political costs of attempting to discuss resources were great in that all realized that the claimants would not be willing to compromise on the sovereignty question if they were also called upon at the same time to forgo all chance of gaining the wealth that would come from mineral exploitation. Since all of the participants expected that actual exploitation of the minerals would not occur within a generation, it is not surprising that they decided to defer the question. Thus, the Antarctic Treaty never addressed it.

This combination of high expected political costs and low urgency persisted until the Sixth Consultative Meeting in 1970.[69] Political inhibitions were laid aside enough to permit discussion of the subject in 1970 because the Australian, New Zealand, and United States governments had all been approached by mining or oil companies interested in the possibilities of Antarctic resources and inquiring how they might get permission to undertake preliminary exploration.[70] Even so, it took the consultative parties several years to arrive at a consensus that the issue would have to be addressed and could be handled without upsetting the compromise on sovereignty. The Report of the Sixth Consultative Meeting did not even mention that mineral resource questions had been discussed. Discussion at the Seventh Consultative Meeting in 1972 did lead to acknowledgment of the issue. Recommendation VII-6 provided that the question should figure on the agenda of the next consultative meeting, and by implication recorded the consultative parties' agreement that none would proceed unilaterally on the question while discussions continued.[71]

Serious discussion began at the Eighth Consultative Meeting in 1975. These discussions continued in additional preparatory meetings devoted to both marine and mineral resources held in Paris during July 1976 and in London during March 1977.[72] These two meetings set the pattern of talks for the next few years by dividing the negotiations between two working groups, one dealing with technical and environmental questions raised by exploitation of fuel and mineral resources, the other dealing with the legal and political implications of such activity. By the end of the Ninth Meeting, the consultative parties had reached agreement on a number of basic principles for the negotiations, which were set forth in Recommendation IX-1.[73]

Negotiations since 1977 have followed much the same pattern. Although resource issues were discussed at the biennial consultative meetings, most of the negotiation has occurred at a series of intersessional meetings culminating in the Third Special Consultative Meeting of June 1982 and the multisession Fourth Consultative Meeting, which first met in July 1983 and now gathers twice a year. Initially, these sessions followed the tradition of the Antarctic Treaty system of writing drafts after wide-ranging discussion among the participants. Thus, the main framework of principles and norms guiding discussions was laid out in Recommendation XI-1 of 1981.[74] The complex nature of the issues involved later forced participants to work from drafts prepared by the chairman of the Fourth Special Meeting, Christopher Beeby of New Zealand, on the basis of informal consultations with all delegations.

The statement of guiding principles in paragraphs 5 and 6 of Recommendation XI-1 includes the following elements: (1) the Antarctic consultative parties will continue to be active in the formulation and implementation of any minerals regime, (2) the Antarctic Treaty is to be maintained in its entirety, (3) protection of the Antarctic environment shall be a "basic consideration" in the minerals regime, (4) the consultative parties should not prejudice the interests of all mankind in Antarctica, (5) nothing in the minerals regime shall be allowed to affect the compromise on sovereignty embodied in Article IV of the Antarctic Treaty, and (6) any minerals regime must be acceptable to both claimant and nonclaimant states.

The consultative parties have also agreed on a number of rules for decision making about the exploitation of mineral and fuel resources. First, they envisioned a two-stage process: an initial determination that a proposed resource activity will be acceptable, to be followed by decisions about who may participate in whatever activity is allowed. Second, they agree that there must be adequate information on likely environmental impacts to guide decisions and that any activity that is allowed must be made subject to binding rules that safeguard the environment.

They also agreed on a number of more specific points. The minerals regime will apply to commercial exploration and exploitation of on- and off-shore resources.[75] Any state interested in Antarctic resource exploitation will be allowed to join the agreement creating the regime, so long as it promises to be bound by the basic provisions of the Antarctic Treaty, which Recommendation XI-1 identifies as including Articles I, IV, V, and VI, and relevant recommendations of the consultative parties. Finally, the "voluntary moratorium" on activity imposed by Recommendation IX-1 pending the completion of a regime will continue to apply.

Since 1981 the consultative parties have continued to widen the areas of consensus.[76] Currently they are agreed that four institutions will be involved in overseeing the exploitation of nonliving resources. The first, added to drafts in early 1985 at the behest of the nonconsultative parties,[77] is a Special Meeting of States Parties, which would include all states that are parties to the mineral and fuel resources agreement. In the initial formulation it would have had the power to decide which areas would be open to resource activity, but later proposals have returned that authority to the commission.[78] At present the extent of Special Meeting authority remains under discussion.

General oversight will be provided by the Antarctic Mineral Resources Commission. It is expected to have two classes of members, permanent (all eighteen current Antarctic Treaty consultative parties) and temporary (other states that become consultative parties, for as long as they retain that status, or are parties to the resources agreement, for as long as their nationals are active in resource activity). Other states that accede to the resources agreement or the Antarctic Treaty may send observers to commission meetings.

The commission will have the power to (a) declare certain areas of Antarctica open or closed to all resource activity, (b) elaborate environmental standards for resource activity additional to those in the agreement, (c) draw up rules for operations, (d) authorize particular exploration and exploitation activities, (e) monitor those activities, and (f) carry out any other function necessary to ensure fulfillment of the objectives and principles of the agreement. Most participants support the proposal that the commission be assisted by a Scientific, Technical, and Environmental Committee consisting of experts appointed by the states that are members of the commission. Environmentalist groups have proposed the creation of an independent Antarctic Environmental Protection Agency, which would, as one of its tasks, assess the environmental acceptability of proposed resource activity and monitor operations,[79] but no consultative party has endorsed the idea.

The current Beeby draft envisions the separate regulation of prospecting, exploration, and development. Prospecting, which seems to denote surveys and small-scale sampling, would operate under a system of prior notification and relatively little regulation. Exploration, which includes larger-scale sampling or the drilling of test wells, and development, that is, actual exploitation, would require filing an application with the commission specifying the area to be worked and many details of the operations to be undertaken. Exploration and exploitation would be subject to increasingly tough, but as yet not fully elaborated, safety and environmental standards. Neither activity could begin until the commission, with advice from the Scientific, Technical, and Environmental Committee, and an ad hoc Regulatory Committee appointed to oversee the drawing up of management plans by a particular applicant, had approved the applicant's plans. These two bodies would also perform the actual monitoring for the commission.

Prospecting became the subject of some controversy in 1984–85 after allegations that the seismic surveys of Antarctic continental-shelf areas being undertaken by various governments were prospecting rather than scientific research and so violate the moratorium adopted in Recommendation IX-1.[80] Though environmentalists are highly worried by this activity, governments are treating it as science. As of mid-1985 all but the French had published results and varying amounts of data.[81]

While the main outline of an agreement on minerals and fuels seems clear, many important points remain to be settled. The most politically difficult involve decision making. While some participants favor allowing the commission to act by majority vote, some want the normal Antarctic rule of consensus applied. The nettlesome problem of maintaining the compromise on sovereignty is being approached through the device of appointing a separate regulatory committee for each application to explore or exploit. As is now being discussed, their composition would ensure representation for any state claiming the area where the applicant wants to work.[82] Decision making in the regulatory committees also remains an issue, with at least some claimants holding out for a veto.

Other questions also remain open. The consultative parties are divided about whether the minerals/fuels regime should be "self-financing," that is, whether it should derive funds for expenses from fees and royalties paid by miners and oilmen or depend on assessing member governments. There also remains much work to be done on defining "prospecting," "exploration," and "development"; on setting forth basic standards for operations; on assuring a balance between commission needs for information and operator desires to keep certain knowledge confidential; on deciding whether there should be provisions on preventing monopoly; on defining operator and sponsoring state liability for damage; and on many of the details of the relationship of commission and committees.

At present, then, the Antarctic regime has these features:

1. The Antarctic Treaty remains the source of the regime's basic principles and norms.

2. The rules and procedures of the Antarctic Treaty are supplemented in the fields of demilitarization, use of nuclear energy, scientific cooperation, logistical cooperation, science and support-related aviation, telecommunications, environmental protection on land, and air- or seaborne tourism by recommendations adopted in consultative meetings and ratified by the governments of states with consultative status.

3. The rules and procedures of the Antarctic Treaty are supplemented for exploitation of marine living resources by the various provisions and regulations established in or under the International Convention for the Regulation of Whaling of 1946 as amended subsequently, the Convention for the Conservation of Antarctic Seals, and the Convention for the Conservation of Antarctic Marine Living Resources.

4. The consultative parties retain general competence; the competence of other bodies is limited to the tasks necessary for applying the provisions of the separate treaty by which they are created.

5. The regime's goals remain modest; no effort is made to regulate activity before it seems likely to occur, and regulation is not made any more complicated than is necessary.

6. Participation in decisions is limited to states that demonstrate a real material interest in Antarctic activity, though others may participate in the preceding discussions.

## Pressures to Replace the Regime

Despite its success, the Antarctic Treaty regime does not enjoy universal support. Some claimants—particularly Argentina, Australia, and Chile—are widely assumed to hope that they will one day be able to exercise the territorial sovereignty they believe is rightfully theirs.[83] A number of academic observers feel that the regime is too fragile to survive the actual exploitation of fuel and mineral resources.[84] A number of environmental groups propose replacing the Antarctic Treaty with an agreement to make the continent a "world park" in which no resource exploitation would be allowed. Some members of the Nonaligned Movement have proposed that the "common heritage" principle discussed in other fora, notably the Third UN Conference on the Law of the Sea (UNCLOS III), be applied to Antarctica as well. They seek to replace the Antarctic Treaty with a new regime in which all states would share in management decisions and the material benefits of resource exploitation. Of the three ideas, only the latter two have current political relevance, at least so long as most of the consultative parties prefer the current regime to the division of Antarctica.

## World Park

The notion of making Antarctica into a "world park" has been sponsored by a number of individuals and nongovernmental groups, mainly environmental organizations, for a decade. It first came to international prominence in 1972 when the Second World Parks Congress cosponsored by UNESCO and the International Union for the Conservation of Nature (IUCN) formally endorsed it. It has received a number of endorsements since, most prominently by the "Forum of Non-governmental Organizations" assembled at Nairobi in May 1982 to observe the UN Environmental Programme (UNEP) "Session of Special Character." This session was intended to combine an evaluation of the program's first decade of activity with establishment of guidelines for its second. Forum members circulated their resolution among the delegations and pressed their arguments with great energy. A number of the environmental groups involved felt that their ideas were received sympathetically by delegates at the UNEP meeting.[85] In January 1986 members of a Greenpeace-sponsored expedition landed on Antarctica, raised the Greenpeace flag, and proclaimed Antarctica a "world park."[86]

Though details sometimes vary, the main features of the "world park" proposal are clear. Basically, it would prohibit any exploration for and exploitation of mineral or fuel resources on the continent or nearby ocean areas on grounds all such activity is extremely dangerous to the environment. Fishing might or might not be allowed, depending on whether conservation of marine species was or was not defined as including managed taking. Current proposals are also unclear about how the "world park" would be administered, though many envision placing it under some UN agency.

Since this is a private initiative, its political future would depend on the extent to which governments chose to adopt it. Many Third World governments support the placing of Antarctica under UN administration because this would mean the creation of a regime in which all states participate in decision making. The allowing of fishing would address their concern with assuring adequate protein for the their countries' growing populations. Yet Third World governments are likely to differ with environmentalists on what constitutes safe levels of fishing. Then, too, Third World governments might also be interested in assuring some resource exploitation. As the activity of many in their own continental margins shows, any Third World state that is a net oil importer is very interested in finding new sources of supply. Other resources might be attractive as import substitutes or sources of revenue. After all, the "common heritage" principle as defined at UNCLOS III is an exploitation concept, not a preservation one.[87]

## Common-Heritage Regime

The more politically significant challenge to the Antarctic regime comes from those members of the Nonaligned Movement hoping to establish international control of the continent along the lines of the seabed mining regime included in the 1982 Law of the Sea Convention. At minimum, these ideas include governing Antarctica through an international organization in which all states participate and where at least the broader policy decisions are taken by a majority operating under a one state–one vote rule. This organization would set the conditions under which various activities could occur, levy charges on any resource exploitation, and divide the revenues among member states on a formula favoring developing countries. Other details vary; some governments would probably prefer a system in which only an entity owned by the international organization (analogous to the International Seabed Authority's Enterprise) undertook resource activity, while others might be content with licensing state-owned or private firms. Other possibilities, like joint ventures, linking resource activity to mandatory technology transfer or the training of Third World nationals, have also been raised.

Third World interest in Antarctica may be traced back to the mid-1950s when India attempted to have the UN General Assembly discuss its future.[88] However, serious and sustained interest appeared only in the early 1970s, after the Nonaligned Movement and the Group of 77 had taken on their contemporary form and vague notions of "common heritage" were being discussed simultaneously for the oceans and outer space. The early 1970s saw attempts to raise Antarctic issues in the Economic and Social Council, the UNEP, the FAO, and the Third UN Conference on the Law of the Sea.[89] There was stiff opposition to all these initiatives from the consultative parties. Yet lack of success also stemmed from divisions within the Third World itself—if not on the main issue, then at least on whether it was useful to bring it up while the Law of the Sea Conference continued. This can be seen in the fact that only in 1983 did the summit meeting of the Nonaligned include any mention of Antarctica in its final communiqué, a document usually referring to any international issue on which the members can find some common ground.[90]

With completion of the UN Convention on the Law of the Sea in December 1982, Third World energies were freed for other initatives. There were soon indications that creating a new Antarctic regime would become one of them. The Final Communiqué of the March 1983 summit metting of the Nonaligned in New Delhi included two paragraphs setting out a joint position on Antarctica:

> The Heads of State or Government noted that the continent of Antarctica has considerable environmental, climatic, scientific, and potential economic significance to the world. They expressed their conviction that, in the interest of all mankind, Antarctica should continue forever to be used exclusively for peaceful purposes, should not become the scene or object of international discord, and should be accessible to all nations. They agreed that the exploration of the area and the exploitation of its resources shall be carried out for the benefit of all mankind, and in a manner consistent with the protection of the Antarctic environment.
> The Heads of State or Government, while noting relevant provisions of the Antarctic Treaty of 1959 related to international cooperation in the area, in view of increasing international interest in Antarctica, considered that the United Nations, at the thirty-eighth session of the General Assembly, should undertake a comprehensive study on Antarctica, taking into account all relevant factors, including the Antarctic Treaty, with a view to widening international cooperation in the area.[91]

Malaysia duly requested inclusion of "The Question of Antarctica" on the General Assembly's agenda in September. Despite opposition from all consultative parties,[92] the General Assembly took up the issue. It was referred to the First Committee, where some sixty governments made comments in debate.[93] In the end, all members agreed to a compromise resolution asking the Secretary-General to prepare a study of the question and report back to the 39th session in 1984.[94]

Debates at the 39th session revealed no greater Third World unity and thorough coordination of position by the consultative and nonconsultative parties.[95] This balance led to some backtracking by proponents of regime replacement. Antigua and Barbuda floated the idea of an "Antarctic resources authority" composed equally of consultative parties and nonparty states to be attached to the existing system.[96] Malaysia, while not giving up, accepted a compromise under which the Secretary-General would be asked to prepare a study of Antarctic questions to be considered at the 40th session.[97]

Continued Third World disarray, together with stronger support for replacement among some states was revealed in the summer of 1985. In July the Organization of African Unity's Council of Ministers declared that Antarctica is "the common heritage of all mankind" and called upon all member states to secure UN General Assembly endorsement of that position.[98] The ministerial meeting of the Nonaligned Movement in early September did not go as far; its resolution stated that the interest of the whole international community in Antarctica would be served best by keeping the UN fully informed of all developments there and called for a more comprehensive debate at the upcoming General Assembly session.[99] The 1986 summit meeting of the Nonaligned included a declaration that Antarctica should be used only for peaceful purposes, not become the "scene or object" of conflict, and be accessible to all states.[100] This still fell short of declaring that the common-heritage principle should apply.

At both the 40th and 41st sessions,[101] the pro-replacement group had to retreat from its maximal plan of establishing a UN special committee on Antarctica. At the 40th session sufficient support could be won only for resolutions requesting further studies and urging the consultative parties to expel South Africa. At the 41st session, the pro-replacement group fared somewhat better by narrowing their target. Resolutions repeated calls for submission of more information and the expulsion of South Africa from the consultative parties. Malaysia and its supporters did, however, win substantial Third World support for a resolution calling upon the Antarctic Treaty states to suspend their resources negotiations "until such time as all members of the international community can participate fully in such negotiations."[102] The phrase "participate fully" indicated that the pro-replacement group would not accept the current Antarctic Treaty group division into voting members and observers, but wanted an entirely new set of negotiations using a one state– one vote rule.

The Antarctic Treaty states reacted strongly against all these resolutions. Resolutions 40/156 A and B, which called for studies, contained preambular formulations that obviously prepared the way for later arguments that they had accepted application of the common-heritage principle in Antarctica. The studies themselves were framed in a way that implied formal accountability to the UN. The preambular formulations in Resolutions 41/88 A and B were no less objectionable to the Antarctic Treaty states. The operative parts were worse from their point of view than the earlier resolutions. Resolution 41/88 A spoke of the UN's functioning as "the central repository" of all information about Antarctica, while the call for a moratorium on negotiations in Resolution 41/88 B directly attacked an ongoing Antarctic Treaty system activity.

The calls for expulsion of South Africa handed the consultative parties a dilemma. Much as they object to South Africa's apartheid policies, they object even more to having an outside body assume the right to tell them who may or may not participate in the Antarctic regime. In addition, expelling South Africa for its domestic policies would violate a major rule of the Antarctic regime: keeping non-Antarctic conflicts from interfering with Antarctic cooperation.

The consultative parties chose to dissociate themselves as far as possible from all these resolutions. First, they requested roll-call votes on all of them and indicated objections in the strongest terms politically feasible in the UN context—concerted nonparticipation in the vote. This led to record levels of nonparticipation—forty-one to forty-four states on the general resolutions and at least twenty on the calls for expelling South Africa.[103] Second, they become less communicative with the UN. They had announced at the 40th session that they would adopt such a policy if other members refused to return to decision by consensus. They carried it out at the 41st session by refusing to supply any of the information requested for the secretary-general's studies and confining themselves to one joint statement and a few explanations of vote in the Assembly debate.[104]

The attack on the Antarctic Treaty regime continues. So far it has widest support among African states, but not enough support that the leaders can propose draft Assembly resolutions declaring Antarctica part of the "common heritage of mankind" or stating that UN bodies should take over its management. The Antarctic Treaty states have remained united on most issues, though the calls to expel South Africa have produced some public divisions among them.

# 6

# Regime Establishment and Maintenance

Once a regime is created, it must be established before it can acquire any significance in world politics. Establishment involves acting on prior verbal agreements, translating their words into political outcomes. The conditions for successful establishment are straightforward. First, the agreements previously made must prove workable in the conditions prevailing at the time they are to be put into effect. Second, a coalition of states able to make the agreements work and maintain them against any outside challenge that arises must continue to support the regime. It is not necessary that every state participating in the initial negotiations ratify the agreements or contribute to the starting up of the regime. It is necessary, however, that those participating in establishment have sufficient power to start the regime and protect it from challenge. Since such a coalition will usually have formed in the course of negotiations, establishment depends heavily on having regime supporters within each government involved—or at least enough of them to start and protect the regime—retain control over the implementation of policies already agreed upon in international negotiations.

Successful establishment usually turns into maintenance within a year or two. Maintenance, then, is the application of a working regime over time. Its continuation depends on satisfying three conditions: (1) continued low salience of the issue, (2) continued perception within participating states' governments of shared or parallel interests that are best served by obeying the regime's prescriptions, and (3) continued participation in the regime by a coalition of states with sufficient overall and issue-specific power to sustain the regime. The first is important because an international regime is intended to solve problems. A later rise in salience, or continued high salience after establishment, indicates that the regime is failing in some way to do that. Participants may then reassess their interests.

## Successful Establishment of the Antarctic Regime

Establishment of the Antarctic Treaty went so smoothly that it is now difficult to think of success as having been doubtful. Yet the Antarctic regime had to overcome the hazards lying in the way of establishing any international regime. The main dangers consist of (1) a reevaluation of interests on the part of enough participating governments to bring the viability of the regime into question even before it is applied and (2) a failure of regime provisions to prove workable in the international conditions prevailing at the time they are to be applied.

The fact that the Antarctic regime was created by a treaty built an interval of uncertainty into the establishment process. Most national constitutions require that treaties be ratified by the legislature before they become binding on the state. Therefore, those involved in the negotiations who have second thoughts—or, more likely, those inside and outside the government who object to the negotiators' handiwork—have a chance to prevent acceptance of the treaty and hence participation in the emerging international regime.

Whether subsequent refusals to ratify affect the establishment of a new regime depends on the number and power of the nonratifying states. Most multilateral treaties contain a safeguard by stipulating that they will come into force only after ratification by a certain number of states. Some go even further. A treaty might stipulate that the minimum number include a certain proportion of states with particular issue-relevant capabilities. A treaty written in a limited-participation conference might even stipulate that it will not come into force until all of the states represented at the conference ratify.

Even so, there are many examples of international regimes being created only to fail at establishment for lack of ratifications. The 1958 Geneva Conventions on the Law of the Sea all specified entry into force when twenty states had ratified. This was a respectable proportion of the approximately sixty states represented at the conference. Yet none of these conventions ever formed the basis of an effective regime in the area they covered, because the coalition of ratifiers was never sufficiently powerful to maintain them against other states. Because of the lapse of time between conclusion and ratification the conventions were rendered obsolete politically and technologically even before they could be applied extensively. The number of independent states in the world doubled in the following decade. Many of these new states were easily recruited into a coalition pressing for additional changes with arguments that they, too, ought to have a say in the writing of the international law of the sea, and with appeals to their material interests. In addition, advances in fishing and offshore drilling technology had made many of the 1958 stipulations irrelevant.

In some cases, one or a few states may be able to prevent the establishment of an international regime. United States failure to ratify the charter of the proposed International Trade Organization in 1947 killed all chance of building an international trade regime along the lines it laid out. The United States controlled so much of the world's trade as a producer of goods and a source of loans that other countries could not maintain any trade regime it rejected. Similarly, refusals of the United States (the largest consumer) and Sierra Leone (the largest producer) to join have seriously weakened the latest International Cocoa Agreement.

In the Antarctic case, the treaty could enter into force only when all twelve original parties had ratified. There was an interval of eighteen months between signature of the treaty in December 1959 and ratification by the last of the twelve in June 1961. Ratifications occurred as follows:

| United Kingdom | 31 May 1960 |
| South Africa | 21 June 1960 |
| Belgium | 26 July 1960 |
| Japan | 4 August 1960 |
| United States | 18 August 1960 |
| Norway | 24 August 1960 |
| France | 16 September 1960 |
| New Zealand | 1 November 1960 |
| Soviet Union | 2 November 1960 |
| Argentina | 23 June 1961 |
| Australia | 23 June 1961 |
| Chile | 23 June 1961 |

Though this was a relatively short interval by the standards of multilateral treaties, the outcome remained in doubt for some time. Many of the participants held back to see if both superpowers would ratify. In the United States, ratification was never a foregone conclusion. A coalition of people worried about allowing Soviet participation, and others advocating that the United

States make a territorial claim, tried hard to prevent Senate approval. The United Kingdom, consistent with its early interest in discussing Antarctica in 1958, thus took the lead. This no doubt helped tip the scales in favor of ratification in the other Commonwealth countries. However, superpower ratifications were probably more important. The Soviets clearly waited to see if the Eisenhower administration could get the treaty approved in the U.S. Senate. When this happened and a few more claimants ratified, they felt safe in doing so. Yet the uncertainty was not over; it took three claimants, those generally deemed most assertive of their rights, another six months to ratify. Though a source of temporary uncertainty, the requirement that all twelve ratify proved useful because it assured that there would be no attempt to establish the regime without a powerful coalition behind it.

Ratification by all twelve states did not solve all the problems of establishing the Antarctic regime. The treaty's provisions had to prove workable. Many international regimes have failed because conditions assumed during negotiations were found not to prevail when the time came to start applying treaty provisions. The whole UN collective security mechanism failed because it was built on a set of assumptions about state conduct that proved false, the well-publicized disagreements between the superpowers being only a symptom of this wider problem. The International Monetary Fund's Articles of Agreement were not fully established until 1958 because most countries' economic circumstances were such that they could not meet the requirement of maintaining freely convertible currencies. The British attempt to do so in 1947 failed so quickly that all other governments—including that of the United States, which was the greatest advocate of convertibility—agreed that this step was best postponed. The financial requirements of postwar reconstruction proved far bigger than anyone expected. Under the circumstances, it was not surprising that establishment failed. In this case, it is more interesting that failure led not to the end of the regime but only to delayed establishment.

Establishment of the Antarctic regime was greatly simplified by the fact that the International Geographical Year (IGY) had provided a test run for most of its features. Science remained the main activity and continued to be coordinated through the Scientific Committee on Antarctic Research (SCAR), just as it had been before. Further, many regime prescriptions were prohibitions, established simply by avoiding the proscribed activity. The only feature of the regime needing a test was the system of political consultation. There, the large scientific and technical portion of the agenda gave the parties a workable program for testing the new institution and perfecting its operation. The nature of the agenda also helped confine Antarctic issues to restricted salience, permitting the same small groups of officials and scientists who had been managing Antarctic affairs before 1961 to continue doing so. Domestic processes of implementation were not captured by rival agencies either unaware or uninterested in the bargains made by the initial negotiators or opposed to the regime. The general disposition to avoid raising new questions before they became pressing was also useful, since it kept the new institution from being swamped before it established regular patterns of work. All this meant that the potential for difficulty inherent in a unanimity rule was not realized.

The strength of perceptions of shared or parallel interest appear in the steps governments took to reorganize the management of their Antarctic affairs. This reorganization was motivated less by interagency struggles for influence than by desires to cope better with the new international regime. It involved bureaucratic restructuring in some countries and legislative adjustments in virtually all.

Coming out of the IGY, all twelve parties had a National Committee on Antarctic Research, usually within their national scientific academy. Yet these committees lacked the resources to supplement their planning with the funding and logistical support necessary to actual research. The resources needed were so large that funding and logistics necessarily became government functions; therefore each government had to find or create some body to take charge of that Antarctic activity. In the USSR the Arctic Institute within the Chief Administration of the Northern Sea Route, a part of the Ministry of Merchant Marine, expanded its mandate and became the Arctic and Antarctic Institute in 1958.[1] In the United States the interagency battles had been fought in 1958 when the newly established National Science Foundation was given responsibility for funding scientific work. The navy, which had hitherto run all U.S. Antarctic programs largely because of the interest and initiative of Admiral Byrd, wanted to keep that task, but had to content itself with maintaining overall charge of logistical operations.[2] In the United Kingdom the British Antarctic Survey (former Falkland Islands Dependencies Survey), which ran British stations, provided logistics, and funded research, remained part of the Foreign and Commonwealth Office.[3]

Other governments created new bodies or shifted responsibilities around. By 1963 Chile had reorganized the parts of its foreign ministry dealing with Antarctica to make them more effective. In a number of ways, excepting a smaller direct role for the military, the resulting organization looked similar to that of the Argentine government. The Foreign Ministry was given a specific Antarctic section to deal with political and legal affairs. A Chilean Antarctic Commission was added as a consultative body for policy planning. Finally, the Chilean Antarctic Institute was set up as an autonomous body within the Foreign Ministry's Department of Frontiers to coordinate and oversee scientific work and other expeditions.[4] In 1962 Japan brought all Antarctic scientific activities together in an Antarctic Section of the National

Science Museum, a research arm of the Ministry of Education. As it grew in the 1960s, the section became successively a division and then a department in the museum.[5] In 1964 the French government reorganized the head office of the Terres australes et antarctiques françaises to include a scientific council to help plan expeditions and a stronger research program of its own as it moved to take over from the privately organized but government funded Expeditions polaires françaises.[6] In South Africa the Department of Transport, which had charge of scientific work and logistics for the Prince Edward Islands, simply expanded its activities to include Antarctica as well. An advisory council reporting to the Secretary of Transport provided advice on planned activity. The old Antarctic Research Committee, established in 1945 and reporting to the government's Center for Scientific and Industrial Research, became South Africa's national committee for SCAR.[7]

Establishment of the Antarctic regime was followed by a number of measures intended to build its prescriptions into domestic routines. The British made one of the clearest revisions when changing the method of administering their Antarctic claim. The United Kingdom sought to separate subantarctic and Antarctic claims disputes with Argentina by organizing all territorial claims south of the 60° line into a separate British Antarctic Territory ruled from the Colonial Office rather than through the governor of the Falkland Islands.[8] Several governments adjusted their domestic legislation to the Antarctic Treaty's requirements. Where domestic legislation normally did not apply to nationals' conduct abroad, special laws were passed to assert jurisdiction over their activity in Antarctica.[9] Claimants also adjusted legislation concerning their territorial claims to exempt foreign scientists, their expeditions or stations, exchange scientists at the claimant's own stations and observers appointed to carry out Antarctic inspections from local jurisdiction.[10]

## Maintenance of the Regime, 1963–1975

For more than a decade the Antarctic Treaty regime satisfied all three conditions of regime maintenance. The salience of Antarctic issues remained low. Participating governments continued to view the principles, norms, rules, and procedures of the regime as serving, or at least compatible with, their interests. The coalition of participants continued to monopolize issue-specific power, inasmuch as any state embarking on serious Antarctic activity acceded or was persuaded at some point to accede to the treaty. Though the original twelve parties possessed enough overall and issue-specific power to defeat any outside challenge to the regime, these accessions were politically significant.

They indicated that governments interested enough in Antarctica to encourage some level of Antarctic activity by their nationals were ready to support
the existing regime rather than any outside challenge that might be raised.
Even with the addition of a few countries, Antarctic affairs remained in the
hands of the same interconnected transgovernmental network of officials and
transnational network of scientists running Antarctic affairs since the IGY.

## Salience

The stability of individual governments' perceptions of Antarctic interests
and the durability of the coalition behind the treaty were both reinforced by
the low salience of Antarctic issues in the 1960s. Antarctic affairs appeared to
be satisfactorily regulated, and no pressing new issues arose. At the same
time, there were plenty of other more pressing issues to worry about in other
parts of the world.

Antarctica continued to have little immediate economic significance until
after 1970, despite two flurries of interest in sealing. Norwegian exploratory
expeditions in the early 1960s and a similar Soviet venture in 1970 both
yielded unfavorable results, so the planned commercial ventures were given
up.[11] Though the rise in salience was brief, these sealing ventures did have
considerable political impact because they helped inspire the Convention on
the Conservation of Antarctic Seals of 1972. A few people expressed interest
in Antarctic offshore hydrocarbon resources in 1969, but real interest arose
only after the first oil crisis in 1973.[12] Exploitation of onshore minerals still
seemed a distant prospect.[13] There was some exploitation of Antarctic fish in
the late 1960s, but this was generally carried on in the northern parts of the
Southern Ocean, around subantarctic islands lying north of the treaty area's
60° limit.[14] Whaling was still governed by the regime created in the International Convention for the Regulation of Whaling. The number of whales
continued to decline, leading to the imposition of stricter quotas and other
limits on activity. Conservationists were interested in these developments but
were not yet expanding their interests to general Antarctic questions.

Only one set of developments increased the salience of Antarctic activity,
and it worked mainly for the benefit of scientists, reinforcing their strong
hold on Antarctic activity. Until the 1960–61 season, scientists wishing to
pursue research at a site away from a coastal station had to spend at least
twelve months away from their home institutions in order to get three
months of working time. They had to leave for Antarctica in February, winter
over at a station, then proceed to their field site at the start of the Antarctic
summer in November. In addition, the choice of inland sites was limited by

the need to carry all personnel, fuel, and supplies overland. With the introduction of large, long-distance, ski-equipped cargo planes in the United States program in 1960, the situation changed dramatically. Their use meant that scientists working with a U.S. field party could leave home in October, be flown directly to the field site, work, be flown out again at the end of the season, and return home by the end of February. Therefore, more scientists could participate in Antarctic work because it was easier to get leave from the home institution for this shorter period of time. Scientists' mobility was further increased in the 1961–62 season with the introduction of turboprop helicopters able to ferry personnel and supplies in the neighborhood of a summer base camp.[15] The pace of research quickened, and the number of different individuals participating over the years increased as other countries shared U.S. transport facilities or established their own.[16]

Developments in the wider international system did not increase the salience of Antarctic affairs. Related international regimes remained stable. Despite considerable coastal-state dissatisfaction with rules limiting maritime jurisdiction to the continental shelf and a twelve-mile band of water adjacent to the coast, the law of the sea did not undergo any real transformation in the 1960s. In 1967 Malta formally proposed that the UN General Assembly either discuss the issue or sponsor a separate conference to do so. All governments were on notice that the law of the sea was going to change, but the form of those changes was not worked out until 1976 for coastal-state jurisdiction, and 1982 for other issues. Nor were there any developments in technology or global resource markets that made Antarctic resources look any more economically interesting than they had looked in 1959.

Though the need to protect the Antarctic environment attracted increased attention in the 1960s, measures to this end were seen largely in terms of maintaining the scientific value of the continent. This made it possible to deal with environmental questions by adding some new rules and procedures to the Antarctic regime through the mechanism of Consultative Parties Recommendations. The main measures in this direction included the 1964 Agreed Measures for the Protection of Antarctic Flora and Fauna, and a form of "zoning" establishing Specially Protected Areas and Sites of Special Scientific Interest where activity was limited by tighter restrictions than those specified in the generally applicable Agreed Measures.

*Interests*

There was no reevaluation of interests on the part of participating governments between 1963 and 1975. All remained committed to upholding the regime's various prescriptions. Though participants had disagreements on particular questions, the only serious ones involved maneuvering for possible future advantage on the claims question.

Nonmilitarization retained universal support in this period. If anything, the nonmilitarization clauses were strengthened by certain developments. The military value of Antarctica to the superpowers decreased in the 1960s as they developed ICBMs and then submarine-launched missiles capable of threatening targets anywhere in the world without the use of Antarctic bases. This removed one of the potential military uses most often discussed in the 1950s. For other parties, particularly those in the Southern Hemisphere, not having to worry about threats on their home territory from the Antarctic continued to have high positive value.

The procedures developed for the consultative parties also enjoyed the advantages of wide support. The unanimity rule spread from adoption of recommendations to the making of other decisions because it assured every participating government that its wishes would not be ignored by some adverse coalition. The distribution of interests among participants was such that none could be sure of being in the majority all the time. The United States had learned in 1948 that having a group of friends and allies involved in the Antarctic did not assure that its views would always prevail. The more adamant claimant governments knew that some other claimants were willing to consider an international administration for the continent, so they did not consider the ratio of seven claimants to five nonclaimants among the original parties as much of a guarantee. They also realized that any additions to the membership of the consultative parties would necessarily be nonclaimants. While they could prevent such additions by refusing to agree, it was politically less costly to rely on the veto to protect interests in a slightly enlarged group than to reject the addition of all new members. Of course, it would be in the claimants' interests to make sure the group did not grow too much or too quickly. Nonclaimant governments knew that they were outnumbered in 1959, and they could not be sure that any augmentation of the consultative parties would result in a cohesive nonclaimant majority, given all the other differences among them.

Confidentiality was rather strictly maintained in the 1960s. Delegates seldom discussed meetings. Reports tended to be dry listings of delegations and working groups, recitals of the agenda, and reproductions of the texts of any recommendations and other decisions adopted. This was particularly congenial to the Argentine and Soviet governments, which were not used to extensive public discussion of political affairs. It did not particularly irk the democratic governments, since there was so little media or public interest in the Antarctic, and the requirements of democratic control over policy could be satisfied by legislative ratification of recommendations and approval of budgets for Antarctic activity. Flexibility and informality were simply very useful rules for negotiating, while maintaining a separation between the Antarctic regime and other international questions permitted the parties to cooperate regardless of other ups and downs in their overall relations.

The only area of difficulty was the compromise on sovereignty. On territorial issues there was a certain amount of cheating at the edges, motivated by the concern of governments to be in a good position should the Antarctic Treaty by terminated later. Most of this concern was expressed by continued assertion of claims to sovereignty in various symbolic ways or by making ostensibly scientific decisions for their potential political usefulness. Although no claimant would attempt to assert jurisdiction over another treaty state's expedition or station within its claim, some have sought opportunities for other symbolic assertions neither so clearly incompatible with the treaty nor so likely to be noticed. Argentina indulged in this tactic the most. It regularly stamped passports of scientists who go to or return from the Antarctic via Argentina with notations that they had been authorized to visit the "Argentine Antarctic Territory,"[17] and issued postage stamps for the area. It also published official maps for domestic consumption, labeling some of its Antarctic stations as "naval outpost" (*destaciemento naval*) or "army base" (*base de ejercito*) despite the nonmilitarization clauses of the Antarctic Treaty.[18] Chile has sometimes inspired and sometimes emulated Argentine gestures. The president of Chile formally visited his country's Antarctic claim in 1948 and 1977, and the president of Argentina did likewise in 1961 and 1974.[19] Chile also designates some of its stations as military bases,[20] but does not print those designations on maps. During the 1960s such activity was a minor irritant ignored by others, as it seemed to have few immediate implications.

The other consultative parties also expended energy on buttressing or maintaining their political positions and widening their options in case the Antarctic regime collapsed. The restrictions on activity imposed in the Fildes Peninsula Specially Protected Area (SPA) were ignored by the USSR when building Bellingshausen Station in 1968 and by Chile when building Presidente Frei Station in 1969. Operations at the two stations affected the area so much that the consultative parties finally withdrew the SPA designation and declared a much reduced area a Site of Special Scientific Interest in 1975.[21] The Australian government was upset when the Soviets set up Leningradskaya Station at 69°30'S, 159°24'E in the smaller portion of the Australian claim in 1970 without prior notice.[22] The Soviets have never proved particularly eager to share data. Polish scientists complain that they could have been saved much effort and expense in the mid-1970s if their Soviet counterparts had shared data on krill acquired earlier.[23]

The regime also faced two free-rider problems, but neither became significant in the 1960s (or later). The first involves the consultative parties. An original party to the treaty might close down its year-round station and suspend other research activity yet still remain eligible to send delegates to consultative meetings, whereas an acceding party was technically eligible to do so only as long as it kept up large-scale research. Thus, an inactive original party could still have a voice in decisions despite the regime norm that decisions be taken by those with a serious stake in Antarctic activity. Neither Belgium (since 1967) nor Norway (since 1959) now maintains a year-round station. This potential problem was reduced indirectly in 1983 when the standards for consultative status were modified to be somewhat less rigorous.[24] Yet even without a requirement for maintaining a year-round station, the problem could still arise.

The second free-rider problem is posed by the activity of states that are not party to the Antarctic Treaty. Such states could take advantage of open access to initiate activity without becoming a party to the treaty and hence not subject to the obligations of the regime. This could present a difficult problem because any effort to make such states comply would involve enforcing the regime on outsiders. Except in special cases, international law specifies that treaties may not be enforced against states that are not parties. Yet the open-access rules of the Antarctic Treaty regime make it difficult to keep third parties out of the area. However, this possibility did not materialize in the 1960s. First, the number of third states interested in Antarctic activity was small. The lack of immediate potential for resource activities other than whaling meant that few others were attracted to activities that cost a good deal but had little immediate return except in some extra scientific prestige. Second, participating states succeeded in getting those few other states showing an interest in Antarctica to accede to the treaty.

At their most literal, structural theories of domestic politics suggest that structural change leads to revised definitions of interest even in the absence of changes in issue salience. This version received little confirmation in the Antarctic case between 1963 and 1975. Only one of the consultative parties has undergone any major structural change in this period. Chile went from center-left to leftist democracy in 1970, and from that regime, whose policies inspired fears of Marxist-Leninist dictatorship in some quarters, to a rightist military dictatorship in 1973. This does not mean that the political structures of all states have remained static, however. In most of the consultative parties, alternations of government have brought different parties backed by a different social coalition into power at different times. These changes are summarized in figure 2.

Analysis of individual governments' policies reveals a mixed pattern. The

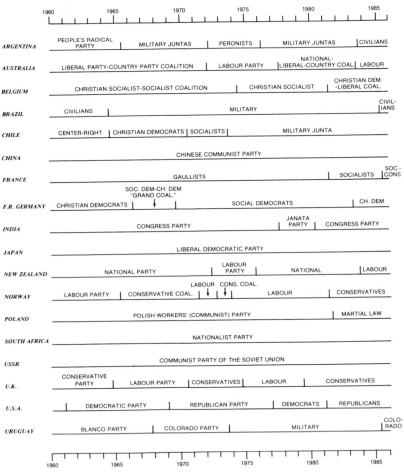

Figure 2. Governments of Consultative Parties, 1960–1985

Chilean case is the most instructive. Chilean Antarctic policy, combining insistence on the right to territorial sovereignty with acknowledgment of the practical advantages of cooperation within the regime, was not changed after either the 1970 elections or the 1973 coup. The shift to rightist military dictatorship did not lead to more assertive rhetoric in or outside consultative parties sessions. In those countries where there have been changes of social coalition represented in the government, only New Zealand has shown a clear relation between the shifts and any aspect of Antarctic policy. There, the Labour party has been more willing than the National party to consider internationalization. Labour Prime Minister Nash advocated trusteeship or some other internationalization in 1959.[25] It was also under a Labour government that New Zealand endorsed the proposal to make Antarctica a world park in 1972.[26] When the National party was in power, from May 1965 through June 1972, and from September 1977 through June 1984, New Zealand displayed more interest in holding its claim or at least asserting special claimant rights over revenues derived from resource activities.[27] The current Labour government has not, however, departed from this policy as yet.[28]

For regime maintenance, the relative strengths of participating governments vis-à-vis their own domestic society become relevant only if weakness prevents one or few from upholding their obligations so much that others get impatient. This did not occur with the Antarctic regime, because it touched so few social interests in each country. The governments were left pretty much alone in supporting the regime and obeying its rules.

Theories of bureaucratic politics suggest that maintenance of the policies that support particular international regimes is easier if the same agency retains authority over the issue and if that authority is not challenged by other agencies. Several consultative parties made important bureaucratic adjustments in the late 1960s. In one case this represented an effort to centralize more of the national Antarctic effort in governmental hands. In three other cases it represented a shift giving government-employed scientists more direct say in policy. In Norway the task of representing the country in SCAR was transferred from the Norsk Videnskapacademie to the Norsk Polarinstitutt, a research body in the Ministry of Industry. This brought the planning and execution of research into the same body.[29] In a more general reorganization, the British government moved the British Antarctic Survey out of the Colonial Office in 1967 and united it with other research bodies in a new National Environmental Research Council.[30] In Australia the operation of stations, logistics, and expeditions was transferred from the Antarctic Division of the Foreign Ministry to a new Antarctic Division of the Department of Supply in 1968. Four years later that Division was transferred to the new ministry in charge of science.[31]

United States Antarctic bureaucracy underwent a number of changes between 1965 and 1971. Occasional proposals to create an independent Antarctic commission failed because of strong opposition by Presidents Kennedy and Johnson. The reorganization that occurred was thus an adjustment among existing agencies. The first move was the creation of an Antarctic Policy Group chaired by the assistant secretary of state for International Organization Affairs and including as permanent members the assistant secretary of defense for International Security Affairs and the director of the National Science Foundation (NSF). Representatives of the Interior Department, the National Oceans and Atmospheric Administration, and the Commerce Department were included when the discussions covered matters within their competence. Though this appeared to be a centralizing move, the relative growth of National Science Foundation influence could be seen in the Defense Department's decision to abolish the Antarctic Projects Office and transfer its personnel and functions to either the assistant secretary of defense for International Security Affairs or to the Commander of the U.S. Naval Support Force, Antarctica. In 1971 all Antarctic activities were placed under the budget and control of the NSF, the navy becoming simply a contractor providing some support and logistics functions. The scientific cast of U.S. bureaucratic organization also increased when the State Department moved its Polar Regions Desk from the Bureau of International Organization Affairs to the Bureau of Oceans and International Environmental and Scientific Affairs.[32]

Except in Argentina, where the navy was the "lead agency," and in Chile, where the foreign ministry was, Antarctic policy was entrusted to agencies not normally among the most influential. Though the foreign ministry had some role in all twelve governments, Antarctic issues were usually too far down the list of its concerns to get much attention. This left the scientists considerable discretion.

Yet neither this fact nor the specific bureaucratic reorganizations undertaken in the late 1960s and early 1970s have any systematic relation to the content of individual states' Antarctic policies. The Norwegian and British changes do not seem to have affected those countries' Antarctic policies. However, a number of commentators believe that the Australian and American changes, by increasing scientific and reducing political-military inputs, did affect Antarctic policy. They believe that the result has been a tendency to overlook the political implications of Antarctic activity and to let policy drift.[33] However, it is impossible to conclude that countries allowing scientists a more autonomous role in policy making have one type of Antarctic policy, and countries that do not, another. Each group is divided by too many other interests. Nor can it be said that allowing a greater scientific role in itself leads to greater policy incoherence. This seems less true in the United Kingdom, perhaps because the overlap with Argentine and Chilean claims and the highly politicized nature of those two countries' Antarctic policies concentrate British attention.[34]

Only in one respect did differences in the domestic restraints on individual governments affect regime maintenance in the 1960s. When faced with particularly far-ranging decisions, a few governments delayed formal approval until they were able to modify domestic legislation. This was most noticeable with the Agreed Measures for the Preservation and Conservation of Antarctic

Flora and Fauna of 1964. Belgium, Japan, and the United States all delayed formal approval for more than a decade on grounds that they had to modify existing law first.[35] Similar considerations may have contributed to the decision to deal with pelagic sealing in a separate treaty rather than in a Consultative Parties Recommendation. A recommendation would not by itself modify existing national law, but acceptance of a treaty could, if the treaty were deemed self-executing.[36]

The relative openness of societies was not significant in the Antarctic discussions of the 1960s. Because of low and restricted salience throughout that decade Antarctic issues captured the attention of small groups in governmental and scientific bodies. In all participating states there was a growing number of "Antarctic hands" who had actually spent time on the continent or in formulating related policy. Although these people could serve as the core around which wider groups of concerned citizens form, this was not yet happening.

*Coalitions*

The coalition behind the treaty held together. There were no defections, though some parties became less active in Antarctic research than they had been. No party withdrew from the treaty and none joined any coalition of outsiders criticizing the regime or seeking its replacement. Yet maintenance of the Antarctic regime neither confirms nor impugns structural theories of coalition formation and maintenance, given the lack of serious change in the international distribution of power between 1963 and 1975. A look at power does, however, reveal a number of interesting points.

Maintenance of the Antarctic regime cannot be explained by the hegemonic-stability version of the overall-power-structure theory. It suggests, rather, the real possibility of organizing cooperation among a small group of the like-minded in the absence of a hegemonial power. In the 1960s the United States was not hegemonial in the political-military realm and was becoming less so in the economic realm. The Soviet Union began the decade in a weaker strategic position, but had achieved rough parity in nuclear weapons by its end. The Soviet Union maintained its lead in conventional weapons and was increasing its ability to project power over long distances by acquiring its first foreign bases, increasing its airlift capability, and building up its navy. The Soviets were closing some technological gaps, though the Americans still kept important advantages in this field. At the same time, U.S. forces were bogged down in a seemingly endless conflict in Vietnam. This war cost heavily in terms of material resources, and also politically by making the U.S. appear as expansionist as and more conservative than its superpower rival. Economically, the relative position of the United States was eroding, though it still enjoyed great preeminence. Its troubles would not become obvious until the unilateral moves to change the monetary regime in 1971 and the OPEC oil embargo and price hike of 1973. Japan and Western Europe both experienced a decade of rapid growth in the 1960s. They also began giving the United States serious competition in many international markets for manufactured goods. A number of developing states, particularly the newly industrializing Asian states and, after 1973, OPEC members, were also beginning to show respectable growth rates.

The irrelevance of the theory of hegemonic stability does not discredit the overall-power variant of structural theory. It is possible to attribute successful regime maintenance to continued Soviet-American cooperation in a bipolar distribution of power. The United States and the Soviet Union continued to have very similar Antarctic policies. Both supported nonmilitarization, opposed division of the continent, wanted to continue scientific cooperation, kept an eye on any resource possibilities that might arise, and preferred the existing regime to any other. Since no coalition of other states—whether active or not in Antarctic affairs—could challenge the superpowers' joint position, a structuralist could legitimately conclude that maintenance was assured until the two split or there arose some third coalition able to overwhelm both. The latter seemed to be a remote possibility, since so many of the world's middle-level powers and so many of the other states involved in the Antarctic were allied to one or the other superpower.

Yet the overall-power-structure theory misses an important dimension of the problem. Regime maintenance is much easier if the regime is not simply imposed but also has geniune support from other states involved, particularly those others possessing significant resources of their own. An imposed regime must deal not only with the normal temptations to take benefits without contributing a share of the costs, but also with efforts to hasten the regime's demise. Maintaining a regime imposed on unwilling participants is more costly than securing willing participation, and will occur only if the strongest participants place a very high value on maintenance of the regime. Further, when an imposed regime needs modification, the dissatisfied participants are as likely to leave the coalition as to join in efforts to repair or modify the regime so that it can continue to function. Thus, it is worth looking at the issue-specific distribution of power and the attitudes of other participants.

In the 1960s issue-specific power in Antarctica stemmed first of all from the level of current activity. For maintenance of the regime, the fact of having previously asserted a territorial claim was less relevant, though political advantage might be derived if amendments extended the regime to new areas.

Proximity remained useful for reducing costs and allowing a greater level of activity than would otherwise have been possible. Historical activity was much less relevant; it had been taken into account when the initial participants were selected. It had continuing relevance in that original participants could remain consultative parties even if their current activity fell to minimal levels, but no new benefits could be derived from a historical record unsupplemented by a fairly high level of current activity.

Throughout the 1960s the superpowers maintained their lead in issue-specific power. They operated more stations than most other participating states and had the largest groups of scientists and support personnel in Antarctica. There were some rearrangements among the other participants. Poland found itself unable to maintain the station it had been given by the Soviets and dropped out of Antarctic activity in 1961.[37] Belgium found it hard to maintain its year-round Roi Baudoin Base (70°25′S, 24°18′E). It was closed from the end of the 1960–61 summer until spring of 1963. Between 1963 and February 1967, it was operated on a year-round basis with a staff of eighteen to twenty-four. It was then closed again, and Belgian scientists worked on summer expeditions near the South African Sanae Base (70°18′S, 2°24′W).[38] Though Norwegian whalers remained active and were allocated 28 percent of the total Antarctic catch allowed by the International Whaling Commission,[39] Norway found it difficult to maintain scientific activity on the continent, maintaining no year-round base after 1959, though sending summer expeditions. Other original parties were able to maintain or increase activity. South Africa established Sanae Base in 1962 and operated it consistently with a staff of about fifteen. It also maintained a summer camp for geological work at Borga, 380 km south of Sanae, beginning in 1969.[40] Japan sent regular expeditions and established its first station, Syowa (69°00′S, 39°35′E) in 1967.[41] Some sense of consultative party activity can be gleaned from the number of winter stations operated and wintering personnel sent by each in 1960, 1965, and 1970, as is shown in table 3.

Some newcomers also appeared on the Antarctic scene. Italian scientists began working in New Zealand bases and expeditions as early as 1958. They also began joining Belgian projects in 1960–61.[42] Czech scientists participated in Soviet expeditions,[43] and the Dutch helped operate the Belgian Roi Baudoin station.[44]

By the late 1960s, then, issue-specific power in Antarctica was coming to resemble more closely the overall distribution of power in the international system. The superpowers had used their great general resources to establish a high level of current activity. Despite being nonclaimants, they were thus the leading Antarctic powers. Argentina was still able to make up for low overall power by a high level of Antarctic activity, but this was harder for Chile.

Table 3.    Winter Activity, 1960–1970

|  | 1960 | | 1965 | | 1970 | |
|---|---|---|---|---|---|---|
|  | stations | staff | stations | staff | stations | staff |
| Argentina | 6 | 76 | 6 | 120 | 7 | 116 |
| Australia | 3 | 59 | 2 | 52 | 3 | 56 |
| Belgium | 0 | 0 | 0 | 0 | 0 | 0 |
| Chile | 4 | 35 | 3 | 39 | 3 | 40 |
| France | 1 | 14 | 1 | 22 | 1 | 26 |
| Japan | 1 | 15 | 0 | 18 | 1 | 32 |
| New Zealand | 1 | 31 | 1 | 12 | 2 | 18 |
| Norway | 0 | 0 | 0 | 0 | 0 | 0 |
| South Africa | 1 | 13 | 1 | 14 | 2 | 20 |
| Soviet Union | 2 | 129 | 4 | 145 | 5 | 220 |
| United Kingdom | 8 | 71 | 6 | 86 | 6 | 59 |
| United States | 3 | 169 | 5 | 290 | 4 | 243 |
| N.Z. and U.S.A. | 1 | * | | | | |

SOURCES: Stations from *Polar Record* 9:467–87; 10:543–44; 12:770–72; and 15:279–80. Staff from Budd, "Scientific Research in Antarctica," 230.
    *Personnel included in separate national totals.

Australia and New Zealand were holding their acivity steady, though at a level too low to satisfy domestic critics who were most concerned with protecting the claims. Japan was beginning to increase its activity, an increase reflecting its growing global economic position. The United Kingdom reduced activity somewhat, but not in the major way it was reducing remaining commitments "east of Suez" in light of its long-straitened economic circumstances.

    Process theories are useful mainly for indicating how little strain was put on the Antarctic regime in the 1960s. Variables captured by looking at the economic process, organizational behavior, related regimes, and ideas held in common by governments showed little change over the period. No strain was imposed on the regime, because there was no reason for participants to redefine their interests or think that they could do better without the regime.

    International organizations were not disturbing the regime or the issue-specific distribution of power in any way. The consultative parties and SCAR lacked permanent international staffs. Hence, they provided none of the usual opportunities for building coalitions between organization staff and national officials or exploiting procedures provided by standing organizations. Outside organizations were not causing any difficulties either. The United Nations agenda was full of other things, and the low immediate economic potential of Antarctica made it an area that countries could ignore for the moment. The now-familiar Third World coalition in the UN was not formed until 1964. It spent most of its energies in the 1960s on such issues as decolonization, economic development, and preparations for a new conference on the law of the sea. The tendency to view virtually all international economic issues in North-South terms did not develop until the early 1970s, and the "new international economic order" platform was not advanced until 1973.

There were changes in the realm of ideas which would begin to affect the Antarctic later. The first stemmed from increased discussion about how to regulate activity in outer space. With both superpowers sending manned and unmanned vehicles into space, and other countries being interested in doing likewise, the issue of creating a legal framework for activity in outer space seemed urgent in the mid-1960s. Here, too, was an area where the rival superpowers were able to agree on a number of principles for cooperation. In 1967 many states accepted the Treaty on Principles Governing the Activities of States in the Exploration and Use of Outer Space,[45] setting agreement on several principles. For Antarctic purposes, the most important of these was contained in Article 1 (1), which stated: "The exploration and use of outer space, including the moon and other celestial bodies, shall be carried out for the benefit and in the interests of all countries, irrespective of their degree of economic and scientific development, and shall be the province of all mankind."

These developments encouraged analogies between outer space, the high seas, and Antarctica as common-use areas that ought not to be divided among individual states but should be governed through some international mechanism. Since most thinking about how those international mechanisms should work had not progressed very far, this imposed no particular strain on the Antarctic regime. Vague calls for internationalization were fully compatible with continued control by the consultative parties, since that could plausibly be regarded as a type of internationalization.

The second change in ideas took shape in proposals before the General Assembly's Committee on Peaceful Uses of the Seabed that any mineral resources found in the deep ocean floor be treated as "the common heritage of mankind," a notion that won General Assembly endorsement in 1970.[46] Though there was wide agreement that claims to national control over the resources should be rejected, there was little agreement on any positive content for the concept. Only later did the notion acquire content that made it a basis for ideological challenge to the whole Antarctic regime.[47]

## Summary

Establishment of the Antarctic regime suggests that the process can be simplified even in a limited-participation regime by borrowing principles, norms, rules, or procedures that have recently proven workable in relation to the geographical area or issue to be governed by a new regime. Few regimes are likely, however, to have as extensive a "dry run" as the IGY gave the Antarctic regime. At the same time, it is important that the experience be fairly recent. There had been convertible currencies in the 1920s, but the postwar international monetary regime would not have worked if all the features of that earlier experience had been adopted.

Maintenance of the Antarctic regime shows that governments' definitions of interests on international issues depend more on actual or likely possessions or activities than on the structure or process of domestic politics. Again, this may stem from the fact that Antarctic affairs had such low domestic salience that governments could decide these matters in private. The example of changing policies in New Zealand shows that different ideologies or social coalitions could lead to different Antarctic policies, whereas the Chilean example shows that Antarctic policy could continue unaffected by large changes in the nature of the government.

Low salience is probably crucial to regime maintenance. Given the large number of questions arising at any time and the limited amount of time and resources available, governments tend to economize effort by reevaluating only when circumstances require and preferring small to large adjustments of policy. So long as an issue has low salience, both processes continue, imparting to the existing international regime the extra strength deriving from inertia.

# 7

# Regime Amendment

Efforts to amend an international regime follow a rise in the salience of the issue or geographical area governed by the regime. Such a rise in salience indicates that the regime is no longer serving the participants as well as it did initially. All or some participants come to perceive gaps in the original regime prescriptions or experience problems following regime prescriptions. These perceptions may stem from any of several causes, but whatever the cause the result is the same: the international regime seems to be a less satisfactory way of handling the issue than it had been in the past.

Though a more than momentary rise in issue salience is sufficient to inspire attempts at amending an international regime, it alone cannot ensure successful amendment. Two other conditions must be met for success. First, the perception that there are problems requiring amendment must be shared by a group of participants having enough power to make amendment a real issue. Second, a coalition of states with sufficient power to maintain an amended regime must be able to agree upon some specific set of amendments. This new coalition need not be identical to that which created the original regime; it only needs to possess the requisite power.

## The Roots of Increased Salience

There are five possible causes of a rise in the salience of an issue: (1) a change in the international distribution of power that favors states unhappy with the regime, (2) changes in the domestic structure that lead to a reassessment of interests in enough states, or in a sufficiently powerful state, to make amendment an issue, (3) developments stemming from operation of the regime that expose some inner tension between its prescriptions which can no longer be ignored, (4) changes in related issues or international regimes that make continuing the same lines of conduct more difficult, and (5) changes in environmental conditions, such as the state of technology, making the regime a less satisfactory mechanism for coordinating cooperation.[1]

Neither the first nor the second cause operated in the Antarctic case. This makes structural theories, whether at the international or the national level, irrelevant to understanding the timing of efforts to amend the Antarctic Treaty system. At the international level, the distribution of military power remained bipolar. Though other states had increased their capabilities to the point where they could deny victory to a superpower in a wider range of circumstances, it remained true that no plausible coalition of other states could defeat even one superpower, given the solidity of the postwar blocs. Additionally, the identities of the superpowers remained the same. Stability of structure was reinforced by continuity in its management; the changes that often accompany the replacement of one power by another within the same basic distribution of power thus could not occur.

There was notable, but not thoroughgoing, change in the distribution of economic power. The United States remained the leading economic power, but its advantages over the second-ranking economies were nowhere near as commanding in 1975 as they were in 1961. Japan and several Western European states had joined the ranks of the strong industrial economies, and OPEC states were enjoying an era of great significance based on their control of one vital resource. This change in the economic hierarchy is sufficient to suggest that the renewed salience of Antarctic issues might stem from the erosion of U.S. economic hegemony. There are, however, two difficulties with this notion. First, the Antarctic Treaty system was not an economic regime deriving its strength from the readiness of the United States to establish and maintain it. It was and remains basically a politico-military regime with provisions for joint peaceful use of a geographical area maintained by the wider set of supporters identified in chapter 2. Second, there is a far more persuasive alternate explanation, to be presented below, for the rise in salience.[2]

While there were minor adjustments in the issue-specific distribution of power, these were not enough to upset the regime. Since the Antarctic Treaty system is a limited-participation regime, the distribution of power as between participants and nonparticipants is as important as the distribution among participants. Even more in 1975 than 1960, issue-specific power was based on the level of current activity. Though the participants did not quite monopolize issue-specific power in the Southern Ocean, because a number of nonparticipant states did take part in the fishery, they continued to monopolize issue-specific power on the Antarctic continent. Thus, the rise in salience of Antarctic issues did not stem from problems of accommodating a large number of nonparticipating states that had somehow acquired significant issue-specific power. Within the group of participants, the superpowers maintained their joint lead over all others. While individual countries were increasing or decreasing activity at the margin, the balance did not change much between 1970 and 1975, though it would do so later after the rise in salience had led to serious negotiations about amending the regime. This is indicated by the maintenance and staffing of winter scientific stations on the continent, as is shown in table 4.

Nor can the rise in salience be attributed to domestic political and economic changes that of themselves led to a reassessment of interests by individual states. Among the consultative parties, only Chile underwent major change of system, shifting to a strongly Marxist government in 1970 and to a right-wing military dictatorship in 1973. Yet Chile alone lacked the overall or specific power to cause any stress in the regime, and the main features of its Antarctic policy were not affected by the changes. Other consultative parties experienced alternations between center-left and center-right electoral coalitions, and Argentina shifted several times between civilian and military rule, but none of these changes affected Antarctic policy very much except in the case of New Zealand, another state with relatively little power.

Nor did the workings of the regime create situations exposing latent tensions between its prescriptions. There was a tension between resource activity and the sovereignty compromise because that was the one issue that could weaken the agreement to disagree about territorial claims which lay at the heart of the Antarctic Treaty. However, this had not opened up before the mid-1970s, because actual activity remained confined to scientific research. Once resource activity began or became highly probable, this latent tension would become manifest. That depended, however, on exogenous change, not on the operation of the regime itself.[3]

Rather, the mid-1970s rise in the salience of Antarctic issues stemmed from environmental changes and, to a lesser extent, from changes in the

Table 4.    Winter Activity, 1970–1985

|  | 1970 | | 1975 | | 1980 | | 1985 | |
|---|---|---|---|---|---|---|---|---|
|  | stations | staff | stations | staff | stations | staff | stations | staff |
| Argentina | 7 | 116 | 5 | 126 | 8 | 179 | 6 | * |
| Australia | 3 | 56 | 3 | 68 | 3 | 76 | 3 | 86 |
| Belgium | 0 | 0 | 0 | 0 | 0 | 0 | 0 | * |
| Brazil | — | — | — | — | — | — | 0 | * |
| Chile | 3 | 40 | 3 | 43 | 3 | 52 | 3 | 90 |
| China | — | — | — | — | — | — | 0 | * |
| France | 1 | 26 | 1 | 35 | 1 | 26 | 1 | 27 |
| West Germany | — | — | — | — | 1 | 5 | 1 | 9 |
| India | — | — | — | — | — | — | 1 | * |
| Japan | 1 | 32 | 1 | 32 | 2 | 34 | 2 | 21 |
| New Zealand | 2 | 18 | 2 | 10 | 1 | 11 | 1 | 11 |
| Norway | 0 | 0 | 0 | 0 | 0 | 0 | 0 | 0 |
| Poland | — | — | — | — | 1 | 19 | 1 | 19 |
| South Africa | 2 | 20 | 1 | 18 | 1 | 16 | 1 | * |
| USSR | 6 | 220 | 6 | 244 | 7 | 288 | 7 | 304 |
| United Kingdom | 6 | 59 | 6 | 54 | 4 | 55 | 4 | 60 |
| United States | 4 | 243 | 4 | 90 | 4 | 111 | 3 | 115 |
| Uruguay | — | — | — | — | — | — | 0 | * |

SOURCES: Personnel through 1980 and 1980 stations from Budd, "Scientific Research in Antarctica," 130; other stations from *Polar Record* 15 (1970): 279–80, 17 (1975): 720–21, and 22 (1985): 733. 1985 personnel from U.S. State Department (non-U.S. as given in prior notifications) and *Antarctic Journal of the United States*, June 1985, p. 7 (actual U.S.).

*Data not available.

international regime of the oceans which together brought resource issues to the fore. This rise in the prominence of questions regarding Antarctic resources had two components: an increase in the significance attached to Antarctic resources themselves, and a shift of Antarctic affairs from restricted toward widespread salience as private groups and additional government agencies not hitherto interested in Antarctic questions sought a role in their countries' decision-making process.

Looking back, the energetic analyst can usually find indications that an issue was rising in salience well before governments and other observers saw it at the time. Politically, however, this retrospective wisdom is less significant than the contemporary perceptions; behavior is influenced by what actors know at the time. At first glance, it is tempting to date the rise in salience of Antarctic resources to 1964 when some Norwegians attempted to revive sealing. Yet it would be misleading to do so, even with negotiation of the Convention on the Conservation of Antarctic Seals between 1966 and 1972. Both the 1964 Norwegian and the 1970 Soviet experiments with sealing were brief ventures that did not lead to the establishment of an ongoing fishery. Nor did they give Antarctic issues widespread salience. Rather, they inspired discussion of regulation because it exposed a gap in the geographical coverage of the regime. The Antarctic Treaty, as supplemented by the Agreed Measures, already protected seals on the continent and in island breeding areas. However, both also contained provisions that protected the status of high-seas areas below the 60°S line. Though this attitude changed later, several consultative parties then doubted the group's right to assert jurisdiction over the Southern Ocean simply by adopting a recommendation— particularly when the activities of a third state's nationals were or might be involved.[4] They felt that efforts to regulate ocean uses were better grounded in a separate treaty linked to the Antarctic regime.

Today there is no commercial sealing in the Antarctic. The Seal Convention thus has no current substantive significance in the regime. Yet it is important to the later evolution of the regime because it provided precedents later adopted in the Convention on the Conservation of Antarctic Marine Living Resources and the negotiations about mineral and fuel resources.

Though occasional interest in offshore hydrocarbons was expressed as early as 1969, interest became widespread enough to acquire political significance only after the 1973 oil crisis and subsequent quadrupling of oil prices. News that the *Glomar Challenger* had found indications of ethane, ethylene, and methane gas in core samples taken from the Ross Sea continental shelf in early 1973 initially sparked interest only in scientific and professional circles.[5] That soon changed. Higher oil prices, coupled for most countries with massive drains on foreign exchange, led many governments to commission hydrocarbon exploration in their own land territories and offshore areas. The same price changes encouraged national and multinational oil companies to consider exploiting fields in locations hitherto considered uneconomic. In mid-1975, when most analysts were predicting steadily increasing oil prices for at least the rest of the century, attention was drawn to Antarctic possibilities by the leak of a U.S. Geological Survey guess that Antarctic offshore areas might contain 45 billion barrels of oil and 15 trillion cubic feet of natural gas.[6] Though based on data so scanty that Robert Rutford later characterized it as "much quoted but poorly supported,"[7] the numbers soon took on a life of their own and were cited in nearly all discussions of Antarctic resources.

Optimism encouraged by developments in offshore drilling and transportation technology led many people to believe that Antarctic operations would begin before the end of the century. Interest in hydrocarbon exploitation remained high through the 1970s, despite a growing awareness of the physical obstacles and high investment costs involved. These were discussed at length in meetings sponsored by the consultative parties, within national policy-making bodies, and in private scientific, commercial, and legal circles.[8] Even so, not everyone was discouraged immediately. Interest acquired its own momentum, in a process well described by Wright and Williams in 1974: "The social and economic costs of search are high, but these costs have not stopped similar ventures in the past once zeal was stimulated, even when the chances of success were small. The danger lies in an unwarranted stimulation of zeal because of either a misinterpretation of terms or a failure to separate appraisal of the resource from the actual costs involved in exploration and development."[9]

More recently, a weak oil market, the realization that Antarctic natural gas is not exploitable with current technology,[10] and very uneven performance of Arctic projects[11] have discouraged much of the earlier interest. However, this has not stopped efforts by the consultative parties to write rules for mineral and hydrocarbon exploitation. Some forms of preliminary exploration are possible today, and most governments of consultative party states realize that exploration raises most of the legal issues about jurisdiction and security of operator tenure that would be raised by exploitation.[12]

The same increases in oil prices provoked speculation about all sorts of alternative energy ventures. Antarctic possibilities discussed included using the Southern Ocean as a site for generating electricity by processes depending on differences in salinity of various levels of water,[13] exploiting solar power as a local energy source in the summer season,[14] or exploiting Antarctica's high winds, waves, or geothermal potential.[15] All of these were speculative ideas never taken very far, given the cost and low local demand for energy. They might revive if other resource activity ever began.

The general excitement about resources spread to onshore minerals as well. Scientific work since 1961 had yielded much new information indicating that Antarctic iron and coal deposits might prove commercially exploitable.[16] However, closer inquiry quickly showed that technological problems, high costs, and environmental hazards posed formidable obstacles to exploitation.[17] Offshore minerals, mainly in the form of polymetallic nodules, never inspired much interest. Since such nodules are richer in mineral content the closer they lie to the equator, Antarctic nodules are the least economically attractive of them.[18] By 1980 the nature of the rules proposed for seabed mining at the Third UN Conference on the Law of the Sea (UNCLOS III), lower mineral prices, reduced fear about maintaining access to supplies of strategic minerals, and increased understanding of the real difficulties involved in recovering and refining them all combined to discourage interest in any nodules. More recently a number of the private mining companies involved in early ventures were actually deferring new operations.[19]

The mid-1970s also witnessed serious proposals for towing Antarctic icebergs to desert areas as a source of fresh water. Later schemes also proposed generating electricity while the iceberg melted by exploiting the temperature difference between the iceberg and the surrounding air or water.[20] However, close looks proved that towing icebergs would be more difficult and costly than was expected, and many questioned the environmental wisdom of the enterprise. This speculation also petered out in about 1980, though it is still occasionally revived.

Interest in fishing, for both the shrimp-like krill and finned fish, rose in the 1970s as well. There had been some research-related harvesting of krill in 1961–62 by Soviet and Japanese vessels,[21] but most observers felt that krill had no immediate economic use. Taubenfeld noted in 1960 that "one other suggestion frequently heard is the conversion into human food of the plankton living in fantastic quantity in these waters, particularly in the area of the Antarctic convergence. This, too, awaits technical developments and probably even for a far greater unsatisfied demand for food than exists today."[22] As late as 1972 Phillippe Van der Essen noted that "krill *may* become one of the most important resources" of Antarctica (emphasis added).[23]

Interest in krill rose rapidly during the mid-1970s. In 1974 the Japanese had developed a trawler capable of catching sixteen metric tons of krill a day. In the 1975–76 summer season, the West German trawler *Weser* once caught thirty-five metric tons in an hour, though its average rate was eight to twelve metric tons an hour.[24] In that same season, a number of distant-water fleets had begun harvesting krill. The New Zealand journal *Antarctic* reported the following numbers of ships active: Japanese, 1 research vessel and 4 or 5 trawlers; Polish, 1 research vessel and 4 trawlers; East German, 1 large trawler; Taiwanese, 1 research vessel; Chilean, 1 trawler; Norwegian, 1 research vessel. The article went on to note that Soviet, American, West German, South African, and British ships were also pursuing occasional research or experimental harvesting.[25]

Krill fishers faced fewer technological problems than drillers or miners. Since krill float on the currents in huge swarms, they need only be scooped up.[26] The maximum rate of scooping is imposed not by limitations of trawling gear but by those of processing equipment. Krill spoil unless processed within four to eighteen hours of being taken from the water.[27] Most of the processing problems have been overcome, but marketing problems have severely limited the fishery. Krill has found few human consumers because of its strong taste[28] and high fluorine content. It has been sold on U.S. markets as food for pet fish,[29] on Soviet markets as paté or in a krill-cheese spread,[30] in

Japan as simply another form of seafood, in Chile as fish sticks, in Australia and New Zealand as one ingredient in a processed seafood imported from Japan,[31] and in West Germany, the Soviet Union, and Japan as a sausage substitute,[32] but only in Japan is there a stable market. Fuel costs and long distances to market usually make it too expensive to use as animal feed, where taste would be less of a problem. The Soviet Union is an exception because its agricultural system is so inefficient.[33]

Krill catches rose rapidly in the 1970s. Total reported catch went from 1,300 metric tons in 1970–71 to 42,130 metric tons in 1976–77,[34] to 530,000 metric tons in 1981–82.[35] At the peak of interest, the UN's Food and Agricultural Organization, (FAO) estimated that the annual sustainable catch could equal the world's fish harvest of 60 million metric tons a year.[36] However this, like all other estimates, was based on guesses from almost nonexistent biological data.[37]

Concern about the lack of accurate information inspired several multinational research programs and helped inspire negotiation of the Convention on the Conservation of Antarctic Marine Living Resources (CCAMLR). More recently, however, krill catches have dropped. In 1982–83 catches fell to 250,000 metric tons and in 1983–84 to 128,000 metric tons.[38] Most of the drop is attributable to decreased Soviet effort, which Soviet scientists and officials both attribute to processing and marketing problems rather than to the difficulty of finding krill to catch.[39] This drop was significant enough that even the London-based International Institute for Environment and Development—which has tended to overestimate the amount of resource activity occurring in efforts to mobilize opinion behind environmentalist proposals for prohibiting such activity—modified its earlier projections and estimated that total krill catches will not exceed 2 to 5 million metric tons a year before 1990.[40] Even this figure looks wildly optimistic today.

A similar pattern affected fin fishing. It is difficult to judge just how much fishing occurred in Antarctic waters before 1976, because FAO data lumped the various parts of the Southern Ocean together with more northerly waters.[41] However, zeal was sufficiently stimulated to cause at least one case of local overfishing. Catches around South Georgia totaled about 30,000 metric tons in 1971, rose to 417,000 metric tons in 1976, then declined to about 130,000 metric tons in 1979.[42] While these figures indicated a long-term problem, in the short term fleets reacted by just spreading out. By 1977 the Soviets, Poles, and East Germans, the most active harvesters of fin fish in Antarctic waters, were together taking 300,000 metric tons of fish a year off South Georgia, the Kerguelens, and other areas.[43] With fin fish, the technology was already well developed, and marketing was not a major problem, since many Antarctic species look and taste similar to more familiar northern fishes.[44]

Overall fish catches did not drop steadily in the early 1980s. In the 1978–79 season 125,091 metric tons of fish were taken, 121,527 in the 1980–81 season, and 197,252 in the 1982–83 season.[45] Unlike those with krill, however, these declines were largely the result of overfishing. The management authorities responsible for various parts of the Southern Ocean began to impose restrictions in hopes of restoring the most threatened stocks.[46]

Market forces were not the only, and in the case of fishing not even the main, source of increased interest in Antarctic resources. Changes in the law of the sea being negotiated during the 1970s at the Third UN Conference on the Law of the Sea (UNCLOS III) also inspired reevaluations of national interests in the Southern Ocean.

Agreements reached at UNCLOS III increased the potential value of Antarctic territorial claims by enlarging the marine area placed under exclusive coastal-state control. When the conference began substantive negotiating sessions in 1974, the Group of 77 had already endorsed the idea of extending coastal-state resource jurisdiction to all waters within 200 nautical miles of the coast.[47] By the spring of 1977 the last resistance from industrial states had been overcome.[48] The concept of the Exclusive Economic Zone (EEZ) then adopted gave coastal states the right to control all resource activity in the water column, such as fishing, ocean thermal energy conversion (OTEC) projects, tidal-power generation, or precipitating of minerals from sea water. This represented a considerable expansion in both the seaward extent and the substantive scope of coastal-state jurisdiction compared with the twelve-mile fishing zones accepted in 1958.

The older continental-shelf concept, redefined at UNCLOS III to include at least all seabed and subsoil within 200 nautical miles of shore, gave coastal states control over all resource activity on the seabed, such as taking sedentary species of marine life or mining surface minerals, and in the subsoil, such as exploiting oil and natural gas. After further negotiations, states with broad geological continental margins won acceptance of the idea that they could extend their jurisdiction over the seabed and subsoil of those margins up to a line 350 miles from shore or 100 miles seaward of the 2,500-meter isobath.[49]

This represented an expansion of the jurisdiction accepted in the 1958 Convention on the Continental Shelf (at least as initially interpreted). The 1958 Convention defined a coastal state's jurisdiction as extending to all areas where the depth of the water did not exceed 200 meters, or where it was possible to exploit the resources of the continental shelf and its subsoil.[50] At that time technology was advancing slowly, so the "exploitability clause" was not viewed as justifying very large extensions of coastal state authority. By 1970, however, advances in technology made it appear that a literal reading of the exploitability clause would allow coastal states to claim control over areas out into the deep ocean.[51] In that respect, then, the agreement to limit such claims to a maximum of 200 or 350 miles (depending on the width of the continental margin) can be viewed as placing a limit on coastal state claims. Yet it did mean giving explicit endorsement to a wider extension of coastal jurisdiction than many (including the government of Malta) expected as late as 1970. Once these agreements were reached, few governments waited for the end of the rest of the UNCLOS III negotiations before asserting the wider jurisdiction.

These changes in the law of the sea had different effects on those interested in exploiting different resources. Oil companies exploit a fixed nonrenewable resource. They need the protection of an enforceable exclusive right to work in a particular place, which can be gotten only from a government or an international authority entrusted with the control of some area. Even allowing for complications arising from the seasonal changes in pack ice,[52] the new continental shelf doctrine would place the most promising Antarctic sites under the control of any state whose territorial claim there was generally accepted. For oil companies, the complications over coastal state jurisdiction created by the Antarctic Treaty were an inhibition rather than an incentive. When a few oil companies approached individual governments with requests for licenses to explore in Antarctic areas, they put both claimant and nonclaimant governments into a quandary. If a claimant government granted a license, this would destroy the compromise on sovereignty and with it the Antarctic regime; yet if it flatly rejected the possibility of granting a license, this might be read as undermining its own claim. Nonclaimants were put into less of an immediate quandary, since they knew they lacked the authority to grant a license on the basis of sovereignty over the area. However, they did not want to concede claimants the right to grant licenses, as this would amount to accepting their claims. Rather, they hoped to preserve their interest in joint use by creating some system of joint regulation within the Antarctic regime. These quandaries gave both claimants and nonclaimants an incentive to discuss the issue within the consultative parties.

The effect of agreements reached at UNCLOS III on seabed miners' activities depends on where they wish to set up operations. If they wanted to mine areas within 200 miles of shore or otherwise within the legal continental margin, they would have to apply for coastal state permission and be subject to coastal state laws. If they wanted to mine in areas of the deep seabed outside national jurisdiction, the legal situation was unclear. If the 1982 Convention won general support, they would be subject to the International Seabed Authority. If not, they might be able to mine under the flag of a state with unilateral seabed-mining legislation or under an alternative arrangement (such as the Reciprocating States Agreement) among a number of states. The complications of deep-seabed mining are not an issue in Antarctic affairs, however, since there is at present no interest in such operations. Because of the extra hazards and relatively low value of the resources compared with similar resources in other areas no one has yet proposed any offshore mining operations. Seabed miners may therefore be left out of the discussion.

For distant-water fishing fleets, the implications of 200-mile zones were obvious. About 99 percent of the world's edible fish live within 200 miles of some coast.[53] Thus, access to fish, which had been assumed in the past, suddenly became an important problem. The governments of states with large distant-water fleets responded in several ways. First, they negotiated fisheries agreements with as many coastal states as were willing to grant access. At the same time, some cast their eyes to the extreme south because the Antarctic Treaty meant that for practical purposes there were no coastal states able to bar access to the fish. Since Article IV put all claims in abeyance for the duration of the Antarctic Treaty, claimant governments could not exercise jurisdiction in the 200-mile zone. In fact, some lawyers read the Law of the Sea Convention[54] in ways that would make even proclamation of an EEZ an "enlargement of claim" banned by the Antarctic Treaty.[55] Therefore, fish within the Antarctic Treaty area could be taken without asking another state's permission. It is not surprising that most of the leading distant-water fishing fleets had ships in the Southern Ocean by 1979.[56]

These changes in the law of the sea placed several distinct strains on the Antarctic regime. The compromise on sovereignty gave fishing fleets greater incentive to develop Antarctic operations than otherwise would have existed. Oil companies, who want a legal regime laying out jurisdictional authority very precisely, aproached a number of the consultative parties for advice or permits, forcing first those governments and then the whole group to define a policy on the question. Claimant governments were given more reason to value their claims, since they would now carry much larger components of maritime jurisdiction. This quickly translated into greater stubbornness on sovereignty-related issues. In the Antarctic case, then, the increased importance attached to natural resources both revealed a gap in the substantive coverage of regime prescriptions and renewed the underlying tension between ongoing use and the sovereignty compromise. The problem could be abated only if the participating states found a way to supplement the existing regime with provisions on resource activity that would succeed in balancing claimant and nonclaimant interests well enough that the tension could be reduced again. The whole process of amendment was actually speeded up by early consensus that there was a gap and a problem of internal tension in the regime prescriptions. Many efforts to amend international regimes bog down in disagreements about whether amendment is needed; it is usually the case that some participants desire change well before others perceive any problem.

## The Speed and Form of Amendment

Agreement on the necessity for change is only the first step in the modification process. It is then necessary to forge agreement on specific changes that will appeal to a coalition of states with the power to implement and maintain the amended regime. In the Antarctic case, such agreement was reached with respect to fisheries in four years of negotiation between 1976 and 1980. Despite discussion since 1975, full agreement on mineral and fuel resources has not been attained. This difference in the speed of negotiations stems largely from a difference in the gap to be bridged between claimant and nonclaimant interests. However, the content of the agreements made to date can be understood only by taking both individual states' interests and patterns of coalition formation into account.

### Interests

On both sets of resource issues, the strength of other shared or parallel interests served by the Antarctic Treaty system encouraged all participants to regard resource issues as revealing gaps to be filled by amending the regime rather than as being reasons for replacing or terminating it.

The stress put on the regime by the revival of differences in claimant and nonclaimant interests is reflected in the increase of political maneuvering after 1975. The Argentine and Chilean governments have both supported their ongoing symbolic assertions of sovereignty with the dispatch of volunteer military and civilian families to year-round settlements at stations in the Antarctic Peninsula area. This allows both governments to argue that they are meeting international law requirements for asserting territorial claims by effectively occupying the area. The Argentine effort began in 1977–78 with a group of families at Esperanza Station (63°24'S, 56°59'W). A child was born to a settlement family in January 1978.[57] The Chilean effort began in the 1983–84 season, with families at Marsh Station on King George Island. In this group, the first Antarctic-born baby arrived in December 1984.[58] However, neither of these is a permanent settlement, because the families involved leave after a few years to be replaced by others. The governments of both Australia and New Zealand have become more assertive of claimant rights.[59] Recently, attitudes of the New Zealand government even led to reports that it would give the Chinese a station site in the Ross Dependency in return for

Chinese recognition of the New Zealand claim. Official spokesmen denied these reports,[60] but they did state that if, as was widely assumed, China wished to stage logistics through Christchurch, it would have to make an agreement with New Zealand similar to those in force with the United States and West Germany.[61] In 1980 the Soviet government inspired fresh rounds of speculation about its intentions by establishing Russkaya Station (74°46'S, 136°51'W) in the western part of the unclaimed area, the first station on that side (the U.S. Palmer Station is at the eastern end).[62] Many Australian commentators saw this as part of a program to bolster political influence by having more stations than anyone else and having them in all parts of Antarctica.[63] Both superpowers have become more assertive, insisting that they belong to a special category of states "which prior to the entry into force of the Antarctic Treaty, had asserted a basis of claim in Antarctica."[64]

This revival of underlying differences is also shown in the fact that a number of governments have been tardy in sharing information. The Soviets remain slow in reporting results of scientific work. During negotiations of CCAMLR, they refused to share data on fishing effort and catch on grounds that both are economic data the 1977 Soviet Constitution says cannot be shared in the absence of clear international obligations.[65] The Norwegians knew about India's plans for Operations Gangotri I and II in 1981 and 1982 respectively, but did not inform fellow consultative parties before the expedition left, as was required both by consultative parties and by SCAR rules on information exchange, because India requested confidentiality.[66] France has been very slow to publish any data or conclusions from its seismic survey work.[67]

Yet despite this revival of old claimant-nonclaiment divergences, there remain wide areas of shared interest among the parties to the treaty. Though mainly interested in different resources, both superpowers support open access to the whole continent and the Southern Ocean. The Soviet Union is interested mainly in protecting access to fisheries. It possesses the largest distant-water fishing fleet in the world, and has a strong interest in keeping that fleet busy. Fish supplement the Soviet protein supply both as a direct meat substitute and as an alternative to spending hard currency to supplement the ever-erratic harvest of feed grains. Finally, Antarctic fishing appears more secure than fishing in other areas where the single coastal state involved might decide to cut off access for political reasons.[68] In the future, Soviet interest might extend to minerals and hydrocarbons. Though the Soviets are a net exporter of both today, many observers believe that they will be net importers of oil before the end of the century.[69] This could create greater Soviet interest in Antarctic resources.

The United States is not interested in Antarctic fishing. It possesses a smaller distant-water fleet, which fishes mainly for tuna, shrimp, and salmon. By far the largest part of the U.S. fleet engages in coastal fishing, and has plenty to exploit in the U.S. Exclusive Economic Zone.[70] American interest focuses more on hydrocarbons and minerals, since it is a net importer of both types of resource and can tap sophisticated technology for their exploitation even in cold climates. Yet American interest in these resources was probably higher in the years 1979–82 than it is today;[71] the fears of oil shortages and cutoffs of access to strategic resources seem to have abated for now.

The Antarctic community norms of limiting participation to those active in Antarctic research and requiring broad agreement before decisions are made retain wide support. Both superpowers have a strong interest in maintaining the Antarctic Treaty rule of limited participation. Neither is comfortable in universal-membership bodies where each member state has an equal number of votes.[72] First, neither can be sure of being able to influence the more numerous Third World states, particularly when the Group of 77 or the Nonaligned Movement act as a united group. Though these Third World groups are less united today than in the 1970s, their internal divisions have not become so great that either superpower can count on being able to split the Third World whenever it wants or needs to. Second, both the United States, with its particularly strong liberal outlook, and the Soviet Union, with its particular interpretation of Marxism-Leninism, are ideologically uncomfortable with the rest of the world. They thus find much Third World rhetoric distasteful. Yet the superpowers are not the only supporters of limited participation. Other consultative parties also value these rules because they maximize their influence within the regime.

The principles of scientific cooperation and nonmilitarization are still supported by all participants. The need for cooperation in science remains clear; not only do some countries share stations and logistics, but in an emergency all must depend on the willingness to help of whoever is nearest. Though the concerns of the 1980s differ from the concerns of the 1950s in many respects, the nonmilitarization clauses of the treaty still serve everyone's interest. This is not contradicted by the fact that a number of Latin American governments have recently become concerned with the Antarctic peninsula because of its relevance to control of the seas off Cape Horn.[73] If anything, this gives them additional reason to keep the area free of military competition. As the Falklands war indicated, none of these states has the ability to fend off a large-scale attack even by a second-rank industrial state operating at the end of long supply lines.

Structural theories of domestic decision making do not identify the states taking an early interest in amendment or identify reliably the differences of position taken in negotiations about the content of the resource agreements.

On the mineral and fuel side, structural explanations would appear to be
borne out by the fact that the states most interested in early discussion—
Australia, New Zealand, and the United States—are all market-economy
democracies. Yet other market-economy democracies were not interested until after the 1973 oil crisis. If a market economy or a democracy explains early
interest, it does so only under particular conditions that have to be specified
as well. When fisheries are considered, this structural explanation loses all
plausibility. It is not clear which countries raised the issue, but it is obvious
that all consultative parties, whatever their domestic structure, were ready to
address the issue and come to an agreement quickly.

The only structural argument borne out in the Antarctic case is the one
maintaining that weak governments are more sensitive to changes in international conditions and so are more likely to take an early interest in regime
modification. The Australian, New Zealand, and United States governments
are all weaker vis-à-vis domestic groups than are those of many other participants. However, the relation is not perfect, because a number of strong
governments involved in fishing, notably the Japanese and the Soviet, were
interested in securing additional security for fishing by the conclusion of an
international agreement that would ensure against claimant assertion of 200-
mile zones in the Southern Ocean.

Two other factors, a difference in the legal norms regulating exploitation
of different types of resources, and a difference in the character of the resources involved, explain why it proved far easier to reach agreement on
fisheries. The effect of both differences was to make disagreements about
claims less of a hindrance in drafting the CCAMLR than in drafting its
mineral and fuel resources counterpart.

The different character of international law regarding the subjects goes far
in explaining the different pace of negotiations on fishery and on mineral and
fuel resources. While most species of Southern Ocean finned fish live in
waters fairly close to shore, krill range around the whole Southern Ocean in
huge swarms that straddle not only the likely borders of claimant EEZs but
also the line 200 nautical miles from the coast. Article 63 of the 1982 Law of
the Sea Convention, a provision probably being adopted into customary law
independently of the fate of the Convention, specifies that fishing of such
species is to be regulated jointly by the various coastal states involved (because of the straddling of EEZ boundaries) and fishing states (because the
species range within and outside the EEZ) interested in the fish. Thus, claimants can agree to the provisions of CCAMLR because they are not really
giving up much more than would be the case under the general law of the sea.
Mining or exploiting hydrocarbons on land or the continental shelf is a
different matter. There, international law specifies that the state that is sover-

eign over the territory has full control over such activity, an idea reinforced by adoption of the Group of 77's doctrine of "permanent sovereignty over natural resources." Accepting joint management, then, means making a clear concession that most claimants find difficult, since it could be read as the first step in abandoning claims.[74]

These legal differences are reinforced by the nature of the resources involved. Fish, if managed correctly, are a renewable resource; taking some today does not necessarily mean leaving none for others in the future. Hydrocarbons and minerals are, so far as is known today, nonrenewable; those taken now are not available for others later. Fish can be managed without assigning exclusive rights to fish in particular areas, but mineral and fuel resources cannot. This, too, adds to the greater toughness of negotiating positions on the exploitation of mineral and fuel resources.

Features of the domestic structure of states also fail to explain the substantive positions taken in negotiations about resource exploitation. These positions depend far more on whether a state has or lacks a territorial claim, has or lacks fishing fleets engaged in Antarctic operations, and is or is not at the cutting edge of technology relevant to other resource activity than on any aspect of domestic structure. This is demonstrated in both the fishery and the mineral and fuel negotiations.

When mineral and hydrocarbon resources first received extended attention at the Eighth Consultative Meeting (Oslo, 1975), six of the twelve participating delegations supported an open-ended complete moratorium on all mining, drilling, and related activity. These six—Argentina, Australia, Chile, Japan, New Zealand, and the Soviet Union[75]—represent a bewildering variety of state structures under any of the usual theories advanced. The United States opposed a formal moratorium and urged instead that each consultative party follow a policy of restraining its own nationals informally (a policy known as "voluntary restraint") until a resource regime was written.[76] At the Ninth Consultative Meeting (London, 1977), the participants arrived at a compromise. While Australia, Chile, Poland, and the Soviet Union still favored a moratorium, the United States shifted position enough to help create a compromise under which the delegates would link abstinence from resource acitivities with progress toward a resource regime.[77] This appeared in paragraph 8 of Recommendation IX-1, reading:

> [The Consultative Parties] urge their nationals and other States to refrain from all exploration and exploitation of Antarctic mineral resources while making progress towards the timely adoption of an agreed regime concerning Antarctic mineral resource activities. They will thus endeavor to ensure that, pending the timely adoption of agreed solutions pertaining to exploration and exploitation of mineral

resources, no activity shall be conducted to explore or exploit such resources. They will keep these matters under continuing review.[78]

Polish and Soviet policy might lead to the conclusion that states with centrally planned economies or Marxist-Leninist governments are more likely than others to support nonexploitation of Antarctic resources. Yet, two considerations weaken this argument. First, these two states supported a moratorium for mineral and fuel resources but not for fisheries. At best, then, there is a biconditional argument depending both on domestic structure and on the type of resource involved. Second, an alternate explanation based on interest accounts better for the behavior. In 1975 both Poland and the Soviet Union were among the leaders in fishing technology but not in technology for the exploitation of mining or hydrocarbons. A number of Western observers have argued that Soviet positions in particular stem from a desire to slow down negotiations until they improve their technology and geological knowledge of Antarctica enough to acquire a better negotiating position.[79]

Certain propositions about the resource regime attracted almost unanimous support from the start, again confounding structural theories. All of the consultative parties were keen to avoid any possibility that a scramble for resources would lead to what one member of the Australian House of Representatives called an "all-time record brawl."[80] They thus agreed that the Antarctic Treaty and the surrounding regime had to be preserved. They also agreed that resource activities should not be allowed to endanger the Antarctic environment,[81] though they differed on just what restrictions its protection would require.

It is true that in Australia, New Zealand, and the United States left-of-center governments have shown more concern on environmental issues than right-of-center ones. Yet there is no systematic correlation between ideology and environmental policy. The right-of-center Thatcher government of the United Kingdom presented a proposal for (a) tougher rules on prior assessment of likely impacts and the continued monitoring of ongoing activity and (b) greater institutional insulation of those taking environmental decisions from the influence of states sponsoring applicants for work permits to the January 1984 minerals meeting.[82] The Soviet government has been identified as opposing the British idea.[83]

A few disagreements can be traced to differences in economic structure. States with a centrally planned economy initially proposed that the state take on the role of "operator" under the resources regime and be held directly responsible for any activity even if actual work was accomplished by private firms. Market-economy states wanted the firms doing the work to be designated as "operators," with state responsibility confined to ensuring that their own nationals obeyed regime rules.[84] A number of participants also favored creating a compulsory joint venture of all private and state-owned firms interested in working a particular area.[85] In the end, the consultative parties agreed to permit activity by individual firms as authorized by the resource-management institution and regulated by their rules.[86]

However, most of the disagreements are rooted in different material interests. At the February-March 1985 meeting at Rio, Chile proposed adopting a norm giving priority to scientific research or fishing over mineral and fuel exploitation any time those activities came into conflict. This was opposed by Japan, Norway, the United Kingdom, the United States, and West Germany.[87] This was an argument, then, among market-economy states where positions depended more on current or near-term ability to join in the various activities. Chile is now an active fishing state, but is not, like the opponents, in a position to join in early mining or drilling ventures. Reports on discussion of regulating exploration, and whether to permit deep drilling of the continental shelf as a form of exploration subject to little regulation, indicate splits among states based more on technological attainment than on ideological division or any other structural difference among governments.[88]

Many of the key arguments over resource activity rest on disagreements between claimants and nonclaimants. Claimant governments initially pushed for authorization to supervise activity within their claims as delegates of the central institutions, whereas nonclaimants insisted on joint supervision.[89] The current Beeby draft proposes a compromise under which supervision would be entrusted to regulatory committees roughly balancing claimant and non-claimant representation.[90] Though the claimant governments still regard themselves as rightfully sovereign,[91] most realize that they are unlikely to get the nonclaimant governments to endorse any form of splitting Antarctica into national areas.[92] At the same time, they expect that in return for agreeing to extend the Antarctic Treaty compromise on sovereignty into the resource field, and thus foregoing the exercise of their sovereign rights, they will be given preferential treatment in the resource regime.[93] However, nonclaimant governments oppose any obviously preferential treatment lest it compromise their position on the sovereignty question.[94]

Examination of the fisheries regime established in the Convention on the Conservation of Antarctic Marine Living Resources also casts doubt on the usefulness of structural theories for predicting policy. It did not take long to get widespread agreement that some sort of fisheries regime was needed, that good management of the resources would be impossible without greater scientific information, and that fishing rules would have to cover all waters up to the Antarctic Convergence if krill and fin-fish species were to be protected effectively.[95]

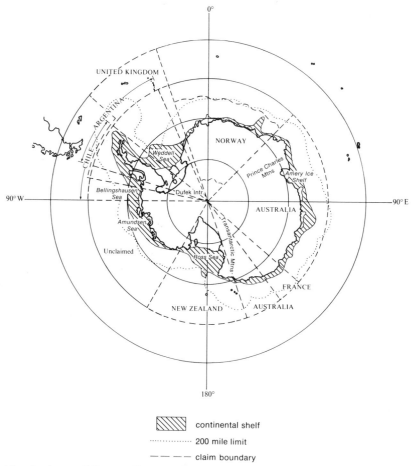

continental shelf
············· 200 mile limit
— — — — claim boundary

Map 2. Areas of Greatest Resource Interest

The long argument in 1977 over whether the fisheries regime should be based on a species-by-species or an ecosystems approach pitted distant-water fishing states against local-fishing and nonfishing states. Japan and the Soviet Union wanted the former while Argentina, Chile, and the United States insisted upon the latter.[96] In the end, the consultative parties agreed to use an ecosystem approach on the grounds that all species of marine life depended on krill directly or indirectly for food. Arguments about creating a system for on-board inspection of fishing activities pitted nonfishing against fishing states. Alignments were a bit fuzzier on rules for decision making in the commission. Poland and the Soviet Union joined Argentina and Chile in opposing proposals from Japan, the United Kingdom, and the United States to permit some form of majority voting.[97]

There also appears to be no relation between domestic structure and the interval between signing and ratifying the CCAMLR. The participants in the Canberra Conference ratified it in the following order:[98]

| | |
|---|---|
| Australia | 6 May 1981 |
| Japan | 26 May 1981 |
| USSR | 26 May 1981 |
| Chile | 22 July 1981 |
| South Africa | 23 July 1981 |
| United Kingdom | 31 August 1981 |
| United States | 18 February 1982 |
| New Zealand | 8 March 1982 |
| East Germany | 30 March 1982 |
| European Community | 21 April 1982 |
| West Germany | 23 April 1982 |
| Argentina | 28 April 1982 |
| France | 16 September 1982 |
| Norway | 6 December 1983 |

On the whole, claimants were a little slower to ratify than nonclaimants. However, the most important conclusion to be drawn is that a number of governments probably waited to see whether the most active fishing states would accept it before they did, since the fisheries regime would be ineffective without them. Early Soviet and Japanese ratification made it easier for other governments to ratify in their turn.

Differences between claimant and nonclaimant governments also sparked a number of arguments during negotiation of the fisheries regime. The negotiation session of July 1978 was marked by "endless arguments about sovereignty,"[99] perhaps encouraged by the fact that the Argentine foreign minister chaired the meeting. The same division also appeared in arguments about quotas, where claimant governments pressed for their immediate imposition while others, especially Japan, Poland, and the Soviet Union, opposed setting them until the commission had begun functioning.[100]

The few bureaucratic reorganizations and more numerous lesser adjustments occurring after 1975 reflected Antarctic or international needs. The increase in Japanese research activity led to the creation of a separate National Institute of Polar Research in 1975, which took over all the work of the National Science Museum's Polar Department. This gave Antarctic activity a boost in prestige because it was now run by an entity with the same status as a national university rather than being buried in a multipurpose entity.[101]

The most extensive reorganization of an existing Antarctic bureaucracy occurred in the United Kingdom after the 1982 Falklands war. There was widespread feeling that the decision to retire HMS *Endurance* after the 1982–83 season had helped bring on the war by encouraging Argentine underestimation of British willingness to defend the Falklands. The war led directly to decisions that Britain should demonstrate its continued interest in Antarctic affairs by maintaining the *Endurance* and increasing the British Antarctic Survey's budget. The government also decided that it needed to create clearer links between political direction from the Foreign Office and scientific activity in the field. It hoped that adding a Foreign Office representative to the National Environmental Research Council would accomplish this. The council oversees all the scientific work of bodies reporting to the Department of Education and Science, including the British Antarctic Survey.[102]

New consultative parties had to establish policy machinery. In Brazil, a private Brazilian Institute of Antarctic Studies had been formed in 1972, but governmental machinery was not organized until 1982. The government then adopted a two-body structure. The National Commission for Antarctic Affairs (CONANTAR), chaired by the minister of foreign affairs, provides political guidance, assisted by the Sea and Antarctic Office within the Foreign Ministry's division of United Nations Affairs. The coordination of university research and provision of logistical support was entrusted to the International Commission for the Resources of the Sea (CIRM), chaired by the minister of the navy.[103] The Indian government similarly entrusts organization and support of Antarctic expeditions to the Department of Ocean Development established in 1981.[104] In China the Foreign Ministry takes care of political questions. Organization and logistics support for research is coordinated through the Chinese National Committee for Antarctic Research. Until activity is further organized by the establishment of a separate polar research institute, operations are being carried out by the National Bureau of Oceanography, which reports to the National Commission for Science and Technology.[105] Uruguay, too, adopted the prevailing split between scientific and political affairs; it established the Uruguayan Antarctic Institute in 1968, and a Commission for Antarctic Studies reporting to the foreign ministry in 1970.[106] Uruguay had thus put a policy structure in place well before it acceded to the Antarctic Treaty in 1980. This meant that, unlike the other new consultative parties whose admission to that status followed closely upon their accession to the treaty, it was not still creating policy machinery when it attended its first consultative meeting.

The increased importance attached to resources and hence the shift of Antarctic affairs from restricted to widespread salience is changing the bureaucratic competition for influence over policy in all participating states. Negotiating on resource questions required the addition of relevant experts to national delegations.[107] Conclusion of the Convention on the Conservation of Antarctic Marine Living Resources brought the ministry or agency handling fisheries matters into the circle of Antarctic policy makers. Seismic surveys aimed at identifying sites meriting full exploration has also brought in new bureaucratic actors. The Australian program is run by the Bureau of Natural Resources, Geology and Geophysics in the Department of Resources and Energy.[108] French work in the Ross Sea and off the Adélie Coast is being undertaken by the Institut Français du Pétrole.[109] The large three-year Japanese effort in the Bellingshausen, Ross, and Weddell Seas is financed by the Ministry of International Trade and Industry (MITI) and executed by the Japan National Oil Corporation.[110] United States work is being carried out by the U.S. Geological Survey, which is part of the Interior Department.[111]

Thus, experience of other governments most likely mirrors that of the United States. Robert Rutford recalled in 1984:

> The [Antarctic Policy Group], through its operating arm known as the interagency Antarctic Group, suddenly flourished. Where previously other agencies had stayed away from meetings, suddenly they had reason to attend. The resource issue brought Commerce, Interior, CEO, EPA, Energy to the table, and suddenly the quiet of the Antarctic Policy Group was broken by advocates from both sides of these issues.[112]

In most governments the department responsible for science is less influential than those responsible for resource questions. These changes mean that the long hold on Antarctic policy enjoyed by a few scientists and diplomats who have been active in Antarctic affairs for years—in many cases since the International Geophysical Year—is now being challenged by a variety of newcomers. While individual members of these new agencies had Antarctic experience, on the whole those newly involved lacked the same longtime commitment to cooperation and an equally good understanding of the bargains on which the Antarctic Treaty had been based.

Difference in the relative openness of national political systems to private lobbying began to have notable policy effects as Antarctic issues acquired widespread salience in the mid-1970s. A few companies were interested in Antarctic prospects during the early 1970s, and it was their inquiries that led the Australian, New Zealand, and United States governments to raise the issue of resources at the Sixth Consultative Meeting in 1970.

The sustained discussion of resource activities inspired a great increase in environmentalist activity. Starting in 1975, the London-based International Institute for Environment and Development sponsored regular press conferences on Antarctic issues at which environmentalists and Third World diplomats or political leaders criticized the consultative parties's discussions and advocated either making Antarctica a world park or applying a common-heritage regime there. Some 120 conservation and environmentalist groups in several countries formed the Antarctic and Southern Ocean Coalition (ASOC) in 1977 to coordinate information-gathering and lobbying efforts on Antarctic issues. By the Tenth Consultative Meeting in 1979, the ASOC and individual organizations were sending people to lobby at consultative meetings and related sessions, distributing material to journalists and the public in efforts to widen knowledge about and concern for the Antarctic environment, and lobbying individual governments. Conclusion of the Law of the Sea Conference in 1982 also released for Antarctic lobbying a good deal of energy that had been going into more general oceans issues.[113]

All this activity received a boost from those governments willing to include environmentalists in the policy process. The United States delegation to the London conference on seals in 1972 included environmentalists among the "advisors."[114] Since then environmentalists have also been included in U.S. delegations to consultative meetings.[115] The Australian delegation to the Canberra Conference on living marine resources included "observers" from Friends of the Earth and the Australian Conservation Foundation.[116] The New Zealand government allowed an observer to accompany the delegation to the 1984 Tokyo minerals meeting at his own expense.[117] The Australian and United States governments also appointed members of nongovernmental groups to their delegations at the mineral and fuel resources talks.[118] The Australian, Danish, New Zealand, and United States delegations to the Thirteenth Consultative Meeting in 1985 also included representatives of nongovernmental groups.[119] Environmentalist interest helped inspire discussions in the Belgian and Dutch parliaments in early 1984.[120]

Environmentalists are numerous, active, and well organized, but their influence is not unlimited. While the governments of Australia, France, Japan, New Zealand, the United Kingdom, the United States, and West Germany are accustomed to them and permit them a political role, governments of other consultative parties are not. Though environmentalist publications often level blanket accusations against all the consultative parties, they actually realize that some—like the Chilean and the Soviet—are less approachable than others.[121] The limits of environmentalist influence can be seen not only in the number of occasions when the consultative parties have not adopted their policy preferences, but also in the fact that delegates from nongovernmental groups are not included in the informal afternoon discussions at consultative meetings and resource negotiation sessions.[122]

Further, the longer-term prospects for maintaining environmentalist influence over even the open governments is unclear. Quigg points out that "the degree of [environmentalist] influence is partly attributable to the absence of any countervailing force. In the United States especially, the public has been unaware of the Antarctic for at least two decades and there are as yet no organized interests."[123]

Industrial groups have not yet formed in comparable numbers, in part because the economics of most Antarctic ventures remain very unattractive, and in part because government policies already reflect many of their concerns. Those governments which have numerous state-owned enterprises, such as the Soviet, the Polish, the French, the British, the Chilean, or the Indian, rather naturally take the concerns of those enterprises into account. In others, interested groups and firms have access through their normal contacts or special fora, such as the Antarctic Section of the U.S. Public Advisory Group on Oceans. Indirectly, environmentalist groups show awareness of these facts when they represent immediate industrial interest as higher than it actually is, as a way to gain more public attention.[124]

In the United States, opportunities for private groups to try affecting policy are particularly large. Congressional hearings provide at least one chance a year for such groups to present their views. Industry and environmental groups are represented in the Antarctic Section of the Public Advisory Group on Oceans. Since the U.S. government believes that the Environmental Protection Act applies to its Antarctic programs, proposals for activity ranging from the normal scientific work to refurbishing stations to international negotiations on resource activities require preparation of an environmental impact statement. The procedures for this preparation always include soliciting views from the general public and interested groups.

Other democracies are less open. Australians have petitioned parliament, but there is not the same hearing process that exists in the United States. The Australian government does not apply the rules for prior assessment included in the Environmental Protection (Impact of Proposals) Act of 1974 to Antarctic activity with any consistency. New Zealand's legislation provides voluntary guidelines for assessing probable impacts, which government departments tend to ignore if the activity is unusual or involves international negotiations.[125] However, public debate in both countries has intensified in recent years, with environmentalist groups very active participants. Though the French government has slowed work and undertaken additional impact studies, it has not forsworn finishing its planned airstrip at Pointe Géologie near Dumont d'Urville Station despite the fact that the ASOC has criticized it as an environmental disaster and a violation of the Agreed Measures.[126] In West Germany there is considerable discussion between scientists active in the Antarctic and environmentalist groups,[127] but it is difficult to ascertain any effects on policy thus far.

The extent and direction in which private opinions affect policy depends on the preferences of the private groups attempting to influence the government, the preferences of the particular policy-makers who are the targets of their lobbying efforts, and the ability of the government to act independently of private pressures. The environmentalist groups provide a strong test of the influence of private groups, since their policy positions, particularly their initial preference for replacing the Antarctic Treaty system, contrast strongly with the known preferences of participating governments. Industrial groups have not challenged governments' views about the future of the regime. Australian industry supports the government's efforts to secure some form of claimant preference in the mineral-and-fuel-resources regime.[128] United States industry also desires assurance of open access on equal terms for nationals of all participating states. Yet to the extent that the scientists and diplomats constituting the national groups of "old Antarctic hands" fear that resource activity will greatly change the nature of Antarctic activity and dilute their influence on policy, they will resist industrial interests. So far, the balance of influence among domestic groups has not had major impact on any state's Antarctic policy, but the political process is far noisier now than it was in the 1960s.

## Coalitions

Earlier discussion showed that changes in the overall or issue-specific distribution of power among states, whether they participate in the Antarctic regime or not, were not relevant to the rise in issue salience inspiring proposals for amending the regime in the mid-1970s. However, the politics of coalition formation and hence the overall and issue-specific distribution of power are important in explanations of why the participating states agreed on amendment as the best form of modification and adopted a number of their positions.

The fact that the Antarctic Treaty system is a limited-participation regime would be more significant in the politics of amendment if any of the participants were attempting to buttress their position on the general question of amendment or on specific proposals before the group by recruiting additional participants from among outside states sympathetic to their views. This would increase the political tensions within the regime considerably, and perhaps even cause its demise, as other states reacted by recruiting additional allies of their own and rival groups fell to bickering over who should be allowed to participate on what conditions. The Antarctic Treaty itself attempts to limit this possibility by imposing qualifications for consultative status, while the rule that all current consultative parties must agree before any more are added provides an additional safeguard. There are, however, no conditions attached to accession as a nonconsultative party, and their recent acquisition of observer status in all regime meetings gives them influence they lacked before.

Twenty-five states have acceded to the Antarctic Treaty since 1961, and six of them have been added to the group of consultative parties.[129] However, these accessions have been caused less by efforts to win intragroup arguments than by efforts to defend the regime against attack by nonparticipating states. All participants have had to take the risk that newcomers would not agree with them in the intragroup arguments in order to shore up their joint position against outsiders. The necessity and effects of this decision will be investigated at length in chapter 8.

Within the circle of participants, adding more states, particularly more consultative parties, poses greater problems for claimants than for nonclaimants. Both general international law and the Antarctic Treaty discourage the raising of additional claims, hence the claimant group will remain at seven no matter what the total number of consultative parties may be. Under general international law, a newcomer could most plausibly make a claim only in the unclaimed area between 90° and 150°W. It would be possible to make claims in other areas by prescription if the newcomer chose an area of a claim far from the claimant's stations and was able to remain active there without inspiring protests and eviction efforts by the original claimant.[130] Obviously, though, the original claimant would be aware of such possibilities and would do what it could to prevent their occurrence. The result would be considerable tension and possibly even armed clashes. The original claimant might decide at some point to accommodate a newcomer, but this would mean abandoning any pretense to defending existing boundaries on the basis of the sector principle, and so it could simply open up a wider scramble to establish stations and make claims on grounds of more effective occupation in the local area than was accomplished by the original claimant.

The Antarctic Treaty changes the normal situation by providing that while it is in force parties may make no new claims or enlarge old ones and that no activity, including running stations, sending expeditions, or establishing "villages" of settler families, will be taken as supporting or eroding claims. This was intended to prevent, and has succeeded in preventing, the sort of unpleasant possibilities just mentioned. However, all the parties know that if the Antarctic Treaty system collapsed without being replaced by a new regime limiting or liquidating claims, at least some countries would use the fact of having operated stations over long periods to stake out and defend claims of their own. Though any of the newcomers, any of the current nonclaimants, or even a third state not party to the treaty could do this, only a few states have the capability to

Occupied Stations

1. Amundsen-Scott
2. Arctowski
3. Artigas
4. Gen. Belgrano I
5. Gen. Belgrano II
6. Gen. Belgrano III
7. Bellingshausen
8. Almirante Brown
9. Byrd
10. Casey
11. Dakshin Gangotri
12. Davis
13. Dome C
14. Druzhnaya I
15. Druzhnaya II
16. Dumont d'Urville
17. Esperanza
18. Faraday
19. Commandante Ferraz
20. Filchner
21. Fossil Bluff
22. Great Wall
23. Halley
24. Jubany
25. Leningradskaya
26. Lillie Marleen Hütte
27. McMurdo

28. Viceomodoro Marambio
29. Teniente Marsh
30. Teniente Matienzo
31. Mawson
32. Mirny
33. Mizuho
34. Molodezhnaya
35. Georg von Neumeyer
36. New Halley
37. Novolazerevskaya
38. Gen. Bernardo O'Higgins
39. Orcadas
40. Palmer
41. Capt. Arturo Prat
42. Primavera
43. Rothera
44. Russkaya
45. Gen. San Martin
46. Sanae III
47. Scott
48. Signey
49. Siple
50. Sobral
51. Soyuz
52. Syowa
53. Vanda
54. Vostok

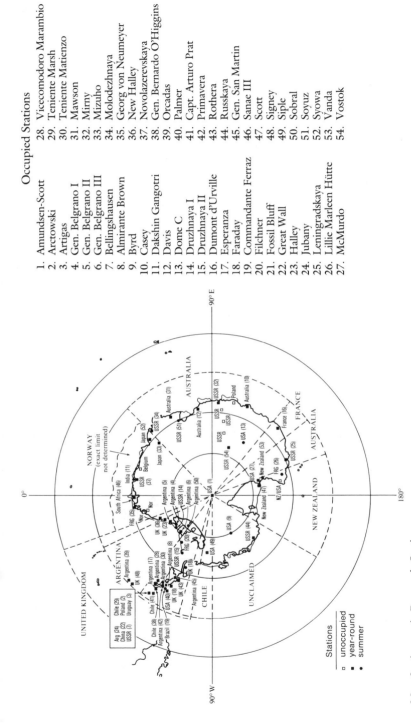

Map 3. Antarctic Research Stations

170

pose a real threat. The most obvious source of new claims would be two of the original parties to the treaty—the superpowers. Among later acceders, only Brazil, where private commentators have discussed possible territorial interests,[131] China, India, and West Germany have the resources for mounting activity of an intensity and duration necessary to challenge a previous claim. Most of the newcomers, including Brazil and China at the moment, have clustered their stations in the relatively accessible Antarctic Peninsula and South Shetland Islands where their activity is still exceeded by that of each of the original claimants—Argentina, Chile, and the United Kingdom.

This being the case, and particularly so long as the Antarctic Treaty stands, most of the additional participants clearly fall within the nonclaimant group on any issue dividing those with plausible territorial pretensions from those without any. One important effect of this balance is that it makes the claimants even more insistent on the retention of the unanimity rule in as many areas of decision making as possible.

Though the claimant-nonclaimant division is very real, the breadth of shared interests among all participating states makes it less significant than it would be otherwise. Most of these shared interests, particularly maintenance of the rules for nonmilitarization and a nuclear-weapons-free-zone, are best preserved by continuing the Antarctic Treaty. Again the outside challenge becomes relevant because both claimants and nonclaimants regard their position as better with the treaty than it is likely to be outside it.

This need to preserve the regime and the protection of unanimity it provides accounts for claimant willingness to accept additional states into the group. Many of them have acquired issue-specific power, first by undertaking fishing operations in the Southern Ocean, which could not be ignored. The rules of general international law specify that treaties are not binding on states that are not parties.[132] That being the case, the Antarctic Treaty states could establish an effective fisheries regime only by getting any state actually fishing in the Southern Ocean to participate. Though the fisheries agreement incorporated major clauses of the Antarctic Treaty, a particularly active and powerful fishing state would also have to be allowed into the Antarctic Treaty's councils if that were made a condition of its accession to the fisheries agreement. This may have been the way Poland finally attained its long-standing ambition of full participation, though it also accepted the condition of establishing a year-round station on the continent as well. Any state beginning sustained activity on the continent would also have to be accommodated. Again, general international law leans against enforcing treaties on third states, making a weak reed of the Antarctic Treaty clause authorizing individual and joint effort to ensure that "no one" violates its terms.[133] Thus the decision to permit acceding states observer status can be read not only as the result of outside pressure but as a way to attract states thinking of increasing their scientific activity, without having to give them all consultative status. That status can still be reserved for those willing to devote substantial resources to Antarctic science over a long period.

For a nonclaimant state lacking the capability to move into the ranks of territorial contenders, such as Belgium, accepting additional participants poses no problems. Rather, it gives advantages by adding a number of countries, like Finland or Papua New Guinea, with compatible interests on questions dividing claimants and nonclaimants.

While the unanimity rule helps preserve the balance between the steady number of claimants and the growing number of nonclaimant participants, it is not the only reason for that balance. Though the numbers of participants now run heavily against claimants—thirty to seven in the whole group and eleven to seven within the consultative parties—the effective distribution of power within the group remains more even. This can be seen in part by comparing the number of stations and staff maintained by each consultative party, summarized in table 4.

The Soviets have increased activity, but so have the Australians, Argentines, and Chileans. The Falklands war prevented a British slackening of effort. Though all of the new consultative parties are nonclaimants, Poland has been hard-pressed to maintain activity,[134] Uruguay's possibilities are limited by its low resources, and Brazil, China, and India will not be able to turn their general potential into very much Antarctic effort for some time, given the needs of their domestic economic programs.

This equilibrium is reinforced by the temporizing policies of both superpowers. Each regards itself as having acquired a "basis of claim" before 1961 and will not foreclose the territorialist option in case the regime does collapse. For the near future, though, each prefers the maintenance of the regime and its provisions for open access and so will not fully endorse territorialist ideas either. Given their high overall and issue-specific power, this ambiguity of position is sufficient to maintain the equilibrium.

If claimant-nonclaimant cleavages were the only divisions of opinion, the Antarctic Treaty system might be in grave trouble. However, specific issues give rise to ad hoc alignments in a way that provides considerable fluidity of coalitions within the group. On fishing, a number of issues divide distant-water-fishing states from the rest, while others—particularly questions of applying the unanimity rule—unite fishing states reluctant to see their efforts limited too much with claimants wishing to retain the appearance of having authority over 200-mile zones. On mining, Soviet interest in slowing the pace of negotiations dovetailed nicely with claimant interest in maintaining unanimity. The ecological issues divide states in confusing ways. Yet in both sets of arguments the effective balance of power has been a rough equilibrium because the Soviets and Americans have been on opposite sides of the argument.

Fluid alignments on particular issues and a wide set of shared interests mean that no one cleavage among the consultative parties becomes so prominent that it threatens to divide them into irreconcilable camps. Shared interests help create common bonds to which any member can appeal during negotiations. Fluid alignments temper the use of power by reminding even the strongest members that today's opponent will probably be tomorrow's supporter. Both help strengthen an international regime by keeping power in the background. Just as in domestic politics, coordination by consent is easier than coordination by coercion. The international system as a whole is more tolerant of coercive self-help than are domestic systems, but a high level of coercion among participants does not enhance an international regime's long-term prospects. Policy coordination based on coercion will be resented; participants viewing an international regime as basically a cover for others' coercion will not cooperate willingly and will leave if the opportunity arises.

## Summary

Both regime creation and regime modification begin when enough governments notice a rise in the salience of some matter. In regime creation the rise in salience generally comes from changes affecting the substantive issue involved. In regime modification the rise may stem from any or all of five sources: (1) changes in the international distribution of power which give greater prominence to states dissatisfied with the regime; (2) changes in domestic system which lead to changed perceptions of existing interests; (3) long-term trends encouraged by the regime's existence which expose tensions or contradictions between different elements of the regime; (4) changes affecting related issues or international regimes; or (5) changes affecting the issue or geographical area regulated by the regime. In the Antarctic case, operation of the fourth and fifth mechanisms later engaged the third. Changes in global markets for fish and fuel, supplemented by changes in the rules of international law governing exploitation of ocean resources, made Antarctic resources appear more attractive in the mid-1970s. This, in turn, inspired concern that the potential tension between resource activity and claimant acceptance of the compromise on sovereignty would become actual and would inspire efforts to terminate the Antarctic Treaty. In sum, all parties realized that changed markets, technology, and related international regimes made the 1959 decision to set resource questions aside obsolete.

A combination of individual government perceptions and the patterns of coalition among participating governments explains both the speed of negotiations and the substantive agreements made in the effort to close the gap. It was easier to reach agreement on fishing because the nature and distribution of the resource and the shape of relevant international rules raised fewer claimant-nonclaimant disagreements than was true in the case of mineral and fuel resources. In addition, the fishery negotiations were spurred on by existing activity. Substantial catches of both krill and finned fish were being taken by the time fishery negotiations started in 1976, while mining and hydrocarbon exploitation remain only future possibilities. Existing activity in itself may make reaching agreement harder or easier, depending on whether it widens or narrows the differences of interests among states, but in either case it requires that the issue be addressed more quickly.

In both sets of resource discussions, though, agreement was facilitated by the importance all governments attached to interests which they believed were best served by maintaining the Antarctic Treaty. This produced rapid agreement that amendment of the regime by extending its prescriptions to resource activity was preferable to either replacement or termination. This allowed the consultative parties to negotiate within a framework provided by the existing principles and norms.

The amendment discussions show that, in the Antarctic case at least, differences in position depended far less often on any facet of domestic structure than on the material interests of each participating government. Claimant-nonclaimant divisions were one important source of disagreements. Others stemmed from whether a particular state was engaged in or had the capability soon to engage in the resource activity under discussion. One facet of domestic structure did begin to acquire significance. The perceived increase in the immediate relevance of Antartic and Southern Ocean resource activity gave Antarctic issues a widespread salience they had lacked before. Various environmentalist and industrial groups sought to lobby for adoption of their policy preferences, while a number of government agencies, heretofore content to let the small group of scientific and diplomatic "Antarctic hands" control policy, took an active interest and sought influence. As resource negotiations continued, the relative openness of domestic political systems to private lobbying and bureaucratic competition became more important. So far it is difficult to assess the effects of this change, though it is safe to say that without the domestic openness of some participant states the private groups, particularly the environmentalists, would have even less influence in Antarctic affairs than they have.

Since the Antarctic Treaty system is a limited-participation regime, the breadth of shared interests among participating governments is very important to its long-term survival. Shared interests decrease the temptation to improve one's own position in intragroup arguments by recruiting sympathetic states from outside. Though the conditions for consultative party status and the unanimity rule limit the significance of recruiting newcomers, serious competitive recruitment could easily lead to abandonment of those rules, changing the nature of the regime substantially.

The breadth of shared or parallel interests among participating governments also explains why they have been able to agree on amending rather than replacing or terminating the regime. Termination is not regarded as desirable; it would produce massive confusion and trigger an all-out scramble for territory. The participating governments also seem to fear that negotiated replacement of the Antarctic Treaty by a territorial division would prove difficult and lead to serious conflict. At the same time, none are attracted by the other alternative regimes proposed so far. This preference is sufficiently strong to have guided the consultative parties to successful conclusion of a fisheries agreement and a considerable portion of the distance to an agreement on mineral and fuel resources. As long as the shared interests outweigh divisive questions, this preference for amendment will persist.

While the breadth of compatible interests goes far in explaining results, the role of coalitions cannot be ignored. The basic stability of the regime also rests on the pattern of coalitions among participating governments. First, coalitions on either side of the most important disagreements are relatively equal in overall and issue-specific power. Second, the coalitions that have formed on specific issues arising in the various resource negotiations are based on crosscutting rather than reinforcing cleavages. Any one participant will find itself allied with a different group of others as particular questions are addressed. Within these ad hoc coalitions, too, there is a fine balance of power. Both of these patterns assure that no one particular disagreement is likely to threaten the regime's existence.

Two more general background conditions are also buttressing the preference for amendment. First, the salience of Antarctic issues has risen, but not so much that participants deem their basic values threatened by continued adherence to the principles and norms of the current regime or by any of the changes in rules and procedures proposed so far. Were basic values (or "vital interests") viewed as threatened, participants would be more tempted to use power for overturning rather than supporting the regime. So far, participants remain confident that no problem has arisen that is too big to be solved within the Antarctic Treaty framework. The slowdown in fishing, particularly for krill, and the spreading realization that mineral and fuel exploitation is decades away at best, and perhaps never going to occur, has helped all parties accept joint management by reducing the size of probable gains from individual control of territory and maritime zones. Second, the fact that outsiders have proposed replacing the regime with one all participants dislike more than the existing regime helps moderate intragroup conflict by reminding them that others will try to step in if amendment efforts falter.

# 8

# Efforts to Replace the Antarctic Regime

$E$fforts to modify an international regime need not be limited to changing rules and procedures. They may go further and seek changes in the principles on which the regime is based. When this is true, the effort is an attempt to replace rather than amend the existing international regime. As with amendment, it is necessary to distinguish the conditions encouraging attempts to replace a regime from those favoring the success of such efforts. Attempts to replace a regime occur when a rise in the salience of the questions regulated by the regime lead some actors, governmental or nongovernmental, to conclude that the existing regime not only fails to serve their interests but cannot be made to do so in the new circumstances simply by tinkering with details. This rise in salience may, as was noted in chapter 7, stem from any of several sources.

Attempts to replace a regime involve more ambitious undertakings than attempts to amend it. Changes in principle also require changes in those norms, rules, and procedures that directly contradict or otherwise fail to express the new principle. While a particular effort to replace may also involve proposals to change other norms, rules, and procedures as well, the cascading effect of changing a principle necessarily produces a more wide-ranging set of changes than does regime amendment. Further, proposals to replace a regime will likely provoke deeper opposition than proposals to amend it. Amendment occurs within a framework of shared principles and norms with arguments centering on how best to preserve them in the changed conditions. Replacement occurs outside such a framework; proponents of change must persuade others that the very principles no longer serve (or never did serve) the common good.

As in efforts to amend, efforts to replace an international regime depend on finding a set of proposals that will serve the interests of a coalition of states possessing sufficient overall and issue-specific power to maintain the new regime. Three scenarios of coalition formation are possible. In the first, applicable equally to universal and limited-participation regimes, all or most of the coalition sustaining the original regime decides that a new one is necessary and agrees on a common set of new principles and attendant modifications. This is usually not a smooth process. There may be considerable lag between the time when a few participants view replacement as necessary and the time when all or most others agree. Additional delay is likely while the early and late acknowledgers of the need agree on a particular set of changes.

In the second scenario, the coalition sustaining the original regime splits. In a universal regime, replacement occurs when one segment of the active sustainers prevails on its own or with the aid of other states hitherto acquiescent in but not actively sustaining the regime. In a limited-participation regime, one part of the original coalition may prevail on its own or by recruiting hitherto nonparticipating states to the coalition sustaining the new regime.

In the third possible pattern, relevant only to limited-participation regimes, a coalition of outsiders with sufficient power coalesces around a new regime and impose it regardless of the desires of those states participating in the original regime. Some of the initial participants may ease this process by defecting to the coalition of outsiders, but the fact that initiative comes from outside creates a different pattern of political conflict than that which occurs when the initiative comes from inside.

The Antarctic Treaty system is a limited-participation regime faced with two challenges of the third sort. The increased salience of Antarctic resource questions has attracted to Antarctic affairs two sets of hitherto uninvolved actors: a group of Third World governments, and a coalition of private environmentalist and conservationist organizations based mainly in the Western industrial states. Each is seeking replacement of the Antarctic Treaty system, though the form and substance of the challenge each poses is different.

The two groups of challengers have sometimes cooperated with one another. In the 1970s, environmentalist groups, most notably the London-based International Institute for Environment and Development, gave developing states not parties to the Antarctic Treaty their main platform for statements on Antarctic affairs.[1] On the other side, representatives of a number of these governments showed considerable sympathy with environmentalist concerns about the impact of resource activity on the Antarctic environment. Yet the interests of the two groups are sufficiently different that these nonparticipant Third World states have stopped short of endorsing the full environmentalist program. The two groups have not, therefore, formed one coalition pursuing a common program of regime replacement.

## Salience

The same rise in the salience of Antarctic resource issues that inspired efforts to amend the regime from within drew the attention of both sets of outside challengers. Environmentalist groups began paying sustained attention to Antarctic and Southern Ocean questions in the mid-1970s. Earlier there had been sporadic discussion of such issues, stemming mainly from the local impact of scientific activity or the implications of continued whaling. However, the first appeared to be covered by rules in the Antarctic Treaty or the 1964 Agreed Measures for the Protection of Antarctic Flora and Fauna if participating states implemented them fully, and the second was an issue already being handled by the International Whaling Commission. The resource-related activities undertaken or discussed in the 1970s, however, raised far wider problems, given their greater potential impact on animal life or the Antarctic biosphere. The increased scale of scientific activity and the impact of tourism might have attracted environmentalist attention in time,[2] but resource possibilities greatly accelerated the process.

Resource possibilities also attracted the attention of nonparticipant states, though the substance of Third World proposals derives more from legal doctrines advanced in UN discussions of the "new international economic order" and at the Third UN Conference on the Law of the Sea. So far, however, the rise in salience of Antarctic resource issues has not been sufficient to overcome intra–Third World divisions based on different material interests in the Antarctic. This has been demonstrated indirectly in the UN General Assembly debates by the amount of attention and effort going into a side issue on which greater Third World agreement is possible: a separate effort to get the consultative parties to drop South Africa from their group. This began as a proposal by Antigua and Barbuda in the 1983 debates, reappeared in African proposals withdrawn in 1983 and 1984, and attained full prominence with adoption of resolutions urging the step, by deeply divided votes in 1985 and 1986.[3] It seems clear that though the Africans took over the issue later, the original discussions were a Malaysian or Antiguan maneuver to spark greater African interest in Antarctic affairs. Third World divisions also appear in policies of Asian states. Members of the Association of Southeast Asian Nations other than Malaysia remain edgy about the whole issue. None has taken a leadership role, because they are not in a mood to start an argument with the consultative parties which would disturb bilateral relations or multilateral cooperation on other issues.[4]

## The Environmentalist Challenge

Many environmentalist and conservationist groups have proposed replacing the Antarctic Treaty system with a regime based on the principle of non-exploitation of Antarctic resources, or at least of Antarctic mineral and fuel resources. Questions of how such a regime would be managed have been secondary, though many of these groups have supported some form of management by the United Nations. As nongovernmental actors, these groups can hope to influence outcomes only by attracting sufficient governmental support for their ideas. They have made efforts to lobby all governments, particularly at environment-related UN conferences,[5] but many have decided to concentrate their efforts on the Antarctic Treaty consultative parties.

### Interests

Efforts to influence government policy necessarily draw environmentalist groups into the domestic political process of each consultative party. On the whole, the prospects of success depend far more on the relative openness of each domestic system to domestic and transnational public pressures than on the political ideology, form of government, economic structure, or other characteristic of domestic systems. The environmentalists themselves realize this; while they attempt to reach representatives of governments running closed polities, they realize that this cannot be supplemented with the public information and administrative or legislative lobbying campaigns that go forward in the open ones.

Even in open polities, the success of their effort varies with the allocation of authority among branches of government and the attitudes of different segments of the leading political bodies or the bureaucracy. The division of authority between executive and legislature in the United States offers maximum opportunity, since it opens up the American policy-making process so widely. Parlimentary systems, with their unification of executive and legislative functions, offer fewer opportunities unless the executive is based on a coalition of parties and unless some member of the coalition whose defection would end the legislative majority were to make adoption of environmentalist views a condition of further participation. This has happened in some countries, most notably at the moment in West Germany, but the environmentaal concerns given such status have been questions of local impact, such as the level of lead emissions from gasoline, rather than the more distant Antarctic ones. Differences of political tradition within the open polities also influence what the environmentalists can do. For example, the dual ethnic structure of Belgium force environmentalist groups to establish coordinate Flemish and Walloon branches, imposing higher internal organization costs than would be incurred otherwise.

The increased salience of Antarctic issues has had mixed effects on environmentalist efforts to win support within governments and among the public. Those fishing or contemplating fishing in the Southern Ocean have an interest in keeping this activity alive. Though they have reason to be very sympathetic to certain environmentalist ideas, such as avoiding marine pollution and providing for adequate long-run management of fish species, they will not support an outright ban on fishing. Mining and oil companies vary considerably in their sensitivity to environmental matters, but none is going to support proposals for a permanent a priori ban on resource exploitation. Calculations of economic costs and benefits might well lead them to leave some or all Antarctic resources alone, but they prefer to have the option of exploiting later if market conditions and changes in technology make exploitation with reasonable environmental safety economically feasible.

The balance of attitudes within governments varies considerably, depending on whether conservationist- or exploitation-oriented segments of the bureaucracy can gain the most influence over Antarctic policy-making. The lack of interest in Southern Ocean fisheries among U.S. fishing fleets permits the conservationist-oriented Marine Mammals Commission more influence than it might otherwise have. This is likely to change as the more use-oriented National Oceans and Atmospheric Administration (NOAA) takes over as lead agency in U.S. implementation of the Convention on the Conservation of Antarctic Marine Living Resources (CCAMLR).[6] Though NOAA supports fairly strong management, it has never supported a ban on fishing before the survival of a particular stock appeared to be in immediate danger. Experience in whaling demonstrates that use interests clearly prevail in Japan and the Soviet Union. Both have resisted efforts to end commercial whaling even in the face of wide agreement that the survival of whale species is at stake. Both will use the CCAMLR unanimity rule to prevent the adoption of any early ban on fishing.

*Coalitions*

One set of coalition calculations accounts for environmentalist interest in a universal-participation Antarctic regime. Such regimes seldom adopt a unanimity rule. Even if they adopt a qualified majority rule for certain questions, the ability of environmentalists to influence international outcomes is greater than it would usually be in any regime operating under a unanimity rule (with the exception discussed below). This can be seen by looking at environmentalist experience with the International Whaling Commission.

That body was established by the 1946 International Convention for the Regulation of Whaling[7] and consists of one member from each state party to the Convention. Since the Convention is open for accession by any state and the commission makes decisions on whaling regulations by a three-fourths majority,[8] it is possible to form a conservationist majority out of states not directly participating in whaling. A shift toward greater restriction of whaling had begun in the early 1970s because a number of the original parties shifted policy, but it gathered far greater momentum afterwards as accessions by nonwhaling states increased commission membership from fifteen in 1978 to forty-three in 1983.[9]

Environmentalists have been interested in UN management of Antarctica because it would most likely occur under a one state–one vote universal agency. Experience with the International Whaling Commission demonstrates that in such a system there is a good possibility of linking up with states having no strong material interest in exploiting some resource and persuading them to support either outright bans or management rules so restrictive as to be the same thing. Yet there is no guarantee that this will occur. As the Third United Nations Conference on the Law of the Sea (UNCLOS III) showed, when enough states can be persuaded that they will share in substantial proceeds from resource activity, any ban is unlikely to be adopted.

Environmentalist influence on a limited-participation regime depends on the voting rules adopted. If some form of majority rule is used, then environmentalist influences operate much as they do in universal-participation regimes, except that a smaller number of governments needs to be lobbied and it will be more difficult to find nonuser acquiescers to convert into active participants in decision making. If a unanimity rule is used, environmentalist influence depends on whether resource activity precedes or follows the making of rules. The Antarctic Treaty system demonstrates the possibilities. On fishing, exploitation of the resource preceded efforts at regulation. Hence current exploiters used the unanimity rule to make sure they could continue. On the extraction of mineral and fuel resources, activity has not yet begun.

This allows the possibility of using the unanimity rule to impose severe restrictions on activity. Severe restriction would follow if participating governments adopted a rule that there would be no activity unless all agreed.[10] Adoption of such a rule would give the advantage to the most environmentally concerned rather than to the actual or potential users.

Nongovernmental actors are aware of international power realities. As long as the Antarctic Treaty parties stick together in defense of their regime, environmentalists know that they have to lobby that group if they want to influence the future of Antarctica. This realization has inspired considerable debate within both the transnational and the various national coalitions of environmentalist organizations. Some have shifted most of their efforts to lobbying the consultative parties, whereas others prefer to press for adoption of a world-park regime.[11] Which course proves most effective in the end depends on whether the Antarctic Treaty system is amended or replaced. Its fate can be assessed only by looking at the state of the concurrent governmental effort to create a "common heritage" regime in its place.

## The Governmental Challenge

The second, and more politically important, effort to replace the Antarctic Treaty system is being attempted by a number of nonparticipant Third World states. They seek to replace the current regime with one based on the principle of the "common heritage of mankind." As currently defined, this principle has two major elements, (a) reservation of a particular geographical area for joint use benefiting all states (and in particular the prevention of appropriation by the most technologically capable under a first come–first served norm), and (b) management by universal bodies operating under one state–one vote and simple or qualified majority rules. This challenge comes from governments, a class of actors able to try influencing the outcome directly. Their problem lies not in getting some other class of actors to do something, but in getting a coalition of similar actors with enough power to agree on a specific form of replacement. In the Antarctic case, however, it is obvious that this challenge can succeed only by dividing the coalition of current regime participants. Both the interests of individual states and the distribution of power among them favor retention of the Antarctic Treaty system over its replacement by a common-heritage regime.

Among the nonparticipant Third World states, the salience of Antarctic issues does not stem from possession of current material stake in Antarctic affairs. Nor would establishment of a common-heritage regime necessarily give them significant individual material interests. It is doubtful that resource

activity would ever yield enough revenue to meet the expenses of an organization like the International Seabed Authority, much less produce a surplus for
distribution to member states. Even with the greater immediate prospects
from seabed resources, experts question whether there would be much to
divide after operations of the International Seabed Authority were paid for.[12]
Admittedly, part of this gloomy situation stems from production controls
imposed at the behest of major mineral-exporting states, but they would
probably secure similar measures under any Antarctic analogue.[13] Experts are
very divided on the prospects for revenue from Antarctic resources. Some
petroleum geologists think that Antarctic hydrocarbons could be economically competitive if the price of oil rose to somewhere between $60 and $70 a
barrel. Yet others believe that the competitive point would not be reached
until prices reached $200 a barrel.[14] Both estimates may be too low; neither
seems to pay enough attention to the effects of conservation and the substitu-
tion of other energy sources at such prices. There is a similar split among
minerals experts, with the more optimistic seeing exploitation beginning just
after the turn of the century and the less optimistic believing that the economics will prove "impossible" even then.[15] The polymetallic nodules on the deep
seabed around Antarctica are of poor quality in relation to similar nodules in
other areas of the world,[16] and even the latter are attracting little interest in
the current state of the minerals market. The only real prospect of revenue
would come from the fishing for krill and Antarctic finned fish. Yet this
would probably mean having to allow the already-equipped fleets to do the
fishing and pay fees in return. This might help less developed countries
indirectly by siphoning off some of the distant-water-fleet interest in access to
their fisheries, leaving more space for the local fishermen. However, the most
promising Antarctic fishery, that for krill, still faces serious problems of developing products that consumers will accept. Even under the regime of relatively open access sponsored by the consultative parties, activity has settled at
about one-fourth of the peak catch of 530,000 metric tons in 1981–82.[17]

Additionally, there are better ways to meet Third World needs for greater
protein supply. Fishing as it is now practiced is a form of hunting: a fishing
crew attempts to capture whatever fish are in the sea. On land such methods
of getting animal protein were largely supplanted long ago by the raising of
domesticated animals. Fish farming, the raising of captive fish in controlled
conditions, has a long tradition in Asia and is spreading to fresh- and saltwa-
ter areas in other parts of the world.[18] Although there are obstacles to its
development, and it is likely to proceed further in some areas than others,
encouraging fish farming is no more economically bizarre than expanding the
Antarctic fishery.

Assuming that there is ever exploitation of Antarctic minerals and hydrocarbons, the material interests of individual Third World governments could be served in a number of ways, such as provisions for joining the minerals regime similar to those governing accession to the CCAMLR, or the adoption of revenue-sharing formulas.[19] Given the huge amount of capital that would be required for these ventures, most Third World states would be better served by putting their efforts elsewhere or, if acquisition of cold-weather skills or another source of income is important to them, by becoming members of consortia or joint ventures.

Although such measures could serve nonparticipant Third World material interests in resources, they would not serve ideological interests. Whether these continued to be important would depend in part on material satisfaction on Antarctic issues, and the relative importance attached to advancing common-heritage ideas in Antarctic as opposed to other foreign policy concerns.

The lack of clear material stake among Third World nonparticipants maximizes the Antarctic impact of ideological notions developed in other areas of international relations. In particular, it has allowed advocates of replacement to unite around the notion of "common heritage" developed in the law of the sea. While this notion has been around as an alternative to national appropriation at least since the late 1960s, there was initially no clear specification of just what such a regime would entail. The first steps toward elaboration were taken at the 1973 Algiers summit of the Nonaligned Movement. The Third World heads of state and government there assembled endorsed a program of securing changes in the international rules governing economic interactions that would provide for (1) greater Third World participation in international decision making, (2) more room for greater control by individual Third World states over economic activity within their own territory, (3) modification of those international rules identified as most regularly putting Third World states at a disadvantage in their dealings with industrial states, and (4) treating as common the resources of any area not yet under the sovereignty of an individual state. The Third UN Conference on the Law of the Sea, which met periodiocally from 1973 through 1982, provided an ideal forum for refining the "common heritage" part of the new international economic order. It dealt with areas of ocean which had so far been treated as outside national jurisdiction and brought industrial and developing states together in the first major international conference beginning substantive work after the 1973 Algiers declaration. The 1982 Law of the Sea Convention, though opposed by some states, did embody a common-heritage regime for deep-seabed mining which provides all the elements needed for an alternative to the Antarctic Treaty system.

The fact that ideology more than material interest drives the governmental replacement effort does not necessarily mean that all domestic-structure explanations of policy are irrelevant. Ideological concerns, too, are affected by the ways states are organized at home. For most Third World states, the rise in salience of Antarctic affairs is restricted only. Few Third World political systems are as open to local private and interest-group pressures as are Western ones. Even in those which are, Antarctic affairs hardly engage the attention of private groups other than the occasional environmentalist affiliate of transnational coalitions. This means that Third World governments can make decisions independent of social pressures.

Though lack of a clear material stake that would be threatened by adoption of common-heritage notions makes it easy for Third World nonparticipants to endorse their adoption in the Antarctic, there are some interesting regularities to be seen in either the domestic structure or the alliance ties of states taking a leading role in efforts to replace the Antarctic Treaty system. Right-wing dictatorships are not found among the leaders. Rather, leaders tend to come from the ranks of the centrist relatively democratic or the left-wing authoritarian Third World states. Perhaps a right-wing government is less interested in "commons" notions generally. It is certainly true that such governments have more trouble influencing other Third World governments, and this decreases their ability to be a public leader of the drive for change. The absence of Marxist-Leninist governments is best explained by the fact that both China and the Soviet Union are consultative parties in the existing regime. Were China a nonparticipant, it might be using the Antarctic issue in anti-Soviet polemics by now, bringing along its Marxist-Leninist and other leftist supporters. Were the Soviet Union a nonparticipant, its various Third World clients would be busy denouncing the Antarctic Treaty system as an imperialist device for arrogating benefits to a few.

There appears to be some correlation between open advocacy of replacement and ambitions to lead the Nonaligned. Algeria was an active proponent of replacement in the mid-1970s while serving as chairman of the Nonaligned. Libyan representatives began advancing similar views at the same time, when Libyan policy had not yet alienated so many Third World states as to make its leadership ambitions unrealistic. Sri Lanka's greatest efforts also coincided with its chairmanship of the nonaligned, though have continued since. Peru even advanced replacement proposals until the government acceded to the Antarctic Treaty in 1979. However, the correlation is not perfect. Cuba did not use the issue while chairman of the Nonaligned between 1979 and 1982, because of its ties to the Soviet Union.[20] The Malaysian interest in 1983 has been traced at least as much to the government's desire to distract attention from a domestic constitutional row as to desires for greater influence within the Nonaligned Movement.[21]

The interests of Third World states participating in the Antarctic Treaty system are different. They have important material stakes in continuing the present regime. For the territorially-minded, interest in replacement runs to division of the continent rather than to adoption of common-heritage notions. Two Third World states, Argentina and Chile, are claimants. Some individuals in at least two others, Brazil and Peru, have shown interest in territorialist ideas.[22] Several, including Argentina, Chile, South Korea, and Taiwan, have fleets in the Southern Ocean fishery. All five Third World consultative parties have put considerable effort into acquiring voting rights in the existing regime. While China and India could reasonably be expected to have significant influence even in a universal regime, the other three could not. Since a universal regime would probably opt for majority voting or for consensus defined as agreement among most members of regional or interest groups, the shift would represent a dilution even of China's and India's influence.

## Coalitions

The interplay of these various interests creates the possibilities of coalition building to further or to oppose replacing the Antarctic Treaty system. Challenges from the nonparticipants have made little progress, because the nonparticipants are divided while the participants are fairly united.

A whole range of negotiations has shown that once questions of material interest arise, it is very difficult to maintain Third World unity even on issues that can be presented in strictly North-South terms. UNCLOS III yielded many examples: landlocked and short-coast states lining up against long-coast ones, states exporting minerals from land-based sources aligning with industrial-state counterparts to ensure that the production of competing seabed minerals was limited, and all states taking positions on questions of maritime boundary delimitation strictly according to how rival formulations would affect their own situation. The fact that six Third World states are consultative parties and another five are nonconsultative parties makes the organization of a pan–Third World effort at replacement very difficult.

This has not stopped efforts to build Third World unity by appeals to the general principle of Third World solidarity. These have been made both by individual commentators[23] and by government officials. The foreign minister of Antigua and Barbuda told his eastern Caribbean colleagues in 1983: "What is sad about this connivance [in appropriating Antarctic resources] between the eastern and western industrial states is that a handful of Third World countries are active participants with them to exclude other Third World nations."[24] In a similar vein, the Ghanaian delegate told the UN

General Assembly in 1984: "We feel particularly insulted by those developing countries, parties to the Treaty in one capacity or another, which have suggested that they will protect the interests of other developing countries not parties to the Treaty or associated with it. Ghana has certainly given no such mandate to any party to the Treaty and will not do so now or in the future."[25]

These appeals have had little success. This conclusion is supported by the fact that the one Third World region formally endorsing replacement by a common-heritage regime, Africa, is the only one having no members among the parties to the Antarctic Treaty. In fact, the region's participation can be seen as negative, given the views on South Africa, one of the consultative parties, held by other African states. Among the Asian and Latin American groups there are consultative and nonconsultative parties arguing against replacement.

Divisions among Third World states have affected every stage of the UN General Assembly's discussion of Antarctic issues. In 1984, 1985, and 1986, only about sixteen Third World delegations explicitly advocated replacement. Another four or five advanced proposals for a more gradual approach that would combine new features with the existing regime, while the others remained silent.[26] Proponents of replacement have had to water down all of their proposals. The Malaysian government initially hoped that the 1983 Secretariat study would pave the way for creation of a special committee on Antarctica the following year, but lack of support forced it to backtrack. No decision was made in 1984, and a new set of studies were commissioned in 1985.[27] There was a partial breakthrough in 1986 after considerable revision of tactics. Rather than attack the Antarctic regime as a whole, the Malaysians and their supporters launched a more discriminating effort aimed at weakening current efforts to extend that regime to mineral and fuel resources. The first prong of this attack began with the 1986 Secretariat study on the application of the 1982 Law of the Sea Convention to the Southern Ocean.[28] Formulations in that study suggested that states parties to the 1982 Convention might be able to use its rules and procedures to challenge Antarctic Treaty states' right to regulate resource activity in any or all of the Southern Ocean. The second prong of this attack is more direct. It was expressed in Resolution 41/88 B, which calls upon the Antarctic Treaty states to cease their resources negotiations until those sessions can be reconstituted on a basis allowing all states, parties to the treaty or not, equal participation.[29] This proposal would leave the Antarctic Treaty in place, but impose upon the resources segment of the regime the UN rules for multilateral negotiation.

These new tactics are more subtle, but have not gotten Malaysia and its supporters any closer to their goal of replacing the Antarctic regime. Though the 1983 and 1984 resolutions were adopted by consensus, the Antarctic

Treaty states refused to accept the more ambitious 1985 and 1986 ones. The ensuing roll-call votes demonstrated a fairly high level of Third World disarray. The votes on Resolutions 40/156 A and 40/156 B, which commissioned the second set of studies, were 96 to 0 with 14 abstaining and 41 not participating, and 92 to 0 with 14 abstaining and 43 not participating, respectively. Since all 159 UN member states are represented in the General Assembly, the delegates of 8 and 10 states respectively were either absent or chose not to respond in any way.[30] The vote on Resolution 41/88 A, calling for submission of additional information to the UN by the Antarctic Treaty states, was 94 to 0 with 12 abstaining and 42 not participating. The vote on Resolution 41/88 B, calling for the moratorium on resource talks, was 96 to 0 with 12 abstaining and 44 not participating. Ten delegates were absent during the first vote, and seven during the second.[31] Allowing for the normal rate of absences, a fully united Third World coalition can muster at least 120 positive votes and bring along some 11 (the Eastern European group) to 25 others as well. Although the total of positive votes on these resolutions is some 20 more than was registered on such divisive questions as the Indonesian incorporation of Eastern Timor or the future of the Western Sahara,[32] the votes are not a good show of Third World solidarity.

At the same time, the Antarctic Treaty states also showed some disunity on the main substantive questions. China and Peru did not follow the common line of nonparticipation on any of the 1985 or 1986 resolutions. Peru voted in favor of the first 1985 study, then joined China in abstaining on the vote about the second. The two also abstained in the 1986 votes. This has led some observers to wonder about their commitment to other joint positions.[33]

In addition, nonparticipation might seem a weaker response than opposition to the resolutions. In the context, however, it was probably the strongest politically feasible stand and carried special symbolic value. The General Assembly has a long tradition of regarding studies as a preliminary step. Despite knowledge that the mere fact of doing a study, as well as the contents of any study produced, can frame subsequent discussion and action, governments find it difficult to oppose the initiation of studies when the question to be examined is clearly an international issue. In addition, nonparticipation remains an exceptional practice in the General Assembly, particularly on the scale adopted in these votes on Antarctic questions. These roll calls were the first time that the number of nonparticipants in any single roll call had exceeded four.

One tactic adopted by the challengers points either to another line of indirect attack or to an expectation that no attack will succeed very quickly. Adopting resolutions calling upon the consultative parties to expel South Africa from their group both wins black African support and tries to divide the Antarctic Treaty states on a side issue. At first glance, this tactic is having some success. In 1985 two consultative parties, China and India, and three nonconsultative parties, Cuba, Peru, and Romania, voted in favor. In 1986, six consultative parties, Argentina, Brazil, China, India, Poland, and the USSR, and five nonconsultative parties, Cuba, Czechoslovakia, East Germany, Hungary and Romania, voted in favor.[34] At this rate, the Third World challengers could expect to have a majority of the consultative parties endorsing expulsion of South Africa in 1987.

This divergence does pose problems for the consultative parties. They have tried to deal with it by allowing the equivalent of a parliamentary "free vote" on the question,[35] thus isolating those votes from others by stating in advance that the group was not attempting to maintain discipline on the issue. This does, however, put an additional burden on those members unwilling to vote for expulsion. Since the consultative parties operate under a unanimity rule, those voting in favor of the resolution can do so, confident that membership in the consultative parties will not be decided by an outside group. In effect, they get to demonstrate "pro-Third World" credentials without actually having to act. This is important; were the consultative parties to expel South Africa, they not only would be violating the prescriptions of their own regime but also would be accepting orders from an outside body. Such a step would be read as the first move toward accepting replacement of the entire Antarctic regime.

Expelling South Africa from the consultative parties would violate regime prescriptions in two ways. First, there is no provision in the Antarctic Treaty for expelling a party or barring an original party from continued Consultative status. The rules of general international law do allow other parties to bar further participation by a state violating its treaty obligations, and they might apply because of the Antarctic Treaty's silence on the matter. However, South Africa has not directly violated that Treaty. Even if it did set off a nuclear explosion on the Prince Edward Islands in September 1979, something not fully proven, this was no violation of the Antarctic Treaty, because the islands are north of the 60° line. Second, expelling South Africa would require the other consultative parties to take an action within the Antarctic regime because of non-Antarctic conflicts. Though nowhere specified in writing, separating Antarctic cooperation from non-Antarctic quarrels has been vital to the maintenance of cooperation. This was demonstrated most vividly during the Falklands war.

Some observers have speculated that the challengers might try a different line of attack, goading one or more claimants into such an outrageous assertion of the territorialist position that the nonclaimants would react by shifting their support to a common-heritage regime.[36] This ignores several realities of the political situation. First, the claimants know that they would be worse off under a common-heritage regime than they are at present. The only time they would have an incentive to attempt breaking up the Antarctic Treaty system is when they can reasonably expect that the superpowers will support some division of the continent. This would pose real risks for the claimants because they would probably have to reduce their claims, but there could still be enough benefit for them to make a redivision preferable to common heritage. Though both superpowers are keeping this option open in all their talk about "states with a basis of claim," both are also some distance from deciding that secure possession of some part is better than open access to the whole. Second, the nonclaimants have no real incentive to opt for a common-heritage regime, since they get more benefits from the current one, particularly in terms of weight in decision making. Third, neither the superpowers nor most of the second-rank states within the Antarctic Treaty group are particularly enthusiastic about common-heritage ideas.[37] The United States has expressed its objections most forcefully, but Soviet and Western European readiness to consider alternatives on seabed-mining issues suggests that those governments are not fully committed to the sort of common-heritage regime adopted in the 1982 Law of the Sea Convention.[38] Even Indian and Brazilian officials have advanced arguments that the "common heritage" notion is not relevant to Antarctica.[39]

Group and individual statements by Antarctic Treaty participants indicate the strength of their unity on the main Antarctic issues. A Soviet participant at the January 1985 Beardmore Glacier workshop on Antarctic affairs, which brought together diplomats, scientists, and others from participating and non-participating states, is said to have warned the Malaysians at one session that attacks on the Antarctic Treaty were "objectively reactionary,"[40] one of the worst condemnations in the Soviet vocabulary. The Soviet delegate in the General Assembly ended his 1985 speech by calling for removal of Antarctic questions from the agenda.[41] In light of the recent decisions allowing wider participation by the nonconsultative parties, the British delegate had hard words for advocates of replacement: "If those criticising the system will not pay the price to go through the open door, whether it be political, economic, or both, my Government can only draw one conclusion: they are not sufficiently interested in the Antarctic, which is, after all, what the Antarctic Treaty system is about, and account of their views should be taken accordingly.[42] The group as a whole, no doubt reacting in part to other states' assertions that discussion in the General Assembly implies accepting the legitimacy of long-term UN involvement in Antarctic affairs,[43] first warned that unless the Assembly returns to its 1983 and 1984 agreement to adopt resolutions only by consensus, it would reconsider its hitherto cooperative attitude,[44] and then stopped sending requested information to the UN Secretariat.

Just as Third World nonparticipants can try dividing the coalition of Antarctic Treaty parties, the latter can adopt policies that accentuate outsiders' differences. They could accommodate additional material concerns by adopting a form of revenue sharing in the fuels and minerals regime.[45] Third World states that have expressed interest in establishment of an international research station[46] could be accommodated in the traditional way by being invited to send scientists to participate in various national programs. This would be a widening of existing practice, not a new departure for the group. Continuing to ensure that those nonconsultative parties caring to comment on particular issues have a chance to do so may not end arguments that the Antarctic Treaty's two-tier membership is wrong because unequal, but it will mean that there is no practical difference between being a nonconsultative party and one of the small members of a universal-participation regime.

The sparse evidence available indicates that the consultative parties are ahead in the competition to build broader coalitions. A number of states indicated their readiness to support the Antarctic Treaty system by joining. Since 1983 four Third World states, Brazil, China, India, and Uruguay, have acquired consultative status. An additional seven states, Cuba, Finland, Greece, Hungary, North Korea, South Korea, and Sweden, have also become parties.[47]

Of course, nonparticipants can always hope that some are joining the regime in order to change it from the inside, as happened in the International Whaling Commission. However, the willingness of states to mount the research efforts necessary for consultative status makes this appear less likely. These research efforts represent, among other things, sunk costs in acquiring influence within the existing regime. To the extent that states follow rational calculations in relating means to ends in their foreign policy, the existence of these sunk costs encourages protecting the investment from the dissipation that would occur in shifting to another form of decision making where it is unlikely to be taken into account in the allocation of influence.

Since power realities so heavily favor the Antarctic Treaty participants, the ability of nonparticipants to raise the issue and keep it alive may seem surprising. This can be explained very quickly by the nature of the UN General Assembly as a global institution. The Assembly has a long tradition of placing on the agenda any plausibly international question any member wishes to discuss, and to remove few things from the agenda later. It therefore gives even very weak coalitions of states a platform for launching proposals and continuing discussion. Without the Assembly the Third World challengers would have trouble finding an intergovernmental forum for their campaign. Attempts to raise Antarctic questions at UNCLOS III were defeated; the already heavy agenda of that conference, together with the fact that Antarctic affairs include activity on land as well as at sea, helped Antarctic Treaty participants defeat the proposal. Attempts to raise Antarctic questions in the UN's Economic and Social Council, Environmental Program, and Food and Agriculture Organization were also turned back.[48]

The Assembly's decision-making rules also make it hard for a group of thirty-seven states to control the substance of discussion. Antarctic Treaty participants did win two concessions in 1983: reference of the issue to the First (Disarmament) rather than the Special Political Committee, and agreement to adopt decisions by consensus. The former meant accepting a more widely political discussion than many of the Treaty participants would have liked,[49] but a less polemical one than some of the Third World nonparticipants might have liked, because of differences in the style of the two committees. The latter agreement meant gaining some control over the content of decisions because resolutions would have to be the product of agreement between the Antarctic Treaty parties and the other members.

The General Assembly tradition of leaving items in the committee where they were originally discussed encourages leaving debate in the First Committee. However, the fact that members can always revert to the Charter rules providing for the adoption of most decisions by a simple majority makes control of decisions more tenuous, as was shown in 1985. Yet this does not mean that the Antarctic Treaty parties have lost control of the outcome. General Assembly decisions are recommendations, which can be implemented only when enough member states with enough power cooperate. The Third World nonparticipants can outvote the Antarctic Treaty parties within the Assembly, but not outdo them outside. They recognized this even in the 1985 and 1986 decisions by not reverting to the idea of creating a special UN committee on Antarctica.[50] Even if, therefore, the General Assembly were to pass a resolution declaring Antarctica "the common heritage of mankind" and recommending a draft treaty for a new Antarctic regime to UN member states, the effects of power would not be diluted. Without powerful states supporting them, that declaration and that draft treaty would remain nothing but noise as far as the real management of Antarctic affairs is concerned.

## Summary

The same rise in salience that inspired efforts to amend the Antarctic Treaty system from within also inspired efforts to replace it from without. Whether a particular state supports the existing regime or seeks its replacement depends heavily on how it perceives its interests. Antarctic Treaty states have clear interests in defending the regime from replacement even as they amend it.

Though the overall salience of Antarctic affairs has risen, it remains true that only a relatively few states have material interests at stake. For most states, the importance of Antarctic affairs lies in the opportunity they afford for advancing the ideological program of universal participation in decisions and common control over resources already embodied in draft treaties on the law of the sea and outer space.

The Antarctic case shows both the extent and the limits ideological concerns as bases for foreign policy. On matters like Antarctic affairs where the whole future of a state's basic ideological tenets is not at stake, ideology weighs less heavily in policy decisions than any identifiable material interests. While there are ideological issues on which it is possible to generate intense commitment, the low absolute and relative salience of Antarctic affairs to most states means that the question of amending or replacing the Antarctic Treaty is not one of them. Rather, the states having identifiable material interests served by retaining the regime have the advantage in generating commitment.

The attitudes of both participant and nonparticipant states demonstrate that governments' definitions of interest are influenced far more by the opportunities a state possesses or lacks than by any aspect of its domestic structure. In the nongovernmental effort to replace the Antarctic Treaty system by a world-park regime, relative openness of domestic systems did indicate where transnational proponents put their greatest effort, but the fact that other social groups could also identify Antarctic interests of their own meant that even in the most open systems the environmentalist supporters of world-park notions could not count on success at influencing the government. In the governmental effort even relative openness has had no significance, because Antarctic affairs have only restricted salience in most countries. Even if more Third World states boasted modern-style interest groups and open political systems, there would probably be little public attention to Antarctic affairs, because of both their lack of relevance to those groups and the pressing nature of other concerns, such as local disputes or making the transition from nonindustrial to industrial society.

The intergovernmental campaign also demonstrates both the extent and the limits of international organizations and changed conceptions of what is proper as levers for bringing change. The General Assembly debates show that even a very weak coalition can succeed in getting regime replacement onto the international agenda and forcing other governments to pay attention to their proposals. Yet those same debates also show that it is a long way from getting an idea discussed to seeing it become the basis of a functioning international regime. Only ideas adopted by a coalition of states with sufficient power to implement them and maintain them against rival coalitions supporting different ideas will form the basis of an effective regime. Hence, the pace and extent of change in the Antarctic Treaty system will be determined by the consultative and nonconsultative parties, in particular the former, as long as they remain united. Thus, a limited-paticipation international regime can survive even in the postcolonial world if it is supported by a sufficiently powerful coalition of states able to remain united in the face of outside challenge.

# 9

# Broader Implications of the Antarctic Experience

The history of the Antarctic Treaty system provides rich material for studying the evolution of international regimes. An unsuccessful attempt at regime creation in 1948–49 was followed ten years later by the Antarctic Treaty. The international regime outlined in that treaty was established by 1963 and maintained with only minor adjustments through the early 1970s. In the mid-1970s, new developments in Antarctic affairs required modifying the regime. Participating governments sought to adjust the regime to the new situation through amendment of its rules and procedures while a number of private groups and a few nonparticipating governments made separate proposals that the Antarctic Treaty system be replaced by a new regime based on different principles. Neither participants nor challengers have proposed termination of the regime. Termination would necessarily let loose a scramble for Antarctic territory according to the normal rules for attributing sovereignty over land territory. Such a division would be further from the preferences of the challengers than the current regime; though some participants might prefer it, they fear that dropping the treaty would lead to extremely costly conflicts, and so at least for now they prefer retaining the regime.

With two attempts at regime creation and the virtually simultaneous efforts to amend and to replace the regime, the Antarctic case provides particularly clear illustration of the dynamics that govern the timing and the success or failure of efforts to create, establish, maintain, and modify an international regime. This history shows more clearly than many that the dynamics governing timing are distinct from those governing success, allowing an examination of why some attempts to create or modify international regimes fail despite the amount of attention devoted to them by international organizations, governments, and private actors.

## The Timing of Regime Phases

The beginning and duration of the various phases of an international regime's existence are governed by changes in the salience of the issue or the geographical area to be regulated by the regime. Attempts to create international regimes follow a more than momentary rise in salience that inspires decisions by one or more governments, or occasionally by an international organization, that there is need for international regulations on the matter. Attempts to establish international regimes follow after successful conclusion of written or tacit agreements creating the regime. If establishment is successful, issue salience should decline and remain low for most of the participating (and for limited-participation regimes, nonparticipating) governments. Attempts to modify international regimes follow a more than momentary renewed rise in the salience of the issue. Such a rise in salience is a clear sign that one or more participants no longer finds the regime prescriptions satisfactory. If modification results in successful amendment or replacement of the regime, issue salience again drops as the modified regime begins its career through the phases. If modification is unsuccessful or leads to termination, issue salience may well remain high and international contention continue.

The question, then, is how salience changes. The Antarctic case highlights the importance of two distinctions in approaching the problem of changing salience. First, issues have both intrinsic and relative salience. Second, issues may have either restricted or widespread salience depending on the number of governmental and nongovernmental actors paying attention to the issue. Both distinctions affect the political behavior inspired by rises and falls in issue salience.

Intrinsic salience refers to the importance of the issue considered in isolation. In the Antarctic case, this has risen three times since 1945: (1) in the immediate postwar period as governments reflected upon wartime experience or began sponsoring a higher level of Antarctic exploration and research than had prevailed in the interwar period, (2) in the mid-1950s with preparations for and the beginning of year-round research during the International Geo-physical Year, and (3) in the mid-1970s as commercial-scale fishing of krill and finned fish in the Southern Ocean began and market changes encouraged greater speculation about the possibilities of exploiting Antarctic mineral and hydrocarbon resources. Each of these caught the attention of officials, scien-tists, and others and inspired thoughts that there was a common problem requiring a new or modified common set of rules for Antarctic affairs.

Relative salience refers to an issue's place in the set of issues competing for governmental attention at any moment. Here it is important to remember that both domestic and international issues vie for attention. Though the two sets are often interconnected, virtually all governments are organized to deal with each set separately. Particular agencies or ministries are thus dedicated either to domestic or to foreign policy. The top political leadership deals with both sorts of issues. Thus at lower levels an international issue generally vies with other international issues for attention, whereas at the highest levels an international issue competes with both international and domestic issues for attention.

Some issues have such high intrinsic salience that they automatically go to the top of the agenda. Invasion by a neighboring state or rebellion within the country demands immediate attention and pushes all other issues aside. Other issues, such as a balance-of-payments deficit or a domestic recession, may rise high on one agenda but not dominate both unless it becomes severe enough to affect other issues on the same half of the agenda or interconnected issues on the other half. Joanne Gowa has argued that the Nixon administration paid sustained attention to international monetary problems and took immediately effective steps only when the deficit became so severe as to hinder pursuit of other foreign policy objectives and threaten the domestic economy.[1]

When an issue does not have such high intrinsic salience that it immedi-ately acquires high relative salience as well, the amount of attention it gets depends on what else is on the agenda at the same time. Here, too, govern-mental organization permits the existence of several simultaneous hierarchies of issues and activity on more than one issue at a time. Most issues with low intrinsic salience can be handled by the particular agency in charge according to previously established guidelines for decision embodied in statute or ad-ministrative orders. Then the amount of attention paid to any one issue depends on what else is on the agency agenda. Yet even an issue with low intrinsic salience may get on the mixed agenda of the top leadership if there is disagreement between agencies responsible for different aspects of the matter or if dealing with the matter requires taking a major legal step such as conclud-ing a treaty or adopting a statute. At this point, then, the issue with low intrinsic salience must compete with everything else on the dual agenda. Since most contemporary efforts to create or amend international regimes require adoption or modification of a treaty,[2] regime creation and modification reaches the mixed agenda at some point. Once there, it may or may not receive the sustained attention needed for maximum chances of success.

The patterns produced by the interplay of intrinsic and relative salience are demonstrated vividly in the Antarctic case. The intrinsic salience of Antarctic issues was greater in 1958 than in 1948, mainly because involvement by both superpowers had changed the nature of the Antarctic game from an intra-allied tension to a potential East-West confrontation. However, most of the rise in relative salience stemmed from the fact that the mid to late 1950s were a fairly quiet time in international politics. The cold war had abated considerably, and the tough issues posed by decolonization and North-South disagreements had not yet emerged. The great postwar burst of regime creation and modification in such fields as finance, trade, transportation, communications, and security had been completed, and most of those regimes were in their maintenance phase. There was, in other words, a much less crowded agenda. In that situation, a modest rise in intrinsic salience translated into a great rise in relative salience. Similarly, the governmental challenge to the Antarctic Treaty system did not take off as soon as the intrinsic salience of Antarctic resource issues rose. Rather, it had to wait until the agendas of the Third World challengers had been cleared somewhat by the obvious failure to secure acceptance of many trade and finance provisions of the "new international economic order" and by the completion of the effort to replace much of the oceans regime at the Third UN Conference on the Law of the Sea.

Salience may also be restricted or widespread. Restricted salience exists when the top leadership or the relevant agency can handle the issue without much pressure from private groups or other government agencies seeking to influence policy. There is no systematic relation between the intrinsic or relative salience of an issue and the restricted or widespread nature of that salience. At least in the first shocks, the top leadership has wide freedom to deal with an invasion; all social groups and bureaucratic agencies tend to "rally 'round the flag" at such times. Issues of similar intrinsic salience may attract very different amounts of private and intragovernmental pressure. In most industrial countries, for instance, international monetary issues have been viewed as arcana best left to the central bank, whereas international trade issues attract attention from a far greater number of private groups and competing agencies.[3]

From this perspective the Antarctic case is somewhat unusual, though not unique. Until the mid-1970s, Antarctic issues had restricted salience. There was no sustained public or interest-group concern. Even government agencies that were given or could claim some competence over some aspect of

Antarctic affairs usually failed to bother. Antarctic policy was generally left to a few people in the foreign ministry and the administrators of the scientific research programs. This was probably less true in Argentina and Chile because the Antarctic claims had strong symbolic value and raised serious foreign policy issues, since they overlapped other countries' claims. In essence, then, one-sixth of the world's land surface has been governed by a few diplomats and part of the staff of normally uninfluential national science agencies. This situation is now beginning to change. Environmentalists and industry groups are now taking an interest, and many of the other agencies that saw no reason to bother with Antarctic affairs are now maneuvering for influence over regulating the current and prospective resource activity. Thus, the intrinsic salience of Antarctic issues has not increased much since 1975, but the pattern of politics is changing considerably because of the shift from a restricted to a more widespread salience.

The rises in salience that inspire efforts to create or modify international regimes stem from many sources. An issue's intrinsic salience may rise because (1) the international distribution of power shifts to favor governments regarding the issue as meriting attention over others that do not; (2) changes in the domestic political or economic structure of one or more states lead to changes in the way those states perceive their interests which then make the issue seem more important; (3) the operation of an international regime produces conditions that expose tensions or contradictions in its prescriptions; (4) changes in related issues or international regimes make continuing the same lines of conduct in an issue area more difficult, and (5) changes in environmental conditions, such as developments in technology or acceptance of new ideas, create a new issue or transform an old one.

The existence of a plethora of explanations for changes in international regimes stems in part from the existence of these multiple and independent pathways to greater issue salience. Structuralists regard one or both of the first two as the most important. Process theorists focus more on any or all of the last three. Economic-determinist theories use a combination in which change in the economy leads to changes in domestic structure or the international distribution of power that in turn lead governments to reformulate goals. No one pathway provides an all-inclusive explanation of rise in issue salience. Each issue has its own evolution involving any or, more often, several of the five.

Particularly since the great acceleration of technological change in the mid-nineteenth century, regime creation is often inspired by environmental changes creating new issues. There was no need for an international civil aviation or an international telecommunications regime until the inventions permitting long-distance controlled flight and extremely rapid long-distance communication were brought into wide cross-national border use.

With previously existing issues, more of the five patterns can apply. While the third relates only to regime modification, any of the others can apply to regime creation. The slow but steady development of international trade in Europe during the twelfth through the fifteenth century led the private actors involved to develop the law merchant. Once the volume grew great enough, governments had an interest in providing institutional backing for these practices through provision of courts for dispute settlement or of enforcement through public agencies.[4] Here, then, a slow environmental change led to the accumulation of a new international regime. The nineteenth-century international agreements banning the slave trade were the product of changes in attitude, aided by a shift in the distribution of power. The journey to agreement began with lobbying by private groups rejecting the long-established idea that one human could under certain conditions treat another as private property to be bought and sold at will. These groups persuaded a number of powerful governments, particularly the British, to couple abolition of slavery at home with efforts to end the international slave trade as a way to hasten the end of slavery abroad. The British, their power greater after 1815, became the main motor of this international effort. The concept of the contiguous zone in the law of the sea received great impetus from United States efforts to prohibit production and consumption of alcoholic beverages in the 1920s. The United States government attached enough importance to stopping maritime smuggling that it was willing to qualify somewhat its normally strong views on freedom of the seas.[5]

The Antarctic case is one where changes in technology increased the salience of previously existing issues. In the 1940s and 1950s, the fact that technology allowed greater activity on the continent worsened two previously existing disagreements among governments. The first was between three of the seven governments accepting the legitimacy of claiming sovereignty over Antarctic territory, and involved where they should draw their respective boundary lines. The second was between the seven claimants, on one side, and other governments interested in Antarctica, on the other, about whether it was legitimate to assert sovereignty in Antarctica at all. This began as an argument between the claimants and the United States, but expanded in the 1950s to become an argument between the claimants, on one side, and the United States, the Soviet Union, and three other states, on the other. Intensification of Antarctic activity inspired several efforts to resolve one or more of these disputes; the British proposed various ways of resolving the boundary disputes, including resort to the International Court of Justice, while the United States sought ways to deal with the wider sovereignty question.

Attempts to modify international regimes are more frequent than attempts to create them; after all, any one regime can be modified several times. They are likely to stem from a wider range of the causes of increased salience, since existing regimes are vulnerable to structural changes in the international system or to domestic changes leading to new policy in individual states.

International structuralists, whether of the general or the hegemonic-stability variety, view changes in the international distribution of power as the most important cause of regime modification. In their view, regimes reflect the distribution of power prevailing at the time of their creation. Once that distribution shifts significantly, demands for modification will arise. The hegemonic-stability theory thus explains the erosion of the interwar effort to retain a liberal international trade regime as the result of declining British power. However, even the earliest exponent of this view, Charles Kindleberger,[6] noted that the refusal of the United States to exert leadership commensurate with its great economic power also contributed heavily to this result. This brings him closer to the modified structuralist views of Robert O. Keohane, who argues that a decline in a hegemon's power need not trigger efforts to modify international regimes (whether or not a hegemon is essential to regime creation) if other states have enough interest in it and enough power to maintain it anyway.[7]

The general wars of the twentieth century have been so productive of new or modified international regimes for two reasons. First, they disrupted previous patterns of interaction, forcing a rise in the salience of the underlying issues great enough to require governmental attention. In this respect, then, the wars represented one type of cataclysmic exogenous change that forces governments to pay attention and make decisions. Second, they have altered the international distribution of power. Though the world remained multipolar after World War I, the identities of the leading powers changed long enough to affect international regimes. World War II changed the distribution of power more thoroughly. The previous multipolar world was replaced by a bipolar one in politico-military affairs and a hegemonic one in economic affairs. Structuralists would expect plenty of regime modification in that circumstance, and it did occur.

Yet there is also an alternative explanation for efforts to replace the liberal trade regime with a far less open one in the 1930s, resting on changes in domestic structure of key states. This has received much attention from historians of the interwar period, but less from students of international regimes. In this view, the distribution of power remained multipolar, as it had been in the nineteenth century, but enough great powers changed policy in the wake of domestic changes to start (and later succeed in) changing the trade regime. The Bolshevik takeover in Russia and the rise to power of economic nationalists in Mexico, Italy, Turkey, and other countries meant the emergence of political leaders rejecting some or all of the tenets of economic liberalism. The balance tipped further against economic liberalism after the Great Depression as new governments emerged in Germany and Japan. Both German economic domination of Eastern Europe and the Japanese "Greater East Asia Co-prosperity Sphere" were alternative programs for regional economies organized by the strongest state. The main differences between them and Stalin's program of "socialism in one country" for the USSR lay in less use of central state planning and in more need to cope with other independent political units. However, all three governments' policies were inward-oriented reactions against being tied to global markets.

International regimes often contribute to their own modification or termination by encouraging developments that expose tensions among regime prescriptions or alter conditions and actor behavior enough to undermine the assumptions on which they were originally accepted. As Robert Triffin noted in 1959, it proved impossible in the long run to satisfy international needs for liquidity by relying solely on the willingness of the United States to trade dollars for gold at $35 an ounce. Once the world economy recovered from the war and grew beyond its predepression size, no one country was able to provide the liquidity needed for its smooth operation.[8] Charles Lipson has argued that the success of regimes for protection of foreign investment encouraged more firms to make direct investments abroad, decreasing the ability of companies to protect themselves against uncompensated or poorly compensated expropriations by raising their number beyond that able to coordinate responses effectively.[9]

An international regime may itself trigger modification efforts by including some internal deadline, such as provision for review of the constituent treaty. The French government used the fact that the North Atlantic Treaty had a twenty-year term and came up for renewal in 1969 to amend the regime significantly by pulling out of the joint arrangements making up the North Atlantic Treaty Organization. The 1982 Law of the Sea Convention provides for review of the "parallel system" under which the International Seabed Authority's commercial arm (the Enterprise) and state-owned or private licensees each mine half the deep seabed fifteen years after the first commercial exploitation of deep-seabed minerals begins. The Antarctic Treaty provides such a possibility in Article XII (2), which permits any consultative party to request a review conference thirty years after the treaty enters into force (1991).

There are many cases of change in related issues leading to a new rise in

salience. Increasing oil prices in 1973–80 worsened a recession in the industrial states and decreased the total flow of aid at the same time they increased
the need of developing countries for funds to pay import bills. Many developing countries sought those and other funds in the private market. They found
banks eager to lend, in part because the OPEC preference for holding funds
in banks rather than in bonds or property meant that the banks had held large
deposits on which they had to pay interest and so needed to make loans. One
important result has been the current international debt crisis.[10]

Finally, changes directly affecting the issue can inspire regime modification. The great improvement in fishing technology after 1945 led to overfishing of more areas and contributed to the acceptance of 200-mile economic
zones in the ocean because efforts to manage through joint regulatory commissions proved ineffective. Development of technology for communications relays and direct broadcasting from satellites led to an attack on the
still-emergent principle that outer space should be treated as a common
realm open to all. Equatorial developing states eager to prevent industrial-
state monopolization of the geosynchronous orbital slots most useful for
satellite communications attempted, among other things, to declare sovereignty over the portion of the geosynchronous orbit directly above their
territories. This effort did not succeed, but it did open an international
discussion that led the International Telecommunications Union's World
Administrative Radio Conferences to qualify to some extent its old rule of
first come, first served.[11]

The Antarctic case is a mixed one, with the mid-1970s rise in issue salience
depending partly on changes within the issue and partly on changes in related
issues. The basic trigger was the increased value attached to Antarctic resources. This increase stemmed partly from changes in the international oil
market that made Antarctic hydrocarbon possibilities more economically attractive than they had ever been, and partly from changes in the law of the sea
that made the Southern Ocean one of the few places distant-water fleets could
operate without limitations imposed by a coastal state. The greater perceived
value of Antarctic resources had two effects. For Antarctic Treaty states it
exposed the tension between economically lucrative uses of Antarctica and
the compromise on sovereignty, inspiring efforts to preserve the latter by
extending regime prescriptions to the former. For nonparticipants, it directed
attention to another area where the lack of definitive national territorial
claims meant that common-heritage principles could be applied. Some of
them then proposed that the existing regime be replaced with one using
universal majoritarian institutions that would assure Third World control of
decision making.

The preceding discussion leaves an oversimplified impression in two respects. First, rises in salience are perceived unevenly. Some governments notice and react to them earlier than others. Second, perceptions of salience need not lead to the creation of an international regime.

The efforts to create an Antarctic regime in 1948 and 1959 demonstrate how uneven perceptions of salience can be. In 1948 the Argentine, British, and Chilean governments saw Antarctic issues as highly salient; their overlapping territorial claims were inspiring armed incidents that could lead to war. Certain United States officials also viewed those issues as salient, mainly out of concern about the negative effects territorial conflicts might have on alliance ties. Other claimant governments were more detached, at least until discussions began inspiring Soviet interest. In 1958 perceptions of salience were more evenly shared among the twelve participants in the Washington Conference. The International Geophysical Year and the prospect of continued year-round Antarctic research forced all of them to formulate positions on the question of what to do when the IGY ended in December 1958.

In most cases international regimes are not created or modified spontaneously; the processes are begun by particular governments. Since the power or identity of the early promoters may affect both the prospects of success and the content of the regime, identifying the governments most likely to act as sponsor has practical significance. There are several hypotheses about which governments are most likely to take on this sponsoring role. One is that the sponsors are most likely to be governments caught in a foreign policy dilemma that would be solved or postponed by creation or modification of an international regime. Both the 1948 and the 1959 Antarctic negotiations bear out this approach. The British government was actively searching for some way to resolve its territorial conflict with Argentina and Chile. It initially hoped to do this by submitting the matter to the International Court of Justice as an ordinary territorial dispute. This proved unsuccessful, however, because ICJ rules allowed the Latin Americans to frustrate British intentions by refusing to accept the court's jurisdiction in the matter. For their part, the Chileans were interested in exploring ways to set the territorial dispute aside if that would weaken the legal significance of the greater amount of Argentine and British activity in the disputed areas. United States interest was also high because a regime would solve both external and internal dilemmas. Internally, it would put off a serious debate about whether the government should assert a territorial claim of its own. Externally, it would allow avoidance of the need to side with either the British or the Latin Americans in their territorial conflicts. The United States initiative of 1958 was prompted by the same concerns, supplemented by a desire to deal with the fact of Soviet entry without triggering another round of serious superpower conflict.

This is not a full explanation, however. On this view, the Argentine government ought also to have been actively promoting a regime. Every bit of its Antarctic claim was contested by either Britain or Chile. Further, the notion that Britain and Chile might team up against Argentina could not be dismissed out of hand. However, Argentina confined its activity to preventing such a coalition through bilateral approaches to Chile and efforts to have other members of the Organization of American States agree that a war with Britain over Antarctic claims would be cause for hemispheric cooperation under the Rio Pact. These considerations made it easier for Argentina to participate in discussions of an international regime, but its emotional attachment to the territorial claim seems to have been deep enough to prevent its taking any initiatives that would reduce the likelihood of dividing Antarctica.

An alternate hypothesis seeking to account for initiative posits that governments which are relatively weak vis-à-vis domestic social coalitions will seek international regimes. Regime prescriptions help such governments control those coalitions by providing international obligations that can be cited against the social pressures to adopt a policy the government wants to avoid. On first glance, the high Chilean and United States interest in promoting an international regime would appear to confirm this hypothesis. On closer inspection, however, the relation disappears. The restricted salience of Antarctic issues in both countries meant that there were no large social groups or coalitions pressing the government to adopt particular policies. There was nothing comparable to the industrial and labor interest in questions of international trade. Internal disunity in the United States case, and the clear inability to deal with a direct external challenge from a more powerful state in the Chilean case, provide better explanations than weakness vis-à-vis domestic social groups.

Perceptions of increased salience are not necessarily perceptions that an international regime is the best solution. In some cases, a problem can be handled on a bilateral basis. Even when multilateral action appears appropriate, an international regime may not be the preferred form. Governments may decide that the problem can be handled through a one-time effort, after which they can revert to their older patterns of behavior. Thus, for instance, several governments decided between 1939 and 1941 that the Axis threat could only be handled through multilateral response, but the response was the forging of a military alliance to smash the Axis and occupy Germany, Italy, and Japan. International regimes are most likely to be chosen when governments perceive a problem as requiring long-term policy coordination to deal with ongoing transactions.

Assuming that governments decide to create, amend, or replace an international regime, issue salience remains high during the establishment phase. Establishment requires attention, since it involves making sure a viable coalition actually ratifies the agreements embodying the original or modified regime and that those agreements prove workable. If both conditions are met, issue salience drops as the original or modified regime enters the maintenance phase. A large and persistent enough rise in salience during maintenance is the signal that the regime is not working well and that questions of modification or termination are going to arise.

The diversity of paths to increased salience of particular international issues makes it impossible to create a unified theory explaining the timing of past and predicting the emergence of future efforts to create or modify international regimes. At best, theory can point out several possible patterns and suggest the signs that skillful policy makers should heed so that they may make decisions in timely fashion. Some of the pathways also warn policy makers that the consequences of decision can be felt not only on the issue being handled but also on related issues.

## The Success of International Regimes

Changes in salience cannot explain either the success or the failure of efforts to create, establish, maintain, or modify international regimes, or the choice of substantive provisions made during creation and modification. Success and content depend, rather, on the ability of governments to assemble a set of prescriptions that will serve the material and political interests of a coalition of states with sufficient power to maintain the international regime.

While any government may initiate an effort to create or modify an international regime, the effort is likely to receive wide and sustained attention only if it comes from or is taken up by a government with considerable issue-specific power. In both 1948 and 1959, United States efforts assured that Antarctic discussions satisfied this condition. Of course, powerful sponsorship does not guarantee success. The various United States proposals made little headway in 1948, but the partly Chilean-inspired United States proposals became basic parts of a regime in 1959.

Though the full landscape of coalition politics cannot be known until sustained discussions have proceeded for a time, ex ante calculations about the number and identity of the states needed in a regime-sustaining coalition affect who is invited to the discussions. This is particularly important during regime creation because there is no previous coalition that can serve as the foundation of a new one or as the target of erosion efforts.

In some cases, decisions about participation can be made fairly quickly. On many issues, universal participation appears necessary even if later on some governments prove more important than others. Though most of the Bretton

Woods negotiations on international monetary and trade regimes in 1944–45 were a conversation between the United States, Britain, and France, the desire to create open global markets required inviting all other states.

Some issues seem best treated by a more limited group, which may or may not be regional. Regional issues are the simpler case; it is usually fairly easy to decide who is inside and who is outside the region. Nonregional issues pose more difficult problems. The group must be defined in a way that does not omit any state with enough issue-specific or overall power to wreck the regime that is interested in participating. The Antarctic case demonstrates this very nicely. By 1950 the Soviet Union was announcing that it would accept no understandings about the future of Antarctica made without its participation. This posed a real problem for the other interested states. On the whole, they would have preferred keeping the Soviets out, but they realized that the Soviets had both the power and the will to challenge any agreement made without them. The others would either swallow their distrust and invite the Soviets in or prepare to keep the Soviets from upsetting their arrangements by whatever means proved necessary. The United States would probably have been able to keep the Soviets out by force in 1948, but this would have required a large effort unlikely to be supported by the public for very long. By the mid-1950s the others had agreed to let the Soviets in. It was impossible to keep the Soviets out of the IGY, since it was based on the cooperative norms of transnational science. At the same time, however, the IGY gave the Soviets a chance to show that they could be trusted to accept certain rules. The abating of cold-war tensions also made it much easier to accept them as a partner.

Both efforts to create an Antarctic regime were assisted by the fact that it was fairly easy to identify the states having a clear interest in Antarctic affairs. In 1948 the states most active in the Antarctic were the seven claimants and the United States. Though a few others complained about being left out, most of them were not powerful enough to cause real problems. In 1959 the group of interested states could be identified very clearly because the IGY had offered states a chance to prove their interest by going to the expense of building stations and sending expeditions.

In general, the success or failure of regime creation and modification depends on forging a coalition of states with sufficient issue-specific power to maintain the regime vis-à-vis any private actors involved and against challenge by other states. Content can thus be predicted through a knowledge of what proposed principles, norms, rules, and procedures appeal to the group of states most likely to forge such a coalition.

Although focusing on issue-specific power provides a good first estimate, there are three reasons why it cannot always provide the definitive estimate.

First, great powers can translate their high overall power into high issue-specific power fairly quickly. The Antarctic case provides two good illustrations of this process. The United States catapulted itself to the first rank of Antarctic powers in the 1930s, and more particularly just after World War II, by maintaining a far greater level of exploration and scientific research than any of the claimants could finance. The Soviet Union used the IGY to do the same thing by establishing and continuing to use several stations.

Second, weaker participants have several ways of limiting the choices or actions of the stronger: they can apply their own issue-specific power, weakening the relative advantage of the strong; they can try to keep too many of the strong from joining one coalition until after their own interests have been secured; they can use various linkage strategies. Logrolling may work when support on one discrete question can be traded for support on another, or cooperation in this negotiation traded for cooperation in another. Calling on emotional ties of alliance, region, or other affinity is often the most effective, particularly when the agenda of negotiations limits the prospects for logrolling. The Antarctic negotiations provide examples of most of these mechanisms. Claimants used the general acceptance of sovereignty over land areas to limit how far nonclaimants would go in attacks on claims. Most of the smaller participants also called on alliance ties with the United States. While logrolling was limited by the decision to postpone consideration of resource issues, the unanimity rule allowed weaker participants to threaten withholding of support if the superpowers went too far.

Third, some results cannot be explained by the international distribution of power, because one or more governments fail to apply their power to the full. This happened in 1948, when internal divisions prevented the United States from adopting a coherent policy and hence from applying its power effectively.

Coalition formation is also affected by the forum in which discussions about creating or modifying an international regime take place. All international fora have formal and informal procedures that affect the ability to make decisions and hence influence the process of discussion. In effect, they require a successful coalition to meet two tests: the ability to assemble a large enough number of members to adopt decisions according to forum rules, and the ability to assemble a powerful enough set of members to sustain the regime outside the forum once it has been created or modified.

Universal participation fora like the UN General Assembly or the UN Conference on Trade and Development have one state–one vote and majoritarian rules. The current emphasis on the norm of sovereign equality of states and the attractiveness of an open agenda make the UN General Assembly the most likely venue for starting discussions of regime creation or modification.

While many of these discussions are then delegated to other UN bodies, the current Third World majority in the Assembly favors using those that also follow one state–one vote and majoritarian rules. This opens the possibility that proposed regime prescriptions supported by a coalition of powerful states may fail to be adopted because a large number of weak states oppose. In both 1958 and 1960, no proposal regarding the breadth of the territorial sea won the two-thirds support needed for adoption. This kept the issue open and helped create the uncertainty about law of the sea that led to convening the Third UN Conference in 1973.[12] Alternatively, proposals accepted by a majority of states may fail to be established, because a small but powerful group opposes. In 1966 the Third World majority won adoption of a General Assembly resolution establishing a UN Capital Development Fund providing that it would be financed by contributions in fixed proportion to each UN member state's national wealth and allocate the money according to the normal one state–one vote simple majority rules. Greece was the only non–Third World contributor, and few of the pledges were actually paid. In the end, the Third World had to settle for a voluntary fund attached to the existing UN technical assistance programs.[13]

Even in the case of universal-participation regimes, some efforts at creation and modification occur in institutions with different voting rules. This is particularly true for modification, which is often channeled through the institutions established to help maintain the regime. Some, like the World Bank and the International Monetary Fund, weight votes according to regime-relevant capabilities. Others have shifted toward a de facto reliance on some form of consensus. In such cases, consensus is usually defined as agreement among most states in the five UN regional groups (Africa, Asia, the Soviet bloc, Latin America, and the West) or other predetermined clusters. Both weighted voting and the use of consensus are efforts to reduce the gap between votes inside the forum and power outside which has grown since the Third World coalition acquired control of the UN in the mid-1960s. Weighted voting is the most direct method, for a group of the weak cannot block decisions. Consensus is indirect, for it allows the weak as well as the strong to block decisions.

Yet many international regimes are created and modified in limited-participation fora. Some, like the Organization of African Unity or the League of Arab States, combine limited participation with one state–one vote and majoritarian rules. Others, like the European Community, combine limited participation with the use of unanimity or of weighted voting on particular questions. In limited-participation fora the requirement for success becomes threefold: not only must the winning coalition have enough votes inside the forum to adopt prescriptions and enough power outside to establish and maintain them, it must also have enough power to fend off attack on the regime by nonparticipant states. The amount of power this third qualification entails depends on the nature of the limited participation. Regional limited-participation regimes, such as those sponsored by the UN Environmental Programme on pollution control in particular ocean areas, the European Community, or the Council for Mutual Economic Assistance, are largely protected by the normative legitimacy of regionalism. Virtually all states accept the idea that clusters of like-minded neighboring states may establish international regimes among themselves. Nonregional limited-participation regimes, however, face serious legitimacy problems once a large number of nonparticipant states get interested in the issue being regulated by the regime. These cannot derive support from regionalist doctrines, so the power of the states sustaining the regime is far more important.

Creation of the Antarctic regime was discussed in a one-time forum of the twelve states supporting Antarctic stations during the International Geophysical Year: the Washington Conference of 1959. Although the participants could have taken the question to the UN General Assembly, they did not, because most of them believed they would be worse off negotiating under General Assembly rules. The Third World coalition that would have challenged this decision did not yet exist. India's proposals that Antarctica be handled through the Assembly were easily turned aside. This was important for all coalition formation within the Antarctic regime because the Washington Conference adopted the unanimity rule normal in small diplomatic conferences. This rule was then carried over into the Antarctic Treaty and has governed decision making within the regime ever since. The practical effect of this rule has been to assure each superpower that the other cannot raise a majority against it. This ensures that any agreement reached has powerful support. At the same time, it provides the other ten participants protection against a superpower duopoly by permitting them to reject prescriptions they find unacceptable. Finally, because it provides claimants and nonclaimants mutual protection against each other, it stabilized the sovereignty compromise. A unanimity rule always carries the risk of deadlock, but limiting the number of participants reduces this by making accommodation easier.

The international regime created at the Washington Conference is a limited-participation regime operating according to a strict consensus rule that effectively amounts to unanimity among the states with voting rights. Despite the fact that the Antarctic Treaty is formally open for accession by any state, it qualifies as a limited-participation regime for two reasons. First, only twenty-five states have chosen to exercise their right to join the original twelve parties. Second, original participation and later addition to the group of states with voting rights (the consultative parties) is based on the functional criterion of supporting "substantial scientific research" on the Antarctic continent. At present, eighteen states have voting rights; the nineteen others are nonconsultative parties having the right to observe and join debate but not the right to be taken into account when it is being determined whether consensus exists.

The limited-participation nature of the Antarctic Treaty system is affecting each effort at regime modification in a different way. Regime amendment remains in intra-group exercise carried out within the special Antarctic institutions. The eighteen voting parties are still operating within the formal rules of unanimity in their efforts to reach agreement on additional rules and procedures. The effort to replace the regime is an outside challenge using the openness of the UN General Assembly agenda to provide an alternate forum. The Third World governments leading the effort hope to take advantage of the fact that the Antarctic Treaty system is not a regional regime in the usual sense and so is vulnerable to postcolonial demands for universal participation. One of their goals is to replace the existing Antarctic institutions with new ones in which the one state–one vote and majoritarian rules giving control to a united Third World would apply.

Yet the change of forum would work to the challengers' advantage only if a powerful group of the thirty-seven participants broke away and endorsed their proposals. Otherwise, given the lack of enforcement mechanisms available to the UN General Assembly and related bodies, the challengers land in the same dilemmas posed by gaps between control of votes inside the forum and possession of power outside which bedevil other Third World efforts to create or modify international regimes. At the same time, the consultative parties' unanimity rule has an important coalition-maintaining effect. Since new consultative parties can be added only with the consent of all current ones, it prevents them from resorting to competitive recruitment drives as a method of solving intragroup differences. Such drives would alter the regime by making it a universal-participation one in the long run, possibly leading some of the original parties to doubt its value for protecting their interests. They might even lead to its demise if original parties decided that the changed balance of voting power would lead to decisions harming rather than protecting their interests.

With these considerations in mind, several possible patterns of coalition formation can be distinguished. The unipolar model posited in hegemonic-stability theory is the simplest. There is no need to forge a coalition if there exists a hegemon willing to create, maintain, or modify an international regime. The mere presence of a hegemon in the system is insufficient. International relations is not like the universe, where laws of physics govern relationships and, for instance, large objects exert a gravitational pull on nearby smaller ones regardless of the desires of each. Rather, it is a realm of human interaction and hence one of human choice. Basic-force models cannot apply; since power acquires political relevance mainly as it is directed toward some goal, force-activation models must be used.[14]

The truth of this proposition about the importance of force activation—or of will—in the interactions of states, is nicely illustrated in the failure to create an Antarctic regime during the late 1940s. Had the pro-claim faction within the U.S. government prevailed, there would not have been a separate Antarctic regime; Antarctica would have become one more landmass covered by the normal rules of territorial sovereignty. Had the anti-claim faction prevailed, the United States would have put its influence solidly behind one of the joint-use proposals and would most likely have secured adoption of a separate Antarctic regime.

When a hegemon possessing a clear purpose is present, then, problems of coalition building do not arise. The success of creation or modification is assured, and the content follows from what the hegemon regards as being in its interest. Yet this need not necessarily lead to a completely imposed regime. Even hegemons do not possess unlimited power. In most cases, particularly if the prevailing norms of international relations discourage the use of military force for resolving conflicts on the particular issue, hegemons find it easier to establish and maintain international regimes that also benefit the other participants. If regime benefits alone fail to attract, then hegemons may offer a range of positive inducements, side payments, to others for their cooperation. Both of these help elicit willing cooperation. Willing cooperation always reduces enforcement costs by eliminating or severely limiting the occasions on which threats must be issued or deprivations imposed to get other participants back into line. This leads hegemons to include prescriptions having wide current appeal or to present their proposals within a doctrine demonstrating convincingly that benefits for all will follow.

The possibilities were demonstrated nicely during the creation of the postwar trade and monetary regimes. The United States presented its proposals for open regimes on the basis of liberal economic theories positing greater growth and efficiency for all from the workings of an open market, but also satisfied the concerns of other states about their ability to protect themselves from major external disruption or to pursue interventionary policies in the domestic economy, by providing a variety of escape clauses permitting temporary or partial suspension of open-market rules.[15] Thus, the interests of the other possible participants are not irrelevant to the success of regimes even in the presence of a hegemon.

When there is no hegemon (or no one is aware of a hegemon's presence because of failure to read the distribution of power accurately), patterns of coalition formation are more complicated. Whenever two or more relatively equally strong powers exist, states involved in an effort to create or modify an international regime must assemble coalitions of the like-minded. This generally entails competition for partners as several clusters of like-minded states seek enough partners to become a winning coalition.

In bipolar systems where there are two relatively equal strong powers, coalition formation may take on one of several patterns, depending on the attitudes of the two great powers. If one is relatively indifferent to an issue, the other will be able to proceed as if it were a hegemon. So long as the other does not try to overturn or disrupt the regime, the one active great power can control developments. However, the possibility that disgruntled weaker participants might recruit the inactive superpower to their cause requires greater flexibility on the part of the active power. If both great powers are interested in the issue, the result may be confrontation or duopoly, depending on whether the two great powers can agree on a set of regime prescriptions. Confrontation, at least on issues of high intrinsic salience, does not promote success in regime creation or modification. This is why few security questions are governed by international regimes in the post–World War II world. Duopoly does promote success. So long as the two great powers act together, other coalitions will have trouble dislodging them. Of course, much depends on the relative power of the united great powers vis-à-vis the rival coalition. Two great powers might not be able to fend off a coalition of all others if the difference between the capabilities of a great and of a second-rank power is not sufficiently wide for power to outweigh numbers. However, bipolar systems seldom function in this way; most of the time each great power has a group of allies, associates, and clients ready to help it against other coalitions.

The Antarctic Treaty system is an example of duopoly in action. Both superpowers continue to have remarkably similar positions on the basic principles and norms governing the Antarctic. Though they disagree on some specific questions, disagreement arises within the framework of common agreement. This does not make Antarctica unique. On at least two other international issues, uses of outer space and nuclear disarmament, progress in forging effective global rules has depended in large part on whether the two superpowers make mutual accommodations. When they agree, they act as a duopoly and bring others along. When they disagree, there is little progress toward making effective rules, much less toward establishing a coherent international regime. Effective duopolies can also occur in particular areas when issue-specific power is detached and insulated from the distribution of overall power. In the 1950s and 1960s, the regime governing international trade in wheat was a United States–Canada duopoly because demand exceeded supply and those two countries together exported at least 85 percent of the wheat traded internationally.[16]

The patterns of coalition building in a multipolar situation where three or more relatively equal great powers exist are yet more complicated. Indifference on the part of some may simplify matters by allowing approximations to hegemony or duopoly.[17] Broad agreement might lead to a "concert" pattern in which all great powers join in maintaining the regime and protecting it against internal or external challenge. Much of nineteenth-century diplomatic history reveals such a pattern, both in areas like the protection of foreign investment that were governed by a regime[18] and in areas like crisis management that were not.[19] Under multipolarity disagreement would lead to competitive coalition building and considerable regime instability as coalitions changed over time. The intensity of the competition and the degree of resulting instability would depend on the depth of the disagreements.

The various international process explanations of regime change say little about the patterns of coalition formation. In general they say more about how states define interests. This does not make them irrelevant to an explanation of coalition formation. However, it is hard to go beyond the generalizations on coalition formation just presented without understanding the interests of each state involved. Additionally, it is impossible to explain the content of newly created or modified regimes without such understanding. States and other actors use their power and find compatible coalition partners on the basis of their material and metapolitical interests. Thus, it is necessary to understand what those interests are and how they arise.

## Content

The literatures on international relations and domestic politics offer many contending theories about how states perceive and act on interests. Some regard the definition of interests as determined by the structure of the state's domestic system; states with similar structures will define interests in similar ways, and a change in structure necessarily occasions a change in the definition of interests. There are at least five such structuralist theories: (1) the Marxist emphasis on organization of the means of production in which the state is simply the "executive committee of the ruling class" and state interests are defined by the preferences of the class controlling the means of production; (2) a form-of-government argument asserting that basic differences in perception of interest stem from whether a government is totalitarian, authoritarian, or democratic; (3) the pluralist assertion that the definition of interest is determined by whatever coalition of social groups is most influential in the political system, distinct from the Marxist in that it does not assume continuing domination by one particular social group; (4) an assertion that definition of interests depends on the extent to which governments act autonomously of social groups or coalitions; and (5) the bureaucratic-politics school asserting that definitions of interest emerge from the priorities of whatever set of bureaucratic actors has the most influence in the policy-making process.

The Antarctic case gives little support to the extreme version of any structuralist theory; there are few correlations between any structural form and Antarctic policies. This does not mean, however, that the case entirely discredits any of them. Most Antarctic issues cannot be analyzed in structuralist fashion, because they do not directly or indirectly pose the metapolitical questions that inspire structure-related differences of opinion among governments. A government espousing some form of socialism would have different attitudes on questions like the regulation of markets or the private ownership of property than one espousing capitalism. Similarly, the implications for basic definitions of loyalty used by each are such that totalitarian states generally prevent the emigration of citizens, whereas democratic governments regard emigration as one of the rights of citizens.

In the Antarctic case, the main issues on the agenda have been very different. During negotiations aimed at creating an Antarctic regime they included treatment of territorial claims, prevention of conflict likely to escalate into warfare, and promotion of scientific research. In the consultative parties' discussions of regime amendment the issues have been how to preserve the valuable features of the existing regime, the procedures for joint decisions on resource activity that should be established, the types and amounts of resource activity that should be permitted, how to protect the environment, and how to balance any conflicting needs of resource activity and scientific research. These generally pose questions that can be solved by rational calculation within either the constraints imposed by the international system or the framework of normative agreement embodied in the Antarctic Treaty, rather than questions with important implications for the basic principles of domestic politics.

Yet in a few instances Antarctic policy does vary by domestic structure. In New Zealand there has been some relation between the willingness to contemplate giving up the claim and the social coalition most strongly represented in the government. In the early phases of the negotiations on mineral and fuel resources a few questions related to the role of state-owned and private firms led to definite socialist-capitalist or left-right differences.

It is very difficult to test theories of bureaucratic politics given the restricted salience of Antarctic issues until recently. A particular agency controlled policy more often by default than by the ability to win contests for influence with others. On the whole, however, the case justifies the skepticism expressed by many analysts about explanations based on the bureaucratic process.[20] In Argentina and Chile the greater military and foreign-ministry control over Antarctic policy does lead to more thorough assertiveness on the claims question. However, that bureaucratic balance stems more from competitive impulses arising from dealing with rival claimants on the international level than from any facet of domestic politics. Neither Chilean shifts between center-left, Marxist, and right-wing governments in the early 1970s nor Argentine shifts between military juntas and elected presidents made any significant difference in the level of assertiveness. In this light, the British case is particularly revealing. The organization of Antarctic policy machinery there resembles that of nonclaimants and claimants enjoying undisputed claim boundaries, with most decisions made by the agency in charge of scientific research. However, British confidence in this system was shaken sufficiently by the Falklands war to inspire some strengthening of the Foreign Office role. The increased importance of resource issues has led to an increase of interagency competition for influence in most countries. It is hard to escape the conclusion that here, at least, international needs and rivalries are more significant for bureaucratic organization than bureaucratic organization is for policy.

On the international plane, structuralist theories of policy making predict that states of differing structure will have more trouble cooperating with one another and will tend to create less comprehensive international regimes than states of similar structure. At first glance, the Antarctic Treaty system appears a case in point; participation by two great powers with markedly different structures seems to limit its possibilities. A closer look at the situation reveals, however, that the main sources of difference on the questions raised by the Antarctic regime are not structural. Rather, most differences stem from whether or not a state had asserted a territorial claim before 1959 and whether or not a state possesses actual or near-term capability to participate in resource activity. Again, structural notions are not fully discredited, but the case does caution that structuralist explanations only apply to certain kinds of issues.

The relatively sparse results of structuralist analysis encourages a closer look at explanations deriving states' definitions of interests from features of the international political process or from differences in their individual domestic political processes. The basic contention here is that the way in which different governments handle issues leads to differences in their definitions of interest. Four schools of thought seem the most prominent: (1) the organizational-process model, which sees governments' choices and perceptions as determined, at least for the short run, by the standard operating procedures of agencies responsible for handling the issue at hand; (2) a wider political-process model, which looks to the constraints imposed by domestic laws and customs; (3) the extent to which a domestic system is open to influence from events occurring in the international system or decisions taken abroad; and (4) the nature of the ideas held by those in charge of policy. At the international level, rival process explanations focus on (1) the way in which general changes at the international level affect individual states; (2) the influence of intergovernmental organizations able to assert a mandate over the issue at hand; (3) the operation of related international regimes; and (4) the nature of ideas winning general acceptance among governments. The second and fourth are in many ways simply the first and fourth domestic-level explanations generalized to a wider set of actors and taking the effects of the international system into account.

The organizational-process model has different relevance in the creation and the later phases of regime existence. In creation, organizational process can refer only to the routines already existing in a government, none of which specifically incorporate the existence or prescriptions of an international regime on the issue at hand. In maintenance and modification, organizational process incorporates the features of the international regime to the extent that they have been adopted into the routines of national bureaucracies.

In the creation of the Antarctic regime, organizational process explains why foreign ministries had control of the issue, since Antarctic affairs were an "international" matter with restricted and low intrinsic salience. Well-established norms of transnational science, such as cooperation, the sharing of data, and the open publication of research, shaped the understandings of the IGY, which in turn influenced the Washington Conference. Yet it is clear that their importance rested on the fact that science was the only possible Antarctic activity at the time. Had resource activity been possible, a rather different set of norms would have been more influential. It is difficult to generalize beyond these points, however, for lack of sufficiently detailed information about the organizational processes of different states.

In regime maintenance and modification, insights from organizational-process theory also have some utility. Success in establishing a regime can be measured by the extent to which regime prescriptions become incorporated into organizational routines. These are the external manifestation of the inertia that buttresses international regimes against immediate erosion when the international distribution of power, the interests of states, related regimes, or conditions influencing the pattern of interaction within the regime change. Establishment of common routines among participating governments also means that in areas governed by effective international regimes, differences of domestic organizational process among governments will decrease. The organizational-process model would then predict a decrease of differences in definitions of interest. However, the discussions of regime modification suggest that this is not a permanent phenomenon, but one that depends on the issue's salience remaining low.

The broader domestic process theory is not particularly relevant to the Antarctic case because of the low and restricted salience of Antarctic issues. Such issues engage few of the limits imposed by national processes. Only on occasion have they made a difference. The particular requirements for environmental impact assessment embodied in United States law have permitted environmentalist groups far greater access to the policy-making process there than in other countries. Yet this does not necessarily mean that they influence United States policy more, because their overall influence depends on how many other private groups with different views mobilize on the issue, how intensely they lobby, and the balance of views among officials responsible for policy. The United States includes the largest number of environmentalists on its delegations to Antarctic meetings, but this has not meant that the United States government constantly takes the most environmentalist positions. One aspect of domestic process is acquiring increasing importance. As the salience of Antarctic issues becomes more widespread, the greater citizen access to decision-making processes allowed in democratic countries will lead to more open contention over policy. As long as government officials and most of the private actors involved remain committed to the basic Antarctic Treaty system, this will not weaken the regime. Yet the example of international trade shows that powerful social groups can over time erode a government's commitment if they oppose a regime.[21]

Relative openness to external influences also fails to explain very much. Again, low intrinsic salience of the issue limits the impact of openness. It is also limited by the fact that the Antarctic regime is regulating activity within a territory rather than transactions across national borders. This removes one of the differences between states that contributes to tensions within many of the global economic regimes. In them, states regarding themselves as vulnerable to external developments seek greater closure than others regarding themselves as able to cope through larger size or greater ability to adjust.

The influence of ideas held by one or many governments depends on whether discussions about a regime occur mainly at the metapolitical or at the relational level.[22] Regime creation necessarily involves metapolitical elements because participating governments must choose the principles and norms that will govern their interactions in the future. Whether this leads to severe differences depends on how states define their preferred principles and norms. There are questions, like emigration or international monetary flows, on which domestic structure affects choice because some choices are more compatible with one structure than another. Yet others, like nonmilitarization, can appeal equally to states with a variety of structures. If an international regime includes lots of these or embodies compromises on the more structure-related principles and norms, even creation will be a time of basically relational behavior in which participants seek principles and norms that maximize their net material benefit.

The metapolitical and relational patterns can be distinguished more clearly in regime modification. When the predominant coalition is satisfied with the existing principles and norms, modification is amendment. Amendment is a relational exercise focused on ensuring that the rules and procedures are modified to better serve material interests. When a coalition with significant power is discontented with the principles and norms, *and* able to articulate a coherent alternative set,[23] modification becomes replacement. Replacement, then, involves a metapolitical challenge to the existing international regime. Negotiations become more "ideological." Whether that means tapping into divergences of opinion resting mainly on differences in some aspect of domestic structure depends on the questions at hand. Once the normative differences are sorted out, discussions on replacement can enter a more relational phase as actors seek to secure maximum net material benefit within the new set of principles and norms.

Of course, an effort to replace a regime may fail. In such cases, supporters of the defeated effort may give up metapolitical challenge and settle for whatever material gains they can acquire from the existing or an amended regime. These need not be trifling; if the stronger participants wish to preserve the regime in order to restrain one another, they may well concede substantial benefits to former challengers.[24] In essence, this is an attempt to reconcile them to the regime enough to make them less likely to join any later attempts at replacement or termination. Some challengers may, however, continue with metapolitical attack even as they maneuver for greater material benefit. Stephen Krasner has argued that this characterizes much Third World behavior vis-à-vis international economic regimes predicated on market allocation of opportunities.[25]

There is no clear relation between continued metapolitical attack and the level of material interests at stake. A lack of material stake allows the luxury of continued crusading. Yet possession of substantial interests that seem to be gravely endangered by the existing regime can also inspire such activity, as is shown by the intensity of Iceland's efforts to secure acceptance of wider coastal-state control over fishing between 1958 and 1977.[26]

Whatever the pattern of negotiation, the ideas held by policy makers have considerable importance for the outcome. Ideas provide a significant portion of the filters that limit governments' choices to particular sets of decisions. In the Antarctic case, the sovereignty compromise is buttressed by the fact that individual national sovereignty is the normal principle governing disposition of land territory. Even the most adamant nonclaimant must argue that Antarctica is an exception, which places the burden of proof on those who would treat Antarctica as a common-use area. The outside challengers labor under the same burden, though they have tried to lighten it by arguing that the fact of common use by the Antarctic Treaty parties since 1961 creates a valid precedent for considering Antarctica as an area "beyond the limits of national jurisdiction." Here the Third UN Conference on the Law of the Sea had contradictory results. It provided the venue for developing the alternate "common heritage" paradigm for Antarctica, but also demonstrated that, on the whole, states still prefer individual appropriation to joint management. Somewhat less of the ocean floor, but far more of its immediately apparent wealth, lies within the extended zones of national maritime jurisdiction accepted at the conference than in the deep seabed deemed common.

Positive or negative examples from other international regimes or organizations also provide a fertile source of the ideas through which governments filter their choices. The early United States proposals to include Antarctica within the UN trusteeship failed, not only because claimants regarded this as an attack on their claims, but also because it would have permitted something both the United States and the seven claimants were then trying to avoid: Soviet involvement in Antarctic affairs. At least one consultative party regards experience in the International Whaling Commission, where a group of states not participating in the resource activity was able to use open-access and majoritarian voting rules to dominate the regime, as a persuasive argument for avoiding a universal-participation Antarctic regime.

Finally, the Antarctic case is only one of many reaffirming the basic point that governments consider their interests and choose their policies on international questions in light of attitudes of other states and the competition for power going on among them. Left alone, claimants would have agreed on dividing the continent even if some then squabbled over how to draw the lines. They agreed to the Antarctic Treaty sovereignty compromise as a second best, preferable to the vague ideas of UN trusteeship or condominium floated by the United States, because they could not hope to prevail in a contest between themselves on one side and both superpowers on the other. Today, the compromise still looks far better to them than the alternative "common heritage" doctrine.

The widespread support for nonmilitarization of the Antarctic cannot be explained without reference to this dimension. In many cases, decisions about acquiring a new weapon or expanding military capability in some geographical area are governed by a set of preferences running from best to worst as follows: (1) only we have, (2) both we and others have, (3) neither we nor others have, and (4) only others have. In these cases, though sole possession gives advantage, mutual possession is not regarded as canceling all the benefits of possession. In the Antarctic case, however, the expense of establishing and maintaining weapons or bases, the small utility they would bring (at least with the technology existing in 1958), and their extreme vulnerability to attack led to a reversal of the middle preferences. Governments had preferences running thus: (1) only we have, (2) neither we nor others have, (3) both we and others have, (4) only others have. The first outcome was deemed unobtainable by either superpower, and Southern Hemisphere states feared that the last was most likely for them if superpower rivalry spread to the Antarctic. All twelve original parties were thus encouraged to agree on the second; hence the nonmilitarization clauses.[27]

As with theories of changes in issue salience and of coalition formation among states, the Antarctic case does not permit complete rejection of any of the most popular theories about how governments make policy. Rather, it suggests that there are conditions under which each is or is not relevant. This does not make for particularly parsimonious theories, but it does help explain why, after so much study, contending theories continue to exist. A sophisticated theory of international affairs may be one that specifies the conditions under which each theory applies, provides signs for recognizing when each set of conditions is occurring, and then specifies how much of international affairs is comprehended under each set of conditions.

## The Future of the Antarctic Treaty System

The Antarctic Treaty system has been and remains a limited-participation international regime in which a group of states with very different domestic structures and individual interests has cooperatively managed a continent and a large area of surrounding ocean for a quarter of a century. The regime has succeeded in serving their interests so well that none of the original or later parties has defected to the coalition of Third World states seeking to replace it with a universal-participation common-heritage regime.

The Antarctic Treaty derives much of its stability from the fact that it permits states to avoid strong common aversions while serving lower-value but still real common interests. All participants want to avoid starting the sort of conflict that would escalate into armed confrontation. They also want to maintain the prohibitions on nuclear weapons placement and testing because these are now important parts of global efforts to limit both horizontal and vertical nuclear proliferation. Unity on these matters has so far been enough to induce compromise on others, such as territorial sovereignty and actual or possible exploitation of resources.

Nonmilitarization provides all participants (as well as nonparticipants) a larger measure of security than they would otherwise enjoy. This security is a public good in the strict definition of the term, since it is indivisible and cannot be made exclusive to the providers. However, the nature of the process by which it is provided reduces the dilemmas usually associated with provision of such goods. The Antarctic Treaty inspection system, supplemented today by satellite observation, provides a mechanism for early detection of violation, but the real buttress of nonmilitarization is the fact that it is far cheaper to provide than any alternate form of security. Nonmilitarization demands that participants abstain rather than act (except in cases where another has violated first). So long as all remain confident that others are not acting, they have no incentive to act themselves. The low cost of compliance is matched by the higher cost and likely small benefit of violation. Except in one case, cheating on demilitarization would yield advantage only in conflicts localized in the Antarctic itself. Yet local advantage in Antarctica is not worth very much, since the continent and the Southern Ocean are relatively far from the main theaters of great- or small-power conflict today.

The one exception relates to the Antarctic Peninsula area where various islands and other places could be used as staging points for attacks on states in the southernmost parts of South America. However, the distance of these staging points from the homelands of any extrahemispheric attacker, and even most hemispheric ones, means they would be operating at the end of long and exposed supply lines. On further reflection, then, the exception is not so much of an exception after all.

A second common aversion also requires abstention. All participants in the Antarctic Treaty system regard the "freeze" on claims as preferable to at least one of the alternate possibilities. Nonclaimants prefer it to endorsement of claims; claimants and probably many of the others prefer it to acceptance of the common-heritage notion. All can avoid their worst choice, though cannot attain their best, by staying within the treaty.

Problems of collective action within the regime remain fairly simple, since the regime rests in the final analysis on a duopoly between two rival great powers. Because of the strength of the common aversions the superpowers have a strong interest in keeping the regime as a way of regulating each other's conduct. Although a duopoly is less stable than a hegemonial structure, it is more stable than a multipolar one as long as the duopolists remain in agreement. While this is the case, there is a two-actor group willing and able to provide the common goods necessary to keep the regime going.

The strength of both common aversions means that differences on how to serve common interests are not taken too far. Although replacing the Antarctic Treaty might not threaten Antarctica's status as the world's oldest nuclear-weapons-free zone, it would greatly increase the chances for other armed conflict. This would happen because it is clear that none of the claimants will accept the common-heritage alternative being proposed in the UN General Assembly. Were the Antarctic Treaty to weaken, the claimants would defect, not to the coalition of Third World states, but to a coalition of themselves bent on terminating any Antarctic regime so that they could make good their claims. In power terms, they might not get away with this on their own, but they would if both superpowers either acted on their recent insistence that they reserve the right to make a claim should circumstances warrant or decided against aiding efforts to impose a common-heritage regime. Their reactions to the 1982 Convention on the Law of the Sea indicates that their enthusiasm for common-heritage regimes is quite limited.

Even consultative parties that might be attracted to common-heritage ideas, such as China or India, are better off within the Antarctic Treaty regime because its unanimity rule gives them a greater voice in management than they would enjoy in the usual sort of universal-participation regime. Even if the Antarctic common-heritage alternate adopted institutions like the International Seabed Authority, which delegates some decisions to specially composed bodies using a variety of qualified majorities for specified decisions, there would still be realms of one state–one vote and majoritarian rule. Even the nonconsultative parties, which have no formal voting rights, are probably better off in the Antarctic Treaty system as long as the total number of participants remains fairly small. They, too, would have to acquire most of their influence informally in a deep-seabed type of common-heritage regime, except during the time they served on the limited-membership organ. Most of them could not expect to serve very often. As long as it persists with domestic policies of apartheid, South Africa is far better off in the Antarctic Treaty system, since a common-heritage regime dominated by the Third World would waste no time in expelling it.

The situation of the challengers is more difficult. They remain a scattering of very weak states. They have not been able to follow normal Third World strategies of using control of the UN General Assembly and similar bodies to shift the terms of international debate by securing adoption of resolutions endorsing their views. Only Africa, which does not include any participants as long as South Africa remains under its present government, has formally endorsed the replacement project. Asia and Latin America, which have Antarctic Treaty states in their ranks, have not. The consensual rules of the Nonaligned Movement and the Group of 77 mean that neither of these pan–Third World fora have endorsed it either.

Unless a fragmentation of the Antarctic Treaty system coalition were to result in significant defections toward the common-heritage replacement, the challengers lack the power to impose such a regime. They cannot muster anywhere near the overall or issue-specific power available to the Antarctic Treaty participants. Yet, as was noted above, the most likely defections are toward a less palatable alternative, termination of the Antarctic regime. Realization of this fact accounts for the slow progress of the replacement effort.

The small prospect of success has not deprived the replacement effort of all impact. The challengers are mounting political pressure through the General Assembly sufficient to inspire certain adjustments of the Antarctic regime. More Third World states have been added to the consultative parties, and the nonconsultative parties have been given more rights than they had enjoyed before in bids to broaden support. The consultative parties have also more actively disseminated information. Antarctic affairs have never been shrouded in as much secrecy as some Third World governments and environmentalists allege, but until recently the participating states made no particular effort to distribute information beyond the small circles of Antarctic specialists.

It is difficult to say how long the current increase in the salience of Antarctic affairs will continue. Fishing, except for certain finned species, is now well below levels that threaten Southern Ocean stocks. The completion of an agreement on mineral and fuel resources is not going to trigger activity, because the current state of oil and mineral markets make Antarctic resource ventures hopelessly uneconomic. The Third World challengers will attempt to keep the issue alive, but in the absence of significant resource activity, the Antarctic is likely to return to its accustomed place below the political horizon for many years to come.

# NOTES

## Chapter 1

1. E.g., Jervis, "Security Regimes"; the section on colonialism in Puchala and Hopkins, "International Regimes"; Mandelbaum, "The First Nuclear Regime"; Jervis, "From Balance to Concert"; and Downs, Rocke, and Siverson, "Arms Races and Cooperation."

2. Initially advanced in Kindleberger, *The World in Depression*, evaluated and refined in Keohane, "Theory of Hegemonic Stability," and evaluated further in Snidal, "Limits of Hegemonic Stability Theory."

3. A "common concern" can be a desire either to ensure a mutually beneficial result or to avoid a mutually costly one. On this point see Stein, "Coordination and Collaboration."

4. See discussion of rejection of Thomas Jefferson's proposal for a joint fleet to subdue the Barbary corsairs, in Szasz, "Thomas Jefferson Conceives an International Organization." The corsairs were not pirates in the strict sense of the term, since their activities were authorized or assisted by various North African rulers, nominally vassals of the Ottoman Sultan but acting with a great degree of independence. However, they were often referred to as "pirates" by nineteenth-century Americans and Europeans.

5. This usage conforms to usage long established among international lawyers. See, e.g., Bowett, *The Law of the Sea*, 17.

6. Cohen, *Organizing the World's Money.*

7. Young, "Regime Dynamics," 282–85, distinguishes three ways regimes can be created: "spontaneously" as participating states evolve common practice without prior negotiation (the process by which customary international law is formed), through negotiations among interested states, or through imposition by one or a few strong states. Since the Antarctic regime has always been a negotiated one, the focus of this study will be on negotiated regimes.

8. See discussions of this issue in Hart, *The New International Economic Order*, and Odell, *U.S. International Monetary Policy.*

9. This definition of amendment is broader than that adopted in Aggarwal, *Liberal Protectionism*, 18–20. He distinguishes between "meta-regimes," which include the principles and norms, and "regimes," consisting of rules and procedures. He

regards a change in the meta-regime as replacement, which restricts amendment to changes in rules and procedures. He uses cognitive theories to explain changes in meta-regimes and structural theories to explain changes in regimes in a way that oversimplifies the mechanisms of regime modification.

10. On the history of the IMF, see Horsefield, ed., *The International Monetary Fund,* and Southard, *The Evolution of the International Monetary Fund.*

11. This is a problem now receiving much attention in the United States and Western Europe as the postwar generation of leaders approaches retirement. Many observers wonder how the next generation, whose formative experiences do not include the Great Depression or World War II, will manage the Western Alliance. See, e.g., "The Present and Future of the Atlantic Alliance."

12. "Outsiders" may even include rival agencies within the same government. For example, L. V. Smirnov, chairman of the Soviet Military-Industrial Commission in 1972, expressed dismay at the American habit of discussing the numbers and capabilities of Soviet weapons in the SALT I talks because this information was not normally shared with Soviet colleagues like Foreign Minister Gromyko. Kissinger, *White House Years,* 1234.

13. This usage treats what Keohane and Nye, *Power and Interdependence,* separate into transgovernmental and transnational interactions as one category. For present purposes their distinction is less significant than the fact that both types of interaction make it impossible to apply the unitary-actor assumptions that can be used when salience is restricted.

14. E.g., Vasquez and Mansbach, "The Issue Cycle and Global Change."

15. E.g., Apter, *Politics of Modernization;* Huntington, *Political Order in Changing Societies.*

16. This tradition can be traced even to Marx in *Eighteenth Brumaire of Louis Bonaparte,* and Hilferding, *Finance Capital.* Contemporary exponents include Cardoso and Felatto, *Dependency and Development in Latin America.*

17. Schurmann, *Logic of World Politics;* Mills, *Power Elite;* Dahl, *Who Governs?*

18. Katzenstein, "Conclusion," in Katzenstein, ed., *Between Power and Plenty,* pp. 295–336.

19. Allison, *Essence of Decision;* Halperin, *Bureaucratic Politics and Foreign Policy.*

20. This theory, too, was discussed in Allison, *Essence of Decision.*

21. Lenin, *Imperialism.*

22. Whittaker, "Concorde Debate."

23. Morgenthau, *Politics among Nations;* Kaplan, *System and Process in International Relations.*

24. E.g., Kindleberger, *World in Depression,* and Krasner, "State Power and the Structure of International Trade."

25. Expositions of this theory in Kindleberger, *World in Depression;* Krasner, "State Power and the Structure of International Trade"; Gilpin, *U.S. Power and the Multinational Corporation.*

26. E.g., Morgenthau, *Politics among Nations.*

27. This is the definition advanced in Keohane and Nye, *Power and Interdependence,* 8–11.

28. Keohane, *After Hegemony*, p. 17.
29. E.g., Volpe, "U.S.–Japan Trade."

## Chapter 2

1. See summary of history in Bush, *Antarctica and International Law*, 2:90–91.
2. See the brief history in "Les Terres australes et l'Antarctide françaises," p. 30.
3. Waldock, "Disputed Sovereignty," 319.
4. Rorquals include Blue, Fin, and Sei whales. See Dawkin, "Whales and Whaling," 155, for a description of this technology.
5. Lovering and Prescott, *Last of Lands . . . Antarctica*, chap. 7, gives a succinct summary of these early expeditions.
6. Letters Patent of 21 July 1908, text in *British and Foreign State Papers* 101 (1912): 76–77. Waldock, "Disputed Sovereignty," 319, discusses earlier claims to Graham Land, South Georgia, and other islands.
7. Letters Patent of 28 March 1917, text in *British and Foreign State Papers* 111 (1921): 16–17.
8. Text of notes in Bush, *Antarctica and International Law* 2:482–83; additional discussion in Prescott, "Boundaries in Antarctica," 89.
9. See documents in Bush, *Antarctica and International Law* 1:575.
10. Comment in Bush, *Antarctica and International Law* 2:301; also discussed in Da Costa, *Souveraineté sur l'Antarctique*, p. 16.
11. Letter from the Colonial Secretary to the Governor-General of Australia, 6 February 1920, text in Bush, *Antarctica and International Law* 2:104.
12. Order-in-Council of 30 July 1923, text in Hackworth, *Digest* 1:462. Da Costa, *Souveraineté sur l'Antarctique*, 14, notes that Victoria Land (the area along the western coast of the Ross Sea between 167° and 150°E) had been claimed in 1913.
13. Da Costa, *Souveraineté sur l'Antarctique*, 14.
14. Report of the Committee on British Policy in Antarctica, Imperial Conference, 1926, Summary of Proceedings, *British Parliamentary Papers (1926)*, Cmd. 2768. Text also in Bush, *Antarctica and International Law*, 2:100–4.
15. Da Costa, *Souveraineté sur l'Antarctique*, 14. Also see Decree of 27 March 1924, *Journal officiel*, 29 March 1924, p. 30004, and Decree of 21 November 1924, *Journal officiel*, 27 November 1924, p. 10452.
16. Memorandum of the Norwegian Minister to the British Foreign Office, 26 January 1934, text in Bush, *Antarctica and International Law*, 2:150. See also Isachsen, "The New Norwegian Dependency in the Antarctic," 73. Norwegians working on Norwegian and foreign-flag vessels then dominated the industry.
17. Order-in-Council of 23 January 1928, text in Norway, *Collection of Laws, etc.*, 1926–30, p. 33.
18. Order-in-Council of 4 May 1931, text in *British and Foreign State Papers* 134:1010.
19. Japan's interest stemmed from the 1911–12 Shirase Expedition in the Ross Sea area. See note to the Norwegian government in Bush, *Antarctica and International Law* 2:318, and discussion in Taijudo, "Japan and the Problems of Sovereignty," 15.

20. Order-in-Council of 14 January 1939, text in *American Journal of International Law* 34 (1940): supp., 83.

21. Walter Sullivan, "Antarctica in a Two-Power World," 156.

22. Sullivan, "Antarctica in a Two-Power World," 158; Hayton, "The 'American' Antarctic."

23. It was to be operated by an Argentine whaling company holding a concession from the British government to operate a land station there. The Argentines viewed this as a cession of sovereignty, the British as simply a condition attached to the concession. See contrasting views in Hunter Christie, *The Antarctic Problem*, 266, and Alzerreca, *Historia de la Antártida*.

24. Da Costa, *Souveraineté sur l'Antarctique*, 6; Hayton, "The 'American' Antarctic," 590.

25. Decree 9844 of 2 September 1946, text in *Boletín oficial*, 19 November 1946, pp. 2–3; translation in Bush, *Antarctica and International Law* 1:630.

26. Supreme Decree 1747, text in *Boletín de leyes y derechos del Gobierno* (Chile), 109 (1940): 2240; translation in Bush, *Antarctica and International Law* 2:318.

27. See correspondence reprinted in Bush, *Antarctica and International Law* 2:321, and accounts in Hayton, "The 'American' Antarctic," 586, and Pinochet de la Barra, *Chilean Sovereignty in Antarctica*, 57.

28. Letter to the Norwegian Minister of 2 April 1924, text in Hackworth, *Digest of International Law* 1:400.

29. Lincoln Ellsworth and Richard Byrd did leave papers purporting to claim for the United States areas sighted during their expeditions in the late 1930s. Department of State Policy and Information Statement, 27 January 1947, text in *Foreign Relations of the United States, 1947*, I:1047. Shapley, *The Seventh Continent*, pp. 43–63, provides further discussion.

30. See the United States Note rejecting French contentions that discovery was a sufficient basis for claim, *Foreign Relations of the United States, 1939*, II:5, and other statements reprinted in Hackworth, *Digest of International Law* 1:399 and 456.

31. On Belgium, see Bush, *Antarctica and International Law* 2:268.

32. An Englishman's summary appears in Hunter Christie, *The Antarctic Problem*, 268–70.

33. Bush, *Antarctica and International Law* 2:321.

34. Hayton, "The 'American' Antarctic," 591. Also see diplomatic correspondence reprinted in *Polar Record* 5:233–37.

35. Bush, *Antarctica and International Law* 2:383–84; John Hanessian, "The Antarctic Treaty," 441.

36. The Rio Pact adopted as the area of application the Interamerican Defense Zone created in 1942, which included all areas lying between 50°S and the South Pole enclosed by the meridians at 24° and 90°W. Both South American governments tended to view this as acceptance of their claims over that of Britain, despite formal United States declarations that the Rio Pact lines had no implications for determining sovereignty over any territory that might lie within them. For further discussion, see Pinochet de la Barra, *Chilean Sovereignty in Antarctica*, 50–51; Auburn, *Antarctic Law*

*and Politics,* 56 and 98; and documents in *Foreign Relations of the United States,* 1947, I:1053–54, and III:75, and 1948, I, pt. 2, pp. 970–71. Argentine notions were further encouraged when the line was shifted eastward to 20°W in a wider set of amendments to the Pact in 1975. Bush, *Antarctica and International Law* 1:489–500.

37.  Texts in *United Nations Treaty Series* 21:175 and 1173.

38.  "Les terres australes et l'Antarctide françaises," 6, says there was some Soviet whaling activity as early as 1932. Soviet fleets began large-scale operations in 1947. See account in *Current Digest of the Soviet Press* 9, no. 4 (6 March 1957): 32–33.

39.  E.g., letter from the Secretary of Defense to the Secretary of State, 12 April 1948, *Foreign Relations of the United States,* 1948, I, pt. 2, pp. 973–74.

40.  Hanessian, "Antarctic Treaty," 442.

41.  See note in *Foreign Relations of the United States,* 1947, I:1050.

42.  Memorandum of Acting Chief of Division of Northern European Affairs, 17 December 1947, *Foreign Relations of the United States,* 1947, I:1059.

43.  *Foreign Relations of the United States,* 1949, I:801 (Argentina), and Bush, *Antarctica and International Law* 2:382–83 (Chile). The Argentines had advertised their hostility to trusteeship ideas at the San Francisco Conference by declaring that "the Argentine Republic will in no case accept that the Trusteeship system can be applied to territories that belong to it, even when those territories are the subject of claim or controversy or even under the control of other States." Argentina, Ministry of Foreign Affairs and Worship, *Memoria,* 1945–46, pp. 69–70. Also in Bush, *Antarctica and International Law* 1:615. Though aimed mainly at the Falkland/Malvinas Islands, the statement can be read more generally.

44.  See statement of the Foreign Minister to the House of Representatives, 25 October 1949, Australia, *Parliamentary Debates,* House of Representatives, 205:1899.

45.  Reactions as summarized in an undated U.S. State Department memorandum, text in *Foreign Relations of the United States,* 1949, I:801. Also see "L'Antarctide et les problèmes soulevés par son occupation," 10.

46.  Bush, *Antarctica and International Law* 2:384.

47.  Speculation to this effect, particularly in Santiago and London, confirmed by the United States on 28 August 1948. *Foreign Relations of the United States,* 1948, I, pt. 2, p. 1007.

48.  References in Bush, *Antarctica and International Law* 2:266.

49.  *Foreign Relations of the United States,* 1948, I, pt. 2, pp. 1007–8.

50.  See the lengthy reports in *Pravda* and *Isvestia,* 11 February 1949. Their significance is discussed in *Foreign Relations of the United States,* 1949, I:794.

51.  Russian text in *Pravda,* 10 June 1950; English translation in *Polar Record* 6:120–21.

52.  Dawkin, "Whales and Whaling," 164–65.

53.  The Soviets themselves had provided a precedent for limited discussions by participating in Arctic negotiations restricted to the six states having territory that actually lies north of the Arctic Circle. Their own legal specialists had presented conflicting views on restricting participation. See Toma, "Soviet Attitudes."

54.  Boczek, "The Soviet Union and the Antarctic Regime," 837.

55. See the draft declaration of August 1949 and related correspondence in *Foreign Relations of the United States*, 1949, I:800–10.

56. These delays are well described in Hanessian, "Antarctic Treaty," 447–48.

57. This was the latest in a number of incidents. Argentines had earlier forced a British party to withdraw from Hope Bay by firing over their heads as they attempted to come ashore. See Hunter Christie, *The Antarctic Problem*, 273–74.

58. On Antarctic aspects of the IGY, see Sullivan, "The International Geophysical Year," 319–26.

59. The main potential problems were allocation of Antarctic station sites, which the Soviets made more severe by requesting sites several other states had already indicated interest in using, and Argentine and Chilean readiness to contest the allocation to any other state of sites within their respective claims. Sullivan, "The International Geophysical Year," 319–20.

60. Text in Whiteman, ed., *Digest of International Law* 1:500–1.

61. E.g., the Australian–United States exchange of 1955 in Whiteman, *Digest of International Law* 2:1243.

62. Sullivan, "The International Geophysical Year," 320.

63. Remarks of John Hanessian in *Proceedings of the American Society of International Law*, 1958, p. 47.

64. Sullivan, "The International Geophysical Year," 323–24.

65. This was generally acknowledged. See, e.g., "Frozen White Elephant?" *Economist*, 13 April 1957, pp. 111–12.

66. A Belgian observer's comments in "Le problème de l'Antarctique," 213; discussion of Commonwealth attitudes in Hanessian, "The Antarctic Treaty," 455–56; remarks of Senator Fulbright, 1 July 1960, in *Congressional Record*, vol. 106, pt. 2, p. 15422; and remarks of Representative Wight, 18 October 1960, in Australia, *Parliamentary Debates*, House of Representatives, 1960, p. 2116.

67. IGY activities forced governments to commit substantial resources to Antarctic research. The United States spent about $500 million (Crary, "International Geophysical Year," p. 2), while even Belgium spent $1 million over the 18 months (*New York Times*, 1 June 1958, p. 31). Spanish, Swedish, and West German scientists had attended the early planning meetings, but their governments had not been able to send expeditions (Guyer, "The Antarctic System," 177).

68. Hanessian, "The Antarctic Treaty," 462; Chilean note of 14 May 1958 accepting the invitation to the Washington Conference, in Bush, *Antarctica and International Law* 2:418.

69. Statement by Representative Duthie, a government supporter, in debates on the treaty, 18 October 1960, in Australia, *Parliamentary Debates*, House of Representatives, 1960, p. 212; and reports of Australian reaction to a Soviet flag-raising ceremony at Mirny Station in 1957, London *Times*, 6 February 1957.

70. French note of 16 May 1958 accepting the invitation to the Washington Conference, as published in Spanish translation by the Chilean Ministry of Foreign Affairs, in Bush, *Antarctica and International Law* 2:540; statement of Prime Minister Nash in New Zealand, *Parliamentary Debates*, House of Representatives, 1960, p.

2890; statement of British Prime Minister Macmillan, 12 February 1958, *New York Times,* 13 February 1958.

71. Typical U.S. statements can be found in Department of State *Bulletin* 16 (16 January 1947): 30–31, or the note of 3 May 1958 inviting others to the Washington Conference, *New York Times,* 4 May 1958, p. 19. A typical Soviet view is expressed in the note of 12 May 1958 accepting the invitation, in Whiteman, *Digest of International Law* 2:1255.

72. Chilean translation of the Belgian note accepting the invitation to the Washington Conference in Bush, *Antarctica and International Law* 2:268; Taijudo, "Japan and the Problems of Sovereignty," 15.

73. *United Nations Treaty Series* 402:71; *United States Treaties,* vol. 12, pt. 1, p. 796; *American Journal of International Law* 54 (1960): 477.

74. See Dater, "Organizational Developments," 26, for a discussion of how IGY norms of cooperation were thus incorporated into the treaty.

75. Burton, "New Stresses on the Antarctic Treaty," 474–75, has an interesting discussion along these lines.

76. This had sometimes been an issue during the IGY. Sullivan, "The International Geophysical Year," 319–20.

77. This is part of a broader rule that treaties normally create neither rights nor obligations for states not parties to them. One exception generally accepted among international lawyers occurs when a treaty rule codifies or has become adopted into customary law. Some claim that a treaty may be enforced against nonparties if it creates an objective regime (e.g., the standard Soviet text, *Kurs medzhdunarodnovo prava,* 3 402 [1967], which claims that status for the Antarctic Treaty), a treaty embodying rules providing general rights and obligations relating to use of a particular area of land, river, ocean, or airspace. On the current rules, see Articles 34–38 of the Vienna Convention on the Law of Treaties, text in *International Legal Materials* 8 (1969): 679, which does not incorporate the concept of objective regimes by name; McNair, *The Law of Treaties,* chap. 14, which discusses a similar concept of constitutive treaties; and *Yearbook of the International Law Commission,* 1966, vol. 2, pp. 226–31. For a full discussion, see Semma, "The Antarctic Treaty as a Treaty Providing for an 'Objective Regime.' "

78. See Lagoni, "Antarctica's Mineral Resources," 26.

79. Remarks of Senator McKenna, 21 September 1960, in Australia, *Parliamentary Debates,* Senate, 1960, p. 583, and discussion in Taubenfeld, "A Treaty for Antarctica," 285.

80. Winter pack ice covers some 19 million square kilometers—an area almost as large as that of the Antarctic continent; summer pack ice covers only about 2.5 million. Central Intelligence Agency, *Polar Regions Atlas* (Washington, 1978), p. 38.

81. Johnson, *Rights in Air Space.*

82. Taubenfeld, "A Treaty for Antarctica," 264–65.

83. Statements of delegates printed in U.S. Department of State, *The Conference on Antarctica,* Washington, October 15–December 1, 1959.

84. Article 31 of the Vienna Convention (text in *International Legal Materials* 8

[1969]: 691); commentary in *Yearbook of the International Law Commission*, 1966, vol. 2, pp. 220–21.

85. Today there are eighteen consultative and nineteen nonconsultative parties. Were this provision absent, a united group of nonconsultative parties could propose an amendment at the review conference on its own.

86. A compromise between Soviet insistence that any state be free to accede and American insistence on limits so that the People's Republic of China and the Soviet-bloc half of divided states could not gain international status by accession. Such arguments over participation were a staple of cold-war competition within international organizations between 1948 and 1973.

87. Poland acceded on 8 June 1961. The treaty thus came into force for Poland along with the twelve original parties when the last three of the latter ratified on 23 June 1961.

88. Longer discussion in McNair, *Law of Treaties*, chap. 31.

89. See codification of the customary rules in Articles 42, 54, 59, 61, and 62 of the Vienna Convention (text in *International Legal Materials*, 8:[1969]: 695, 699, 700, and 702). Also discussed in McNair, *Law of Treaties*, chaps. 30–35, and *Yearbook of the International Law Commission*, 1966, vol. 2, pp. 249–51. Since it came into force before the latter, the Antarctic Treaty is not directly covered by the provisions of the Vienna Convention. Where, however, they codify preexisting custom, they may be used in discussion of the treaty.

90. Denied in, e.g., Triggs, "Australian Sovereignty in Antarctica," 319–20; deemed possible in Hanevold, "The Antarctic Treaty Consultative Meetings," 88; accepted in Honnold, "Thaw in International Law?" 849.

91. Guyer, "Antarctica's Role," 278; rejected in Lagoni, "Antarctica's Mineral Resources," 26.

92. A Boeing 747SP, one of the longest-distance airliners now in service, can fly 12,000 kilometers nonstop. This range would permit direct flights using austral great-circle routes between the capitals of Argentina or Chile and those of Australia or New Zealand if there were adequate navigation and emergency landing facilities in Antarctica.

93. Guyer, "The Antarctic System," 223–26, has the best discussion of reasons for this omission. It will be examined at greater length in chapter 3.

## Chapter 3

1. Letter from the Acting Secretary of the Navy to the Secretary of State, 3 May 1949, *Foreign Relations of the United States*, 1949, I:796.

2. *United Nations Treaty Series* 157:157.

3. Rao, *The New Law of Maritime Zones*, 181–99.

4. See letter from the Acting Secretary of State to the British ambassador, 13 April 1948, setting out a belief that the United States was in a completely different position regarding Antarctica than the Soviets because of its far greater level of activity, *Foreign Relations of the United States*, 1048, I, pt. 2, p. 974. A flurry of concern in

early 1949 was not followed by rapid action on any proposal. See memorandum of conversation between the counsellor of the French embassy and the chief of the State Department's Bureau of Northern European Affairs, 16 February 1949, in ibid., 1949, I:794.

5. Discussed in Auburn, "Legal Implications of Petroleum Resources," 503.

6. Taubenfeld, "A Treaty for Antarctica," 249.

7. Hanessian, "The Antarctic Treaty, 1959," 440–42.

8. Australia, France, New Zealand, and the United Kingdom have mutually recognized one another's claims at least since 1938 when they concluded an agreement on air navigation in the Antarctic. Bush, *Antarctica and International Law* 2:507–9.

9. Letter from the Secretary of the Interior to the Acting Secretary of State, 8 January 1948, *Foreign Relations of the United States,* 1948, I, pt. 2, p. 962.

10. Letter from the Secretary of Defense to the Secretary of State, 12 April 1948, *Foreign Relations of the United States,* 1948, I, pt. 2, pp. 973–74.

11. See documents in Bush, *Antarctica and International Law* 1:504, and 2:418.

12. Argentine statement to the San Francisco Conference (quoted in Bush, *Antarctica and International Law* 1:615). The Australian government was still using the argument in 1976. See the Australian Senate's *Report on United Nations Involvement with Australia's Territories,* p. 113. Also quoted in Bush, *Antarctica and International Law* 1:504.

13. See British objections on this ground in the report of a conversation between the counsellor of the British embassy in Washington and the Acting Chief of the U.S. State Department's Bureau of Northern European Affairs, 17 December 1947, in *Foreign Relations of the United States,* 1947, I:1059, and similar arguments in a letter from the U.S. Secretary of Defense to the U.S. Secretary of State, 12 April 1948, in ibid., 1948, I, pt. 2, pp. 973–74.

14. See references in note 27 to chapter 2. Recall, too, that the Chilean proposal coupled the "freeze" on claims with cessation of British efforts to assert jurisdiction in areas where claims overlapped.

15. Suggested by discussion in Wijkman, "Managing the Global Commons," 515.

16. U.S. Proposals in *Foreign Relations of the United States,* 1948, I, pt. 2, p. 1003, and 1949, I:801. British attitudes discussed in ibid., 1947, I:1050, and Hanessian, "The Antarctic Treaty, 1959," 440–41. New Zealand attitudes discussed in Hanessian, 442.

17. See an undated U.S. State Department paper in *Foreign Relations of the United States,* 1949, I:801, and Hanessian, "The Antarctic Treaty, 1959," 442–44. "L'Antarctide et les problèmes soulevés par son occupation," 10, also sets out French views. For Australian views, see the Foreign Minister's statement of 25 October 1949 in Australia, *Parliamentary Debates,* House of Representatives, 1949, p. 1899.

18. A dependency theorist would probably put Argentina in the third category because of the government's position in the world. However, at least vis-à-vis domestic actors, the Argentine government was stronger than the Chilean.

19. Rankings of industrial states follow the essays in Peter Katzenstein, ed., *Between Power and Plenty.*

20. It might be that adventures occur when a once domestically stronger government seeks to prevent further erosion of its domestic position, whereas a consistently weak government is used to weakness and so is less prone to adventure.

21. Argentine organization discussed in Bush, *Antarctica and International Law* 2:9, and *Polar Record* 2:225.

22. Bush, *Antarctica and International Law* 2:310 and 385.

23. *Polar Record* 17:427.

24. Bush, *Antarctica and International Law* 2:147–49, and *Polar Record* 4:396.

25. *Polar Record* 9:586.

26. Bush, *Antarctica and International Law* 2:495 and 516; Le Schack, "French Polar Effort," 3–5.

27. *Polar Record* 9:35–36 and 159–60.

28. Plott, "Development of U.S. Antarctic Policy."

29. Noted in *Polar Record* 2:52.

30. As noted in Roberts, "Chronological List of Antarctic Expeditions."

31. Tonnessen and Johnsen, *A History of Modern Whaling.*

32. On actual and planned operations in the immediate postwar period, see notes in *Polar Record* 6:2–27 (U.K.), 80–84 (Australia), 382–84 (France), 656–62 (Argentina), and 662–69 (Chile).

33. E.g., Odell, *U.S. International Monetary Policy.*

## Chapter 4

1. *United Nations Treaty Series* 499:311.

2. Today 54 states are parties. Parties and dates of ratification or accession are listed in Status of Treaties to which the Secretary General is Depositary, UN Doc. ST/LEG/Ser.E/4, 1985, p. 694.

3. *North Sea Continental Shelf Cases* (Federal Republic of Germany v. the Netherlands, Federal Republic of Germany v. Denmark), Judgment, *ICJ Reports,* 1969, p. 3, at para. 19.

4. Australia: Proclamation of 10 September 1953 in Bush, ed., *Antarctica and International Law* 2:174, or *American Journal of International Law* 48 (1954): 102. Argentina: Decree 1386 of 24 January 1944, in Bush, 2:73. Chile: Declaration of Santiago, 18 August 1952, in Bush, 2:449.

5. This was still the U.S. position in 1975. See State Department memo on "The Legal Status of Areas south of 60° South Latitude" in Hearings on "U.S. Antarctic Policy" before the Senate Foreign Relations Committee's Subcommittee on Oceans and International Environment, 94th Cong. 1st sess., May 1975, p. 19.

6. Marcoux, "Natural Resource Jurisdiction," 392.

7. E.g., *The Times Atlas of the Oceans,* plate 6.

8. *United Nations Treaty Series* 516:205, and 599:285, respectively.

9. See Argentine Declaration of 11 October 1946 in UN Doc. ST/LEG/Ser.B/1, p. 5, and Chilean Declaration of 23 June 1947 in ibid., p. 6.

10. With ratification of the International Convention for the Regulation of Whal-

ing in 1960, Argentina reserved all rights as against any other state attempting to exercise maritime jurisdiction in waters off coasts it considered its own, listing the Antarctic claim along with the islands disputed with the United Kingdom but made no mention of 200-mile zones. Chile accompanied its 1979 ratification with reservation of rights in the Chilean Exclusive Economic Zone without naming territories. Birnie, ed., *The International Regulation of Whaling* 2:768–70.

11. See chart in *Offshore*, 20 June 1983, p. 35.

12. On Alaska, see T. Miller, "Mineral Resources: Arctic Alaska," 59–61; on Svalbard (Spitzbergen), see Mathisen, *Svalbard in the Changing Arctic*.

13. *United Nations Treaty Series*, 161 (1953):80.

14. Remarks of Dr. Laurence M. Gould, in Hearings on "The Antarctic Treaty" before the Senate Foreign Relations Committee, June 1960, 86th Cong., 2d sess. (CIS No. 1403–14), p. 74.

15. U.S. statement in note of 3 May 1958 inviting the eleven others to the Washington Conference, text in Whiteman, *Digest of International Law* 2:1254; Soviet statement in note of 12 May 1958 accepting the invitation, text in ibid., 2:1255.

16. Andrews, "Antarctic Geopolitics," 5; Sullivan, "Antarctica in a Two-Power World," 162–63 (mainly for the future). Even then, the largest tankers and aircraft carriers could not use the Panama Canal.

17. Lepotier, "Les routes de recharge antarctiques," 62–63; Senator Laughton, 21 Sept. 1960, in Australia, *Parliamentary Debates*, Senate, 1960, p. 589; Da Costa, *Souveraineté sur l'Antarctique*, 78.

18. Sulzberger, "Foreign Affairs" column, *New York Times*, 2 November 1959, p. 30.

19. Lepotier, "Les routes de recharge antarctiques," 75; Sullivan article, *New York Times*, 5 April 1959, sec. 4, p. 6. Wide-angle-view satellites had not been developed, so an orbit over the poles was the only way a satellite could observe the entire world.

20. Lepotier, "Les routes de recharge antarctiques," 75.

21. E.g., Remarks of Senator Dodd (an opponent of the treaty) in debates over U.S. ratification, in *Congressional Record* 106 (1960): 16059–60; Taubenfeld, "A Treaty for Antarctica," 261–62; Gould, "Antarctica in World Affairs," 31–32.

22. In more extended analysis, each superpower's preferences can be listed in the order (1) only we have, (2) neither has, (3) both have, and (4) only they have. Since each could be sure that a move to establish an Antarctic military facility of any kind would bring the other onto the continent, the first preference was unattainable. This left the second as the best attainable outcome.

23. Tunkin, "An Example of International Cooperation," 44. His assertion that it was initially a Soviet idea is further evidence of Soviet interest.

24. See diplomatic correspondence reprinted in *Polar Record* 8:48–56 and 127–51, and reports of related ICJ activity in *ICJ Reports*, 1956, pp. 12 and 15.

25. On these disputes, see Lagos Carmona, *Historia de las Fronteras de Chile*, and Sabaté Lichtschein, *Problemas Argentinos de Soberanía Territorial*.

26. E.g., remarks of Senator Laught, 21 September 1960, in Australia, *Parliamentary Debates*, Senate, 1960, p. 598.

236 NOTES TO PAGES 73–84

27. See Taubenfeld, "A Treaty for Antarctica," 285, on the Latin Americans. See remarks of Senator McKenna, 21 September 1960, Australia, *Parliamentary Debates, Senate,* 1960, p. 583, for discussion of the dangers, including in his view a strong possibility of disrupting the climate.

28. The Australian government, at least, seems to have accepted such a calculation. See the government's answer to a question in the Senate about Antarctic policy, 28 February 1957, in Australia, *Parliamentary Debates, Senate,* 1957, pp. 121–22.

29. Taubenfeld, "A Treaty for Antarctica," 270.

30. See remarks of Lord Lansdowne, 18 February 1960, in *Parliamentary Debates, House of Lords,* 221:188–91.

31. Guyer, "The Antarctic System," 190.

32. Rubenstein, *The Soviets in International Organizations,* chap. 6; Franck, *Nation against Nation,* 104–110; Tunkin, *Theory of International Law,* chaps. 14 and 15.

33. E.g., I. Wallerstein, *The Modern World System,* 91.

34. This classifies South Africa as a partial dictatorship because its apartheid measures exclude much of the population from political participation while allowing elections and constrained debate among the white minority.

35. E.g., Tiano, *La dialectique de la dépendence.*

36. Such arguments about the strength of governments appear in, e.g., Becker, *The New Bourgeoisie and the Limits of Dependency;* Evans, "Transnational Linkages and State Capacities"; Tugwell, *The Politics of Oil in Venezuela;* and Moran, *Multinational Corporations and the Politics of Dependence.*

37. E.g., American interest in Japan's Ministry of International Trade and Industry (MITI) as a mechanism for industrial policy (C. Johnson, *MITI and the Japanese Challenge*), or Western European interest in the U.S. Office of Technology Assessment as a way of better coordinating science policy (*Economist,* 13 September 1986, p. 95).

38. These changes are noted in Bush, *Antarctica and International Law,* 2:11–31, and *Polar Record* 8:419, and 9:360.

39. On Chilean changes, see Bush, *Antarctica and International Law* 2:403–4, and *Polar Record* 9:360 and 362.

40. French changes noted in Bush, *Antarctica and International Law* 2:526–28 and 550; Le Schack, "The French Polar Effort," 5–6; and *Polar Record* 9:360.

41. Changes noted in *Polar Record* 9:360 and 586, and 13:343–44.

42. Changes noted in *Polar Record* 5:205 and 9:360 and 589.

43. Addition noted in *Polar Record* 9:361–62 and 589.

44. Changes noted in Quigg, *A Pole Apart,* 59–60; *Polar Record* 9:360 and 362, and 14:856; and Rutford, "The U.S. Antarctic Program," 58–59.

45. Changes noted in *Polar Record* 9:360 and 362, and 10:297.

46. Changes noted in *Polar Record* 3:285 and 9:360 and 362.

47. *Polar Record* 9:360 and 11:197.

48. *Polar Record* 7:306–16; 8:365; and 9:350–1 and 361–62.

49. This can be seen in the fact that the Soviets did not launch any extended press campaigns denouncing the decision. Further evidence in Tunkin, "An Example of

International Cooperation," 42, which notes the initial Soviet position without polemical comment.

50. See Hanessian, "The Antarctic Treaty, 1959," 462.

51. See the references in note 71 to chap. 2.

52. In 1958 the UN had 82 members, of which 9 were African, 27 Asian, and 10 Soviet bloc. In 1960 the UN had 99 members, of which 25 were African, 22 Asian, and 10 Soviet bloc.

53. "Ice Rush," *Economist*, 30 November 1957, p. 762.

54. See statements by the Australian Minister of the Navy, 8 September 1960, in Australia, *Parliamentary Debates*, Senate, 1960, 491, and Representative Duthie, 18 October 1960, in Australia, *Parliamentary Debates*, House of Representatives, 1960, 2112.

55. Robert Wilson, "National Interests and Claims in the Antarctic," 27–28.

56. The whole question of how states acquire sovereignty over territory and the precise definition of standards of "effective occupation" that ought to apply when determining which of competing states has a better claim has long been a favorite topic of debate among international lawyers. For discussions focused on Antarctic applications of the rules, see Smedal, *Acquisition of Sovereignty over Polar Areas;* Hunter Christie, *The Antarctic Problem;* Pinochet de la Barra, *Chilean Sovereignty in Antarctica;* Da Costa, *Souveraineté sur l'Antarctique;* Mouton, "The International Regime of the Polar Regions"; and Bernhart, "Sovereignty in Antarctica."

57. Before the IGY, claimants maintained the fiction that any expedition operating within their claim was there by permission. This caused no great problems among the claimants themselves, but led to several exchanges with the United States. U.S. policy avoided asking or acknowledging permission, since the United States recognized no claims and in consequence asserted a right of Americans to go anywhere in Antarctica as they wished. For examples of correspondence on such questions, see Whiteman, *Digest of International Law* 2:1243. Also see Auburn, *The Ross Dependency,* 57–58, for a discussion of New Zealand reaction to the Byrd expeditions of 1928–30 and 1933–35.

58. For arguments referring to outdated colonial notions, see Guyer, "The Antarctic System," 164; and Taubenfeld, "A Treaty for Antarctica," 258.

59. See, e.g., Jessup and Taubenfeld, *Controls for Outer Space and the Antarctic Analogy,* or McDougal, Lasswell, and Vlasic, *Law and Public Order in Space.*

60. Indian memoranda explaining requests that Antarctic issues be put on the General Assembly agenda, UN Docs. A/3118/Add.2 (September 1956) and A/3852 (September 1958).

61. D. Miller, "Contributions of the UN to International Security," 36, claims that the 1956 Indian initiative precipitated the Antarctic Treaty. It seems more accurate to say that Indian interest, like that of others, was increased by the IGY.

**Chapter 5**

1. See descriptions in Guyer, "Antarctic System," 185–86; A. Van der Essen, "Réunions consultatives," 20–22; Colson, "Antarctic Treaty System," 875–84; Heg,

"Conference," 45–46; Hanevold, "Antarctic Treaty Consultative Meetings," 183–99; Auburn, *Antarctic Law and Politics,* chap. 5; and Sollie, "Development of the Antarctic Treaty System," 31.

2. Colson, "Antarctic Treaty System," 877, notes that one report was adopted on a less than unanimous decision.

3. Hence delay of the 8th Consultative Meeting from 1974 to 1975.

4. E.g., the Third UN Conference on the Law of the Sea, described in Buzan, "Negotiating by Consensus," 324–48.

5. Compare the reporting of consultative meetings in *Nature, Science, Polar Record,* newspapers, legal journals, and books now and in 1970.

6. Auburn, "Legal Implications of Petroleum Resources," 505. More severe criticisms have been made by leaders of environmentalist groups. See, e.g., "Secrecy on Ice," *ECO* 20, no.1 (June 1982).

7. A. Van der Essen, "Réunions consultatives," 21. See also remarks by U.S. Acting Assistant Secretary of State Brewster, 20 December 1977, quoted in U.S. Department of State, "Final Environmental Impact Statement" (1978), B-22.

8. The SCAR began as the Special Committee on Antarctic Research, set up in 1958 to coordinate post-IGY collaboration in research. Its name was changed in 1961, but its status as a subsidiary body of the ICSU remains unchanged. James H. Zumberge, "Antarctic Treaty as a Scientific Mechanism," 153–68, gives a fuller description.

9. Zumberge, "Antarctic Treaty as a Scientific Mechanism," 166–68.

10. See, e.g., a note in *Antarctic Journal of the United States* 14, no. 3 (September 1979): 20 about the status of consultative party recommendations in the United States. Stating that the U.S. had just gotten around to ratifying a number of recommendations, it explained that "even before ratification, the United States adhered informally to most recommendations. Now adherence is official."

11. Recommendation III-8, text in *Polar Record* 12:457–62.

12. Different states' legislation varies on the extent to which the government may exercise jurisdiction over nationals who commit offenses outside the state's territory. Some, like France, claim comprehensive jurisdiction in this regard; others, like the United States, claim only a limited jurisdiction. For a good example of this problem as applied to the Agreed Measures, see the discussion of Belgium's situation in A. Van der Essen, "Réunions consultatives," 22–23.

13. This second agreement is in Recommendation III-9, text in *Polar Record* 12:462. As of 1981 Japan had not yet ratified the Agreed Measures (*Polar Record* 20:587).

14. E.g., the question of mineral exploitation at the 6th Consultative Meeting. See text in chapter 5 after note 70.

15. For one U.S. official's (rather complicated) scheme of differing weights given to various levels of mention in Reports and Recommendations, see Colson, "Antarctic Treaty System," 882.

16. Auburn, *Antarctic Law and Politics,* 163, calls them "failed recommendations" and "prototype recommendations," respectively.

17. Auburn, *Antarctic Law and Politics*, 163.

18. At the 10th Consultative Meeting, one member proposed amending the rules of procedure to require unanimous approval. The proposal was deferred to the 11th meeting, where it received little, if any, attention. See Report of the 10th Meeting, par. 19 (text in *Polar Record* 20:86), and absence of mention in Report of the 11th Meeting *Polar Record* 21:58–93.

19. Bush, *Antarctica and International Law* 1:88.

20. A. Van der Essen, "Réunions consultatives," 22.

21. Text in *Polar Record* 16:607.

22. Text in *Polar Record* 11:75.

23. Text in *Polar Record* 12:457–65.

24. Colson, "Antarctic Treaty System," 868.

25. P. Van der Essen, "L'économie des régions polaires," 437.

26. Canada had declined an invitation to participate. Heg, "Conference," 45.

27. Poland became a consultative party in 1977, and West Germany in 1981. East Germany has not attained that status.

28. Roberts, "International Cooperation," 116–17. Poland initially asserted the same view by naming the scientific head of its 1975–76 marine expedition as an "observer" entitled to carry out inspections under Article VII of the Antarctic Treaty. Later it accepted the date when Arctowski Station opened as the day it qualified. See Auburn, *Antarctic Law and Politics*, 151.

29. Sollie, "Development of the Antarctic Treaty System," 24.

30. Continuity of original parties' consultative status is implied in Article IX (1); limits on the duration of acceding state consultative status in Article IX (2). Similar rules appear in both the CCAMLR and the draft minerals/fuel resources agreement. However, the consultative parties have not applied it rigorously where financial difficulty rather than loss of interest forces a drop in activity. In recent years Poland has had to reduce its Antarctic commitments and has kept Arctowski Station open only by sharing it with Brazilian expeditions (*Antarctic* 10:134).

31. Sollie, "Development of the Antarctic Treaty System," 24.

32. Shapley, "Antarctic Problems," 505. The station was named for Henryk Arctowski, a member of the Belgian-led Gerlache expedition in 1899, who was the first Pole to set foot on the Antarctic continent.

33. *Antarctic* 9:10.

34. *Antarctic* 9:403, 407, and 446; and 10:114.

35. *Antarctic* 10:114; and 11:187–90.

36. *Antarctic* 9:353–54; and 10:37 and 110; and "New Toe in the Snow," *Economist*, 30 January 1982, p. 48.

37. Stations discussed in *Antarctic* 10:283 and 308–9; consultative status in Kimball, "Report, November 1985," 6.

38. *Antarctic* 10:283 and 308–9; *New York Times*, 25 June 1985, sec. 3, p. 4.

39. *Antarctic* 10:306.

40. It also made obsolete the whole legal literature on conditions for the inclusion among the consultative parties that had developed since 1977. See, for example,

Shapley, "Antarctic Problems"; Bush, *Antarctica and International Law* 1:332–36; Roberts, "International Cooperation," 116–17; Honnold, "Thaw in International Law?" 833–34; and Auburn, "Consultative Status," 514–22.

41. Text in *Polar Record* 23:152.

42. Richard Woolcott (Australian ambassador to the UN), "The Future of the Antarctic Treaty System," 228.

43. *ECO* 30, no. 1, pp. 2–3; Kimball, "Report, November 1985," 6.

44. On Antarctic tourism, see Reich, "Development of Antarctic Tourism," 203–14; and Codling, "Sea-borne Tourism in the Antarctic," 3–9.

45. Text in *Polar Record* 19:272–78.

46. Quigg, *A Pole Apart*, 101–1. All 257 aboard were dead by the time rescue parties arrived.

47. Text in *Polar Record* 16:272–79; and *International Legal Materials* 11 (1972): 251.

48. This is not one of the current terms of art in fisheries management. It means avoiding levels of exploitation that will lead to depletion of current seal populations, and can also cover efforts to increase certain populations before exploitation is allowed.

49. Any party may propose an amendment to the Convention at any time. The amendment enters into force when all parties have indicated acceptance. If one-third of the parties so request, a special meeting can be called to discuss the proposal. The Convention may also be amended in any regular meeting of the parties, or in a special meeting requested by one-third of the parties any time after commercial sealing begins. The meeting may propose an amendment by a unanimous vote so long as representatives of at least two-thirds of the parties are present. These amendments enter into force when ratified by all the parties.

The Annex may be amended on the proposal of any party. The proposed amendment enters into force for all parties six months after being proposed if two-thirds ratify and none files a formal objection within 120 days of receiving the proposal. If a formal objection is raised, the amendment is discussed at the next meeting of the parties. The meeting can accept the proposal or make a substitute proposal by unanimous vote. The same rules of ratification apply as with the initial proposal, except that this time the amendment enters into force only for those states approving it.

50. This remains the most usual rule on accession to multilateral treaties among a limited number of states.

51. Text in *Polar Record* 20:383–402; and *International Legal Materials* 19 (1980): 837.

52. This means management to assure stable populations not only of fished species but also of unfished species living in the same area (hence likely to be caught in any fishing) or dependent on the fished species for food.

53. For on-board observers of fishing operations, e.g, Section 1821(c) (2) (D) of the United States Fisheries Conservation and Management Act of 1977 (*United States Code* 16:1801–82); Brazilian Decree No. 68,459 of 1 April 1971, Article 4 (*Diario Oficial*, 2 April 1971; also in *National Legislation and Treaties Relating to the Law of the Sea*, 1974, UN Doc. ST/LEG/Ser.B/16, p. 271). For inspections by authorized offi-

cers, see the Joint Enforcement Schemes of the North East and North West Atlantic Fisheries Commissions, text (as incorporated into British law) in *National Legislation and Treaties,* pp. 353–56 and 360–61.

54. Argentina, Australia, Belgium, Chile, France, East Germany, West Germany, Japan, New Zealand, Norway, Poland, South Africa, the Soviet Union, the United Kindom, and the United States.

55. On the development of consensus in the Antarctic Treaty system, see Zegers, "Camberra Convention," 155–56.

56. E.g., Mitchell and Tinker, *Antarctica and Its Resources,* 68; Barnes, "Emerging Convention," 261–69.

57. There are few examples of states acting like West Germany in the 1970s and cutting the size of their own distant-water fleets on the high seas unilaterally. Rudolf Illing of the West German government argues that seen from this perspective, 200-mile zones are a logical consequence of the failure to prevent overfishing by international regulatory bodies. He is thus skeptical of CCAMLR's prospects for success. Comment in Wolfrum, ed., *Antarctic Challenge,* 111.

58. Lagoni, "Convention," 103 and n. 44; comments of Richard H. Wyndham, Counsellor of the Australian embassy in Bonn, in Wolfrum, ed., *Antarctic Challenge,* 117.

59. The Soviets dropped opposition to South Korean participation in 1985. South Korea's position as an acceder does mean that it can be a member of the commission only as long as it is active in Southern Ocean fishing or marine research.

60. Quigg, *A Pole Apart,* 173.

61. Auburn, *Antarctic Law and Politics,* 219–23.

62. South Georgia and the South Sandwich Islands, ruled by the U.K. but also claimed by Argentina, also lie within the CCAMLR area of application.

63. Text in *Polar Record* 20:384.

64. These problems are discussed and some interim rules suggested in Butterworth, "Antarctic Marine Ecosystem Management."

65. Chittleborough, "Nature, Extent, and Management of Antarctic Living Resources," 160, notes that the French-Soviet fisheries agreement of 1979 limits the Soviets to an annual catch of 48,000 metric tons off the Crozets and Kerguelens.

66. Accounts of commission activity in remarks of Robert J. Hofman in U.S. Senate Hearing on Antarctica, 24 September 1984 (Serial No. 98–111), pp. 15–16; remarks of R. Tucker Scully in ibid., pp. 11–12; Kimball, "Report, November 1985," 9–12; and Barnes, "Background Paper," pp. 16–18.

67. See discussions of resources in "Les terres australes et l'Antarctide française," p. 9; Tunkin, "An Example of International Cooperation," 42; Fairbridge, "Geology of the Antarctic," 62–63; and *New York Times,* 26 October 1958, p. 23, col. 1.

68. See, e.g., Lepotier, "Les routes de recharge antarctique," 65, or remarks of Dr. Laurence M. Gould in U.S. Senate, Committee on Foreign Relations, Hearings: The Antarctic Treaty, 14 June 1960 (86th Cong., 2d sess.) (CIS No. 1403–14), p. 74.

69. See remarks of the Australian Minister for Air, 18 October 1960, in Australia, *Parliamentary Debates,* House of Representatives, 1960, p. 2115; also remarks of U.S.

Assistant Secretary of State Dixy Lee Ray, May 1975, in U.S. Senate, Committee on Foreign Relations, Hearings: U.S. Antarctic Policy, 15 May 1975 (94th Cong., 1st sess.), p. 5.

70. Colson, "Antarctic Treaty System," 884. A French oil company asked the French government for a license to explore the Gaussberg-Kerguelen Plateau in May 1972. Auburn, *Antarctic Law and Politics*, 135, n. 349.

71. Text in *Polar Record* 16:610.

72. The Paris meeting was deemed so confidential by participants that they did not announce it in advance or even admit that delegates were in Paris until after it had ended. See Pallone, "Resource Exploitation," 412.

73. Text in *Polar Record* 19:85.

74. Text in *Polar Record* 20:590.

75. The consultative parties use a variety of vague formulations to describe the area involved because they do not want to be seen as endorsing either territorial claims (by using phrases like "continental shelf") or "common heritage" notions as currently defined by the Group of 77 (by using phrases like "international area" or "shallow and deep seabed").

76. For post-1971 details, see *Antarctic* 9:408 and 10:31; chapters by Beeby, Brennan, González-Ferrán, and Guillaume in Orrego-Vicuña, ed., *Antarctic Resources Policy*; chapter by Beeby and ensuing discussion in Polar Research Board, *Antarctic Treaty System*, 269–302; Kimball, "Report, July 1985"; Kimball, "Report, November 1985"; The Antarctica Project, "Status of Antarctic Minerals Negotiations," *Antarctica Briefing* no. 8 (30 July 1986); Greenpeace International, "Antarctica Briefing, No. 12" (24 March 1987); and Laughlin, "Minerals Regime in Antarctica." The Antarctic and Southern Ocean Coalition also prints accounts and commentaries in its newsletter *ECO*. The account in vol. 23, no. 1 (1983) was criticized by Richard H. Wyndham, Counsellor of the Australian embassy in Bonn, in Wolfrum, ed., *Antarctic Challenge*, 182, for factual errors and failure to reflect accurately the agreed statements of the consultative parties.

77. "Beeby's Package Deal," *ECO* 33, no. 1 (October 1985): 1.

78. Unofficial (that is, leaked) copies of successive negotiating texts have appeared as follows: the first Beeby draft ("Beeby I") in *Environmental Policy and Law* 11 (1983): 47–52; and the second Beeby draft ("Beeby II") in Greenpeace International, *The Future of the Antarctic: Background for a UN Debate* (1984), appendix 8, and Mhyre, *The Antarctic Treaty System*, appendix B. The "Package Deal" of 1985 has not been published but is discussed at length in *ECO* 33, no. 1 (October 1985). The 1986 draft ("Beeby III") has not yet been published, though copies have circulated among environmentalists and others who follow Antarctic affairs.

79. See discussion of the idea in *ECO* 27, no. 3 (May 1984).

80. Discussed in Auburn, "Antarctic Minerals Regime" 283–84.

81. Comment by R. J. Tingey, a geologist in the Australian Bureau of Mineral Resources, Geology, and Geophysics, in Harris, ed., *Australia's Antarctic Policy Options*, 211–12.

82. Article XX of Beeby I (n. 78 above) proposed equal representation as between

claimant and nonclaimant states, with any claimant having a claim to the territory where the resource activity would occur being included. The Beeby III draft (n. 78 above) proposes inclusion of both superpowers, any claimant to the territory where resource activity would occur, four other claimants, and four other nonclaimants. This provision would lead to a 6 to 4 advantage for nonclaimants in the unclaimed area, a 5 to 4 advantage for nonclaimants in most areas, and a 6 to 6 tie or a 7 to 6 claimant advantage in areas where claims overlap. Since a two-thirds majority is needed for substantive decisions, claimants and nonclaimants as groups, though not individual claimants, would have a veto over decisions.

83. See, e.g., Milenky and Schwab, "Latin America and Antarctica," 90 (on Argentina and Chile). Yet division would require acceptance by other participants. The superpowers are unlikely to agree as long as they value access to the whole continent and Southern Ocean more than exclusive control over a part. If the superpowers did agree to division, they would probably not content themselves with sharing the unclaimed sector. This would mean lengthy negotiations on reallocation of territory before division took place. Such discussions would also attract other contenders, such as Brazil (see discussion of Brazilian territorial interest in "Brazil Enters Antarctic Club," *Latin American Times,* February 1983, p. 27).

84. E.g., Wilson, "Antarctica," 73; or Burton, "New Stresses on the Antarctic Treaty," 421–511.

85. See, e.g., *ECO* 19, no. 1 (1979): 1.

86. *Antarctic* 11:30.

87. This is clear in Article 137 (2) of the 1982 Convention, which states: "All rights in the resources of the Area are vested in mankind as a whole, on whose behalf the Authority shall act. These resources are not subject to alienation. The minerals recovered from the Area, however, may only be alienated in accordance with this Part and the rules, regulations, and procedures of the Authority."

88. Bush, *Antarctica and International Law* 1:504, and Guyer, "Antarctic Treaty System," 174–75.

89. See Bush, *Antarctica and International Law* 1:504; Lagoni, "Antarctica's Mineral Resources," 33–34; 1975 Hearings on U.S. Antarctic Policy, 20–21; Remarks of Senator Puplick, 7 April 1981, in Australia, *Parliamentary Debates,* Senate, 1981, p. 1157; Moneta, "Antarctica," 30; and *Newsweek,* 3 October 1977, p. 95.

90. See Remarks of Senator Puplick, 7 April 1981, in Australia, *Parliamentary Debates,* Senate, 1981, p. 1157; and Triggs, "Australian Sovereignty in Antarctica," 13.

91. Nonaligned Document NAC/CONF.7/INF.11, Section XVIII bis, paras. 87, ter and quater. Text in *Environmental Policy and Law* 11 (1983): 54.

92. Statement by the United Kingdom on their behalf to the General Committee in UN Doc. A/BUR/38/SR.2, 21 September 1983. See also discussions in Clad, "Breaking the Ice," 26.

93. Records of debates in *General Assembly Official Records* [*GAOR*], 38th sess., First Committee, 42d through 45th meetings, 28–30 November 1983.

94. General Assembly Resolution 38/77 of 1 December 1983. Text in *GAOR,* 38th sess., Supp. 47, pp. 69–70.

95. Record of debate in *GAOR*, 39th sess., First Committee, 50th through 55th meetings, 28–30 November 1984.

96. *GAOR*, 39th sess., First Committee, 50th meeting, pp. 6–7.

97. Assembly Resolution 39/152, text in *GAOR*, 39th sess., Supp. 51, p. 94.

98. Discussed in Kimball, "Report, 8 November 1985," p. 7.

99. Discussed in ibid.

100. Declaration of the Harare summit, September 1986, para. 202. Text in UN Document A/41/679.

101. Records of these debates in *GAOR*, 40th sess., First Committee, 49th through 55th meetings, 25 November–2 December 1985, and 117th plenary meeting, 16 December 1985; 41st sess., First Committee, 49th through 51st meetings, 18–19 November 1986; and 96th plenary meeting, 4 December 1986.

102. Texts of resolutions in *GAOR*, 40th sess., Supp. 53, pp. 105–6, and UN Press Release GA/7463, 21 January 1987, pp. 190–92.

103. Results of votes reported in *GAOR*, 40th sess., 117th plenary meeting, pp. 56–66, and 41st sess., 96th plenary meeting, pp. 34–39.

104. Remarks of Australian delegate on behalf of the Antarctic Treaty states in *GAOR*, 40th sess., First Committee, 55th meeting, pp. 46–47; UN Doc. A/41/688 and Add.1; Remarks of Australian delegate on behalf of Antarctic Treaty states in *GAOR*, 41st sess., First Committee, 51st meeting, p. 11.

**Chapter 6**

1. *Polar Record* 9:350–51.

2. Quigg, *A Pole Apart*, 59.

3. *Polar Record* 16:591–92.

4. *Polar Record* 11:465; 12:311; and Bush, ed., *Antarctica and International Law* 2:433–44 and 441.

5. *Polar Record* 13:485.

6. Le Schack, "The French Polar Effort," 13–14; *Polar Record* 13:81.

7. *Polar Record* 4:212; 11:197–98; and 12:97.

8. Hayton, "The 'American' Antarctic," 588. Text of the relevant Order in Council in *Polar Record* 11:306, and Bush, *Antarctica and International Law* 1:647. The Argentine government had long viewed Britain's Antarctic claim as being closely related to its Falklands claim. This stems from the fact that the Argentines define their claim as a sector drawn between the parallels of longitude corresponding to their easternmost and westernmost non-Antarctic territory and the South Pole. Including the Falklands, South Georgia, and the South Sandwich Islands in their territory justifies the 24°W line they currently use. They may also have been confused, as are some private observers, by the British decision to administer the British claim through the governor of the Falklands. The Argentines have clearly believed that this represented a British opinion that sovereignty over the two areas was connected, despite the fact that the British can maintain their Antarctic claim by independent arguments stemming from discovery and subsequent activity. Some

commentators, like Toma, "Soviet Attitudes," 611, n. 1, have even treated the decision as a grant of sovereignty, analogous to those turning Antarctic areas over to Australia and New Zealand.

9. E.g., the South African Citizens in Antarctica Act, 1962, text in *Polar Record* 11:313.

10. E.g., the Australian Antarctic Treaty Act, 1960, text in *Polar Record* 11:302; the British Antarctic Treaty Order in Council, 1962, text in *Polar Record* 11:309; and the Norwegian Law of 2 June 1964, text in *Norge Lover*, no. 17 (1964), pp. 1847–48, and discussed in Johnson, "Quick, Before It Melts," 186, n. 60.

11. Colson, "The Antarctic Treaty System," 868 (Norway), and Mitchell, "The Southern Ocean in the 1980s," 351 (USSR).

12. See Auburn, "Legal Implications of Petroleum Resources," 500–1.

13. E.g., Potter, "Economic Prospects of the Antarctic," 61–68.

14. FAO, *Yearbook of Fisheries Statistics*, reports no catches in Antarctic areas before 1976. Catches below the Antarctic Convergence were not identifiable, because the main fishing areas—South Georgia and the Kerguelens—were included in the southernmost Atlantic and Indian Ocean statistical areas respectively. Additionally, most Antarctic species were included in the miscellaneous category rather than being listed separately.

15. Dater, "Organizational Developments," 29.

16. Argentine, Chile, and the U.K. maintain small planes for local flights in the Antarctic Peninsula area. Chile and Argentina also maintain direct air links between Punta Arenas and Ushuaia, respectively, and Antarctic stations. Australia and New Zealand pool transport with the United States, which maintains its main logistics operations in Christchurch, N.Z., and McMurdo Station. The Soviets had small planes only until 1978 when they built compacted-snow airstrips at Molodezhnaya and Novolazarevskaya Stations capable of handling Ilyushin-18s. *Current Digest of the Soviet Press* 30, no. 39 (25 October 1978): 18, and *Antarctic* 9:29–30.

17. See Op-Ed piece by Charles Neider in *New York Times*, 9 April 1982, p. A27.

18. E.g., Argentina, Ministry of Economy, Coordination, and Economic Planning, *Economic Information on Argentina*, no. 91 (December 1978), map facing p. 3.

19. See discussion of Argentine and Chilean activity in Auburn, *Antarctic Law and Politics*, 48–61; and Quigg, *A Pole Apart*, 116–17.

20. See, e.g., Barros Gonzalez, "Decechos de Chile en la Antarctica," 691–94. Jack Child argues that since 1973 the military character of station organization has been accentuated. Lecture at Harvard University, 19 May 1987.

21. Auburn, "The Antarctic Environment," 259.

22. Auburn, *Antarctic Law and Politics*, 80.

23. Quigg, *A Pole Apart*, 189; Frank, "The Convention," 344, n. 219.

24. See the text in chapter 5 at notes 32–38.

25. See speech to the opening session of the Washington Conference, 15 October 1959, in U.S. State Department, "Conference on Antarctica, 15 October–1 December 1959," p. 11.

26. Quigg, *A Pole Apart*, 180.

27. See discussion in Mitchell, "Resources in Antarctica," 97, and speech by Foreign Minister Talboys in *New Zealand Foreign Affairs Review* 29 (1978): 29.

28. Roger Wilson of Greenpeace expressed doubts that the Labour Party will make any changes in New Zealand Antarctic policy, in Polar Research Board, *Antarctic Treaty System,* 285–86.

29. *Polar Record* 12:623. The Polarinstitutt's role was foreshadowed in the fact that its director was alternate delegate to the First Consultative Meeting (*Polar Record* 11:74).

30. *Polar Record* 16:591–92.

31. *Polar Record* 16:415, and 21:71. This latter ministry has had several names; it is currently called the Department of Science.

32. Quigg, *A Pole Apart,* 59–60 and 215–16; *Polar Record* 13:82.

33. On the U.S.: Quigg, *A Pole Apart,* 214–16; and Westermeyer, *The Politics of Mineral Resource Development in Antarctica,* 99. On Australia: F. M. Auburn, "Submission on the Development of Australian Antarctic Bases," letter to the Parliamentary Standing Committee on Public Works, 16 February 1981.

34. In the wake of the Falklands war many British commentators criticized the Foreign Office and Defense Ministry for failing to anticipate that reductions of Antarctic activity might encourage Argentine aggressiveness on the Falklands dispute. See Beck, "Britain's Antarctic Dimension," 429–44.

35. See the text in chapter 5 at note 12.

36. In the United States, for example, where treaties and federal statutes are deemed equal sources of law and where international obligations can even directly override contrary state law. See *Missouri v. Holland,* U.S. Supreme Court, 1920, 252 U.S. 416.

37. Auburn, *Antarctic Law and Politics,* 83 and n. 258.

38. P. Van der Essen, "L'économie des régions polaires," 495–60.

39. Barrie, "The Antarctic Treaty," 213.

40. Ibid.

41. See note in *Polar Record* 14:204–6.

42. *Antarctic* 9:245 and 364.

43. *Polar Record* 14:47–48.

44. P. Van der Essen, "L'économie des régions polaires," 458–59.

45. *United Nations Treaty Series* 510:205.

46. General Assembly Resolution 2749 (XXV), adopted by a vote of 108 to 0 with 14 abstentions. Text in *General Assembly Official Records,* 25th sess., Supplement 28, p. 24.

47. See the text in chapter 8 after note 19.

**Chapter 7**

1. The first, third, and fifth mechanisms are discussed in Young, "Regime Dynamics," 290–97.

2. This rejection of declining hegemony in favor of a stronger alternative explanation follows suggestions in Keohane, "The Theory of Hegemonic Stability."

3. Inspired by Lipson, *Standing Guard,* 156.

4. Auburn, *Antarctic Law and Politics,* 130–34; Myhre, *The Antarctic Treaty System,* pp. 55 and 58–59.

5. Auburn, "Legal Implications of Petroleum Resources," 501.

6. First noted publicly in the *Washington Post,* 3 March 1975.

7. Rutford, "United States Antarctic Program," 61.

8. E.g., Zumberge, "Possible Mineral Resource Availability," 115–54; Parker, ed., *Conservation Problems in Antarctica;* or Ohio State University, Institute of Polar Studies, "Framework for Assessing Environmental Impacts of Possible Antarctic Mineral Development."

9. Wright and Williams, "Mineral Resources of Antarctica," 1.

10. Remarks of petroleum geologist John Garrett in Alexander and Hansen, eds., *Antarctic Politics and Marine Resources,* 188. He does believe, though, that the necessary technology could be developed were Antarctic fields to prove economically viable. Today, this remains a distant prospect. British Petroleum Company executive Geoffrey F. Larminie estimates that drilling one exploratory well on an island near Antarctica would cost some $300 million. Remarks during discussion on hydrocarbon prospects, in Polar Research Board, *Antarctic Treaty System,* 265.

11. See chapters by Dugger and Garrett in Westermeyer and Shusterich, eds., *United States Arctic Interests;* the *Wall Street Journal,* 27 January 1984; and the chapter by K. R. Croasdale in U.S. Polar Research Board, *Antarctic Treaty System.*

12. This is the reasoning used in U.S. State Department, "Final Environmental Impact Statement" (1982), 1–7.

13. Kesteven, "The Southern Ocean," 484.

14. Report on "Polar Energy Resources Potential" prepared for the Committee on Science and Technology of the U.S. House of Representatives, September 1976, p. 16.

15. Kesteven, "The Southern Ocean," 489; "Polar Energy Resources Potential," 15–16, and Wright and Williams, "The Mineral Resources of Antarctica," 12 and 14.

16. Wright and Williams, "The Mineral Resources of Antarctica," 10.

17. SCAR Group of Specialists, "Possible Environmental Effects"; Colson, "The Antarctic Treaty System," 843.

18. Wright and Williams, "The Mineral Resources of Antarctica," 12; Zumberge, "Possible Mineral Resource Availability," 128–29.

19. Broadus and Hoagland, "Conflict Resolution," 542.

20. E.g., Lundquist, "Iceberg Cometh?"; Wright and Williams, "Antarctic Mineral Resources," 15; Wasserman, "The Antarctic Treaty and Natural Resources," 178–79; Lovering and Prescott, *Last of Lands . . . Antarctica,* 56–61 and 196–97.

21. El-Sayed and McWhinnie, "Antarctic Krill," 14.

22. Taubenfeld, "A Treaty for Antarctica," 264.

23. P. Van der Essen, "L'économie des régions polaires," 461.

24. El-Sayed and McWhinnie, "Antarctic Krill," 14.

25. *Antarctic* 8:328.

26. El-Sayed and McWhinnie, "Antarctic Krill," 14.

27. Four to eight hours if used for human consumption, up to eighteen hours if used to make fish-meal feed. McElroy, "The Economics of Harvesting Krill," 96.

28. Barry Jones, Australian M.P., described krill as having "a strong flavour, which may charitably be described as revolting." Remarks of 1 April 1981 in Australia, *Parliamentary Debates,* House of Representatives, 1981, p. 1217. It even defeated the first French attempt to cook it. The members of the 1951 expedition to Adélie Land had a meal of krill that tasted good but made everyone so sick that no work was done for two days afterward. Sullivan, *Quest for a Continent,* p. 288.

29. Remarks of Dr. Richard Wilson of MIT, in Hearings on various fish and wildlife measures before the House Committee on Merchant Marine and Fisheries, 35th Cong., 2d sess., 1978, p. 180.

30. Wasserman, "The Antarctic Treaty and Natural Resources," 178.

31. *Antarctic* 10:413.

32. El-Sayed and McWhinnie, "Antarctic Krill," 14.

33. Young and Sebek, "Red Seas and Blue Sea," 260, claim that fish provides 30 percent of the protein in the Soviet diet and is an important source of fertilizer as well.

34. Everson, "Antarctic Fisheries," table 7 (p. 245).

35. Remarks of Robert M. Hofman in U.S. Senate, Committee on Science and Transportation, Hearing on Antarctica, 24 September 1984 (Ser. No. 98–111), p. 16.

36. Everson, "The Living Resources of the Southern Ocean."

37. U.S. State Department, "Final Environmental Impact Statement" (1978), 28. Reaffirmed in National Research Council, Committee to Evaluate Antarctic Marine Ecosystem Research, *An Evaluation of Antarctic Marine Ecosystem Research.*

38. Kimball, "Report, 8 November 1985," 11. The 1982–83 catch represents 0.16 percent of the annual world fish catch (Knox, "The Living Resources of the Southern Ocean," 38–39).

39. Hofman remarks in U.S. Senate Hearings on Antarctica, 1984, 16; Quigg, *A Pole Apart,* 85, notes earlier Soviet complaints about the weakness of domestic demand for krill foods.

40. "Fishing in Oily Waters," *Economist,* 3 May 1980, p. 69.

41. FAO statistical zones conformed neither to the Antarctic Treaty line of 60°S nor to the Antarctic Convergence, which lies in an irregular circle north of 60°, until 1976, when they were revised to coincide roughly with the Convergence. Further, most Antarctic species were included in the "miscellaneous" category, since catches were not large enough to merit separate listings. Reporting has improved since 1976.

42. Everson, "Antarctic Fisheries," table 9 (p. 246); FAO *Yearbook of Fisheries Statistics,* 1980, table C-48.

43. Joyner, "Antarctica and the Law of the Sea," 427.

44. This can be seen from many of their common names:

| Scientific Name | Common Name |
|---|---|
| *Micromesistius australis* | Southern Poutassou |
| *Merluccius hubbsi* | Argentinian or Patagonian hake |
| *Dissostichus eleginoides* | Antarctic cod |
| *Notothenia rossi* | white perch or white bass |

45. FAO *Yearbook of Fisheries Statistics,* 1983, table C-00 (pp. 245–51).

46. See the text in chapter 5 at notes 65 and 66.

47. See, e.g., the Lima Declaration of August 1970 by eighteen Latin American states, text in UN Doc. ST/LEG/SER.B/16, p. 586; the Santo Domingo Declaration of 9 June 1972 by fifteen Caribbean and Central American States, text in ibid., p. 599; the OAU Declaration of 1974, text in UN Doc. A/CONF.62/33; and the 1973 Algiers Declaration of the Nonaligned, text in *Review of International Affairs* (Belgrade), 20 September 1973, pp. 38–39.

48. Informal Composite Negotiating Text, Articles 55–59 (UN Doc. A/CONF.-62/WP.10 of 1977).

49. Compare Article 76 in the Informal Composite Negotiating Text of 1977 (UN Doc. A/CONF.62/WP.10) to the longer and more detailed text in the Revised ICNT of 1979 (UN Doc. A/CONF.62/WP.10/Rev.1).

50. 1958 Convention on the Continental Shelf, article 1, *United Nations Treaty Series* 499:311.

51. On advances in offshore technology in the 1960s, see Spangler, *New Technology and Marine Resource Development.*

52. See discussions of the legal status of ice in Mouton, "The International Regime of the Polar Regions," 187–209; Swan, *Australia in the Antarctic,* 321–32; Da Costa, *Souveraineté sur l'Antarctique,* 35; Auburn, *The Ross Dependency,* 45–55; and Bernhart, 'Sovereignty in Antarctica," 300–10.

53. Gulland, "Developing Countries and the New Law of the Sea," 36–42.

54. Text in UN Doc. A/CONF.62/122 of 10 December 1982; also in *International Legal Materials* 21 (1982): 1261–1354.

55. Lagoni, "Antarctica," 399. Others, however, read the Convention as making no distinction between EEZ and continental-shelf claims. See, e.g., Harry, "The Antarctic Regime," 733; Oxman, "Antarctica and the New Law of the Sea," pp. 225–26; and *Australian Foreign Affairs Record,* 1980, p. 10. Lagoni rests his argument on the different formulations used in Articles 55 and 76. Article 76 describes the continental shelf as "the natural prolongation of land territory," whereas Article 55 specifies that the EEZ "is an area beyond and adjacent to the territorial sea . . . under which the rights and jurisdiction of the coastal State and the rights and freedoms of other States are governed by the relevant provisions of this Convention." Harry and Oxman read Article 55 as limiting the amount of authority claimed but not the right to a 200-mile zone.

56. In 1976 the world's largest distant-water fleets, in descending order, flew the flags of the USSR, Japan, the United States, Spain, Norway, the United Kingdom,

France, and South Korea. Kaczynski, "Distant Water Fisheries and the 200 Mile Economic Zone," table 4.

57. *Antarctic* 8:169–70.

58. *Boston Globe Sunday Magazine,* 16 December 1984, p. 42.

59. Discussion in the Australian Senate, 11 October 1979, in *Parliamentary Debates,* Senate, 1979, p. 1131; Bush, *Antarctica and International Law* 2:207; and Remarks of Foreign Minister Talboys, 16 April 1978, in *New Zealand Foreign Affairs Review* 29 (1978): 34.

60. Antarctic 10:198–99 carried the reports. This may have been in part wishful thinking because many members of the New Zealand Antarctic Society, which publishes the journal, support greater assertiveness.

61. Remarks of William R. Mansfield, Deputy Permanent Representative of New Zealand to the UN, in Alexander and Hansen, eds., *Antarctic Policy and Marine Resources,* 38.

62. Auburn, *Antarctic Law and Politics,* 80. See Australian reaction in Bush, ed., *Antarctica and International Law* 2:210. The United States had intended to establish stations at both ends of the unclaimed area in 1940, but ice conditions forced the expedition to build one on Stonington Island, 450 miles east, and the other 200 miles west inside the New Zealand claim instead. (Sullivan, "Antarctica in a Two-Power World," 158.)

63. E.g., Auburn, *Antarctic Law and Poltics,* 80. Australian press outcry was strong enough to inspire a stiff riposte in *Pravda,* 2 April 1980, p. 5, reprinted in *Current Digest of the Soviet Press* 34, no. 13 (30 April 1980): 16.

64. The phrase used in Article XX of the First Beeby Draft on mineral and fuel resources. Text in *Environmental Law and Policy* 11 (1983): 50. The corresponding phrase in the third Beeby Draft is "the two members of the Commission which, at the time of the entry into force of the Antarctic treaty, maintained the largest presence in Antarctica" (Article 29[2][b]).

65. Quigg, *A Pole Apart,* 189.

66. *Antarctic* 9:354. Notifications of plans to SCAR, due the preceding June, and to the consultative parties, due the preceeding November, discussed in Zumberge, "The Antarctic Treaty as a Scientific Mechanism," 161–62, and Rybakov, "Juridical Nature of the 1959 Treaty System," 41.

67. Comments of R. J. Tingey, in Harris, *Australia's Antarctic Policy Options,* 212.

68. Except for the operation of joint ventures, the United States cut all Soviet fishing quotas to zero after the invasion of Afghanistan. Kaczinski, "Distant Water Fisheries," 22 and 40.

69. E.g., Jensen and Shabad, eds., *Soviet Natural Resources in the World Economy;* Sivard, *World Energy Survey,* 23.

70. See U.S. Department of Commerce, National Oceanic and Atmospheric Administration, *Fisheries of the United States,* 1984, for statistics relating to U.S. and foreign catches in the U.S. Exclusive Economic Zone.

71. Official statements on this theme include Joint Chiefs of Staff, *United States Military Posture for Fiscal Year 1982,* supp., p. 3.

72. American feelings have been made clear in reactions to the Law of the Sea Convention's provisions on deep-seabed mining. Indications that the Soviets incline toward similar views may be gleaned from the fact that though they have signed the Law of the Sea Convention, they have also passed legislation authorizing unilateral deep-seabed mining. (Text in *International Legal Materials* 21 [1982]: 551.)

73. Discussed in Milenky and Schwab, "Latin America and Antarctica," 90.

74. The Australian lawyer Triggs in "Antarctic Treaty Regime," 204, n. 44, concludes that blanks left in the articles about management institutions in the first Beeby draft demonstrate that there is no way to reconcile conclusion of the resources agreement with maintenance of territorial claims.

75. Hawkes, "Moratorium," 711.

76. Colson, "Antarctic Treaty System," 890 attributes this to fears that talks would go nowhere once a moratorium was declared. Shapley, *The Seventh Continent,* pp. 160–61, attributes it to a compromise between pro-development forces wanting maximum leeway and old Antarctic hands worried about maintaining the regime.

77. Hawkes, "Moratorium," 711. See also remarks of R. Tucker Scully in Hearings on "U.S. Antarctic Program" before the House Committee on Science and Technology, 36th Cong., 1st sess., May 1979, p. 37.

78. Text in *Polar Record* 19:85.

79. Both Mitchell, *Frozen Stakes,* 69, and Gonzalez-Ferran, "Geological Data," 164, argue this view.

80. Representative Curtin, interrupting remarks by Representative Bandidt, 18 October 1960, Australia, *Parliamentary Debates,* House of Representatives, 1960, p. 2114.

81. See speeches by delegates in Report of the 8th Consultative Meeting.

82. Remarks of Ian Nicholson in Harris, ed., *Australia's Antarctic Policy Options,* 302.

83. *ECO* 26, no. 1 (January 1984): 3. If Vasilchikov, "Prospects for the Industrial Development of Antarctica," as excerpted in *Current Digest of the Soviet Press,* 28, no. 52 (26 January 1977): 1, 3, and 14, is any indication, the Soviets are fairly unconcerned about the Antarctic environment.

84. Nicholson remarks in Harris, ed., *Australia's Antarctic Policy Options,* 301.

85. *Antarctic* 9:408, and Beeby, "An Overview of the Problems," 198.

86. Doc. ANT/XI/34/Add.1 (7 July 1981), p. 3, discussed in Quigg, *A Pole Apart,* 199.

87. *ECO* 30, no. 1 (April 1985): 2.

88. Ibid., p. 3, summarizes these.

89. Beeby, "An Overview," 195–96.

90. Beck, *Politics of Antarctica,* 257; and Laughlin, "Minerals Regime in Antarctica," 10.

91. See statements of Australian, Argentine, and Chilean delegates in Report of the 10th Antarctic Treaty Consultative Meeting (1979), 69–72 and 73–75.

92. See discussion in Beck, *Politics of Antarctica,* 255–58.

93. New Zealand attitudes in Foreign Minister Talboy's speech, *New Zealand*

*Foreign Affairs Record*, 1980, 59; Australian views in "Antarctica—Continent of International Harmony," *Australian Foreign Affairs Review* 51 (1980): 42.

94. U.S. attitude (at least as regards granting permits to explore and exploit), remarks of Assistant Secretary of State Ray, 15 May 1975, in Hearings on "U.S. Antarctic Policy" before the Subcommittee on Oceans and International Environment of the Senate Committee on Foreign Relations, 94th Cong., 1st sess., May 1975, p. 5.

95. See Shapley, "Antarctic Problems," 504, for report of U.S. officials' surprise at the breadth of support at London Preparatory Meeting of March–April 1977.

96. Hawkes, "Moratorium," 712.

97. Barnes, "The Emerging Convention," 254.

98. U.S. State Department, *Treaties in Force*, 1 January 1986, p. 224.

99. *Antarctic* 8:237–38.

100. Barnes, "The Emerging Convention," 253.

101. *Polar Record* 17:166.

102. Beck, "Britain's Role in the Antarctic," 85–87.

103. Brazilian comments in UN Document A/39/583, part II, vol. 2, pp. 7 and 9, 28 October 1984; list of participants in Wolfum, ed., *Antarctic Challenge*, 251.

104. *Antarctic* 9:253.

105. *Antarctic* 10:52 and 309.

106. *Antarctic* 10:137.

107. See lists of delegations in the full versions of Consultative Meetings Reports. (The abridgments in *Polar Record* give names but not organizational affiliations of delegates.)

108. Bergin, "Recent Developments," 189.

109. Rose, "Antarctic Condominium," 19.

110. Mitchell, *Frozen Stakes*, 16. Both she and Auburn (*Antarctic Law and Politics*, 246) say the National Institute of Polar Research first learned about the project when it was publicly announced in late summer 1979.

111. Work described in Eittrim et al., "Marine Geological and Geophysical Investigations of the Antarctic Continental Margin, 1984," U.S. Geological Survey Circular no. 935 (1984).

112. Rutford, "United States Antarctic Program," 61.

113. As seen in the United States, where the Citizens for Ocean Law began serious Antarctic work after 1981.

114. Heg, "Conference," 45.

115. See delegation lists printed in full versions of Consultative Meeting Reports.

116. *Australian Foreign Affairs Record* 51 (1981): 144.

117. Alley, "New Zealand and Antarctica," 930.

118. Discussion in U.S. Polar Research Board, *Antarctic Treaty System*, 326.

119. Kimball, "Report, 8 November 1985," p. 3.

120. Discussed in U.S. Polar Research Board, *Antarctic Treaty System*, 319, 323, and 331, n. 3.

121. *ECO* 22, no. 4:5; Barnes, "The Emerging Convention," 259.

122. Noted and complained about in *ECO* 30, no. 1 (April 1985): 3, for minerals talks; Kimball, "Report, 8 November 1985," 3 for consultative meetings.

123. Quigg, *A Pole Apart*, 179.

124. Compare assessments in Mitchell, *Frozen Stakes*, 7–24, and Pontecorvo, "The Economics of Resources of Antarctica," 155–65.

125. Auburn, "Legal Implications," 512.

126. *Antarctic* 9:402–3, and 11:16–17. For ASOC views, see, e.g., *ECO* 26, no. 2 (January 1984): 1.

127. Conversation with Dietrich Sarhage at the Center for Ocean Management Studies, University of Rhode Island, 19 June 1984.

128. Remarks of John Reynolds of the Western Mining Company of Australia in Harris, ed., *Australia's Antarctic Policy Options*, 305.

129. U.S. State Department, *Treaties in Force*, 1 January 1986, p. 226, and *Department of State Bulletin*, February 1987, p. 86, and March 1987, p. 90.

130. Brownlie, *Principles of Public International Law*, 156–66.

131. See discussion in Auburn, *Antarctic Law and Politics*, 59, and *Latin American Times*, February 1983, p. 27.

132. In certain circumstances, a widely accepted multilateral treaty may come to be accepted as stating customary law binding even on nonsignatories, but such occasions are infrequent.

133. The Vienna Convention on the Law of Treaties, Article 52.

134. They have been able to keep Arctowski Station open by sharing it with Brazilian expeditions (*Antarctic* 10:134).

## Chapter 8

1. See, e.g., Earthscan Press Briefings between 1975 and 1980; Tinker, "Antarctica: Towards a New Internationalism"; Mitchell, "The Politics of Antarctica," 20–21. Discussed in Quigg, *A Pole Apart*, 168–69.

2. The local impact of French construction of an airstrip at Pointe Géologie near the Dumont d'Urville Station has generated considerable environmentalist concern, since it involves linking five islets near an Adélie penguin breeding ground. See, e.g., *ECO* 22, no. 1 (January 1983): 2; 26, no. 2 (January 1984): 1; 30, no. 1 (April 1985): 1. Yet issues raised by United States construction and later dismantling of a small nuclear power reactor at McMurdo Station received little publicity. See Wilkes and Mann, "The Story of Nukey Poo."

3. Remarks of Antigua and Barbuda's delegate on 28 November 1983, in *General Assembly Official Records (GAOR)*, 38th sess., First Committee, 42nd meeting, p. 7. African group withdrawals of proposals to that effect in 1983 and 1984, in *GAOR*, First Committee, 38th sess., 46th meeting (30 November 1983), pp. 10–13, and 39th sess., 55th meeting (30 November 1984), p. 21. Adoption of resolutions urging expulsion in *GAOR*, 40th sess., 117th plenary meeting (16 December 1985), pp. 65–66, and 41st sess., 96th plenary meeting (4 December 1986), pp. 38–39.

4. Clad, "Breaking the Ice," 26.

5. Mitchell, *Frozen Stakes*, 83.

6. Remarks of John V. Byrne, NOAA Administrator, in U.S. Senate, Committee on Commerce, Science and Transportation. Subcommittee on Science, Technology, and Space. Hearing: Antarctica, 24 September 1985 (Serial No. 98–111), pp. 39–40.

7. Text in *United Nations Treaty Series* 161 (1953): 72–99.

8. International Convention for the Regulation of Whaling, Articles III (1) and (2).

9. International Whaling Commission, "Status of the International Convention for the Regulation of Whaling, July 1983," reprinted in Birnie, *International Regulation of Whaling* 2:766–67.

10. Article III (a) of the second Beeby draft, 29 March 1984; text in Greenpeace International, "The Future of the Antarctic: Background for a Second UN Debate" (London, 22 October 1984), Appendix 8, had such a rule. Articles 23 and 39 of the third Beeby draft provide for decision by two-thirds of the commission.

11. See comments by Annette Horsler of the Australian Fund for Animals in Harris, ed., *Australia's Antarctic Policy Options*, 327–38.

12. Annual costs of running the International Seabed Authority have been estimated at about $14.5 million (UN Doc. A/CONF.62/C.1/L.19, 18 May 1977, table after para. 16. Reprinted in Platzoder, comp., *Third United Nations Conference on the Law of the Sea: Documents* 6:481–83). Of course, nothing requires that a new Antarctic regime set up anything quite that expensive, but the UN has a strong tendency to indulge in expensive organizational forms.

13. By 1980, delegates at UNCLOS III generally accepted an estimate that the International Seabed Authority would secure a total revenue of $240 to $300 million a year from a well-established deep-seabed-mining industry, given the production controls (Lowe, "The International Seabed: A Legacy of Mistrust," 212). It would have far larger revenues, possibly running $3 to $6 billion a year, from contributions in respect of resource exploitation in areas of the continental shelf beyond 200 nautical miles from shore (Wijkman, "UNCLOS and the Redistribution of Ocean Wealth," 36).

14. See discussion in *ECO* 24, no. 2 (April, 1983): 5. In 1982 the U.S. State Department was inclined to view exploitation before the turn of the century as likely. See its "Final Environmental Impact Statement" (1982), D-37.

15. Gonzalez-Ferrán, "Geologic Data," 163 (turn of century). Robert Rice, consulting geologist to Rio Tinto Zinc, quoted in *Financial Times*, 26 August 1983, p. 3. "Impossible" is his characterization.

16. Wright and Williams, "Mineral Resources of Antarctica," 12.

17. See the reference in notes 35 and 37 to chap. 7.

18. See Smith and Peterson, eds., *Aquaculture Development in Less Developed Countries*.

19. This appears acceptable to a number of consultative parties, though no details have been discussed. See Moneta, "Antarctica, Latin America, and the International System in the 1980s," 34, and Brennan, "Criteria for Access," 277.

20. Coll, "Functionalism and the Balance of Interests," discusses the extent to which Soviet preferences shaped Cuban diplomacy at the Third UN Conference on the Law of the Sea. In that conference Cuba could often espouse Third World positions without directly countering Soviet preferences, but Cuba cannot support replacing the Antarctic Treaty without challenging strongly held Soviet preferences.

21. See discussion in Clad, "Breaking the Ice," 26.

22. On Brazil, see Fraga, *Introducción a la Geopolítica Antártica*, 36 (for the area between 28° and 49°50′ W), or Villarroel, "Brazil y la Antartida Sudamerica," *El Mercurio*, 1 March 1973 (for the area between 28° and 53° W). On Peru, see remarks of the Director of the Peruvian Antarctic Studies Institute quoted in Pinto, "Battle for the Treasures," 39, and discussion in Milenky and Schwab, "Latin America and Antarctica," 89.

23. E.g., Pinto, "Battle for the Treasures," 38–39.

24. Remarks at meeting of foreign ministers of the Organization of Eastern Caribbean States, 26 May 1983, quoted in Mitchell, *Frozen Stakes*, 43.

25. *GAOR*, 39th sess., First Committee, 53rd meeting (27 November 1984), p. 51.

26. Records of debates in *GAOR*, 39th sess., First Committee, 50th and 52nd through 55th meetings (27–29 November 1984), 40th sess., First Committee, 51st through 55th meetings (25 November–2 December 1985), and 41st sess., 49th through 51st meetings (18–19 November 1986).

27. Malaysian delegate remarks in *GAOR*, 39th sess., First Committee, 50th meeting (20 November 1984), pp. 16–17, and 40th sess., First Committee, 55th meeting (2 December 1985), p. 36.

28. UN Document 41/722 (14 November 1987).

29. Text in UN Press Release GA/7463 (21 January 1987), pp. 191–92.

30. Roll calls in *GAOR*, 40th sess., 117th plenary meeting (16 December 1985), pp. 56–65.

31. Roll calls in *GAOR*, 41st sess., 96th plenary meeting (4 December 1986), pp. 34–35.

32. The politics of voting in the General Assembly is discussed at greater length in Peterson, *The General Assembly in World Politics*, chap. 3.

33. Letter from Christopher C. Joyner, 16 March 1987.

34. Roll calls in *GAOR*, 40th sess., 117th plenary meeting (16 December 1985), pp. 65–66, and 41st sess., 96th plenary meeting (4 December 1986), pp. 38–39.

35. Remarks of Australian delegate on behalf of the Antarctic Treaty parties in *GAOR*, 40th sess., First Committee, 55th meeting, pp. 46–47 (29 November 1985).

36. *ECO* 22, no. 3 (January 1983): 1, presents this as a scenario for destroying the demilitarization clauses of the treaty.

37. Private citizens' advocacy of accepting common heritage in Australia and Norway has not affected government policy. See remarks of Philip Law, quoted in *ECO* 26, no. 3 (May 1984), p. 8 (Australia); Johan J. Holst, article in *Arbeiderbladet* (Oslo), 30 April and 13 May 1982; also discussed in Sollie, "Jurisdictional Problems," 335 (Norway).

38. British doubts about the usefulness of universal regimes where most member states have no direct material interest in the issues regulated appear in remarks of government spokesman Lord Trefgarne using the International Whaling Commission as a model to be avoided, 21 May 1980, in debates about ratification of CCAMLR, *Parliamentary Debates,* House of Lords, 5th Series, vol. 409, p. 1001.

Texts of the various unilateral deep-seabed-mining laws can be found in *International Legal Materials* as follows: USSR, vol. 21, pp. 551–53; France, vol. 21, pp. 808–14; United Kingdom, vol. 20, p. 1219; West Germany, vol. 20, p. 393, and vol. 21, p. 832; United States, vol. 19, p. 1003; and Japan, vol. 22, pp. 102–22. The Reciprocating States Agreement among the United States, the United Kingdom, France, and West Germany is in ibid., vol. 21, pp. 958–62.

39. Soares Guemaraco, "The Antarctic Treaty System from the Perspective of a New Consultative Party," 342, and Qasim and Rajan, "The Antarctic Treaty System from the Perspective of a New Member," 368–69.

40. Quoted in Jeff Wheelwright, "Endpaper: Antarctica as Utopia," *Discover,* June 1985, p. 96.

41. *GAOR,* 40th sess., First Committee, 53rd meeting (29 November 1985), pp. 24–25.

42. *GAOR,* 40th sess., First Committee, 53rd meeting (29 November 1985), p. 18.

43. In 1985 the Nepali delegate argued that joining in adoption of resolutions by consensus in 1983 and 1984 amounted to acceptance of long-term UN involvement in Antarctica. *GAOR,* 40th sess., First Committee, 53rd meeting (30 November 1985), p. 28. The consultative parties are thus understandably eager to define very clearly the terms under which they are willing to cooperate.

44. Remarks of the Australian delegate in *GAOR,* 40th sess., 117th plenary meeting (17 December 1985), pp. 53–55.

45. Beeby, "Overview," 197; Moneta, "Antarctica," 34; Berlin, "UN Launches Debate," *Washington Post,* 1 December 1983, p. A33.

46. E.g., Mexican and Zimbabwean responses in UN Document A/39/583, Part II, vol. II, p. 46, and vol. III, p. 139, respectively. Chile indicated support for such ideas, and for providing part of the funding from resource revenues, in ibid., vol. II, p. 40.

47. See references in note 129 to chap. 7.

48. See references in note 89 to chap. 5.

49. Puchala, ed., *Issues before the 39th General Assembly,* 106.

50. Remarks of Malaysian delegate in *GAOR,* 40th sess., First Committee, 55th meeting (2 December 1985), p. 36.

## Chapter 9

1. Gowa, *Closing the Gold Window,* particularly chap. 6.

2. This is not intended to ignore the possibility of what Young, in "Regime

Dynamics," 282–84, calls "spontaneous regimes." It does, however, reflect most governments' preference for embodying basic agreements in written form.

3. This is apparent from the vastly different amount of attention given to social groups in accounts of changes in the trade regime, e.g., Lipson, "The Transformation of Trade," or Aggarwal, *Liberal Protectionism* and in accounts of change in the monetary regime, e.g., Cohen, "Balance-of-Payments Financing," or Odell, *U.S. International Monetary Policy.*

4. E.g., Trakman, *The Law Merchant,* chap. 1.

5. Hyde, *International Law* 1:777–94.

6. Kindleberger, *The World in Depression,* 297–98.

7. Keohane, *After Hegemony,* particularly chap. 9; Krasner, "State Power and the Structure of International Trade."

8. Robert Triffin's 1961 book, *Gold and the Dollar Crisis,* elaborated on points he initially made in congressional testimony two years ealier.

9. Lipson, *Standing Guard,* 156.

10. E.g., Cohen, "Balance-of-Payments Financing," 471.

11. Krasner, *Structural Conflict,* 228–30.

12. O'Connell, *The International Law of the Sea* 2:161–64.

13. Krasner, *Structural Conflict,* 169–71.

14. The distinction comes from March, "The Power of Power," 39–70.

15. Ruggie, "International Regimes, Transactions, and Change."

16. Hopkins and Puchala, *Global Food Interdependence.*

17. Oye, "Explaining Cooperation under Anarchy," 21–22, discusses the possibility of reducing collective-action problems by lowering the number of states involved. This is simply a voluntary method of securing that result.

18. Lipson, *Standing Guard.*

19. Jervis, "From Balance to Concert," 58–59.

20. E.g., Art, "Bureaucratic Politics."

21. E.g., Aggarwal, *Liberal Protectionism.*

22. These terms are being used as defined in Krasner, *Structural Conflict,* 14–15, where metapolitical behavior refers to "efforts to change the institutions" within which states interact, and relational behavior refers to "efforts to maximize values within a given set of institutional structures."

23. Krasner, *Structural Conflict,* 9.

24. Ruggie, "Political Structure and Change," 464–65.

25. Krasner, *Structural Conflict,* 5–6.

26. Jonsson, *Friends in Conflict,* is very revealing of Icelandic attitudes.

27. Based on the discussion of weapons-procurement decisions in Schelling, *Choice and Consequence,* pp. 244–45.

# WORKS CITED

Aggarwal, Vinod K. *Liberal Protectionism: The International Politics of Organized Textile Trade.* Berkeley and Los Angeles: University of California Press, 1985.

Ahluwalia, K. "The Antarctic Treaty: Should India Become a Party to It?" *Indian Journal of International Law* 1 (1961): 473–84.

Alexander, Lewis M., and Lynn Carter Hansen, eds. *Antarctic Politics and Marine Resources: Critical Choices for the 1980s.* Kingston: Center for Ocean Management Studies, University of Rhode Island, 1985.

Ali, Salamat, and Michael Richardson. "An Eye on Antarctica." *Far Eastern Economic Review,* 27 January 1983, pp. 32–33.

Alley, Roderic. "New Zealand and Antarctica." *International Journal* (Toronto) 39 (1984): 911–31.

Allison, Graham. *The Essence of Decision.* Boston: Little, Brown, 1971.

Alzerecca, Carlos Aramayo. *Historia de la Antártida.* Buenos Aires: Editorial Hemisferio, 1949.

Andrews, John. "Antarctic Geopolitics." *Australian Outlook,* September 1957, pp. 3–9.

*Antarctic.* Wellington: New Zealand Antarctic Society. Vols. 8 (1978); 9 (1982); 10 (1984); 11 (1986).

"Antarctica—A Continent of International Harmony?" *Australian Foreign Affairs Record* 51 (1980): 4–12.

"Antarctica in the 1980s." *Australian Foreign Affairs Record* 52 (1981): 4–13.

"L'Antarctide et les problèmes soulevés par son occupation." *Documentation française,* no. 1098, 24 March 1949.

Apter, David. *The Politics of Modernization.* Chicago: University of Chicago Press, 1965.

Arbuct Vignali, Heber, et al. *Antartida: Continente de los mas para los menos.* Montevideo, Uruguay: Fundación de cultura universitaria, 1979.

Archdale, H. E. "Legality in the Antarctic." *Australian Outlook,* September 1957, pp. 10–16.

———. "Claims to the Antarctic." *Yearbook of World Affairs,* 1958, pp. 242–63.

Argentina. Ministry of Economy. *Economic Information on Argentina,* no. 91, December 1978. Section: "The Argentinian Presence in the Antarctic."

Art, Robert J. "Bureaucratic Politics and American Foreign Policy." *Policy Sciences* 4 (1973): 467–90.

Auburn, Francis M. "The Antarctic Environment." *Yearbook of World Affairs,* 1981, pp. 248–65.

———. *Antarctic Law and Politics.* Bloomington: University of Indiana Press, 1982.

———. "The Antarctic Minerals Regime." In *Australia's Antarctic Policy Options,* edited by Stuart Harris, 271–300. Melbourne: Centre for Resource and Environmental Studies, Australian National University, 1984.

———. "A Sometime World of Men: Legal Rights in the Ross Dependency." *American Journal of International Law* 65 (1971): 578–82.

———. "Consultative Status Under the Antarctic Treaty." *International and Comparative Law Quarterly* 28 (1979): 514–22.

———. "Legal Implications of Petroleum Resources of the Antarctic Continental Shelf." *Oceans Yearbook* 1 (1978): 500–21.

———. *The Ross Dependency.* The Hague: Martinus Nijhoff, 1972.

Australia. Parliament. House of Representatives. Debates.

———. Senate. Debates.

Bankes, N. D. "Environmental Protection in Antarctica." *Canadian Yearbook of International Law* 19 (1981): 303–19.

Barnes, James N. "The Emerging Convention on the Conservation of Antarctic Marine Living Resources." In *The New Nationalism and the Use of Common Spaces,* edited by Jonathan I. Charney, 239–86. Totowa, N.J.: Allanheld, Osmun, 1982.

———. "Resources and Environment in Antarctica." Paper presented to the Seminar on the Polar Regions, Center for Oceans Law and Policy, University of Virginia, March 1987.

Barrie, G. "The Antarctic Treaty: Example of Law and Sociological Infrastructure." *Comparative and International Law Journal of South Africa* 8 (1975): 212–24.

Barros Gonzalez, Vice Adm. Guillermo. "Derechos de Chile en la Antarctica." *Revista de Marina,* June 1983, pp. 691–94.

Beck, Peter J. "Britain and Antarctica: The Historical Perspective." *Fram: Journal of Polar Studies* 1 (1984): 70–75.

———. "Britain's Antarctic Dimension." *International Affairs* (London) 59 (1983): 429–44.

———. "Britain's Role in the Antarctic: Some Recent Changes in Organization." *Polar Record* 22:85–87.

———. *The International Politics of Antarctica.* New York: St. Martin's, 1986.

———. "Securing the Dominant Place in the Wan Antarctic Sun." *Australian Journal of Politics and History* 29 (1983): 448–60.

———. "The United Nations' Study on Antarctica, 1984." *Polar Record* 22:499–504.

Becker, D. *The New Bourgeoisie and the Limits of Dependency: Mining, Class, and Power in Contemporary Peru.* Princeton: Princeton University Press, 1983.

Beeby, Christopher D. "The Antarctic Treaty." Wellington: New Zealand Institute of International Affairs, 1972.

———. "The Antarctic Treaty System as a Resource Management Mechanism—Nonliving Resources." In *Antarctic Treaty System: An Assessment,* edited by Polar Research Board, 269–302. Washington, D.C.: National Academy Press, 1986.

———. "An Overview of the Problems Which Should be Addressed in the Preparation of a Regime Governing the Mineral Resources of Antarctica." In *Antarctic Resources Policy,* edited by Francisco Orrego Vicuña, 191–98. Cambridge: Cambridge University Press, 1983.

Behrendt, John C. "Petroleum Resources of Antarctica." *Antarctic Journal of the United States* 14 (1981): 17.

Bergin, Anthony. "Recent Developments in Australia's Antarctic Policy." *Marine Policy,* July 1985, pp. 180–91.

Berlin, Michael J. "UN Launches Debate on Antarctica." *Washington Post,* 1 December 1983, p. A33.

Bernhart, J. Peter A. "Sovereignty in Antarctica." *California Western International Law Journal* 5 (1975): 297–349.

Bertram, G. C. L., and J. D. M. Blyth. "The Fisheries of Antarctica." *FAO Fisheries Bulletin* 3 (1956), no. 2, pp. 79–84.

Bilder, Richard B. "Control of Criminal Conduct in Antarctica." *Virginia Law Review* 52 (1966): 231–85.

———. "The Present Legal and Political Situation in Antarctica." In *The New Nationalism and the Use of Common Spaces,* edited by Jonathan I. Charney, 167–205. Totawa, N.J.: Allanheld, Osmun, 1982.

Bindschedler, Rudolf. "La délimitation des competences des Nations Unis." Hague Academy *Recueil des cours* 108 (1963): 307–423.

Birnie, Patricia. *The International Regulation of Whaling.* 2 vols. New York: Oceana Publications, 1985.

Boczek, Boleslaw Adam. "The Protection of the Antarctic Ecosystem: A Study in International Environmental Law." *Ocean Development and International Law* 13 (1983): 347–424.

———. "The Soviet Union and the Antarctic Regime." *American Journal of International Law* 78 (1984): 834–58.

Bouton, Katherine. "A Reporter at Large, South of 60 Degrees South." *The New Yorker,* 23 March 1981, pp. 42–122.

Bowett, D. W. 1960. *The Law of the Sea.* Manchester, Eng.: Manchester University Press.

"Brazil Enters the Antarctic Club." *Latin American Times,* February 1983, p. 27.

Brennan, Keith. "Criteria for Access to the Resources of Antarctica." In *Antarctic Resources Policy,* edited by Francisco Orrego Vicuña, 217–27. Cambridge: Cambridge University Press, 1983.

Broadus, James M., and Porter Hoagland III. "Conflict Resolution in the Assignment of Area Entitlements for Seabed Mining." *San Diego Law Review* 21 (1984): 541–76.

Brook, John. "Australia's Policies towards Antarctica." In *Australia's Antarctic Policy Options,* edited by Stuart Harris, 255–64. Melbourne: Centre for Resource and Environmental Studies, Australian National University, 1984.

Brownlie, Ian. *Principles of Public International Law.* 3rd edition. Oxford: Oxford University Press, 1979.

Bruckner, Peter. "The Antarctic Treaty System from the Perspective of a Nonconsultative Party to the Antarctic Treaty." In *Antarctic Treaty System: An Assessment,* edited by Polar Research Board, 315–35. Washington, D.C.: National Academy Press, 1986.

Budd, W. A. "Scientific Research in Antarctica and Australia's Effort." In *Australia's Antarctic Policy Options,* edited by Stuart Harris, 217–47. Melbourne: Centre for Resource and Environmental Studies, Australian National University, 1984.

Bull, Hedley. *The Anarchical Society.* New York: Columbia University Press, 1977.

Burton, Steven J. "New Stresses on the Antarctic Treaty: Toward International Legal Institutions Governing Antarctic Resources." *Virginia Law Review* 65 (1979): 421–512.

Bush, W. M., ed. *Antarctica and International Law.* 3 vols. London: Oceana, 1982–.

Butler, S. O. "Owning Antarctica: Cooperation and Jurisdiction at the South Pole." *Journal of International Affairs* 32 (1977): 34–51.

Butterworth, Douglas S. "Antarctic Marine Ecosystem Management." *Polar Record* 23:37–47.

Buzan, Barry. "Negotiating by Consensus: Developments of Technique at the United Nations Conference on the Law of the Sea." *American Journal of International Law* 75 (1981): 324–48.

Cameron, Ian. [Donald Gordon Payne.] *Antarctica: The Lost Continent.* London: Cassel, 1974.

Cardoso, Fernando, and Enzo Felatto. *Dependency and Development in Latin America.* Translated by M. M. Urquidi. Berkeley and Los Angeles: University of California Press, 1979.

Carr, Beverley May. "Claims to Sovereignty—Antarctica." *Southern California Law Review* 28 (1955): 386–400.

Carroll, James E. "Of Icebergs, Oil Wells, and Treaties: Hydrocarbon Exploitation Offshore Antarctica." *Stanford International Law Journal* 19 (1983): 207–27.

Carter, Russel A. "Alaska: Mining's Chilly Future in the Land of the Midnight Sun." *Mining Engineering,* November 1976, pp. 20–29.

Castles, A. C. "The International Status of the Australian Antarctic Territory." In *International Law in Australia,* edited by D. P. O'Connell, 341–68. London: Stevens and Son, 1965.

Charney, Jonathan I., ed. *The New Nationalism and the Use of Common Spaces.* Totawa, N.J.: Allanheld, Osmun, 1982.

Chittleborough, Graham. "Nature, Extent, and Management of Antarctic Living Resources." In *Australia's Antarctic Policy Options,* edited by Stuart Harris, 135–61. Melbourne: Centre for Resource and Environmental Studies, Australian National University, 1984.

Clad, James. "Breaking the Ice." *Far Eastern Economic Review,* 1 December 1983, pp. 25–26.

Codling, R. J. "Sea-borne Tourism in the Antarctic." *Polar Record* 21:3–9.

Cohen, Benjamin J. *Organizing the World's Money.* New York: Basic Books, 1977.

———. "Balance-of-Payments Financing: Evolution of a Regime." *International Organization* 36 (1982): 457–78.

Colson, David A. "The Antarctic Treaty System: The Mineral Issue." *Law and Policy in International Business* 12 (1980): 841–901.

Coll, Alberto J. "Functionalism and the Balance of Interests in the Law of the Sea: Cuba's Role." *American Journal of International Law* 79 (1985): 891–911.

Comerci, S. M. "La Sociedad Científica Argentina y una iniciativa precurosa de nuestros actividades antarcticas." *Antartida* (Buenos Aires), no. 13 (February 1984), pp. 55–56.

Crary, Albert. "International Geophysical Year: Its Evolution and U.S. Participation," *Antarctic Journal of the United States* 17, no. 4 (1982): 1–4.

Croasdale, K. R. "Arctic Offshore Technology and Its Relevance to the Antarctic." In *Antarctic Treaty System: An Assessment,* edited by Polar Research Board, 245–63. Washington D.C.: National Academy Press, 1986.

Da Costa, J.-F. *Souveraineté sur l'Antarctique.* Paris: Viellanard Librairie générale de droit et de jurisprudence, 1958.

Dahl, Robert. *Who Governs?* New Haven: Yale University Press, 1961.

Danzig, A. "A Funny Thing Happened to the Common Heritage on the Way to the Law of the Sea." *San Diego Law Review* 12 (1975): 655–64.

Dater, Henry M. "Organizational Developments in the U.S. Antarctic Program."
    *Antarctic Journal of the United States* 1 (1966): 21–32.
Davis, Bruce. "Australia and Antarctica: Aspects of Policy Process." In *Australia's
    Antarctic Policy Options,* edited by Stuart Harris, 339–54. Melbourne: Centre for
    Resource and Environmental Studies, Australian National University, 1984.
Dawkin, W. H. "Whales and Whaling in the Southern Ocean." In *The Antarctic
    Today,* edited by Frank A. Simpson, 151–94. Wellington, N.Z.: A. H. and A. W.
    Reed, 1952.
Dell, R. K. "Marine Biology." In *The Antarctic Today,* edited by Frank A. Simpson,
    129–50. Wellington, N.Z.: A. H. and A. W. Reed, 1952.
Deperov, Y. "Antarctica: A Zone of Peace and Cooperation." *International Affairs*
    (Moscow), November 1983, pp. 29–37.
Downs, George W., David M. Rocke, and Randolph M. Siverson. "Arms Races and
    Cooperation." In *Cooperation under Anarchy,* edited by Kenneth A. Oye, 118–46.
    Princeton: Princeton University Press, 1985.
Dufek, Rear Adm. George I. "What We've Accomplished in Antarctica." *National
    Geographic,* October 1959, pp. 526–57.
Dupuy, René-Jean. "The Notion of the Common Heritage of Mankind Applied to
    the Seabed." *Annals of Air and Space Law* 8 (1983): 347–55.
———. "Le Traité sur l'Antarctique." *Annuaire française de droit international,* 1960,
    111–24.
Earthscan Press Briefings. Issued irregularly. London: International Institute for Envi-
    ronment and Development.
*ECO.* Occasional newsletter of the Antarctic and Southern Ocean Coalition.
Eilers, Stephan. "Antarctica Adjourned?" *International Lawyer* 19 (1985): 1309–18.
Eittrim, S., et al. "Marine Geological and Geophysical Investigations of the Antarctic
    Continental Margin, 1984." U.S. Geological Survey Circular no. 935 (1985).
El-Sayed, Sayed Z., and Mary Alice McWhinnie. "Antarctic Krill: Protein of the Last
    Frontier." *Oceanus* 22 (1979): 13–20.
Evans, Peter. "Transnational Linkages and State Capacities." In *Bringing the State
    Back In,* edited by P. Evans, F. Rueschmeyer, and T. Skocpol. Cambridge: Cam-
    bridge University Press, 1984.
Everson, Inigo. "The Living Resources of the Southern Ocean." Rome: Food and
    Agriculture Organization (FAO) Report GLO/SO/77/1, 1977.
———. "Antarctic Fisheries." *Polar Record* 19:233–51.
Fairbridge, Rhodes W. "The Geology of the Antarctic." In *The Antarctic Today,* edited
    by Frank A. Simpson, 56–101. Wellington, N.Z.: A. H. and A. W. Reed, 1952.
Ferraro, A. A. "La Antartida como fin de una estrategia." *Antartida* (Buenos Aires),
    no. 13 (February 1984), pp. 18–27 and 30.
"Fishing in Oily Waters." *Economist,* 3 May 1980, p. 69.
Fogleman, Valerie M. "Antarctic Krill: Problems and Potential." *Marine Technology
    Society Journal* 17 (1983): 29–35.
Food and Agriculture Organization. *Yearbook of Fisheries Statistics.* 1975, 1976, 1980,
    1983.
Fraga, J. A. *Introducción a la Geopolítica Antártica.* Buenos Aires: Instituto Antárctico
    Argentino, 1978.
Francis, Henry S., Jr. "The Antarctic Treaty: A Reality Before its Time." In *Antarctic
    Politics and Marine Resources: Critical Choices for the 1980s,* edited by Lewis M.

Alexander and Lynn Carter Hansen, 87–98. Kingston: University of Rhode Island, 1985.

Franck, Thomas M. *Nation against Nation.* Oxford: Oxford University Press, 1985.

Frank, Ronald F. "The Convention on the Conservation of Antarctic Marine Living Resources." *Ocean Development and International Law* 13 (1983): 291–345.

"Frozen White Elephant?" *Economist,* 13 April 1957, pp. 111–12.

Fuchs, Sir Vivian. "Evolution of a Venture in Antarctic Science." In *Frozen Future,* edited by R. Lewis and P. Smith, 233–48. New York: Quadrangle Books, 1973.

Germany, Federal Republic. Bundestag. *Verhandlungen des Deutschen Bundestages.*

———. Foreign Ministry. "Überblick über Mitgleidschaften in antarktischen System." 5 April 1984.

Gilpin, Robert. *U.S. Power and the Multinational Corporation.* New York: Basic Books, 1975.

Goldblat, Jozef. "Troubles in the Antarctic." *Bulletin of Peace Proposals,* 1973, pp. 286–88.

Goldie, L. F. E. "A Note on Some Diverse Meanings of 'The Common Heritage of Mankind.' " *Syracuse Journal of International Law and Commerce* 10 (1983): 69–110.

González-Ferrán, Oscar. "Geologic Data and Its Impact on the Discussion of a Regime for Mineral Resources." In *Antarctic Resources Policy,* edited by Francisco Orrego Vicuña, 159–66. Cambridge: Cambridge University Press, 1983.

Gould, Lawrence M. "Antarctica in World Affairs." Foreign Policy Association Headline Series, no. 128 (1958).

Gowa, Joanne. *Closing the Gold Window: Domestic Politics and the End of Bretton Woods.* Ithaca, N.Y.: Cornell University Press, 1983.

Graubell, R. "Whale Conservation—the Role of the International Whaling Commission." *Marine Policy* 1 (1977): 301–10.

Greenpeace International. "Antarctica Briefing No. 12. Status of Antarctic Minerals Negotiations." Mimeograph, 24 March 1987.

Guillaume, Gilbert. "Oil as a Special Resource." In *Antarctic Resources Policy,* edited by Francisco Orrego Vicuña, 185–90. Cambridge: Cambridge University Press, 1983.

Gulland, J. "Developing Countries and the New Law of the Sea." *Oceanus* 22 (1981): 36–42.

Guyer, Roberto E. "The Antarctic System." Hague Academy *Recueil des cours* 139 (1973): 149–226.

———. "Antarctica's Role in International Relations." In *Antarctic Resources Policy,* edited by Francisco Orrego Vicuña, 267–79. Cambridge: Cambridge University Press, 1983.

Hackworth, Green H. *Digest of International Law.* 10 vols. Washington, D.C.: U.S. Government Printing Office, 1940–44.

Halperin, Morton. *Bureaucratic Politics and Foreign Policy.* Washington, D.C.: Brookings Institution, 1974.

Hambro, Edward. "Some Notes on the Future of the Antarctic Treaty Collaboration." *American Journal of International Law* 68 (1974): 217–26.

Hanessian, John. "Remarks." *Proceedings of the American Society of International Law,* 1958, p. 47.

———. "The Antarctic Treaty, 1959." *International and Comparative Law Quarterly* 9 (1960): 436–80.

Hanevold, Trub. "The Antarctic Treaty Consultative Meetings—Form and Procedure." *Cooperation and Conflict* 6 (1971): 183–99.

Harris, Stuart, ed. *Australia's Antarctic Policy Options*. Melbourne: Centre for Resource and Environmental Studies, Australian National University, 1984.

Harry, Ralph L. "The Antarctic Regime and the Law of the Sea Convention: An Australian View." *Virginia Journal of International Law* 21 (1981): 727–44.

Hart, Jeffrey H. *The New International Economic Order: Conflict and Cooperation in North-South Economic Relations 1974–77*. New York: St. Martin's Press, 1983.

Haskell, Barbara. "Access to Society: A Neglected Dimension of Foreign Policy." *International Organization* 34 (1980): 89–121.

Hawkes, Nigel. "Moratorium Set on Antarctic Oil at October Meeting." *Science* 198 (1977): 709–12.

Hayton, Robert D. "The 'American' Antarctic." *American Journal of International Law* 50 (1956): 583–611.

Heap, John A. "Cooperation in the Antarctic: A Quarter of a Century's Experience." In *Antarctic Resources Policy*, edited by Francisco Orrego Vicuña, 103–8. Cambridge: Cambridge University Press, 1983.

Heg, James E. "Antarctic Treaty: Eighth Consultative Meeting." *Antarctic Journal of the United States* 9 (1976): 1–2.

———. "Conference on the Conservation of Antarctic Seals." *Antarctic Journal of the United States* 7 (1972): 45–46.

Hilferding, Rudolf. *Finance Capital*. London: Routledge and Kegan Paul, 1981 [1910].

Honnold, Edward E. "Thaw in International Law? Rights in Antarctica under the Law of Common Spaces." *Yale Law Journal* 87 (1978): 804–59.

Hopkins, Raymond F., and Donald J. Puchala. *Global Food Interdependence*. New York: Columbia University Press, 1980.

Horsefield, J. Kenneth. *The International Monetary Fund, 1945–65*. 3 vols. Washington: International Monetary Fund, 1969.

Hunter Christie, E. W. *The Antarctic Problem: An Historical and Political Study*. London: George Allen & Unwin, 1951.

Huntington, Samuel P. *Political Order in Changing Societies*. New Haven: Yale University Press, 1968.

Hyde, Charles Cheney. *International Law, Chiefly as Interpreted and Applied by the United States*. 2d rev. ed. 3 vols. Boston: Little, Brown, 1951.

"Ice Rush." *Economist*, 30 November 1957, p. 762.

Infante, Maria Theresa. "The Continental Shelf of Antarctica." In *Antarctic Resources Policy*, edited by Francisco Orrego Vicuña, 253–64. Cambridge University Press, 1983.

Institute of Polar Studies, Ohio State University, Columbus. "A Framework for Assessing Environmental Impacts of Possible Antarctic Mineral Development," 1977.

International Institute for Environment and Development. "Antarctica: A Continent in Transition." Set of materials, 1983.

Isachsen, Fridtjov. "The New Norwegian Dependency in the Antarctic." *Le Nord* (Revue International des Pays du nord) 4 (1939): 67–78.

Jackson, Richard. *The Nonaligned, the UN, and the Superpowers*. New York: Praeger, 1983.

Jain, Subhash C. "Antarctica: Geopolitics and International Law." *Indian Yearbook of World Affairs*, 1974, 249–78.

Jensen, Robert C., and Theodore Shabad, eds. *Soviet Natural Resources in the World Economy*. Chicago: University of Chicago Press, 1983.

Jervis, Robert. "From Balance to Concert: A Study of International Security Coopera-tion." In *Cooperation under Anarchy*, edited by Kenneth A. Oye, pp. 58–79. Prince-ton: Princeton University Press, 1985.

———. "Security Regimes." *International Organization* 36 (1982): 357–78.

Jessup, Philip C., and Howard J. Taubenfield. *Controls for Outer Space and the Antarc-tic Analogy*. New York: Columbia University Press, 1959.

Johnson, Chalmers. *MITI and the Japanese Challenge*. Stanford: Stanford University Press, 1973.

Johnson, D. H. N. *Rights in Air Space:* Manchester, Eng.: Manchester University Press, 1965.

Johnson, Eric W. "Quick, Before It Melts: Toward a Resolution of the Jurisdictional Morass in Antarctica." *Cornell International Law Journal* 10 (1976): 173–98.

Jonsson, Hannes. *Friends in Conflict: The Anglo-Icelandic Cod Wars and the Law of the Sea*. London: C. Hurst, 1982.

Joyner, Christopher C. "Anglo-Argentine Rivalry after the Falklands/Malvinas War." *Lawyer of the Americas* 15 (1984): 467–502.

———. "Antarctica and the Law of the Sea: Rethinking the Current Legal Dilem-mas." *San Diego Law Review* 18 (1981): 415–42.

———. "Oceanic Pollution and the Southern Ocean: Rethinking the International Legal Implications for Antarctica." *Natural Resources Journal* 24 (1984): 1–40.

Kaczynski, Vladimir. "Distant Water Fisheries and the 200 Mile Economic Zone." Occasional Paper, no. 34, Law of the Sea Institute, Richardson School of Law, University of Hawaii, 1983.

Kaplan, Morton. *System and Process in International Relations*. New York: Wiley, 1964.

Katzenstein, Peter, ed. *Between Power and Plenty*. Madison: University of Wisconsin Press, 1978.

"Keep Off the Ice!" *Economist*, 5 August 1961, p. 554.

Kelsen, Hans. *The Law of the United Nations*. New York: Praeger, 1950.

Keohane, Robert O. *After Hegemony*. Princeton: Princeton University Press, 1984.

———. "The Theory of Hegemonic Stability and Changes in International Economic Regimes, 1967–77." In *Changes in the International System*, edited by Ole Holsti et al., 131–62. Boulder, Colo.: Westview Press, 1980.

Keohane, Robert O., and Joseph S. Nye, Jr. *Power and Interdependence*. Boston: Little, Brown, 1977.

Kesteven, G. "The Southern Ocean." *Oceans Yearbook* 1 (1978): 467–99.

Kimball, Lee A. "Report on Antarctica, July 1985." Mimeograph. Washington, D.C.: International Institute for Environment and Development.

———. "Report on Antarctica: United Nations Focus 1984 and Recent Develop-ments in the Antarctic Treaty System." Washington, D.C.: International Institute for Environment and Development, 1 November 1984.

———. "Report on Antarctica, 8 November 1985." Washington, D.C.: International Institute for Environment and Development, 1985.

Kindleberger, Charles P. *The World in Depression*. Berkeley and Los Angeles: Univer-sity of California Press, 1973.

King, J. "South Africa in the Subantarctic." In *The Antarctic Today*, edited by Frank A. Simpson, 304–12. Wellington, N.Z.: A. H. and A. W. Reed, 1952.

Kish, John. *The Law of International Spaces*. Leiden, Neth.: Sijthoff, 1973.

Kissinger, Henry A. *White House Years*. Boston: Little, Brown, 1979.

Knox, George A. "The Key Role of Krill in the Ecosystem of the Southern Ocean." *Ocean Management* 9 (1984): 113–56.

———. "The Living Resources of the Southern Ocean." In *Antarctic Resources Policy,* edited by Francisco Orrego Vicuña, 21–60. Cambridge: Cambridge University Press, 1983.

Krasner, Stephen D. "State Power and the Structure of International Trade." *World Politics* 28 (1976): 317–47.

———. *Structural Conflict: The Third World against Global Liberalism.* Berkeley and Los Angeles: University of California Press, 1985.

Lagoni, Rainer. "Antarctica: German Activities and Problems of Jurisdiction over Marine Areas." *German Yearbook of International Law* 23 (1980): 392–400.

———. "Antarctica's Mineral Resources in International Law." *Zeitschrift für ausländisches öffentliches Recht und Völkerrecht* 39 (1979): 1–39.

———. "Convention on the Conservation of Marine Living Resources: A Model for the Use of a Common Good?" In *Antarctic Challenge,* edited by Rudiger Wolfrum, 93–113. Berlin: Dencker and Humblot, 1984.

———. "Die Vereinten Nationen und die Antarktis." *Europa-Archiv* 16 (1984): 473–82.

Lagos Camona, Guillermo. *Historia de las Fronteras de Chile: Los Tratados de Limites con Argentina.* Santiago: Editorial Andres Bello, 1982.

Laughlin, Thomas L. "Minerals Regime in Antarctica." Paper presented at the Seminar on the Polar Regions, Center for Oceans Law and Policy, University of Virginia, March 1987.

Lenin, Vladimir Illich. *Imperialism: The Highest Stage of Capitalism.* New York: International Publishers, 1939 [1916].

Lepotier, Admiral A. "La démilitarisation de l'Antarctide." *Revue de défense nationale* 17 (1961): 788–807.

———. "Les routes de recharge antarctiques." *Revue de défense nationale* 24 (1961): 62–76.

Le Schack, Leonard A. "The French Polar Effort and the Expeditions Polaires Françaises." *Arctic* 17 (1964): 3–14.

Lindsey, G. "Strategic Aspects of the Polar Regions." *Behind the Headlines* Series (Canadian Institute of International Affairs), vol. 35, no. 6, 1977.

Lipson, Charles. "The Transformation of Trade: The Sources and Effects of Regime Change." *International Organization* 36 (1982): 417–56.

———. *Standing Guard: Protecting Foreign Capital in the 19th and 20th Centuries.* Berkeley and Los Angeles: University of California Press, 1985.

Lissitzyn, Oliver J. "The American Position on Outer Space and Antarctica." *American Journal of International Law* 53 (1959): 126–31.

Lonergan, Steven J. "The Legal Status of the Antarctic Airspace." L.L.M. thesis, McGill University, 1972.

Lovering, J. F., and J. R. V. Prescott. *Last of Lands . . . Antarctica.* Melbourne: Melbourne University Press, 1979.

Lowe, A. V. "The International Seabed: A Legacy of Mistrust." *Marine Policy* 5 (1981): 205–16.

Lundquist, Thomas R. "Iceberg Cometh? International Law Relating to Antarctic Iceberg Exploitation." *Natural Resources Journal* 17 (1977): 1–41.

McDougal, Myres P., Harold Lasswell, and Ivan Vlasic. *Law and Public Order in Space.* New Haven: Yale University Press, 1963.

McElroy, Seamus. "The Economics of Harvesting Krill." Chapter 8 of Barbara Mitchell and Richard Sandbrook, *The Management of the Southern Ocean*, pp. 81–103. London: International Institute for Environment and Development, 1978.

McKenzie, Garry D. "Geopolitical and Scientific Roles of the United States in Antarctica." Unpublished paper, Mershon Center, Ohio State University, October 1983.

McNair, Arnold Duncan. *The Law of Treaties*. 2d ed. Oxford: Oxford University Press, 1963.

Mandelbaum, Michael. "The First Nuclear Regime." In *Nuclear Weapons and World Politics*, edited by David Gompert, 15–83. New York: McGraw-Hill, 1977.

Maquiera, Christian. "Antarctica prior to the Antarctic Treaty." In *Antarctic Treaty System: An Assessment*, edited by Polar Research Board, 49–54. Washington, D.C.: National Academy Press, 1986.

March, John G. "The Power of Power." In *Varieties of Political Theory*, edited by David Easton, pp. 39–70. Englewood Cliffs, N.J.: Prentice-Hall, 1966.

Marcoux, J. Michael. "Natural Resource Jurisdiction on the Antarctic Continental Margin." *Virginia Journal of International Law* 11 (1971): 374–405.

Marx, Karl. *The Eighteenth Brumaire of Louis Bonaparte*. New York: International Publishers, 1964 [1852].

Mathisen, Trygve. *Svalbard in the Changing Arctic*. Oslo: Universitetsforlaget, 1954.

Menon, K. S. R. "The Scramble for Antarctica." *South*, April 1982, pp. 11–13.

Milenky, Edward S., and Steven I. Schwab. "Latin America and Antarctica." *Current History*, February 1983, pp. 52–53 and 89–90.

Miller, Debra. "Contributions of the UN to International Security." In *The US, the UN, and the Management of Global Change*, edited by Toby Trister Gati, 131–62. New York: New York University Press, 1983.

Miller, Thomas P. "Mineral Resources: Arctic Alaska." In *U.S. Arctic Interests: The 1980s and 1990s*, edited by William E. Westermeyer and Kurt M. Shusterich. New York: Springer Verlag, 1984.

Mills, C. Wright. *The Power Elite*. New York: Oxford University Press, 1956.

Mitchell, Barbara. *Frozen Stakes: The Future of Antarctic Minerals*. London: International Institute for Environment and Development, 1983.

———. "Resources in Antarctica." *Marine Policy* 1 (1977): 91–101.

———. "The Politics of Antarctica." *Environment*, January–February 1981, pp. 20–21.

———. "The Southern Ocean in the 1980s." *Oceans Yearbook* 3 (1982): 349–85.

Mitchell, Barbara, and Richard Sandbrook. *The Management of the Southern Ocean*. London: International Institute for Environment and Development, 1980.

Mitchell, Barbara, and Jon Tinker. *Antarctica and Its Resources*. London: International Institute for Environment and Development, 1980.

Moneta, Carlos J. "Antarctica, Latin America, and the International System in the 1980s." *Journal of International Studies* 23 (1981): 29–68.

Moran, Theodore. *Multinational Corporations and the Politics of Dependence: Copper in Chile*. Princeton: Princeton University Press, 1974.

Morgenthau, Hans. *Politics among Nations*. 5th ed. New York: Knopf, 1978.

Mouton, M. W. "The International Regime of the Polar Regions." Hague Academy *Recueil des cours* 107 (1962): 176–284.

Müller, Scharnhorst. "The Impact of UNCLOS III on the Antarctic Regime." In *Antarctic Challenge*, edited by Rudiger Wolfrum, 169–80. Berlin: Dencker and Humblot, 1984.

Munch, Ingo von. "Völkerrechtsfragen Antarktis." *Archiv des Völkerrechts* 7 (1958–59): 225–52.
Murphy, Robert Cushman. "The Oceanic Life of the Antarctic." *Scientific American* 207 (1962): 187–212.
Myhre, Jeffrey D. *The Antarctic Treaty System: Politics, Law, and Diplomacy.* Boulder, Colo: Westview, 1986.
Neider, Charles. Letter to Editor, *New York Times,* 26 January 1978, p. 20, col. 4.
———. Op-Ed piece, *New York Times,* 9 April 1982, p. A27.
"New Toe in the Snow." *Economist,* 30 January 1982, p. 48.
New Zealand. Parliament. House of Representatives. *Debates.*
Nye, Joseph S., Jr., and Robert O. Keohane, eds. *Transnational Relations and World Politics.* Boston: Little, Brown, 1974.
O'Connell, D. P. *The International Law of the Sea.* 2 vols. Oxford: Clarendon Press, 1982.
Odell, John S. *U.S. International Monetary Policy: Power, Markets, and Ideas as Sources of Change.* Princeton: Princeton University Press, 1983.
Olsen, Magnus L. *Saga of the White Horizon.* Lymington, Eng.: Nautical Publishing Co., 1972.
Orrego Vicuña, Francisco. "The Application of the Law of the Sea and the Exclusive Economic Zone to the Antarctic Continent." In *Antarctic Resources Policy,* edited by Francisco Orrego Vicuña, 243–51. Cambridge: Cambridge University Press, 1983.
———. "The Definition of a Regime on Antarctic Mineral Resources." In *Antarctic Resources Policy,* edited by Francisco Orrego Vicuña, 199–215. Cambridge: Cambridge University Press, 1983.
Orrego Vicuña, Francisco, ed. *Antarctic Resources Policy.* Cambridge: Cambridge University Press, 1983.
Oxman, Bernard H. "Antarctica and the New Law of the Sea." *Cornell International Law Review* 19 (1986): 211–47.
Oye, Kenneth. "Explaining Cooperation under Anarchy." In *Cooperation under Anarchy,* edited by Kenneth Oye, pp. 1–24. Princeton: Princeton University Press, 1985.
Pallone, Frank. "Resource Exploitation: The Threat to the Legal Regime of the Antarctic." *Connecticut Law Review* 10 (1978): 401–17.
Pardo, Arvid. "The Evolving Law of the Sea: A Critique of the Informal Composite Negotiating Text (1977)." *Oceans Yearbook* 1 (1978): 9–37.
Parfit, Michael. "Nations Are Debating the Future of Antarctica's Frozen Assets." *Smithsonian,* November 1984, pp. 47–58.
Parker, B. C., ed. *Conservation Problems in Antarctica.* Lawrence, Kans.: Alen Press, 1972.
Peterson, M. J. *The General Assembly in World Politics.* Boston and London: George Allen and Unwin, 1986.
Pinochet de la Barra, Oscar. *Chilean Sovereignty in Antarctica.* Santiago: Editorial del Pacifico, 1955.
Pinto, Clarence Da Gama. "Battle for the Treasures of the Last Frontier on Earth." *South,* December 1983, pp. 38–39.
Plott, Barry M. "The Development of U.S. Antarctic Policy." Ph.D. dissertation, The Fletcher School of Law and Diplomacy, 1969.
*Polar Record.* Cambridge, Eng.: Scott Polar Research Institute. Vols. 2 (1935–38),

3 (1939–42), 4 (1943–46), 5 (1947–50), 6 (1951–53), 7 (1954–55), 8 (1956–57), 9 (1958–59), 11 (1960–61), 12 (1964–65), 13 (1966–67), 14 (1968–69), 16 (1972–73), 19 (1978–79), 20 (1980–81), 21 (1982–83), and 23 (1986–87).

Polar Research Board, U.S. National Research Council. *Antarctic Treaty System: An Assessment.* Washington, D.C.: National Academy Press, 1986.

Pontecorvo, Guilio. "The Economics of the Resources of Antarctica." In *The New Nationalism and the Use of Common Spaces,* edited by Jonathan I. Charney, 155–66. Totowa, N.J.: Allanheld, Osmun, 1982.

Potter, Neal. "Economic Prospects of the Antarctic." *Antarctic Journal of the United States* 4 (1969): 61–68.

Prescott, J. R. V. "Boundaries in Antarctica." In *Australia's Antarctic Policy Options,* edited by Stuart Harris, 88–89. Melbourne: Centre for Resource and Environmental Studies, Australian National University, 1984.

"The Present and Future of the Atlantic Alliance." *Atlantic Community Quarterly* 20 (1982): 307–26.

"Presentation du territoire des terres australes et antarctiques françaises." Paris, 1983. Mimeograph.

"Le problème de l'Antarctique." *Chronique de politique étrangère* (Brussels) 9 (1956): 212–27.

Public Issues Law Committee, Auckland District Law Society (N.Z.). "How Strong Is New Zealand's Claim to the Ross Dependency?" *New Zealand Law Journal,* 4 March 1980, pp. 76–77.

Puchala, Donald J., ed. *Issues before the 39th General Assembly.* New York: United Nations Association of the USA, 1984.

Puchala, Donald J., and Raymond F. Hopkins. "International Regimes: Lessons from Inductive Analysis." *International Organization* 36 (1982): 245–80.

Purver, Ron. "Security and Arms Control at the Poles." *International Journal* (Toronto) 39 (1984): 888–910.

Qasim, S. Z., and A. P. Rajan. "The Antarctic Treaty System from the Perspective of a New Member." In *Antarctic Treaty System: An Assessment,* edited by Polar Research Board, 345–74. Washington, D.C.: National Academy Press, 1986.

Quigg, Philip W. *A Pole Apart: The Emerging Issue of Antarctica.* New York: McGraw-Hill, 1983.

Rao, P. C. *The New Law of Maritime Zones.* New Delhi: Miland, 1982.

Reich, R. J. "The Development of Antarctic Tourism." *Polar Record* 20: 203–14.

Rich, Vera. "Soviet Antarctica: When Will the Miners Move South?" *Nature* 301 (1983): 457.

Roberts, Brian B. "A Chronological List of Antarctic Expeditions." *Polar Record* 9:96–124, and 191–239.

———. "International Cooperation for Antarctic Development: The Test for the Antarctic Treaty." *Polar Record* 19:107–20.

Roots, E. F. "Resource Developments in Polar Regions." In *Antarctic Resources Policy,* edited by Francisco Orrego Vicuña, 297–315. Cambridge: Cambridge University Press, 1983.

Rose, Julia. "Antarctic Condominium: Building a New Legal Order for Commercial Interests." *Marine Technology Society Journal* 10 (1976): 19–27.

Rubenstein, Alvin Z. *The Soviets in International Organizations.* Princeton: Princeton University Press, 1964.

Ruggie, John G. "International Regimes, Transactions, and Change." *International Organization* 36 (1982): 379–416.

———. "Political Structure and Change in the International Economic Order: The North-South Dimension." In *The Antinomies of Interdependence*, edited by John G. Ruggie, 423–88. New York: Columbia University Press, 1983.

Rutford, Robert H. "The United States Antarctic Program." In *Antarctic Politics and Marine Resources: Critical Choices for the 1980s*, edited by Lewis M. Alexander and Lynn Carter Hansen, pp. 55–64. Kingston: University of Rhode Island, 1985.

———. "Summary of Science in Antarctica prior to and including the International Geophysical Year." In Polar Research Board, *Antarctic Treaty System*, pp. 375–90. Washington, D.C.: National Academy Press, 1986.

Rybakov, Yuri M. "Juridical Nature of the 1959 Treaty System." In *Antarctic Treaty System: An Assessment*, edited by Polar Research Board, 33–45. Washington, D.C.: National Academy Press, 1986.

Sabaté Lichtschein, Domingo. *Problemas Argentinos de Soberanía Territorial*. Buenos Aires: Cooperadore de Derecho y Ciencias Sociales, 1976.

Sanderson. T. J. O. "Offshore Oil Development in Polar Regions." *New Zealand Antarctic Record* 5 (1983): 30–44.

Schelling, Thomas C. *Choice and Consequence*. Cambridge: Harvard University Press, 1984.

Scheville, William, ed. *The Whale Problem: A Status Report*. Cambridge: Harvard University Press, 1975.

Schurmann, Franz. *The Logic of World Politics*. New York: Pantheon, 1974.

SCAR Group of Specialists on the Environmental Impact Assessment of Mineral Resource Exploration and Exploitation in Antarctica. "Possible Environmental Effects of Mineral Exploration and Exploitation in Antarctica." Cambridge, Eng.: Scientific Committee on Antarctic Research, 1979.

Scully, R. Tucker. "Alternatives for Cooperation and Institutionalization in Antarctica." In *Antarctic Resources Policy*, edited by Francisco Orrego Vicuña, 282–96. Cambridge: Cambridge University Press, 1983.

Sechrist, Frank. "With the Soviets in Antarctica." *Antarctic Journal of the United States* 12 (1977): 4–11.

Semma, Bruno. "The Antarctic Treaty as a Treaty Providing for an 'Objective Regime.' " *Cornell International Law Journal* 19 (1986): 189–209.

Shapley, Deborah. "Antarctic Problems: Tiny Krill to Usher in New Resource Era." *Science* 196 (1977): 503–5.

———. "India in Antarctica." *Nature* 301 (1983): 362.

———. "North Pole, South Pole Resources Eyed." *Science* 189 (1975): 365.

———. *The Seventh Continent: Antarctica in a Resource Age*. Washington, D.C.: Resources for the Future, 1986.

Simmonds, K. R. "Le Traité sur l'Antarctique de 1959." *Journal du droit international* (Clunet), 1960, pp. 668–701.

Sivard, Ruth. *World Energy Survey*. 2d ed. Leesburg, Va.: World Priorities, 1981.

Smedal, Gustav. *Acquisition of Sovereignty over Polar Areas*. Translated by C. Meyer. Oslo: J. Dybwad, 1931.

Smith, Leah J., and Susan Peterson, eds. *Aquaculture Development in Less Developed Countries*. Boulder, Colo.: Westview Press, 1982.

Snidal, Duncan. "The Limits of Hegemonic Stability Theory." *International Organization* 39 (1985): 579–614.

Soares Guimaraes, L. F. Macedo de. "The Antarctic Treaty System from the Perspective of a New Consultative Party." In *Antarctic Treaty System: An Assessment*, edited by Polar Research Board, 337–44. Washington, D.C.: National Academy Press, 1983.

Sollie, Finn. "The Development of the Antarctic Treaty System—Trends and Issues." In *Antarctic Challenge*, edited by Rudiger Wolfrum, 17–37. Berlin: Dencker and Humblot, 1984.

———. "Jurisdictional Problems in relation to Antarctic Mineral Resources in Political Perspective." In *Antarctic Resources Policy*, edited by Francisco Orrego Vicuña, pp. 317–35. Cambridge: Cambridge University Press, 1983.

Southard, Frank. *The Evolution of the International Monetary Fund*. Princeton Essays in International Finance, no. 135 (1979).

Spangler, M. B. *New Technology and Marine Resource Development*. New York: Praeger, 1970.

Spencer, Cisca. "The Evolution of Antarctic Interests." *Australia's Antarctic Policy Options*, edited by Stuart Harris, 113–29. Melbourne: Centre for Resource and Environmental Studies, Australian National University, 1984.

Spero, Joan. *The Politics of International Economic Relations*. 3d ed. New York: St. Martin's Press, 1985.

Stein, Arthur A. "Coordination and Collaboration: Regimes in an Anarchic World." *International Organization* 36 (1982): 299–324.

Sudbury, John. D. "Submerged Barges for Arctic Transportation?" *Ocean Industry*, March 1973, pp. 22–24.

Sullivan, Walter. "Antarctica in a Two-Power World." *Foreign Affairs* 36 (1957–58): 154–66.

———. "The International Geophysical Year." *International Conciliation*, no. 521 (1959).

———. *Quest for a Continent*. New York: McGraw-Hill, 1957.

Swan, R. A. *Australia in the Antarctic*. Melbourne: Melbourne University Press, 1961.

Szasz, Paul. "Thomas Jefferson Conceives an International Organization." *American Journal of International Law* 75 (1981): 138–40.

Taijudo, Kanae. "Japan and the Problems of Sovereignty over the Polar Regions." *Japanese Annual of International Law* 3 (1959): 12–17.

Talboys, Brian (then foreign minister). "New Zealand and the Antarctic Treaty." *New Zealand Foreign Affairs Review* 29 (1978): 29–35.

Taubenfeld, Howard J. "A Treaty for Antarctica." *International Conciliation*, no. 531 (1961).

"Les terres australes et l'Antarctide françaises." *Documentation française*, no. 1326, 13 May 1950.

Tiano, André. *La dialectique de la dépendence*. Paris: Presses universitaires de France, 1977.

The *Times* (London). *The Times Atlas of the Oceans*. New York: Van Nostrand Reinhold, 1983.

Tinker, Jon. "Antarctica: Toward a New Internationalism." *New Scientist*, 13 September 1979, pp. 799–801.

Toma, Peter A. "Soviet Attitudes towards the Acquisition of Sovereignty in the Antarctic." *American Journal of International Law* 50 (1956): 611–26.

Tonnessen, J. N., and O. A. Johnsen. *A History of Modern Whaling*. Abridged English edition. Berkeley and Los Angeles: University of California Press, 1982.

Trakman, Leon E. *The Law Merchant: The Evolution of Commercial Law*. Littleton, Colo.: Fred B. Rothman, 1983.

Triffin, Robert. *Gold and the Dollar Crisis*. New Haven: Yale University Press, 1961.

Triggs, Gillian. "The Antarctic Treaty Regime: A Workable Compromise or a 'Purgatory of Ambiguity'?" *Case Western Reserve Journal of International Law* 17 (1985): 166–228.

———. "Australian Sovereignty in Antarctica." *Melbourne University Law Review* 13 (1981): 123–58 and 302–33.

———. "Australian Sovereignty in Antarctica: Traditional Principles of Territorial Acquisition versus a 'Common Heritage'." In *Australia's Antarctic Policy Options*, edited by Stuart Harris, 29–66. Melbourne: Centre for Resource and Environmental Studies, Australian National University, 1984.

Tugwell, F. *The Politics of Oil in Venezuela*. Stanford: Stanford University Press, 1975.

Tunkin, Grigori I. "An Example of International Cooperation." *International Affairs* (Moscow) 6 (1960): 42–45.

———. *Theory of International Law*. Translated by William E. Butler. Cambridge: Harvard University Press, 1974.

United Kingdom. Foreign Office. *British and Foreign State Papers*.

———. Parliamentary Debates. House of Commons.

———. Parliamentary Debates. House of Lords.

*United Nations Treaty Series*. Vols. 21, 402, and 499.

United States. Central Intelligence Agency. 1978. *Polar Regions Atlas*.

United States. Congress. *Congressional Record*.

———. House. Committee on Foreign Affairs, Subcommittee on National Security Policy and Scientific Developments. 1973. Report: The Political Legacy of the International Geophysical Year. November 1973.

———. Committee on Merchant Marine and Fisheries, 35th Cong., 2d sess., May 1978. Hearings on various fish and wildlife measures, including polar living marine resources (H.R. 10905).

———. Committee on Science and Technology, 34th Cong., 2d sess., September 1976. "Report on Polar Energy Resources Potential."

———. Committee on Science and Technology, Subcommittee on Science, Research, and Technology. 36th Cong., 1st sess., May 1979. Hearings: "U.S. Antarctic Program."

———. Senate. Committee on Armed Services, 83rd Cong., 2d sess., July 1954. Hearing: "Antarctic Expedition."

———. Committee on Energy and Natural Resources. 36th Cong., 1st sess., April 1979. Hearing: "U.S. Activities in Antarctica."

———. Committee on Foreign Relations. 86th Cong., 2d sess., June 1960. Hearings: "The Antarctic Treaty."

———. Committee on Foreign Relations, Subcommittee on Oceans and International Environment. 94th Cong., 1st sess., May 1975. Hearings: "U.S. Antarctic Policy."

———. Committee on Commerce, Science, and Transportation. Subcommittee on Science, Technology, and Space. 98th Cong., 2nd sess., 24 September 1984. Hearing: "Antarctica." Serial No. 98–111.

United States. Department of State. "The Conference on Antarctica, October 15–December 1, 1959."

———. "Final Environmental Impact Statement for a Possible Regime for Conservation of Antarctic Living Marine Resources." June 1978.

———. "Final Environmental Impact Statement on the Negotiation of an International Regime for Antarctic Mineral Resources." August 1982.

———. *Foreign Relations of the United States.*

———. Treaties in Force. 1 January 1986.

Van der Essen, Alfred. "The Application of the Law of the Sea to the Antarctic Continent." In *Antarctic Resources Policy,* edited by Francisco Orrego Vicuña, 231–42. Cambridge: Cambridge University Press, 1983.

———. "Réunions consultatives du Traité sur l'Antarctique." *Revue belge de droit international* 15 (1980): 20–27.

Van der Essen, Philippe. "L'économie des régions polaires: Réalisations et perspectives." *Chronique de politique étrangère* (Brussels) 25 (1972): 391–545.

Vane, Gregg. "Soviet Antarctic Research, 1972–73." *Antarctic Journal of the United States* 8 (1973): 324–32.

Vasilchikov, N. V. "Prospects for the Industrial Development of Antarctica." *Current Digest of the Soviet Press* 28 (1977), no. 52, pp. 1, 3, and 14.

Vasquez, John A., and Richard W. Mansbach. "The Issue Cycle and Global Change." *International Organization* 37 (1983): 257–80.

Vernon, Raymond. "International Trade Policy in the 1980s." *International Studies Quarterly* 26 (1982): 483–510.

Villarroel, E. G. "Brazil y la Antartida Sudamerica." *El Mercurio,* 1 March 1973.

Volpe, John. "U.S.–Japan Trade and the Yen/Dollar Relationship." *Journal of the American Chamber of Commerce of Japan* 21 (1984): 59.

Waldock, C. H. M. "Disputed Sovereignty in the Falkland Islands Dependencies." *British Yearbook of International Law* 25 (1948): 311–53.

Wallerstein, Immanuel. *The Modern World System: Capitalist Agriculture and the Origins of the European World-Economy in the Sixteenth Century.* New York: Academic Press, 1974.

Wasserman, Ursula. "The Antarctic Treaty and Natural Resources." *Journal of World Trade Law* 12 (1978): 174–79.

Watts, Arthur D. "The Antarctic Treaty as a Conflict Resolution Mechanism." In *Antarctic Treaty System: An Assessment,* edited by Polar Research Board, 65–75. Washington, D.C.: National Academy Press, 1986.

Wellborn, Stanley, N. "Antarctic's Riches: For Some or for All?" *U.S. News and World Report,* 24 January 1983, pp. 70–74.

Westermeyer, William E. *The Politics of Mineral Resource Development in Antarctica.* Boulder, Colo.: Westview Press, 1984.

Westermeyer, William, and Kurt Schusterich, eds. *United States Arctic Interests: The 1980s and 1990s.* New York: Springer Verlag, 1984.

Whiteman, Marjorie M., ed. *Digest of International Law.* 13 vols. Washington, D.C.: U.S. Government Printing Office, 1963–73.

Whittaker, Christine R. "The Concorde Debate." *Law and Policy in International Business* 9 (1977): 959–83.

Wijkman, Per J. "Managing the Global Commons." *International Organization* 36 (1982): 511–36.

————. "UNCLOS and the Redistribution of Ocean Wealth." *Journal of World Trade Law* 16 (1982): 27–48.

Wilkes, Owen, and Robert Mann, "The Story of Nukey Poo." *Bulletin of the Atomic Scientists,* October 1978, pp. 32–36.

Wilson, Gregory, P. "Antarctica, the Southern Ocean, and the Law of the Sea." *JAG Journal* 30 (1978): 47–86.

Wilson, Robert, E. "National Interests and Claims in the Antarctic." *Arctic* 17 (1964): 15–31.

Wolfum, Rudiger. "The Use of Non-Living Resources." In *Antarctic Challenge,* edited by Rudiger Wolfrum, 143–63. Berlin: Dencker and Humblot, 1984.

Wolfrum, Rudiger, ed., *Antarctic Challenge.* Berlin: Dencker and Humblot, 1984.

Woolcott, Richard. "The Future of the Antarctic Treaty System: One Consultative Party Outlook." In *Antarctic Politics and Marine Resources: Critical Choices for the 1980s,* edited by Lewis M. Alexander and Lynn Carter Hansen, pp. 225–32. Kingston: University of Rhode Island, 1985.

————. "The Interaction between the Antarctic Treaty System and the United Nations System." In *Antarctic Treaty System,* edited by the U.S. Polar Research Board, pp. 375–90. Washington, D.C.: National Academy Press, 1986.

Wright, N. A., and P. L. Williams. "Mineral Resources of Antarctica." U.S. Geological Survey Circular no. 705 (1974).

Young, Elizabeth, and Victor Sebek. "Red Seas and Blue Sea: Soviet Uses of Ocean Law." *Survival* 20 (1978): 255–62.

Young, Oran. "Regime Dynamics." *International Organization* 36 (1982): 277–98.

Zegers, Fernando. "The Canberra Convention: Objectives and Political Aspects of Its Negotiation." In *Antarctic Resources Policy,* edited by Francisco Orrego Vicuña, 149–56. Cambridge: Cambridge University Press, 1983.

Zumberge, James H. "The Antarctic Treaty as a Scientific Mechanism—The Scientific Committee on Antarctic Research." In *Antarctic Treaty System: An Assessment,* edited by Polar Research Board, 153–68. Washington, D.C.: National Academy Press, 1986.

————. "Possible Mineral Resource Availability and Possible Environmental Problems in Antarctica." In *The New Nationalism and the Use of Common Spaces,* edited by Jonathan I. Charney, 115–54. Totowa, N.J.: Allanheld, Osmun, 1982.

# INDEX

Adelie Land, 33, 34, 60, 81, 164
Agreed Measures for Conservation of Antarctic Flora and Fauna, 95, 104, 107, 130, 136–37, 147, 166, 177
Air New Zealand, 103
Alfred von Wegener Institute for Polar Research, 101
Algeria, 184
All-Union Geographical Society (USSR), 38
Alternative energy ventures, 148
Amendment: conditions for, 12, 13, 143, 154, 172–74, 218; process of, 7–8, 12–13, 97–117, 143–74, 195, 223, 225 n.9
"American Antarctic", 35
Amundsen, Roald, 33, 64
*Antarctic* (journal), 149
Antarctic and Southern Ocean Coalition, 165, 166
Antarctic Convergence, 106
Antarctic Division (Australia), 59, 135
Antarctic Division (New Zealand), 59, 81
Antarctic Environmental Protection Agency (proposed), 115
Antarctic Mineral Resources Commission (proposed), 115, 116
Antarctic organization (proposed), 75
Antarctic Peninsula, 32, 33, 64, 73, 113, 154, 221
Antarctic Policy Group (USA), 135, 164
Antarctic policy machinery: Argentina, 59, 60, 61, 80, 136; Australia, 59, 61; Belgium, 82; Brazil, 163; Chile, 59, 60, 61, 80–81, 127, 136, 165, 166; China, 163; Denmark, 165; France, 60, 61, 81, 128, 165, 166; India, 163, 166; Japan, 82, 127–28, 162, 165; New Zealand, 59, 61, 81, 135, 136, 165, 166; Norway, 60, 81, 135, 136; Poland, 166; South Africa, 82, 128; Soviet Union, 82, 127, 165, 166;

United Kingdom, 59, 60, 61, 81, 127, 135, 136, 163, 166; United States, 60, 61, 81–82, 127, 135, 136, 164, 165, 166; Uruguay, 163; West Germany, 165, 166
Antarctic Projects Office (USA) 82, 136
Antarctic Research Committee (South Africa), 128
Antarctic Treaty: Article I, 42, 45, 46, 115; Article II, 41, 46; Article III, 44, 45; Article IV, 42, 43, 68, 85, 104, 107, 110, 114, 115, 153; Article V, 45, 115; Article VI, 42, 45, 107, 115; Article VII, 43, 44, 45, 46; Article VIII, 41, 44; Article IX, 42, 43, 44, 47, 101; Article X, 44; Article XI, 41, 44, 107; Article XII, 47, 48, 201; Article XIII, 47; claims and 42, 43, 48, 168; enforcement of, 43–44, 49, 133, 170, 321 n.77; provisions summarized, 41–49; ratifications, 125; review conference, 47, 72
Antarctic Treaty System: future of, 220–23; norms, 41–42, 93–95, 106, 117; principles, 41–42, 106, 114, 117; procedures, 46–48, 95–97, 100, 107–8, 114–17; omissions, 48–49; rules, 42–46, 100–105, 106–7, 117
Antigua and Barbuda, 177, 178, 185
Arctic and Antarctic Institute (USSR), 82, 127
Arctowski Station, 101
Argentina: to 1949, 33, 36, 38, 51, 52, 62, 64; 1950–59, 38, 40, 69–70, 73, 76, 77; 1961–, 103, 110, 131, 132, 139, 158, 161, 171, 185. *See also* Antarctic policy machinery; Claims
Argentine Antarctic Institute, 80
Argentine Antarctic Territory, 132. *See also* Claims

Auburn, F. M., 94
Australia: to 1949, 32, 64; 1950–59, 40, 73, 77; 1961–, 103, 113, 132, 140, 150, 158, 159, 171. *See also* Antarctic policy machinery; Claims
Australian Conservation Foundation, 165

BANZARE Expedition, 64
Beagle Channel dispute, 36, 54, 73
Beardmore Glacier Workshop (1985), 189
Beeby, Sir Christopher, 114
Beeby drafts, 114, 116, 160
Belgium: to 1949, 37, 38, 64; 1950–59, 87, 71–73; 1961–, 139, 171. *See also* Antarctic policy machinery
Bellingshausen, Adm. Thaddeus von, 31, 38
Bellingshausen Sea, 164
Bellingshausen Station, 132
Biscoe, 31
Borga Station, 139
Bouvet Island, 34, 81, 111
Brazil, 101, 171, 185, 188. *See also* Antarctic policy machinery; Claims
Brazilian Institute of Antarctic Studies, 163
British Antarctic Survey, 127, 135, 163. *See also* Falkland Islands Dependencies Survey
British Antarctic Territory, 128. *See also* Claims
Bureaucratic politics model, 19, 58, 79, 82–83, 135–36, 162–64, 179, 214
Byrd, Adm. Richard E., 34, 64, 127

Cheating, 116, 132, 154–55, 221
Chile: to 1949, 33, 36, 38, 62, 64; 1950–59, 38, 40, 69–70, 73, 77; 1961–, 103, 110, 132, 133, 134, 139, 149, 150, 158, 160, 161, 171, 185. *See also* Antarctic policy machinery; Claims
Chilean Antarctic Commission, 59, 127
Chilean Antarctic Institute, 127
China, 155, 171, 185, 187, 222. *See also* Antarctic policy machinery
Chinese National Committee for Antarctic Research, 163
Civil aviation, 46, 49, 103, 232 n.92
Claimant states, 35–36, 38, 39, 40, 53–54, 57, 61, 62, 69, 71, 74, 75, 76, 83, 84, 110, 117, 126, 128, 131, 152, 153, 154, 158, 160, 162, 168, 188, 209, 221
Claims: Argentina, 33, 35, 51, 53, 70, 80, 117, 154, 229 n.43, 234 n.10; Australia, 32, 53, 117, 154, 244 n.7; Brazil (potential), 170; Chile, 33, 35, 51, 53, 56, 70,

80, 117, 154; France, 32, 33, 34, 53, 81, 83; "freeze" on, 37, 38, 40, 58, 62; Germany (potential), 34; Japan (potential), 34; New Zealand, 32, 51, 53, 54, 57, 81, 154, 244 n.7; nonrecognition of, 35–36; Norway, 34, 35, 53, 83; origins of, 33–37, 40; overlapping, 32, 54, 58, 62, 73, 199, 203; possible, 168; question of renouncing, 40, 53, 54, 55, 57, 58; significance of, 58, 68, 87–88, 97, 138–39, 151; Soviet Union (potential), 38, 155, 170; United Kingdom, 33, 34, 35, 51, 53, 54, 57, 244 n.8; United States (potential), 34, 37, 53, 57, 70, 232 n.4
Coalition formation: conditions influencing, 11, 22, 23–29, 174, 205–7, 210–13; in 1945–49, 62–65; in 1950–59, 84–88; in 1963–75, 137–41; in 1975–, 167–72, 180–81, 185–91
Coastal state jurisdiction. *See* Maritime jurisdiction
Common aversions, 220, 221–22
Common heritage: defined, 117, 119, 181; proposed regime, 119–22, 141, 165, 189, 191, 219, 256 n.38
Commission for Antarctic Studies (Uruguay), 163
Commission of the Conservation of Antarctic Marine Living Resources: authority, 105, 106, 107–8; decisions, 111–13, 161, 162
Committee on Polar Research (USA), 82
Confidentiality of negotiations, 93, 94, 131, 223
Congress of Berlin (1885), 57
Consultative Parties; attitudes of, 131, 140, 178, 181, 188, 190; authority of, 42, 46, 47, 95–97; procedures, 84, 93–94, 95–97, 188; resource regime, 113–16, 120–21
Consultative status, 43, 96–97, 100–102, 133, 167–68, 173, 210, 223
Continental shelf, 52, 68, 69, 111, 151, 152, 157
Convention on Conservation of Antarctic Seals (Seal Convention, 1972), 99, 100, 104–5, 129, 147
Convention on Fishing and Conservation of the Living Resources of the High Seas (1958), 69
Convention on the Conservation of Antarctic Marine Living Resources (CCAMLR, 1978), effectiveness, 109–13; enforcement, 107, 109–10; origins of, 100; provisions of, 106–8; ratifications, 162, sig-

Ice, 46, 231 n.80
Icebergs, 149
Ideas, political influence of: domestic, 14, 76,
   159, 184, 192, 198, 216; international,
   20, 28, 56, 66, 76, 89, 140–41, 182–83,
   184, 192, 198, 217, 218–19
Ideology. See Ideas
Imperial Conference (1926), 34
Incidents, 37, 38, 51, 73, 97, 230 n.57
India: 1950–59, 86; 1961–, 101, 119, 155,
   171, 185, 188, 209, 222. See also Antarc-
   tic policy machinery
Industry groups, 166, 167, 173
Inter-agency rivalry, 164–65
Interdependence, 14, 25, 26, 217
Inspection: in Antarctic Treaty, 42, 44, 221;
   in CCAMLR, 107, 161
Interests: defined, 11, described, 53–62,
   130–37, 154–67, 181–83; how per-
   ceived, 16–21, 173–74, 178–79, 183–
   85, 191–92, 213–20; influence of shared,
   171–72, 174, 189, 212, 213, 220
International Convention on the Regulation
   of Whaling (1946), 51, 70, 129, 180
International Council of Scientific Unions
   (ICSU), 39, 79
International Court of Justice (ICJ), 36, 44,
   69, 73, 108
International Geophysical Year (1957–58):
   generally, 65, 164; planning, 38, 39, 206,
   230 n.67; significance, 67, 68, 74, 79, 84,
   126, 142, 196, 203, 206, 207, 216
International Institute for Environment and
   Development, 164, 176
International law, 15, 44, 88, 133, 168, 188
International organization process model,
   26–27, 140, 192, 207–9, 219
International regimes: defined, 2–6, 204; dynamics of, 9–29, influence of deadlines
   on, 201; internal tensions of, 145, 145,
   153, 201, 202; phases of, 6–9, 195–200.
   See also Amendment; Creation; Establishment; Maintenance; Modification; Replacement; Termination
International Whaling Commission, 105,
   139, 177, 180, 190, 219, 256 n.38
Internationalization of Antarctica (proposed),
   57, 74, 85, 89, 135, 141
Issue salience. See Salience
Issue-specific power: components of, 43–49,
   87–88, 138–40, 145, 170; distribution
   of, 63, 138–40, 145; model, 18, 24, 54,
   62, 87–88, 90, 138–40, 167, 206–7,
   212
Italy, 139

Japan: to 1949, 32, 64; 1950–59, 71, 73,
   76, 85, 87; 1961–, 139, 140, 149, 150,
   158, 160, 161, 162
Jurisdiction: generally, 42, 43, 49, 128, 147;
   over Antarctic resources, 104, 107, 147,
   148. See also Maritime jurisdiction

Keohane, Robert O., 200
Kerguelen Islands, 32, 34, 36, 81, 111, 113,
   150
Kindleberger, Charles P., 3, 200
King Geoge Island, 102, 154
Krasner, Stephen D., 218
Krill, 110, 132, 149–50, 157, 160, 182. See
   also Fisheries
Krill catches, 150, 182

Laurie Island, 35, 64
Law of the sea, 45, 51, 68, 130, 141, 146,
   148, 151, 152, 157–58, 183, 202
Law of the Sea Convention. See Convention
   on the Law of the Sea
Lazarev, M. P. 38
League of Nations, 36, 56
Leningradskaya Station, 132
Libya, 184
Limited participation regimes, 84–85, 156,
   167–68, 176, 206, 208–10
Lipson, Charles, 201

McDonald Island, 111
McMurdo Station, 103
Macquarie Island, 32
Maintenance: conditions of, 12, 123, 128–
   41, 142, 216; defined, 6–7, 93
Malaysia, 120, 121, 178, 184, 186
Marine living resources, 103–13. See also Fish-
   eries; Krill; Sealing; Whaling
Maritime jurisdiction, 69, 111, 151, 152,
   153. See also Continental shelf; Exclusive
   Economic Zone; Territorial sea
Marsh Station, 154
Marxist models, 16, 17–18, 56, 57, 75–76,
   213–14
Mawson, Sir Douglas, 64
Military aviation, 46
Military personnel, 45
Military uses of Antarctica, 51, 72–73, 131,
   219–20, 235 n.22
Mineral and fuel resources: generally, 99,
   100, 113–17, 147–48, 171, 173; regime
   for exploiting, 113–17, 157, 183, 186
Minerals, 129, 148–49, 152–53, 155, 157,
   158, 182
Mining companies, 179

| | |
|---:|:---|
| Compositor: | Huron Valley Graphics, Inc. |
| Text: | 10/13 Galliard |
| Display: | Friz Quadrata |
| Printer: | Braun-Brumfield, Inc. |
| Binder: | Braun-Brumfield, Inc. |